Asia's Turning Point

AN INTRODUCTION TO ASIA'S DYNAMIC ECONOMIES AT THE DAWN OF THE NEW CENTURY

Asia's Turning Point

AN INTRODUCTION TO ASIA'S DYNAMIC ECONOMIES AT THE DAWN OF THE NEW CENTURY

Ivan Tselichtchev
and
Philippe Debroux

WILEY

John Wiley & Sons (Asia) Pte. Ltd.

Other Wiley Editorial Offices

John Wiley & Sons Inc., 111 River Street, Hoboken, NJ 07030, USA
John Wiley & Sons Ltd., The Atrium, Southern Gate, Chichester, West Sussex, P019 8SQ, United Kingdom
John Wiley & Sons (Canada) Ltd., 5353 Dundas Street West, Suite 400, Toronto, Ontario, M9B 6HB, Canada
John Wiley & Sons Australia Ltd., 42 McDougall Street, Milton, Queensland 4064, Australia
Wiley-VCH, Boschstrasse 12, D-69469 Weinheim, Germany

Library of Congress Cataloging-in-Publication Data
ISBN : 978-0-470-82360-6

Typeset in 10.5/13pt Palatino by Macmillan

Printed in Singapore by Markono Print Media Pte Ltd
10 9 8 7 6 5 4 3

Dedication

To
Olga, Maxim, Galina,
Yasuko, Amelie, and Tatsuro

Contents

Acknowledgments

This book would have never been written without cooperation, encouragement, and advice from our friends and colleagues. They are our co-authors.

We would like to give special thanks to Dr. Frank-Yurgen Richter, president of the Geneva-based Horasis consultancy and one of the opinion leaders on today's Asia, for actively supporting the idea and making many valuable comments.

Working on the book required three intensive research sessions at the Singapore campus of INSEAD, one of the world's best business schools, famous for its edge in the area of Asian business and economic studies. We take this opportunity to express our gratitude to Professor Hellmut Schutte who was our host there. He not only let us in, but also offered a lot of food for thought, generously sharing his innovative ideas, and kindly supplied very important materials and data.

Brain-storming discussions with INSEAD's leading scholars Peter Williamson, Michael Witt, and Philippe Lasserre provided precious intellectual inputs.

We are also very grateful to people from the INSEAD staff, especially the Tanoto Library team, who made the research work there an unforgettable experience.

Outside INSEAD, we had very fruitful discussions with Dr. Chia Liu Sien, a distinguished expert on Asian affairs, who was part of the academic staff of the National University of Singapore for thirty years until 2001 before spending two years at the Waseda and Soka Universities in Japan as a visiting professor, and Mr. Wong Meng Quang, who served as a senior officer at Singapore's Economic Development Board in the 60s and early 70s and then as a senior diplomat in Japan and China. Also in Singapore, we had a valuable exchange of views with the researchers at the Institute of Southeast Asian Studies.

Important contributions to the book came from the contacts with many Japanese researchers, business people, politicians, and ministries' staff. We'd especially like to mention Ken'ichi Imai, Senior Fellow Emeritus of Stanford University, and Hisao Kanamori, Adviser of the Japan Center for Economic Research.

Special thanks to the colleagues and friends from the Institute of World Economy and International Relations (IMEMO) of the Russian Academy of Sciences, whose advice and support are always important whether they are near or far: Alexander Dynkin, Vyacheslav Amirov, and Sergei Chugrov. Gratitude and tribute to late Vladlen Martynov and Yakov Pevzner.

Finally, thank you, Maxim Tselichtchev, for timely and efficient technical assistance.

Prologue

A unique cluster of highly performing Asian economies[1] produced the biggest economic sensation of the postwar decades. They shook the world with their high growth rates, rapid industrial development, and quick rises in living standards. In 1993, the World Bank called their success the "East Asian miracle." The cluster was steadily enhancing its role in the world economy, opening enormous trade and investment opportunities. The trend was dramatically amplified when China joined its ranks in the 1980s.

Successful Asian economies set an example for developing countries around the world. Furthermore, led by Japan, they created a model of capitalism, which was largely an alternative to the one established in the West. The pillars of the economic model—the role of the state and its relations with the private sector; corporate ownership, governance, and management; intercompany and company–bank links; and labor relations—in their Asian version were quite different from American and European patterns.

There is a great deal of literature covering the many aspects of the East Asian miracle and the specificity of Asian capitalism. The region's remarkable growth was interrupted by the Asian crisis of 1997–98: the first financial crisis of the globalization era. At that point the focus of attention, naturally, shifted to the reasons which led to the crisis and to its implications, and many books and articles appeared where the issue was thoroughly analyzed from various angles.

By 1999 the crisis was over. The question was: what now? What is the relevant angle from which to view the Asian economies at the dawn of the new century?

They are growing fast again, and their role in the world economy continues to increase. As of late 2008, most have retained growth dynamics in spite of global financial turmoil, initially caused by subprime loan troubles in the US and the deteriorating performances of the American and European economies. Many new features and developments have emerged. Industrialization, the major driver of growth in the miracle years, was, by and large, finished by the 1990s. Growth has become decisively dependent on the ability to produce higher value-added goods and on the performance of the service sector. Singapore, Hong Kong, South Korea, and Taiwan have joined the ranks of the developed economies. China has emerged as the new economic superpower

1

with the second-largest gross domestic product (GDP) in the world if the recalculation into dollars is made on the basis of the purchasing power parity (PPP) of national currencies, not their nominal exchange rates (in other words, if it takes into consideration that with the same amount of dollars in your pocket you can buy many more goods and services in China than in Japan or Germany because of much lower prices). India is following suit. In terms of GDP (PPP), it has climbed to number four, overtaking Germany. Asian regionalism is on the rise, and the contours of the East Asian Community are becoming more and more visible. Finally, the model of Asian capitalism is no longer a workable alternative to the system established in America and Europe. Asian countries are undergoing a far-reaching structural change, which adapts their systems to global standards and brings them much closer to Western capitalism. (It means neither that the system of Western capitalism is "perfect," nor the West's triumph over the East). Accommodating such a change has become a necessary precondition for economic success. This is the way we see the changing face of today's Asia, and these are also the major angles of the book.

After the Asian crisis the regional economies have entered a new stage of their development. Ten years have passed—a period long enough to try to articulate its major features and trends. The exercise is especially exciting as there are still no other books directly addressing this task.

This book consists of two parts. The first one deals with the region as a whole. We start with a brief retrospective of the East Asian miracle. To understand and explain the present you have to remember the near past. The second chapter presents a picture of the region's growth from 1999 to present, and examines its new features. Chapters 3, 4, and 5 are especially important for us, as there we dig into the three major aspects of the systemic, or structural, transformation of Asian economies. We trace the transformation of: the economic role and policies of the state; ownership, governance, and management of Asian companies; and Asian-style labor relations. Chapter 6 addresses one more major aspect of structural change: intensifying regional integration and the prospects for the East Asian Community.

In the second part we look in depth at a wide selection of national economies. Seeking to make this book a one-stop read for both business and nonbusiness people, and in an attempt to present the regional panorama in all its diversity, we made the range of countries covered as extensive as we could. Fourteen economies will be discussed.

Existing terminology complexities make it necessary to clarify the meaning of the basic geographical terms and the geographic scope of the book. It is focused on East Asia. We stick to the framework where this includes Northeast Asia (China, Japan, Mongolia, North and South Korea, and the Russian Far East) and Southeast Asia (the ten members of the Association of Southeast Asian Nations (ASEAN): Brunei, Cambodia, Indonesia, Laos, Malaysia, Myanmar, the Philippines, Singapore, Thailand, and Vietnam, and nonmember East Timor). The two "tiger territories" of Hong Kong and Taiwan, as well as Macau, do not belong to either Northeast or Southeast. They are just "East."

In various literary and statistical sources quite often Northeast Asia is called East Asia and, consequently, East Asia and Southeast Asia turn out to be two different regions.

As for the division of East Asian economies into groups depending on the level of their development, we basically follow the conventional pattern. East Asia's ten major economies, traditionally the focus of attention, are: Japan; the four newly industrialized economies (NIEs)—Hong Kong, Singapore, South Korea, and Taiwan; the ASEAN 4—Malaysia, Thailand, Indonesia, and the Philippines; and China. Nine of them (Japan excluded) are usually defined as East Asia's emerging-market economies. We do not insist on changing this conventional approach, though it may already be a bit outdated. As far as today's per-capita GDP and other major indicators are concerned, the four NIEs have to be included in the category of developed economies. That is why we will also use the term "developed Asia," meaning Japan plus the four NIEs. Brunei, a small oil-rich sultanate, which in 2007 had the highest per-capita GDP in the region, is a very peculiar case, requiring special research. It is not dealt with in this book.

To the list of ten major economies, we added four more "heroes." The first one is Vietnam—a big country which joined the ranks of Asia's fastest runners in the 1990s and is attracting attention worldwide as a place to invest and to do business. The second one is North Korea—a nation with significant economic potential still unrealized due to political and ideological constraints. Today, the North Korean theme is dominated by the nuclear issue. It is unavoidable. Still, we believe that the time is ripe to have a much closer look at its present economic transformation. In time this may lead to the creation of a market economy, and our book encourages discussions about the ways to stimulate it. The third "hero" is the Russian Far East. In our view, it is an indivisible part of East Asia's economic space. It is hardly relevant to leave it out just because Russia's major economic centers are located in its European part—especially as its economic ties with its East Asian counterparts are visibly expanding. Finally, we add Asia's new economic giant, India, whose growth story commands attention all around the world. Geographically, it is in South Asia. However, economically it is becoming increasingly interlinked with the East. Also, it is participating in the East Asian Community creation process.

This time we have not included in our list the economies of Cambodia, East Timor, Laos, Macau, Mongolia, and Myanmar. This will remain a task for the future.

The chapters on each national economy start with some basic data about the country's population, natural resources, GDP, major industries and companies, administrative divisions and economic regions, economic agencies, and political system. We hope it will help our readers to get on this particular country's "frequency." Next we present a brief overview of the major postwar economic developments. Third, we look at structural reforms and this begins the major part of each national economy's story. This section complements Chapters 3, 4, and 5, on regional structural transformation, in the first part of the book. Fourth, we proceed to the economy's present performance. We have done our best to present the latest data and facts. Along with macroeconomic developments, we discuss each country's economic policies and medium- and long-term strategies, major challenges and tasks, and important events in the economic and business worlds. Readers will also find descriptions of everyday life, which, we hope, will help them not only to understand economic developments, but also to feel the country's pulse and national flavor. The fifth section discusses foreign trade. In the sixth section we look at foreign direct investment (FDI) and the country's business environment. The latter covers a range of issues from investment-related laws, regulations, and incentives to costs and business culture. We finish with concluding remarks—mostly an evaluation of the results of the post-crisis period and a summary of the major issues on the agenda.

We hope that this book will be of interest and use to a wide readership. It is written for businessmen who are either working in or planning to work in, or with, East Asia; for academics and students who study the region, as well as international economics and business; and for anyone, anywhere whose activities are East Asia-linked or who simply wants to know more. Though the book is not written in accordance with the strict canons of the academic genre, we hope that scholars researching these topics will also find something here that is new and deserving of attention.

Endnote

1 Japan; four newly industrialized economies (NIEs)—South Korea, Taiwan, Hong Kong, and Singapore—often called the "tiger economies," and three ASEAN economies—Malaysia, Thailand, and Indonesia. The performance of one more major ASEAN economy, the Philippines, did not merit inclusion in this group.

Part 1
Region

1

The East Asian Miracle in Retrospect

Similarity in Diversity

East Asia is the most diverse region in the world. It is comprised of nations that are very different in size: from China with its 1.3 billion people to the 4-million-strong city-state of Singapore. Development and wealth gaps are bigger here than anywhere else. Singapore, Hong Kong, and Japan are among the wealthiest nations in the world while Cambodia, Laos, and Myanmar are among the poorest. In 2007, per-capita gross domestic product (GDP) in Singapore was 48 times greater than in Myanmar and the gap between the average per-capita GPD for Japan and the newly industrialized economies (NIEs) on the one hand and the four countries with the lowest per-capita incomes (Cambodia, Laos, Myanmar, and Vietnam) on the other reached 19 times (International Monetary Fund (IMF) 2008; per-capita GDP is calculated on the basis of the purchasing power parity (PPP) of the national currencies).

Political systems also vary. Some East Asian nations are parliamentary democracies while others are ruled by authoritarian regimes or even military dictators. Sometimes, formally democratic countries are governed in an authoritarian way as one party or political organization has a de facto monopoly on power and the activities of the opposition parties and groups are restrained.

Finally, there is a unique diversity of religious cultures—Brunei, Indonesia, and Malaysia are mostly Muslim, the Philippines is Christian, and Thailand is Buddhist. However, the latter two also have Muslim majorities in their southern provinces. Cambodia, Laos, and Myanmar are Buddhist as well. South Korea is both Christian and Buddhist. The Japanese never hesitate to point out that in their country Buddhism, Shintoism, and Christianity coexist in a most peaceful and positive way. Various traditional religions and beliefs also retain their influence. Above all, Confucian values and philosophy are very important throughout the region, especially among the Chinese and Koreans.

The question arises: If East Asian countries are so different from one another, is it relevant to view the region as an entity in any sense other than purely geographical?

The answer is "yes, most of these countries do." Their major common feature is rapid economic growth and development. East Asia has established itself as the most dynamically growing region in the world (see Table 1.1). In the postwar decades, practically all of the region's major economies joined the ranks of the fastest runners. Japan started the spurt in the 1950s and was the most dynamic developed economy until the early 1990s. The four newly industrialized economies (NIEs)—Hong Kong, Singapore, South Korea, and Taiwan—and Thailand and, at a lower growth rate, Malaysia began their rapid economic development in the 1960s, followed by Indonesia in the 1970s, China in the 1980s, and Vietnam in the 1990s. In the latest developments, Russia, including its Asian part, has been growing fast since 1999 and Cambodia and Mongolia have reached the level of double-digit growth in this decade. As far as growth dynamics are concerned, until recently, only the Philippines was an exception among the region's emerging-market countries.

The combined share of Japan, the four NIEs, the ASEAN 4 (Indonesia, Malaysia, the Philippines, and Thailand), and China in the world GDP increased from 13.6 percent in 1970 to 19.4 percent in 1990 (the author's calculations based on: NationMaster 2008; Council of Economic Development and

Table 1.1   Average real growth rates of major East Asian economies (%)

Country	1960s	1970s	1980s	1990–97
Industrially developed countries average (North America, Western Europe, Japan, Australia, New Zealand)	5.2	3.2	3.0	2.2
Japan	10.9	5.0	4.0	1.5
South Korea	8.6	9.5	9.7	7.2
Taiwan	9.2	8.0	8.0	5.2
Hong Kong	10.0	9.3	7.1	5.3
Singapore	8.8	8.5	6.1	8.5
Thailand	8.4	7.2	7.9	7.4
Malaysia	6.5	7.8	5.2	8.6
Indonesia	3.9	7.6	6.0	7.5
Philippines	5.1	6.3	1.0	3.3
China	5.0	6.3	9.4	11.2

Source: Data from Azia Joho Center, Takushoku University, "Higashi Azia Choki Keizai Tokei," 9, (Tokyo: 2000) p.27; for China: National Bureau of Statistics of China, *China Statistical Yearbook 2004*; "National Bureau of Statistics of China Plan Report," (http://www.chinability/com/GDP.htm).

Planning, Republic of China 2008), and their share in world exports surged from 9.0 percent in 1960 to 21.4 percent in 1990 (Takushoku 2000).

In 1968, Japan rose to the position of the second-largest market economy after the US and in the late 1980s was practically number one in terms of competitiveness and financial might. East Asia's emerging-market economies—the NIEs, ASEAN 4, and China—developed into one of the world's four major centers of production and trade, along with North America, Europe, and Japan. Their share of world exports went up from 5.9 percent in 1960 to 12.9 percent in 1990 (Takushoku 2000). In the 1990s, China established itself as the world's factory, capable of producing an almost full set of industrial products from sneakers to personal computers.

The World Bank labeled the remarkable growth of eight East Asian economies—Japan, the four NIEs, Malaysia, Thailand, and Indonesia—as the "East Asian miracle" and defined them as high-performing Asian economies (HPAE) (World Bank 1993). Presumably, the rapid growth of China, and later Vietnam, which gained momentum after the publication of the Bank's famous report, can be viewed as the continuation of the miracle—if you accept this metaphor.

East Asia's developing economies performed much better than their counterparts in other regions. Between 1960 and the early 1990s the eight HPAE were growing roughly three times as fast as the economies of Latin America and South Asia. They managed to visibly enhance living standards and reduce poverty. During 1960–85 real per-capita income increased more than four times in Japan and the NIEs and more than doubled in Indonesia, Malaysia, and Thailand (World Bank 1993). Poverty incidence, defined as the proportion of families living below the poverty line (comparisons between countries are not recommended because the poverty threshold criteria vary from one country to another), between the years 1970 and 1990, fell in South Korea from 23 percent to 5 percent and in Indonesia from 58 percent to 19 percent. In Malaysia it dropped from 37 percent in 1973 to 14 percent in 1987 and in Thailand from 59 percent in 1962 to 22 percent in 1988 (Gerson 1998, 46).

Economic growth was accompanied by a visible reduction of income inequality—opening new opportunities for, and giving hope to, families in the lower income bracket. Many social indicators characterizing people's well-being improved dramatically—infant mortality fell and school enrollment increased.

East Asia's postwar growth also played a very important role in world economic history because its major developing economies successfully pursued industrialization, joining the group of leading exporters of manufactured products. In 1980, the share of manufacturing as part of the GDP was 36.2 percent in Taiwan, 28.6 percent in South Korea, 28.0 percent in Singapore, and 22.0 percent in Hong Kong versus 28.2 percent in Japan and 21.5 percent in the US. In 1990, it reached 27.2 percent in Thailand, 26.5 percent in Malaysia, and 25 percent in the Philippines (Takushoku 2000, 27). Thus, not only Japan, but also the majority of East Asian economies, proved that industrialization was not an exclusive characteristic of Europe and North America.

Why Rapid Growth?

Why did major East Asian economies grow so fast? Why was their industrialization successful?

First, East Asia's saving rates—the highest in the world—provided a sound financial basis for domestic investment. Investment from overseas was also actively promoted.

Second, the demographic situation was favorable. A high share of the population was of working age, in particular the young generation, and this enabled necessary labor inputs, while falling population growth rates made it easier to fight poverty and create jobs.

Third, most of these workers proved to be diligent and quick to learn. In this regard it cannot be denied that values—or to be more specific, attitudes, toward work—also matter a great deal, though their influence is impossible to measure. For many East Asians, working hard for long hours, with few and short holidays was, and is, a normal way of life. Of course, generalizations are risky—within the region itself attitudes toward work differ greatly depending on the country, generation, and social or ethnic group. Not all East Asians are hard workers.

Fourth, in East Asia both the state and private households willingly invested in education. As a result, in the field of basic (primary) education, its emerging-market countries outperformed developing nations in other regions: their ratio of children attending primary and secondary schools was higher and education itself more intensive.

Fifth, in relative terms, East Asian countries were politically stable—at least they experienced fewer cataclysms, such as civil wars, coups, uprisings, or riots, than developing states in other regions—though the guarantor of stability was usually a dictatorship or at least an authoritarian regime.

Finally, the governments were pursuing sound macroeconomic policies—keeping public spending, budget deficits, and inflation relatively low—which were valued by both domestic and foreign investors. Also, the state worked to ensure the security of banks through prudent regulation, restrictions on competition, and administrative guidance.

Next comes a factor of a very special character—East Asia gave birth to a peculiar type, or model, of capitalism (different from Western, especially Anglo-Saxon capitalism in a number of important respects).

The East Asian Model of Capitalism: An Outline

The East Asian Model Exists

In the 1950s and 1960s, in times when a bitter rivalry between capitalist and socialist systems stood behind all the major collisions in the world economy and politics, economically successful East Asian countries opted for capitalism, recognizing the key role of market competition and private entrepreneurship. China, under Mao Zedong, Mongolia, North Korea, and North Vietnam[1] chose Soviet-style socialism, or a state-dominated planned system, and were economically unsuccessful. China in the 1980s and Vietnam in the 1990s started growing fast after transitioning to a market-style—actually capitalist— economy, though they preserve the Communist Party rule and call their systems "socialist market" for political and ideological reasons.

Capitalism in East Asia, however, turned out to be largely different from the conventional American or European patterns. As far as the economic system is concerned, the major differences emerged in such key areas as the role of the state and its relationship with the private sector, corporate ownership and control, corporate finance patterns, and relations between companies and their employees.

There is no consensus about the contents of the East Asian economic model and, perhaps, even about the relevance of the term itself. The East Asian economic model is sometimes interpreted as almost a synonym of the Japanese model because Japan, the region's economic leader, was the first to create a complete and cohesive alternative version of highly developed capitalism.[2] In our view, in spite of substantial differences between the economic systems of the various countries around the region, their common features are important enough to say that the East Asian model of capitalism exists and that this notion goes beyond the Japanese model.[3]

The Role of the State

The first major feature of the East Asian model of capitalism is the leading role of the state in the process of economic development. As mentioned, unlike former socialist countries, in the economically successful countries of East Asia the state recognized the primary role of the private sector. Yet, contrary to conventional capitalist wisdom, it did not seek to limit its involvement in the economy to adopting and enforcing laws, providing public services (police, diplomacy, national security, public schools, and so on), and building infrastructure, leaving everything else to private business. Instead, it was actively guiding the private sector, articulating development visions and plans, and, especially important, creating and supporting strategically important industries, as well as particular companies and business groups: national champions. This type of state is called a "developmental state."[4]

The developmental state led the shift of East Asian economies from import substitution to export-led industrial growth, introducing a wide range of financial and other incentives for exporters. Also, it actively intervened in resource allocation, complementing and correcting the market mechanism. Yet, as time went by, it pursued deregulation, privatization, and import and foreign investment liberalization, creating a more competitive business environment and encouraging private companies to become less dependent on its support.

In spite of the active involvement in their national economies, the governments in East Asia were usually rather compact. The region opted for low taxes and self-reliance for those who are physically capable of earning their living. Among other things, it stimulated work motivation.

Asian Companies

The second major feature of East Asian capitalism is the dominant position of large, widely diversified, financial–industrial groups and companies (conglomerates) with ownership and control structures, business goals, and management practices largely different from those of big corporations in the West. The latter are mostly owned by a large number of dispersed shareholders seeking maximization of profits and company value. Ownership and management are separated and shareholders exercise control over employed managers through boards of directors and other institutions. Large companies with a founder family as a dominant shareholder are not an exception, especially in continental Europe, but in these companies too the interests of minority shareholders are well protected by law. They are run mostly by professional managers personally unrelated to the founder family.

In a large East Asian corporation, on the contrary, the founder family is usually not only a major owner but also a dominant stakeholder, exercising complete control. The voice of other minority, or, to be more precise, outside shareholders (this latter definition is more precise because their share combined may be quite high and even exceed that of a founder) is practically unheard. Legal protection of their rights is weak. Management is not separated from ownership—key managerial posts are occupied by the founder, his family members, and close friends. Corporate governance mechanisms don't work or can be applied only on a very limited scale. Most (but not all) East Asian conglomerates also have very close ties with politicians and bureaucracy and capitalize on the state support.

Japan is different from other East Asian nations as it has very few strong founder families as dominant owners of big corporations. Most of them were ousted in the wake of postwar economic and political reforms. In this regard, the Japanese economic system is sometimes called "capitalism without capitalists" or "corporate capitalism." The majority of shares used to be held by corporate shareholders, mutual shareholding being very popular. Between 1970 and 1990, the share of stock of listed corporations owned by other domestic corporations—both nonfinancial companies and financial institutions—went up roughly from 55 percent to 70 percent of the total in terms of value (Cabinet Office 2006, 175). In China, leading domestic corporations were born mostly as a result of the corporatization of state-owned enterprises (SOEs) started in the second half of the 1990s. For the time being the state remains their major stakeholder.

While Japanese and Chinese companies were mostly focused on particular industries, founders of other large East Asian companies and groups definitely preferred a conglomerate-style organization. They would be engaged in a wide variety of businesses which typically included property development, real estate, hotels, catering, banking and finance, telecommunication services, retailing, and, possibly, some sectors of manufacturing, such as food, textiles, construction materials, or maybe even auto assembly. South Korean conglomerates established a very strong edge in heavy industry too. Conglomerates in other East Asian economies, mostly owned by overseas Chinese, were stronger in the services than in manufacturing, and in light industry rather than in heavy industry.

Western corporations and their shareholders are wary about conglomerate-style business organization because maximization of profits and company value requires focusing the firm's activities on the areas where it can do its best.

However, for East Asian conglomerates and their founders, maximization of dividends and company value was not necessarily the first priority. The stability and expansion of the organization; presence, market share, and influence in a wide range of industries; prestigious jobs for family members; or just personal ambition could well be more important.

Corporate Finance

The third feature of the model is the corporate finance pattern. To raise external funds, East Asian corporations relied mostly on debt finance, or borrowing from banks, rather than on equity finance, or the issue of stock. In this regard, the situation in most continental European economies looked similar. However, East Asia's pattern had two more distinctive features. First, the share of connected lending was high—a significant portion of bank loans went to companies either belonging to the same business group as the lender bank or having close long-term links with it (personal ties, shareholding, the bank's executives on the company board, and so on). Second, a significant role was played by directed lending—lending orchestrated by the state.

Labor Relations

The fourth feature of the East Asian model is the "not quite market" relationship between companies and their employees. It is largely based on the notions of "company as a family," loyalty, and harmony within the organization. In the East Asian social context, firing a regular worker was difficult because companies were supposed to be responsible for stability of employment and to care about employees' everyday lives.

The Reliance on Inward FDI

Finally, the fifth feature of the model is the leading role of foreign-affiliated companies in the most technologically advanced, export-oriented sectors of the economy. East Asia's growth was largely driven by inward foreign direct investment (FDI). Foreign firms, mostly leading multinational companies (MNCs), provided not only capital, but also technologies and managerial expertise, as well as the opportunity to use their international distribution networks, sales promotion systems, brands, and so on. Japan and South Korea were the only major countries in the region which did not actively promote inward FDI. However, both were keen to import foreign technology.

The East Asian Model as an Alternative

So, here are the pillars of the East Asian economic model: a developmental state, family-owned and family-controlled conglomerates (in Japan, corporations which own and control one another) as the core players in the private sector, bank lending (especially, connected and directed lending) as the major source of corporate finance, labor relations emphasizing the notions of family and loyalty, and foreign-affiliated companies as leaders in the technologically advanced, export-oriented industries.

The fifth feature aside, this model turned out to be an alternative and even a challenge to conventional Western (especially Anglo-Saxon) capitalism. The most controversial point was the role of the state and its relationship with the private sector. The model questioned such basic principles of Western capitalism as the freedom of private entrepreneurship, resource allocation determined by the invisible hand of the market, a level playing field for all enterprises and industries, and profit maximization as the major goal of company management. Yet, for several postwar decades, all the features of the model contributed to the region's economic growth.

The East Asian Model of Capitalism: How It Worked for Growth

Developmental States: Promoting Industries

First, the state fixed economic development as the major national goal and worked to concentrate limited financial, material, and human resources in the strategically important industries which were leading growth and structural modernization.

In Japan, South Korea, and Taiwan—in close cooperation with domestic private companies—it managed to create and develop a range of manufacturing industries, including technologically advanced heavy industries, which became highly competitive internationally.

Japanese companies in the 1960s, and South Korean ones a decade later, joined the ranks of the world's major producers in most sectors of manufacturing—largely due to successful industrial policy. In Singapore and China, actively promoting inward FDI, foreign-affiliated firms played, and are playing, a leading role as exporters of manufacturing products—especially in technologically advanced sectors—but a group of competitive domestic companies has also emerged. Notably, they are mostly state-owned or government-linked.

In ASEAN 4 countries, production and exports in the electronic, auto, and other heavy industries are dominated by foreign subsidiaries. A cohort of internationally competitive domestic firms has emerged, mostly in food and textile industries, as well as in the sectors leveraging natural resources, such as wood processing or production of palm oil. The policy of creating and promoting heavy industries by establishing large, state-owned companies and injecting public funds, adopted in Malaysia and Indonesia, was not that successful. Newly created industries were internationally uncompetitive in terms of both cost and quality.

Economists' evaluation of the state's contribution to growth in these countries is rather mixed. Many of them attach the major growth-stimulating role to inward FDI. The key role of the latter can hardly be denied. Yet, for East Asian countries, the fact that they managed to nourish domestic companies in heavy industry, such as Malaysia's automaker Proton or Indonesia's Krakatau Steel, had its own significance. At least they proved to be capable of industrializing on their own and created a significant amount of jobs in the manufacturing sector. It is still not too late to try to make such companies internationally competitive.

Conglomerates: Bringing Dynamism to the Private Sector

Second, family-owned conglomerates contributed greatly to economic growth as the leaders of the private sector. Their founders vigorously expanded the range of business activities, giving a boost to many sectors of the economy at one and the same time.

Companies belonging to the same conglomerate, and operating in various business sectors, supported each other's growth in times when a still immature legal system, weak law enforcement, and underdeveloped financial markets made it difficult to rely on arm's-length transactions to provide the necessary material and financial inputs.

Japanese corporations' business philosophy—prioritizing long-term stability and the expansion of the organization, market shares, and production volumes over profit rates—also stimulated economic growth. One more distinctive feature of Japan's corporate world was the emphasis on long-term transaction ties between major industrial producers, such as Toyota or Hitachi, and their medium- and small-scale suppliers of parts, materials, and equipment. Constant, close interaction between final-product makers and their suppliers enabled growing technological sophistication and scrupulous quality control (Asanuma 1992; Tselichtchev 1992; 1994).

Massive Bank Lending

Third, massive bank lending played a pivotal role in the financing of industrial growth as stock markets in the region were mostly underdeveloped. Connected and directed lending minimized risks and helped lenders to monitor their borrowers, overcoming such hurdles as weak corporate governance and lax disclosure standards.

Labor Relations: Creating Commitment

Fourth, labor relations—emphasizing the notions of family, loyalty, organizational harmony, and long-term employment—were helpful to enhance work motivation and prevent labor conflicts. Their most sophisticated version, developed in Japan, emerged as a cohesive human resource management system with such distinctive features as long-term strategies of personnel training, on-the-job rotation, information sharing, and effective delegation of authority within a firm. This system contributed greatly to nurturing highly skilled and strongly committed laborers who were looked upon as the companies' most precious resource.

The East Asian Model: Working Better Than Western Capitalism?

Initially, the East Asian model of capitalism looked like a transitional system which could be appropriate just for the catch-up economies with still immature market institutions. In the 1970s, and especially the 1980s, the perception changed. In the late 1960s, Japan became one of the world's economic leaders and subsequently often outperformed the US and Western Europe not only in terms of growth rates but also in terms of quality of products and production efficiency. The four NIEs, and later Malaysia, Thailand, and, with reservations, Indonesia, emerged as successful followers. Therefore, East Asian capitalism, with Japan as its leader, began to be perceived as an alternative model, in many respects superior, to Western capitalism and relevant not only for a catch-up but also for a mature, developed economy. It looked capable of not only providing faster growth and stronger competitiveness but also effectively fighting with such evils of Western (especially, American-style) capitalism such as large income gaps and social inequality, rising unemployment, marginalization and low labor motivation of workers, destructive labor conflicts, and, consequently, social unrest, growing crime rates, moral degradation, and so forth.

The school of thought emphasizing the superiority, or at least substantial advantages, of the East Asian (especially, the Japanese) model found a growing number of supporters, not only in the East but also in the West.

The Asian Crisis: The Final Curtain

Crisis Overview

By the 1990s, the adoration of the East Asian model of capitalism was over and the discussion of its advantages also faded.

The Japanese economy entered a long and painful *Heisei* depression which lasted from 1991 to 2002. In the 1990s, its average growth rate was only a little more than 1 percent. Then, during 1997–98, the Asian crisis erupted sending the economies of South Korea and the ASEAN 4 into meltdown and posing enormous problems for the region as a whole. In 1998, GDP fell by 6.9 percent in South Korea, 10.5 percent in Thailand, 7.4 percent in Malaysia, and 13.1 percent in Indonesia (ADB 2008).

The crisis played a crucial role in the region's economic history: it marked the end of its growth within the framework of the model described. The nature of the crisis was both financial—the first financial crisis of the globalization era—and structural—the crisis of the model itself.

The major manifestations of the crisis were abrupt falls in the value of currencies and stocks—mainly in South Korea and the ASEAN 4—as foreign portfolio investors and lenders started to repatriate their capital on an unprecedented scale. The change from an upswing of inward investment to a massive withdrawal of funds was extremely dramatic. While, in 1995, the net inflow of capital in South Korea, Thailand, Malaysia, and Indonesia combined (total financial account surplus of the four countries) reached US$36.973 billion and in 1996—US$63.733 billion; in 1998 the four countries suffered a total net outflow (financial account deficit) of US$25.293 billion (ADB 2008).

Before the crisis, many East Asian currencies, pegged to the US dollar, were effectively overvalued. Central banks maintained the exchange rates through market interventions, buying their national currencies and selling US dollars and other foreign exchange. In early July 1997, having run short of foreign exchange, Thailand eventually floated the baht—which had been pegged at 25 baht for US$1 since 1985. In January 1998, it hit its lowest level of 56 baht for US$1, having lost 53 percent of its value. In 1997, the country's stock market plunged by 75 percent. In the summer of the same year, the crisis spread to other countries. In 1998, at their lowest levels the Indonesian rupiah lost 83 percent of its value, the South Korean won 47 percent, the Malaysian ringgit (which had not been pegged) 42 percent, and the Philippine peso 40 percent (Cheong 2006, 164). The Hong Kong dollar also faced strong downward pressure from October 1997 but the range of its fall was smaller: just 19 percent.

Stock prices, at their bottom, lost 65 percent of the pre-crisis high in South Korea and Indonesia, 67 percent in the Philippines, and 79 percent in Malaysia.

Singapore and Taiwan floated their currencies to maintain competitiveness of exports in the wake of the currency falls in neighboring states. Both economies, though not hit by the crisis as strongly as South Korea and the ASEAN 4, also experienced a very big drop in stock values: 72 percent and 46 percent respectively (Cheong 2006, 165).

The operations of many banks and other financial institutions in the crisis-impacted countries were paralyzed due to skyrocketing foreign debts (those debts were denominated in foreign currencies but the earnings necessary to pay them back were made mostly in the national currencies—thus, abrupt depreciation of the latter made the debt burden heavier) and nonperforming domestic loans. A number of leading conglomerates collapsed, many others found themselves on the verge of bankruptcy. Currency falls resulted in high inflation, household purchasing power was squeezed, domestic demand curtailed, production fell, and unemployment rose to unprecedented levels.

The Financial Side of the Crisis

Politicians, scholars, and business people in the region often emphasized the purely financial side of the crisis. Sometimes it was argued that it was engineered by international financial capital—mainly hedge funds and other speculators. According to this school of thought, international speculators deliberately crushed the Thai baht causing a chain reaction of subsequent depreciations. The toughest rhetoric of this kind came from then Malaysian prime minister, Mahathir bin Mohamad. However, it did not find many supporters.

In broader terms, a dramatic rise in the cross-border movement of short-term funds, which can easily come but also easily go, was often viewed as the major reason for the crisis. Yes, financial globalization did intensify the cross-border flow of short-term funds and, in 1997–98, East Asia's high dependence on those funds did make it vulnerable. Yes, in the age of globalization the exchange rate of every national currency is influenced by the moves of big players on the international money markets much more so than ever before. However, it is hardly relevant to stop here to explain the reasons. After all, the region's financial problems were rooted in its structural deficiencies.

Before discussing those faults and weaknesses, however, one more factor of the crisis has to be assessed—the policy of pegging national currencies to the US dollar. It was adopted by most East Asian countries to avoid currency risks and prevent import inflation, which was considered vital to boost investors' confidence. It is very difficult to say, even in retrospect, whether pegging was a good idea or not. It had its rationale, but, presumably, the governments overdid it by failing to show enough flexibility when it was necessary. Keeping exchange rates at high pegging levels significantly reduced the cost of foreign borrowing. As a result, its scale increased and this exacerbated the crisis. Also, it became a deterrent for exports, squeezing foreign exchange revenues.

In the early 1990s the US economy started to recover, boosted by growth in the IT sector. From 1995, the Federal Reserve Board began to raise interest rates to neutralize inflationary pressures. It made the US a more attractive place to invest and raised the value of the US dollar to which many East Asian currencies were pegged. Respectively, the latter appreciated too, hitting the exporters. Consequently, current account deficits soared. In 1996, the deficit of the five crisis-impacted economies combined reached US$55 billion (Economic Report of the President 1999, 241).

Current account deficit can be sustained only as long as the inflow of foreign capital, or the surplus of the financial account, remains sufficient to finance it. As the inflow stops, interest rates go up leading to economic contraction. As foreign capital runs away, downward pressure on the national currencies grows stronger, making it difficult to maintain the peg. A decline in export revenues worsens the problem even further.

Under these conditions the following mechanism starts to work. Expectations of the currency fall arise. Financial market players begin massive selling, which forces the government to terminate the peg. Free currency fall starts. Speculators benefit as now they can buy the same currency cheaper for settlements or acquire the respective countries' assets for "a discount price."

They act fully in accordance with the logic of the market, using the mechanism because it exists. However, they don't create it. It has been created by the financial authorities of the respective Asian countries.

The Structural Side of the Crisis

In a way, in 1997–98, foreign lenders and portfolio investors reckoned that, obsessed with East Asia's high growth rates, they had lent or invested there a bit too much. Massive repatriation of funds and sales of East Asian currencies began, not least because investors became concerned about the financial condition of local companies and banks. Many of them were on the verge of a default. This was the result of poor management and governance rooted in the following flaws of the East Asian model.

First, a by-product of large-scale state involvement was widespread cronyism. Often, government support was not extended to the most dynamic and, at least potentially, competitive sectors and companies but to well-connected firms and business groups.

Second, as East Asian conglomerates deliberately blocked control by outside shareholders, their managers could often afford to ignore the "discipline of the market" without being penalized. The close relationship with the state and the mutual support within business groups eased natural market pressures even further.

Third, connected and directed lending made East Asian companies addicted to large-scale borrowing. The basic premise of their founders and managers was that money would be "at hand" any time it was needed and the capital cost would be low. Getting a wider access to external borrowing in the wake of globalization and financial liberalization exacerbated the problem even further. Too many East Asian companies did not care that much about the risk of becoming unable to pay back their debts.

East Asian corporations became "famous" for their high and, in most countries, growing leverage, or ratio of total debt to equity. In South Korea it increased from 2.82 in 1988 to 3.47 in 1996 (in other words, in 1996, the total debt of South Korean corporations was 3.47 times as big as their equity capital), in Thailand from 1.60 to 2.36, and in Malaysia from 0.73 to 1.18. In the Philippines, leverage went up from 0.83 in 1991 to 1.29 in 1996, and in Indonesia, over the same period, it slightly decreased from 1.94 to 1.87, still remaining at a high level (Claessens 2000). For a cohort of leading conglomerates the leverage was much higher.

Especially risky was East Asian companies' high dependence on short-term debt, not least because short-term borrowing was often used for investment projects that basically required long-term financing.

Founders of the conglomerates were too confident that they wouldn't fail. If grave financial problems emerged, either the government would help or the continuous rise of the market prices of their assets would provide the necessary liquidity, offsetting the losses they made. Many Japanese corporations, especially in the latter half of the 1980s, adopted a similar mode of behavior.

Fourth, Asian-style labor relations also had its faults. Inflexibility of employment made it extremely difficult to fire a poorly performing, incapable, or simply lazy or irresponsible worker. Rigid remuneration schemes reflected an inability or unwillingness to effectively link individual remuneration and promotion to skills and performance.

The Asian crisis, along with the *Heisei* depression in Japan, was a signal to East Asian economies that they could no longer operate as they used to.

China, though not directly hit by the Asian crisis, had to address structural problems of a similar nature, especially posed by weak banks with huge nonperforming loans (NPLs) and ailing big enterprises—in China's case state-owned.

Entering a New Stage

The Asian crisis was over within a very short period of time—since 1999 practically all major East Asian emerging-market economies have started growing fast again. (However, Japan needed more than a decade to get out of the *Heisei* depression.) Therefore, sometimes it is argued that it was not a crisis of a structural nature. We disagree.

The return to growth was quick because one of the major manifestations of the crisis—a brisk fall of the currencies—also provided the way out. Currency depreciation boosted exports. It led the regional economies back to the familiar path—export-led, industrial growth.

However, it was not a return to the pre-crisis status. East Asia would hardly restore its ability to grow if it did not come out with anti-crisis policies that dramatically accelerated its structural transformation—a transformation which marked the beginning of the end to the East Asian model of capitalism. In the following chapters we will show that post-crisis growth itself is taking place within a new, gradually forming, systemic framework.

The specifics of anti-crisis policies, worked out under the guidance of the International Monetary Fund (IMF), varied from country to country, but their major contents were largely the same.[5]

First, the governments had to drastically cut, or eliminate, subsidies supporting particular industries or the consumers of basic products, such as fuels or foodstuffs, as well as curb public expenditure in general.

Second, they were to give up supporting ailing banks and companies with dim prospects of revitalization.

Third, the core of anti-crisis policies was a drastic rationalization of the banking sector. The crisis-hit countries established powerful state institutions, responsible for the disposal of nonperforming loans and the restructuring of the troubled banks, and authorized them to put the banks under direct control. Supervision of banks was strengthened, the criteria of a nonperforming loan tightened, and the requirements regarding the ratio of own capital to assets became strict as never before.

Fourth, East Asian countries took big steps to liberalize imports and inward investment, especially into the service sector.

Fifth, they moved to introduce laws and regulations improving corporate governance, disclosure standards, foreclosure, and bankruptcy procedures.

This set of measures should be viewed in a wider context than just policies to overcome the crisis of 1997–98. It was the start, or at least an accelerator, of a big systemic shift, imposing a much tougher market discipline on the governments, companies, and workers—a shift needed to eliminate East Asia's structural biases and to make it capable of meeting the challenges of the globalization era. This systemic shift was being undertaken throughout the region, not only in the crisis-hit countries.

In other words, the launch of anti-crisis policies marked the beginning of a new stage in the region's economic development.

Endnotes

1 North Vietnam, or the Democratic Republic of Vietnam, was proclaimed by Ho Chi Minh in 1945. It was ruled by Communists and was an ally of both the Soviet Union and China. In 1976, after the Vietnam War, the single nation, known as the Socialist Republic of Vietnam, was formed. Like China, it pursues market-oriented economic reforms under a Communist regime.

2 One of the recognized theoretical interpretations of the East Asian model, based mostly on the analysis of the Japanese economy, was suggested by Murakami in 1992. He defines three major economic features of the model: market competition based on private property; industrial policy pursued by the government in order to create industries counted upon as future leaders; and the policy of income redistribution aimed at reducing inequality and softening shocks resulting from structural change (Murakami 1992). We are trying to present a wider version.

3 It has to be remembered that not all the features mentioned are applicable to all the major East Asian economies.

4 We interpret a "developmental state" as one which puts economic development on the top of its priority list and actively intervenes in the economy to promote it. Sometimes this notion is associated only with the role of "honest technocrats"—ministerial bureaucracy shielded from political pressures and having the authority to articulate economic policy. We agree that this was part of the "developmental state" story, though, of course, honesty and freedom from political pressures have to be perceived in relative terms. However, the story as a whole has wider issues.

5 Malaysia was an exception. Officially, it rejected the IMF-proposed package and took some steps which ran contrary to its approach. Mainly, it pegged the ringgit to the US dollar, imposed restrictions on the cross-border movement of short-term capital, and refused to pursue speedy liberalization of imports and inward investment. Yet, regarding all the rest, it turned out to be not that different from others.

2

A New Wave of Growth

Having overcome the Asian crisis of 1997–98, East Asian economies entered a new phase of economic growth which started in 1999 and continues for the time being (see Tables 2.1 and 2.2). Once again, East Asia has emerged as the fastest growing region in the world (along with Central Asia), steadily increasing its share of global gross domestic product (GDP) and world trade.

Table 2.1 Average real GDP growth of the East Asian economies and India (1999–2007) (%)

Country	%
Japan	1.5
South Korea	5.6
Taiwan	4.3
Hong Kong	5.0
Singapore	6.1
Malaysia	5.6
Thailand	4.9
Philippines	4.8
Indonesia	4.6
China	9.6
Vietnam	7.3
India	6.4

Source: Calculated on the basis of the annual growth rates data presented in the chapters on the national economies in the Part 2.

Table 2.2   Average real GDP growth for East Asia and other regions* (%)

Country/Region	1985–90	1991–96	1999–2004
ASEAN 4 (Indonesia, Malaysia, Philippines, Thailand)	6.2	7.3	4.6
China (incl. Hong Kong)	8.2	10.5	7.8
Japan	4.8	1.8	1.4
NIEs 3 (Singapore, South Korea, Taiwan)	11.1	7.4	5.2
European Union	3.4	1.2	1.9
US	2.4	1.4	2.0
World	1.9	0.9	1.6

Source: METI. Tsusho Hakusho 2006.
*GDP is measured in US dollars.

East Asia in the World: Its Present Position

East Asia's Shares of the World's GDP and Exports

Without Japan, the region's share (the share of the four NIEs, ASEAN 4, and China combined) of the world's GDP went up from 7.8 percent in 1999 to 11.0 percent in 2007. However, it increased mostly due to a dramatic rise in the share of China. The share of the ASEAN 4 elevated only a little and the share of the four NIEs was practically unchanged. With Japan included, the region's share dropped from 22.4 percent to 19.1 percent (see Table 2.3).

The share of East Asia in the world's exports was higher: in 2007 it reached 26.8 percent including Japan and 21.7 percent excluding it versus, respectively, 25.6 percent and 17.9 percent in 1999. As with East Asia's share of the world's GDP, the increase occurred due to the remarkable 5.2 percentage point increment of China's share. The shares of the NIEs, ASEAN 4, and Japan all fell.

In other words, growth dynamics in post-crisis East Asia come mainly from China. China leads the growth, others follow—capitalizing on its rise. We will return to this crucial point later on.

Ranking by GDP (PPP)

The position of East Asian countries in the world economy turns out to be much stronger if the GDP in US dollars is calculated on the basis of the purchasing power parity (PPP) of national currencies, not their exchange rates (see Table 2.4). As a measure of the size of a particular national economy the PPP-based GDP is more adequate than the GDP calculated on the exchange rate basis, as the latter ignores the fact that goods or services of the same type and quality would cost you less US dollars in China than in Germany. The PPP-based calculation eliminates this disparity.

Table 2.3   East Asia's share of world GDP and world exports, 1999–2007 (%)

Country/Region	Share of world GDP, 1999 (%)	Share of world exports, 1999 (%)	Share of world GDP, 2007 (%)	Share of world exports, 2007 (%)
NIEs 4	3.2	10.1	3.1	9.2
ASEAN 4	1.4	4.2	1.9	3.7
China	3.2	3.6	6.0	8.8
Japan	14.6	7.7	8.1	5.1
East Asia total (excl. Japan)	7.8	17.9	11.0	21.7
East Asia total (incl. Japan)	22.4	25.6	19.1	26.8
European Union*	28.0	39.8	31.0	42.5
US	30.3	12.7	25.5	8.4

Source: World Economic Outlook Data Base, International Monetary Fund (IMF), September 2004, April 2008; World Trade Organization (WTO) (www.wto.org); Government of Philippines (www.census.gov.ph).
*EU-15 for 1999, EU-27 for 2007.

In terms of nominal GDP on a country basis, China recently rose to number four, overtaking all European economies except Germany. India is in twelfth position, South Korea in thirteenth.

In terms of GDP (PPP), China runs second after the US with a GDP 1.6 times bigger than that of Japan. India is fourth, ahead of Germany. Three Asian economies are in the top five and six in the top twenty.

Table 2.5 shows where the regional economies stand in terms of wealth, or per-capita GDP (PPP). Today, two "tigers," Singapore and Hong Kong, follow oil-rich Brunei and are clearly ahead of others. Japan runs fourth and is followed very closely by Taiwan. This cohort of countries and territories is in the world's top thirty. South Korea is a little bit behind, but, definitely belongs to the ranks of developed economies. Its per-capita GDP is a bit lower than that in Greece (US$29,172) and a little higher than in Portugal (US$21,701).

These days, it is no longer relevant to call the four "tiger economies" NIEs. As far as the share of industry in the GDP or the total number of persons employed is concerned, they had already become industrialized three decades ago. However, for the readers' convenience, we will stick to the conventional terminology.

Malaysia and Thailand are middle income countries. Their per-capita GDP is much higher than the developing nations' average. Yet, they still have to do much to narrow the gap with the developed world.

Table 2.4   GDP of East Asian countries, India, and other major economic powers, 2007 (US$ millions)

Country	Nominal GDP	Ranking	GDP (PPP)	Ranking
US	13,843,825	1	13,843,825	1
Japan	4,383,762	2	4,289,809	3
Germany	3,332,147	3	2,809,603	5
China	3,250,827	4	6,991,036	2
UK	2,772,570	5	2,137,421	6
France	2,560,255	6	2,046,899	8
Italy	2,104,666	7	1,786,429	10
Spain	1,436,959	8	1,351,608	11
Canada	1,432,140	9	1,265,838	13
Brazil	1,313,590	10	1,835,642	9
Russia	1,289,582	11	2,087,815	7
India	1,098,945	12	2,818,867	4
South Korea	957,063	13	1,200,879	14
Indonesia	432,944	20	837,791	16
Taiwan	383,307	24	695,388	19
Thailand	245,659	33	519,362	24
Hong Kong	206,707	Not ranked	206,707	Not ranked
Malaysia	186,482	38	357,391	29
Singapore	161,349	45	228,116	44
Philippines	144,129	46	299,626	37
Vietnam	70,022	59	221,397	46

Source: World Economic Outlook Database, IMF, April 2008.

East Asia's economic performance is often compared with another cluster of major emerging market countries, Latin America. From the data presented in Tables 2.5 and 2.6 we can clearly see that, as far as per-capita GDP is concerned, the East Asian NIEs definitely outperformed the leading Latin American nations but Malaysia and Thailand are in the same cohort.

The next pair, Indonesia and the Philippines, remains in the low-middle-income countries league. Thus it is not surprising that, for example, Indonesians perceive modern Malaysia as a rich neighbor and those who manage to find a job

Table 2.5   Per-capita GDP (PPP) in East Asian countries and India, 2007(US$)

Country	Per-capita GDP (US$)	Ranking
Brunei	51,005	4
Singapore	49,714	5
Hong Kong	41,994	Not ranked
Japan	33,577	22
Taiwan	30,126	26
South Korea	24,783	34
Malaysia	13,315	56
Thailand	7,900	81
China	5,292	99
Indonesia	3,725	120
Philippines	3,378	122
Mongolia	3,203	124
Vietnam	2,587	126
India	2,659	126
Laos	2,060	136
Cambodia	1,806	143
Myanmar	1,039	162

Source: World Economic Outlook Database, IMF, 2007.

there are looked upon as lucky people. On the other hand, in the Malaysians' eyes, Indonesia is the supplier of a low-cost labor force (including illegal immigrants, which can cause some social tension) for plantations, construction sites, or catering enterprises.

As for China, for the time being it remains in the group of low-middle-income countries, but its per-capita GDP is growing at the fastest pace in the region. In the post-crisis years it managed to overtake and clearly exceed Indonesia and the Philippines.

Of the remaining East Asian countries, Vietnam's per-capita GDP has also been growing fast, though its world ranking is still low and Cambodia, Laos, and Myanmar are in the group of low income, or less-developed countries.

Size Matters

When comparing per-capita GDP we have to keep in mind that larger developing nations usually find it more difficult to raise it than smaller ones. They

Table 2.6   Per-capita GDP (PPP) of major Latin American economies, 2007 (US$)

Country	Per-capita GDP (US$)	Ranking
Chile	13,936	54
Argentina	13,308	57
Mexico	12,775	60
Costa Rica	10,300	75
Brazil	9,695	78

Source: World Economic Outlook Database, IMF, 2007.

have many more poor households in their vast territories, and a much longer time is required for the fruits of industrial progress to reach those areas and significantly elevate their living standards. In this regard, small city-states, such as Singapore and Hong Kong, are "lucky," while China, India, Indonesia, or the Philippines face the toughest challenges.

For the time being, China and the major Southeast Asian countries have achieved a very significant increase of wealth in and around the capitals and other large cities (as well as in the international resort areas), while the rest of their territories remain at a earlier stage of economic development.

Running Fast But Slowing Down

East Asia's average growth rates in the post-crisis period of 1999–2007 were several times higher than those in the "old developed economies."

Yet, after the crisis, growth in the region has been decelerating. Compared both to the average for the whole East Asian miracle period (from the 1960s to the mid-1990s) and to the pre-crisis period of 1990–96, with the exception of Hong Kong and the Philippines, growth rates during 1999–2007 fell. On the other hand, growth in the US, European Union (EU), and the world economy in general accelerated (see Table 2.2).

Growth ranking within the region remains mostly the same as in pre-crisis years. China is leading, followed by the four NIEs, and the growth of the ASEAN 4 economies is the slowest (see Table 2.1). After the crisis, Vietnam became the second-fastest runner among the major regional economies. The NIEs are almost repeating—with a time lag—the growth pattern of Japan. Growth rates decline somewhat as the economy matures. For Malaysia and Thailand, deceleration may pose problems. It looks like they are losing their ability to sustain high growth rates long before their economies have matured—among other things, this may prevent them from solving their poverty problems. For Indonesia, in this regard, the situation is even more critical.

The Philippines, the only slow runner of the miracle era, turns out to be the only major regional economy visibly accelerating in the post-crisis period. However, the acceleration achieved is hardly sufficient for a low-middle-income country with about 40 percent of the population living below the poverty line.

Finally, in China, average growth rates for 1999–2007 were lower than for 1990–1996 but from 2003 they began to go up again, becoming double-digit and the highest among the world's major national economies.

The future growth potential of the East Asian economies can be seen from the forecast presented in Table 2.7.

Table 2.7 Growth forecasts for the Asian economies, US, and EU (%)

Forecaster	Japan	NIEs	ASEAN 4	China	India	US	EU
World Bank, 2006–15	1.7	6.1	6.1	6.1	5.5	3.6	2.0
IEA, 2004–30	1.9	3.8	3.8	5.0	4.7	2.3	2.1
Cabinet Office of the Government of Japan, 2004–30	1.5	4.1	3.1	6.9	4.1	3.1	1.8
Average of the above three[1]	1.7	4.7	4.3	6.0	4.8	3.0	2.0

Source: METI. Tsusho Hakusho 2006, p.60.[2]
Notes.
[1] As forecasts cover different periods, averages presented in the fourth line have to be viewed with caution.
[2] The data is presented the way it was arranged in the White Paper on International Trade by METI. As there is no World Bank forecast separately for ASEAN 4, China, and the NIEs the growth rates for these economies presented in the table's World Bank line are the forecasted growth rates for East Asia and the Pacific. For the same reason, the World Bank's forecast for South Asia is used instead of the forecast for India and the forecast for the Eurozone instead of the forecast for the EU. In the IEA line, the forecast for "Asia, OECD" is used instead of the forecast for Japan, the forecast for the US and Canada instead of the forecast for the US, the forecast for "Europe, OECD" instead of the forecast for the EU, and the forecast for East Asia instead of the forecasts for the ASEAN 4 and the NIEs. The forecast of the Cabinet Office of the Government of Japan for the EU covers its 15 members. The World Bank's forecasts for Japan, the US, and the EU cover the period from 2003 to 2015.

Labor and Capital: Inputs and Productivity

Economic growth rates depend on the increase in the number of workers and capital stock and on the rise in productivity of labor and capital.

Labor Resources are Still Abundant

In the post-crisis years, the situation with the supply of labor resources remains favorable throughout the region, with the exception of Japan. First, most of the region's major countries maintain fairly high population growth rates. In 2000–04 population growth rates averaged: 2.6 percent in Malaysia and 2.3 percent in the Philippines (very rapid growth); 1.9 percent in India, 1.5 percent in Indonesia, and 1.4 percent in Thailand (rapid growth); 0.8 percent in South Korea and

Hong Kong, 0.6 percent in China, and 0.5 percent in Taiwan (moderate growth); and 0.2 percent in Japan (slow growth). Second, the region retains by far the highest employment participation rates in the world—in other words, its share of people at work in the whole population is large by global standards. On the other hand, the share of elderly people is low (see Table 2.8).

In a number of East Asian countries favorable demographic conditions are not expected to last long. Especially in the NIEs and China, the decline in the share of the population of working age is expected to start as soon as the beginning of the 2010s (Cheong 2006, 2). By contrast, in the ASEAN 4 and India conditions are likely to remain favorable for several decades ahead. For more details see Chapter 5.

The Deficit of Highly Skilled Laborers

As far as quality of the labor resource is concerned, East Asia's pool of literate, diligent, motivated, and easily manageable workers retains its role as an important driving force of growth.

Yet, an important new problem is emerging—an unfavorable change of the labor cost-quality mix. On the one hand, labor costs in major East Asian economies are going up, gradually but steadily. On the other, the region is facing a severe shortage of skilled human resources, especially highly qualified specialists.

Still, the region, especially the Northeast Asian countries, is leading the world in terms of growth of labor productivity. In post-crisis 2003, Northeast Asia's labor

Table 2.8   Population by age group (%)

Country	Date of survey	0–14 years old (%)	15–64 years old (%)	65 years and older (%)
Japan	October 1, 2005	13.6	65.3	21.0
South Korea	July 1, 2003	20.3	71.4	8.3
Taiwan	December 31, 2004	19.3	71.2	9.5
Hong Kong	July 1, 2003	15.7	72.6	11.7
Singapore	July 1, 2003	20.8	71.5	7.7
Malaysia	July 1, 2004	32.9	62.9	4.2
Thailand	December 31, 2002	24.7	68.8	6.4
Philippines	July 1, 2003	34.7	61.1	4.2
China	December 31, 2004	21.5	70.9	7.6
Vietnam	April 1, 1999	33.1	61.1	4.2

Source: Sekai Kokusei Zue 2006–07, p.71.

productivity (measured as GDP per person employed) was 75 percent higher than in 1993, which means that average annual productivity growth within this period was 5.8 percent across the whole region (6.3 percent in China, 4.3 percent in South Korea, 3.6 percent in Taiwan, and 1.7 percent in Hong Kong). In Southeast Asia productivity went up 21.6 percent and its average growth rate was 2.0 percent. For South Asia the figures were 37.9 percent and 3.3 percent respectively (see Table 2.9).

Table 2.9 Labor productivity and GDP average growth rates, 1993–2003 (%)

Region	Labor productivity growth (%)	GDP growth (%)
World	1.0	3.5
Northeast Asia[1]	5.8	3.5
Southeast Asia[2]	2.0	4.4
South Asia	3.3	5.5
Middle East and North Africa	0.1	3.5
Sub-Saharan Africa	0.2	2.9
Latin America and the Caribbean	0.1	2.6
Industrialized economies	1.4	2.5

Source: International Labor Organization (ILO), World Employment Report 2004–05, Chapter 1, p.27.
Notes:
[1] Includes China, Hong Kong, Mongolia, North and South Korea, and Taiwan.
[2] Includes all ASEAN member states and also adjacent economies of the Pacific region.

Investment Ratios

As far as capital supply is concerned, since the miracle years, East Asia has been "famous" for its high rates of savings and investment. The exceptions are Indonesia and the Philippines where investment rates (investment ratio of GDP) are lower than in the "old developed countries," and Taiwan, where they are about the same (see Table 2.10). In the post-crisis period, most East Asian economies maintained investment rates higher than those of other regions.

In comparison with the 1960–94 average, in China investment rates for the period of 1996–2006 almost doubled, in South Korea they increased significantly, and in Indonesia and Thailand they only increased a little. In the Philippines, Malaysia, and Singapore they fell. The Philippine economy, especially, is underinvested. In Taiwan, they are practically unchanged and in Hong Kong they are mostly declining in this decade.

Notably, a number of regional economies (especially the ASEAN 4) are facing inward foreign direct investment (FDI) constraints unthinkable in the miracle years. This is largely because of the investors choosing alternatives, such as China

Table 2.10   Investment* ratio of GDP (%)

Country	1960–94 (av.)	1999–2006 (av.)	1999	2000	2001	2002	2003	2004	2005	2006
South Korea	23.5	28.8	26.8	31.0	26.7	26.0	29.4	30.2	30.1	29.8
Taiwan	20.0	20.2	24.3	23.3	18.2	17.2	17.2	20.7	20.2	20.3
Hong Kong	–	23.9	25.4	27.5	25.8	24.2	22.8	23.0	20.5	21.6
Singapore	33.2	22.5	32.8	33.3	24.3	20.6	13.4	18.3	18.6	18.8
Malaysia	25.6	22.8	22.3	26.9	24.0	24.4	21.8	22.5	19.8	20.7
Thailand	25.1	25.8	20.7	22.8	24.0	23.8	25.2	27.1	31.6	31.5
Indonesia	18.1	18.8	11.6	22.2	17.0	14.3	16.0	22.8	22.2	24.6
Philippines	19.8	17.8	18.6	21.2	17.6	19.3	18.9	17.0	15.7	14.3
China	22.3	41.5	38.3	36.1	37.9	41.0	44.4	45.3	44.1	44.9

Source: For 1960–94: Collins and Bosworth 1996; for 1999–2006: Asian Development Bank (ADB), Key Economic Indicators.
*Gross capital formation.

and India, and, to a certain extent, the emergence of Vietnam as a new popular investment destination. New investment constraints are interrelated with the above-mentioned skilled labor shortages. The latter impede the launch of investment projects in many areas that require highly skilled professionals and personnel capable of using advanced technologies.

The Falling Productivity of Capital

As shown in Table 2.11, marginal capital coefficients (calculated as the share of gross capital formation in the nominal GDP divided by the real GDP growth rate) in the post-crisis years were higher than the 1960–94 average in all the major East Asian economies, except Singapore and the Philippines. This means that today East Asian countries have to invest a higher share of their GDP per every percent of their real growth. Partly, this can be explained by the rising share of capital-intensive industries in the total output. Falling productivity of capital can be offset by the rising productivity of labor.

Yet, low efficiency of capital has become an issue in the focus of attention in the region—especially in China, though its marginal capital coefficient is lower than in most other countries.

Total Factor Productivity

One of the hot issues for the region is the contribution to growth made by the rise in total factor productivity (TFP). Basically, economic growth is achieved by the increase of either inputs of labor and capital or of the output per unit of those inputs. Rising TFP means the growing output per unit. It becomes possible, mainly, because of increments in knowledge and technological progress. Debate about the contribution of TFP to growth in East Asia was boosted by the publication of Paul Krugman's famous article "The Myth of Asia's Miracle"

Table 2.11 Average marginal capital coefficients

Country	1960–94	1999–2006
South Korea	3.46	5.05
Taiwan	2.30	4.93
Singapore	4.00	3.81
Malaysia	3.66	4.07
Thailand	3.26	5.27
Indonesia	3.17	4.37
Philippines	5.21	3.79
China	3.28	3.84

Source: For 1960–94: Collins and Bosworth 1996; for 1999–2006 Asian Development Bank (ADB), Key Economic Indicators.

(Krugman 1994). Based on the calculations made by A. Young, the author argued that growth in the Asian NIEs was prompted simply by the quantitative expansion of the inputs of capital and labor, not by the rise in their productivity. In other words, the contribution of the TFP rise was very low. That's why, according to Krugman, the Asian miracle is a myth. The region's rapid growth is doomed to end as the law of falling marginal returns on investment is at work.

Krugman's conclusions were criticized by many economists. Among other things, opponents insisted that much depended on the calculation methodology and the period the calculations cover. Alternative estimates showed that TFP was an important factor of growth in the region, at least in the NIEs and China, and that compared to other regions the situation in East Asia, in this respect, looked quite favorable.

One of the latest studies by International Monetary Fund (IMF) experts covered the period from 1970 to 2005 and also, for every major group of Asian countries (in this survey Asia includes South Asian states, but excludes Japan), the period between the start of their dynamic growth take-off and the mid-2000s (IMF 2006).

The results show that though the increase in the number of laborers provided an important stimulus, growth in Asia was driven mainly by the rise in labor productivity. The contribution of productivity was larger than in Latin America.

Also, compared to other developing regions, Asia had both faster capital accumulation and a more rapid rise in TFP. However, its progress in catching up with the developed economies was achieved mainly due to capital accumulation. In other words, TFP growth in the developed economies was more significant.

Most of all, TFP contributed to growth in the the NIEs, China, Thailand, and India. As a whole, the contribution of the ASEAN 4 was low, largely due to the poor performance of particular economies, especially the Philippines (see Figure 2.1).

The results of the numerous studies on the contribution of TFP to economic growth have to be viewed with caution. Their authors themselves don't hesitate to point out that they are highly dependent on the methodology (assumptions the estimates are based upon), period of time chosen, statistical data used, and so on. Furthermore, TFP as such is not a universally accepted economic indicator.

Still, the TFP debate helped the countries of the region grasp and articulate a problem of crucial importance. While the increases in their labor inputs and, especially, capital stock were remarkable, they may not have been necessarily that successful in raising the efficiency of their utilization.

Let us not forget that East Asian companies (excluding Japanese), even in the NIEs, let alone the rest, often specialize in the production of lower value-added items and more simple technological processes compared to Japanese, US, or European firms. Quite often they may just assemble an electronic device, or a vehicle, or produce their more simple parts, while the key components, requiring more advanced technologies, are manufactured overseas.

Acquiring the capability to produce more value-added items domestically is the key to East Asia's future growth.

Sources of growth in output per capita (%)

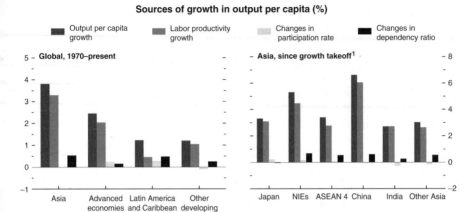

Sources of growth in labor productivity (%)

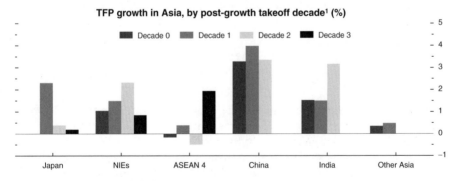

[1] The growth takeoff is defined as occurring in 1955 for Japan, 1967 for the newly industrialized economies (NIEs), 1973 for the ASEAN 4 (Indonesia, Malaysia, the Philippines, and Thailand), 1979 for China, 1982 for India, and 1990 for other Asian economies. Each decade corresponds to a 10-year period following the takeoff years stated above.
[2] The crisis countries group consists of Indonesia, South Korea, Malaysia, the Philippines, and Thailand.

Figure 2.1   Sources of growth in Asia

Source: IMF, World Economic Outlook: Financial Systems and Economic Cycles, September 2006.

Growth Drivers on the Demand Side

Private Consumption Becomes More Important

On the demand side, the emergence and expansion of the middle class, mainly in large cities, results in a rapid rise in private consumption.

The NIEs have already entered the mass consumption stage. Furthermore, their growing middle class is becoming increasingly sophisticated in its requirements with regard to goods and services. Consumers want more and more high-grade, expensive items and care about brands. This trend is intensifying in China and Southeast Asia too (for instance, China is becoming one of the biggest importers of designer clothing, footwear, and cosmetics), but here it is mostly limited to major cities.

In 2005, the total number of consumers with significant purchasing power (meaning annual household income of more than US$3,000) was 160 million in China and a little more than 40 million in the ASEAN countries (METI 2006).

Still, Growth Remains Export-led

Though the role of domestic demand is rising, East Asian growth remains largely export-led. In most major Asian economies the ratio of merchandise exports to GDP is increasing, in some cases dramatically. For example, between 2000 and 2007, it grew from 119.4 percent to 166.3 percent in Hong Kong, from 146.5 percent to 185.3 percent in Singapore, from 56.3 percent to 61.9 percent in Thailand, from 33.7 percent to 38.3 percent in South Korea, from 20.9 percent to 37.1 percent in China, and from 10.3 percent to 16.3 percent in Japan.[1]

The share of intraregional exports is rising, mainly due to the dramatic growth of trade between China and other East Asian states (see Table 2.12).

China-led Growth

Why China-led?

China's growth is the core of East Asia's growth. It influences the growth of all of the region's other national economies through both opening new opportunities and posing new challenges. Why?

First, China has by far the highest growth rates in the region and is among the fastest economic runners in the world. It has risen to the position of the world's fourth-largest economy by nominal GDP and the second-largest in terms of GDP (PPP).

Second, China has become a major competitor for practically all other East Asian economies. It has created a full set of industries and made most of them internationally competitive. Every other country in the region has to think about

Table 2.12   Trade flows between East Asia and its major counterparts (US$ millions)

Trade flow	1994	2004	2004/1994
From East Asia[1] to China	43,075	196,703	4.6 times
From China to East Asia[1]	60,248	202,103	3.4 times
From East Asia[2] to East Asia[2]	329,629	682,490	2.1 times
From East Asia[1] to East Asia[1]	226,306	281,684	1.2 times
From East Asia[2] to Japan	90,875	196,348	2.2 times
From Japan to East Asia[2]	63,206	101,902	1.6 times
From East Asia[2] to the US	146,737	367,873	2.5 times
From East Asia[1] to the US	107,956	171,181	1.6 times
From East Asia[2] to the EU15	130,983	293,589	2.2 times
From East Asia[1] to the EU15	109,878	146,921	1.3 times

Source: METI, Tsusho Hakusho 2006.
Notes:
[1]NIEs+ASEAN 4.
[2]NIEs+ASEAN 4+China.

how to differentiate from China in the world markets or otherwise face dire consequences for its exports and future growth.

Third, China is the region's leader in terms of attracting FDI. Producing in China and exporting worldwide is a pattern for a growing number of multinational companies.

Fourth, rapidly growing China opens a lot of market and investment opportunities. Exporting to China, doing business there, and providing a wide range of services for China—for instance, for the rapidly growing number of Chinese tourists—stimulates growth around the region.

China's Share in Regional Trade

Let's have a look at the change in the amount of East Asia's trade with various parts of the world between 1994 and 2004 (see Table 2.12). In these calculations, East Asia includes either the NIEs, the ASEAN 4, and China or, when it is necessary to detect the share of China, only the NIEs and ASEAN 4.

Some remarkable developments can be traced. First, the share of China in the total amount of intraregional trade in East Asia (NIEs+ASEAN 4+China) increased dramatically from 31.3 percent in 1994 to 58.7 percent in 2004. In other words, almost 60 percent of the intraregional trade is accounted for by China's trade with its East Asian counterparts. By contrast, trade within East Asia without China (NIEs+ASEAN 4) grew very little, only 1.2 times.

Second, in 2004, exports by the NIEs and ASEAN 4 to China exceeded their own and China's combined exports to Japan. In 1994, by contrast, the latter were about twice as big as the former. In 2004, the NIEs and ASEAN 4 exported to China more than to the US and to the EU, while, in 1994, exports to the US were almost 3.4 times, and to the EU 2.6 times, greater.

On the other hand, the present configuration of the region's growth, with China at its core, contains a substantial risk as every other East Asian economy, including the Japanese, becomes China's economic hostage. If, for whatever reason, China stumbles, the whole region may suffer a severe shock.

The Growth of Poor Quality: Energy Inefficiency and Environmental Unfriendliness

East Asia's growth is high, but its "quality" is still low. The rapidly growing regional economies perform poorly in terms of their efficiency in using natural, especially energy, resources and the preservation of the natural environment.

Low Energy Efficiency

Japan, in the wake of the first oil shock of 1973–75, started to drastically reduce energy consumption per unit of production. It successfully introduced energy-saving technologies and changed the industrial structure in favor of knowledge-intensive industries consuming relatively little energy. Environmental issues were placed very high on the policy priorities list. At this point, other East Asian economies, even after a longer period of rapid growth are still far from making a similar shift.

Figure 2.2 shows a big difference in the growth patterns of "old developed economies" and East Asian countries between 1980 and 2003. The former, having already drastically reduced energy consumption per unit of production in the late 1970s, continued along that line and in 2003 consumed less energy per US dollar of nominal GDP than in 1980. In most East Asian countries, by contrast, energy consumption per US dollar of GDP went up.

Even South Korea, an energy-efficient country by regional standards, consumes per US dollar of its GDP 15–22 percent more energy than the US and Europe. In other Asian countries, with the exception of the less industrialized Philippines, energy consumption levels are three to four times higher than in the "old developed states."

Energy Resource Constraints as Growth Impediments

Energy resource constraints are becoming growth impediments. The rapid economic rise of energy-hungry Asia—particularly giants like China and India, but also other large countries such as Indonesia—has caused an unprecedented hike in the world demand for oil and other energy resources on a global scale. Consequently, world prices have been beating one record after

(1980 in Japan = 1)

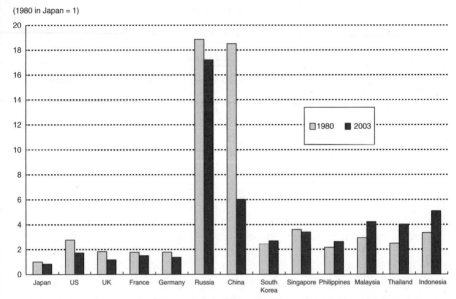

Notes: The above figures have been obtained with energy consumption per US$1 of nominal GDP in Japan in 1980 (5,508Btu) as 1.
        1 Btu equals about 0.25Kcal. The figures for Russia are for 1992 and 2003.

Figure 2.2   Energy consumption per US$1 of nominal GDP

Source: METI, White Paper on International Economy and Trade, 2006, p.82.

another, influencing costs, consumption, and investment in almost every East Asian economy in the negative.

China Has Become the World's Greatest Polluter

High energy-consumption rates are closely linked with exacerbating environmental problems. China has become the largest polluter in the world.

As the country is still far from solving basic economic development tasks, it is very difficult to make environment protection the number one national priority. China's giant economy has a very high share of energy-intensive heavy industries, even by East Asian standards, while its energy efficiency is the lowest.

One more reason for the rise of greenhouse gas emissions is the modernization and Westernization of consumption patterns. At present the living standards of the vast majority of Chinese families are still far below those of an average Western household. For instance, as of 2005, even in the cities there were only 3.4 cars per 100 families, (METI 2006, 29). Yet, they are doing their best to approach Western standards and, as time goes by, more and more of them succeed.

Today, an average Western household emits three times as much carbon dioxide as an average Chinese one. Imagine if the majority of the 1.3 billion Chinese reach, or approach, the living standards of an average Westerner. The result would be an environmental disaster. The only realistic solution is to search for alternative, environmentally friendly lifestyles and modes of consumption.

Greenhouse Gas Emissions in the Region's Other National Economies

Other East Asian countries' records on greenhouse gas emissions are also not that encouraging. South Korea's share in global carbon dioxide emissions is 1.9 percent compared to 1.8 percent for Italy and 1.6 percent for France (this data is for 2002) while its GDP, measured on the PPP basis, is less than 60 percent of the French and 70 percent of the Italian GDP. Indonesia's 1.3 percent share of world emissions is only slightly lower than in these two countries, while its GDP is less than half of theirs (Mitsuhashi 2007, 530).

Environmental Constraints on Growth

As time goes by, environmental constraints on growth are likely to become stronger. The countries of the region will face growing international pressure to accept numerical targets for the reduction of carbon dioxide emissions. To halt the deterioration of the natural environment their governments will increasingly resort to administrative regulation of investment and production.

Another group of constraints concerns labor inputs. A deteriorating natural environment, especially air pollution, exacerbates health problems. As a result many people of working age, suffering from "environmental diseases," become unable to work or educate themselves to their full potential, or even to work at all. Also, environmental problems increase the probability that highly skilled, especially knowledge, workers would prefer to live and work not in East Asia but in other, less polluted, areas.

One more growth impediment comes from environment-related social unrest, especially when and where environmental problems have grave consequences for people's traditional economic activities, most of all in agriculture.

Redirecting the Chinese and other East Asian national economies toward a more pro-environment development pattern may stimulate growth because of the expanding demand for environmentally friendly products and services.

The Impact of the Global Financial Turmoil

In the period from 2006 until the first half of 2008, rapidly rising world prices for oil, other natural resources, and foodstuffs emerged as a serious impediment to the growth of most Asian economies. Inflation was on the rise, ramping up production costs for companies and restraining private consumption. Shortages of energy resources and raw materials became a visible threat. In the medium and long terms, these issues pose some of the biggest challenges for Asian economies.

However, in the short term, after the autumn of 2008, they temporarily disappeared. On the contrary, oil and other commodity prices began to fall at an enormous speed and inflationary pressures largely eased. That said, these are no more than clouds with silver linings as Asian economies have been hit by the global financial turmoil, rooted in the US subprime mortgage loans crisis, which (the turmoil) started with the Lehman Brothers' collapse in September.

At the time of writing (December 2008), the turmoil is far from being over. Still, it would be safe to say that, by and large, Asian economies proved to be structurally strong enough to minimize its negative effects. Yet, Japan, Hong Kong, and Singapore have entered a recession, which is defined as two or more quarters of negative growth in a row, and South Korea and Taiwan are on the brink of it. On the other hand, in China and the developing ASEAN economies, as well as India, growth continues, though, on a year-to-year basis, around 2-3 percentage points of it have been lost (see country pages in Part 2).

Definitely, in these hard times, Asia is doing much better than the US and Europe. Its present economic performance shows that the structural transformation the region underwent after the Asian crisis has brought clear results.

Asian economies are showing their strength in the following respects. First of all, today, contrary to 1997–98, Asian countries' financial sectors are resilient and essentially healthy. Their exposure to the US subprime loans market, and the toxic financial products linked to it, has generally been low. Prudential regulation is in place and the management of banks is sound and reasonably conservative. Asian banks are mostly well-capitalized and the ratio of their nonperforming loans (NPLs) does not pose a problem. Also, the fact that the variety of financial products circulating in the region, especially complicated structured products, is smaller than in the West, is doing Asian economies a good turn.

Consequently, in Asia, this time there have been practically no bank failures and no rescue operations to save particular financial institutions.

Second, the significant current account surpluses and foreign currency reserves that most Asian countries have, along with healthy national budgets, have created a cushion, making it easier for the governments to launch economic stimulus packages and for the central banks to provide ample liquidity or loan/deposit guarantees which help to mitigate the impact of the global credit crunch.

Third, household consumption, though slowing down, remains quite dynamic and continues to support growth in some major Asian economies at least. The turmoil has not stopped the middle-class families' consumption rush.

Yet, the blows from the turmoil are heavy. The major one comes from a decline in exports, caused by the falling demand in the US and Europe. High dependency on exports, especially on those to the West, has backfired. Though, as mentioned, domestic markets and East Asia's intraregional trade are expanding and absorb an increasing share of made-in-Asia goods, exposure to the Western, especially the US, market remains significant. The United States is the most important export market for five out of eleven major East Asian economies (China, Japan, Malaysia, Thailand, and Vietnam) and the second most important one for the other six (South Korea, Hong Kong, Taiwan, Singapore, Indonesia, and the Philippines). The shares of the EU countries combined in the exports of all major East Asian countries and territories, except Hong Kong, are also significant, ranging (in 2006) from 11.3 percent for Singapore to 19.6 percent for

China. Besides, in East Asia's intraregional trade a very substantial role is played by intermediary goods (such as parts and materials) and equipment used in the manufacturing of final products which are exported to the US and Europe. Naturally, this trade segment has also been adversely affected by the downturn in the West.

The second blow has been dealt by the credit crunch and liquidity constraints. Overseas banks often refrain from rolling over their loans to Asian companies and financial institutions and are cutting new lending. The countries with a higher level of external corporate indebtedness, such as South Korea, Indonesia, or India, are hit most. In Asian countries themselves, banks are largely losing confidence in one another due to uncertainties about the counterparts' exposure to toxic financial products and the status of their balance sheets in general. As a result interbank loans get squeezed, adding to the credit constraints.

In some countries, outstanding bank loans are close to, or even exceeding, the amount of deposits, which makes them especially vulnerable to the drop in the inflow of funds from overseas. In South Korea, the loan-to-bank deposit ratio is 136 percent and in Indonesia it is 95 percent (Tejada 2008).

Finally, the third blow is the withdrawal of funds by international investors. For example, according to Citigroup, since the beginning of 2008 until late November, foreign mutual funds sold US$61.8 billion in emerging-market Asian equities (Tejada 2008). Contrary to 1997–98, this time the major reason for the sell-offs is not the structural weakness of Asian economies, but investors' fears caused by instability in the world financial markets in general, which create a strong risk aversion trend. Even though Asian emerging market economies are doing relatively well, their capital markets are perceived as riskier and funds are transferred to the markets considered to be safer, such as Japan or the US.

The investors' exodus exacerbates the plunge of stock values around the region. However, in this regard it is worth noting that the stock values in Asia had mostly begun to fall from late 2007 and had already declined quite a lot before the Lehman shock, largely due to uncertainties caused by growing oil and food prices. Besides, by the middle of the decade, in most Asian countries a speculative asset bubble had emerged and from late 2007 it had begun to burst.

The outflow of capital, along with deteriorating current account balances in some countries (particularly Thailand and South Korea), has led to the depreciation of nearly all national currencies (the fall in the currency values, in turn, prompts the outflow of capital). The only exceptions are Japan, Hong Kong, and China. For example, in January–November 2008, the South Korean won lost 38 percent against the US dollar, the Indonesian rupiah 23 percent (both currencies approached the level registered in the days of the Asian crisis), and the Indian rupee 21 percent (Tejada 2008). Unlike in the late 1990s, depreciation has had a very limited stimulative effect on exports due to the fall in global demand, while its negative effects—rising costs of imported raw materials, materials and parts, growing overseas borrowing costs, and the increasing burden of the debts, denominated in US dollars and other foreign currencies—are significant.

To support the currencies, the central banks of Indonesia, India, the Philippines, Malaysia, and even Singapore have had to intervene in the currency markets.

On the other hand, the yen, considered by international investors to be a safe-haven, sharply appreciated, and the Hong Kong Monetary Authority had to sell US dollars so as not to let the local currency go beyond the fixed trading band. One of the major reasons for the appreciation of both currencies was the unwinding by international investors of their transactions in which they borrowed the yen and Hong Kong dollars, at relatively low interest rates, to fund their high-yield operations in US dollar-denominated assets.

There is a strong impression that the world business community, the mass media, and also some business analysts, initially, had too high expectations regarding Asia's economic performance under the global turmoil. The so-called "decoupling theory" suggested that even though the Western economies were in trouble, Asia could do well on its own due to its countries' sound fundamentals, expanding domestic markets, and growing intraregional trade. In our view, those expectations were unrealistic from the very start. First, as mentioned, Asia's dependency on the Western, especially the US, market remains too high for the latter's squeeze to be offset by the sales within the region. Second, in the globalized economy the behavior of major banks and international investors has worldwide repercussions that no region can escape.

As it became obvious that there would be no decoupling and that Asia was also hard hit, disappointment surfaced and the assessments of Asia's prospects grew quite pessimistic.

For example, in its report issued in late November 2008 the investment bank, UBS, stated: "We knew Asian economies would be caught in the direct highlight of two ongoing trains: the weak global demand and a global credit freeze.... What has surprised us was the extent and speed with which these shocks have hurt what we still maintain were/are strong Asian fundamentals as the credit storm approached" (Thaichareon, Seo 2008).

Our viewpoint is a bit different. Definitely, Asian economies have suffered a severe blow. However, rather than be surprised by its strength and disappointed that they cannot continue to grow the way they did, we should credit them for managing to limit the turmoil's negative effect on growth and to prevent big troubles in the financial sector.

Together with the rest of the global economy, Asia has gone through the economic upturn of 2002–07 and entered the downturn in 2008. The most important thing is that, as in the upturn years, during the global downturn it retains its position as one of the world's fastest runners. All the factors of growth presented in this chapter remain in place, which means that the preconditions are set for returning to higher growth rates in the next decade after the financial turmoil is over.

It is also notable that, though the global turmoil started in the United States and the biggest setback was suffered by Western economies, in today's Asia practically no calls are heard to address the problems that emerged by the revival or creation of some kind of peculiar, Asian-style, economic model. This time much of the criticism of American-style capitalism and the free market system is coming from the US and Europe themselves.

Let us make it clear. It would be wrong to suggest that the turmoil manifests the failure of either the market economy in general or its American, or Anglo-Saxon, model in particular. It does not.

It is no more than the result of the failure of one sector, by the name of banking and finance, most of all in the US—the failure of its institutions, their managers and regulators, as well as their corporate governance mechanisms—to provide an adequate management of risks in times of an asset bubble. Another big problem is that, while addressing those issues, the US and also West European governments have bailed out the ailing financial institutions using taxpayers' money, without properly requiring the management and shareholders to bear responsibility for their failures. This is contrary to the very basic principles of the market economy and Anglo-Saxon values. It also, strikingly, contrasts with the policies Asian countries were required to adopt, and did adopt, in the years of the Asian crisis.

After all is said and done, the 2008 financial turmoil in no way changes the major track Asian economies have taken since 1997–98—structural transformation aimed at building economic systems where markets are at work, companies are self-reliant, and profitable and relevant corporate governance is in place.

Concluding Remarks

After the Asian crisis, East Asia quickly restored its position as practically the fastest-growing region in the world, providing promising new business opportunities. Yet, post-crisis growth has a number of specific features making it different from the growth in the miracle years.

In most major East Asian economies growth rates fell while growth in other regions around the world, and the world economy, as a whole accelerated.

By the standards of the developed economies, however, the growth rates of the NIEs are high. For ASEAN 4, the deceleration of growth should be a matter of concern. To become developed in the foreseeable future they have to accelerate again, but their ability to do so is not a given.

China is strengthening its position as an indisputable growth leader, dragging forward other East Asian economies. Vietnam deserves attention as a new and important fast runner. India is a rapidly growing, new economic giant, expanding and deepening its ties with East Asia.

Demographic conditions in most countries of the region remain favorable for the time being, providing an increase of labor inputs. Yet, in a number of the major economies they are expected to worsen in the near future.

To preserve and accelerate growth, it is crucial for East Asian countries to speed up the rise of TFP and pursue the upgrading of their economies, introducing advanced technologies, producing more high value-added items, and developing more products and technologies of their own.

With the formation and expansion of the middle class, private consumption, especially in the major cities, has become one of the major growth drivers. However, East Asia's growth remains largely export-led.

Finally, the post-crisis regional economy is growing amidst structural reforms that are radically transforming the East Asian economic model itself. Not all of the reforms started in the crisis years. Some of them were launched earlier, some afterward. Also, they are not limited to crisis-impacted countries. The point, however, is that the crisis surfaced the weaknesses of the East Asian model, underlining the urgent need for its rapid and radical transformation.

Endnote

1 Authors' calculations. Data sources: ADB, "Key Economic Indicators 2008," NationMaster.com, 2008.

3

Structural Transformation: The State

The Developmental State Is Yesterday

Reassessment was Inevitable

The developmental state played a crucial role in orchestrating the East Asian miracle. Having fixed economic development as the major national goal, the governments articulated short-, medium-, and long-term development plans and used a wide spectrum of tools to make their growth targets achievable.

The main job done by the developmental state was creating, often from scratch, and promoting the manufacturing industries which lead economic growth. To fulfill this task, the governments pursued various kinds of industrial policy, actively intervening in resource allocation.

The developmental state is different from the state in a conventional capitalist economy, which is supposed to limit its involvement at the industry level, entrusting the resource allocation job to market forces. Still, with the exception of the countries ruled by Communist parties—notably, China and Vietnam, before the start of market reforms—East Asian states remained basically "true" to the capitalist paradigm. As time went by and private businesses became stronger, the state gradually restrained and narrowed its involvement, opening more room for private enterprise and competition.

The Asian crisis dramatically accelerated this shift. It explicitly showed that the developmental state, with its traditional set of industrial policy tools, had become outdated and at that point was already doing more harm than good. The role of the state had to be reassessed.

First, the "favor for money" relations of politicians and bureaucrats with particular companies and politicians' involvement in business reached a scale threatening the very foundation of social ethics and morale. Economically, a state industrial policy based on cronyism becomes an impediment to growth.

Second, governments often made mistakes when choosing industries and sectors to be promoted. More often than not, industry promotion schemes based on the subjective judgment of political leaders and state bureaucracies turned out to be too ambitious, costly, and lacking in economic rationale.

Third, the changing economic environment made the preservation of the developmental state difficult in practical terms. Globalization, liberalization of trade and foreign investment, World Trade Organization (WTO) rules, and a dramatic rise in the number of free trade agreements did not allow the developmental state to protect and promote domestic industries in the way it used to.

Shock Therapy Asian-Style

The Asian crisis undermined one of the pillars of the developmental state—cooperative relations between government and business. Instead of supporting businesses through various kinds of preferential treatment governments had to initiate speedy reorganization and restructuring using a stick rather than a carrot.

It was dramatic shock therapy Asian-style. For instance, in South Korea as many as 347 financial institutions (16.5 percent of their total number) with big non-performing loans were liquidated between late 1997 and early 2000 (Tselichtchev 2004, 36). In Thailand, in spite of very strong opposition from influential business and political groups, in October 1997, the government shut down 56 financial companies (non-bank lending institutions). The following year it temporarily nationalized four leading commercial banks, replaced their managers, and reduced capital (Tselichtchev 2004, 38–39). In Indonesia, to pursue restructuring the government nationalized or injected funds into eleven banks, including Bank Central Asia (BCA), a key financial institution of the Salim Group, a leading conglomerate turned flop.

Within a very short period of time the focus of government policy abruptly changed from supporting domestic businesses through tax incentives, soft loans, subsidies, and so on to encouraging or, rather forcing, them to become self-reliant and competitive without direct state support and guidance.

Cultural Deterrents

Yet, though the transformation described has been gaining momentum, cultural constraints exist. People, or public opinion, in the East Asian countries expect governments to play a pivotal role in economic development and bear responsibility for the well-being of every household, rather than emphasize the responsibility of the household itself. Furthermore, as globalization progresses, they expect and demand that the governments protect them from the mounting competitive pressures and the uncertainties it brings.

Finally, significant parts of the ruling elites and government bureaucracies are "addicted" to the state's tight control over the economy and interested in preserving it, though maybe in a different form.

All this keeps the door open for substantial involvement on the part of the state and sometimes may cause politically driven waves of escalating government intervention. Yet, it does not change the major trend.

"Less Government, More Market"

Koizumi's Motto

Japan's former prime minister, Junichiro Koizumi, liked a catchphrase expressing the gist of his structural reforms philosophy—"everything that the private sector can do better than the state has to be done by the private sector." Reforms launched by his cabinet in 2001–06 have significantly changed the Japanese economy in this direction.

In a TV program, broadcast in the second half of the 1990s, an owner of a small construction firm, looking directly into the television camera, made an emotional plea to the then prime minister, Ryutaro Hashimoto, "Hashimoto-san, I want work, that's all." He expressed a popular sentiment of the time—the government has to provide "work" for businesses, mainly by boosting public works expenditure. Today, you don't hear pleas of this kind. The public sentiment has changed.

Restructuring *Zaito*

Changes in government policy are accompanied by a far-reaching institutional transformation. In Japan, probably the most important shift is the overhaul of *Zaito*—the Fiscal Investment and Loan Program (FILP)—which was the cornerstone of the system of state support for domestic industries and companies.

Zaito used to be called the "second budget" as it reached half the size of the general account. Its major source of finance was postal savings. The Japan Post Network, besides operating as the postal system, happens to be the biggest financial institution in the world by the amount of money in its deposit accounts. It also provides small-scale life insurance (*kampo*) services. The postal insurance fund, along with the national pension funds, was FILP's second most important financial source. The funds allocated for the program were accumulated on the special account of the Ministry of Finance called the Trust Fund Bureau and then channeled, as investments or low-interest loans, to public companies and about a dozen state-owned financial institutions, such as Japan Development Bank; Small Business Finance Corporation; Agriculture, Forestry and Fisheries Finance Corporation; or Japan Bank for International Cooperation (JBIC). The latter, in turn, extended low-interest loans to particular sectors of the economy in accordance with the government's set of priorities. *Zaito* was a very powerful tool of industrial policy and practically every major industry received some support through the program at a certain, mostly early, stage of its postwar development. As time went by and large private companies were growing stronger, especially from the 1970s, FILP became increasingly focused on the financing of small and medium-sized firms, agriculture, forestry, and fisheries, housing construction, infrastructure projects, utilities, and less economically advanced regions. In the 1990s the loans extended by state-owned banks and financial corporations often comprised around one-third of the total lending by all Japanese financial institutions to nonfinancial companies.

The program contributed a lot to Japan's economic growth and structural modernization. However, it was criticized for the vague criteria for extending loans and evaluating the performance of the state financial institutions involved. Another problem was the adverse effect on private banks—the postal network absorbed as much as one-third of the total amount of household deposits and state-owned financial institutions enjoyed such privileges as access to public funds, implicit state guarantees, and a tax-free operating regime.

After 2001, the Koizumi cabinet started the reforms. The Trust Fund Bureau was liquidated. Mandatory allocation of postal savings and insurance and pension funds surpluses for financing the program were abolished. State-owned financial institutions and other companies supported through FILP were prescribed to raise funds directly on the capital market, issuing their own bonds—FILP agency bonds. However, as the latter could hardly provide the amount of funds needed the government introduced a seven-year transitional period until 2007 to support their fund-raising by issuing special FILP bonds (*Zaitosai*) partly bought by the postal savings, pensions, and insurance funds.

The scale of the program has dramatically declined—in 2007, its outlays (original budget) amounted to only 14,112 billion yen or less than one-third of the 48,190 billion yen in 1995 (MIC 2008).

Privatizing the Post

The step of primary importance was the enactment, in 2005, of the law on the privatization of the postal system. It paved the way for the biggest privatization project since the 1980s, when the cabinet of Prime Minister Yasuhiro Nakasone privatized the National Railways (*Kokutetsu*) and the National Telephone and Telegraph Corporation (*Denden Kosha*). The privatized Japan Post Group was born in October 2007. From the very beginning it emphasized its intention to operate as other private commercial organizations and to seek new business opportunities.

Finally, in June 2006, the government came out with the reorganization plan for the state-owned financial institutions. In October 2008, Japan Development Bank became a corporation. It will be privatized within five to seven years. The Small Business Finance Corporation; the National Life Finance Corporation; the Agriculture, Forestry and Fisheries Finance Corporation; and the Japan Bank for International Cooperation were merged into the Japan Finance Corporation, which will remain the only state financial facility.

Most other countries are moving along a similar transformation path.

Reconsidering Established Practices

In Indonesia the policy of supporting strategic industries, associated with the worst cases of cronyism of the Suharto era, was effectively stopped after the change of the regime in 1998.

Similarly, South Korea put an end to the established practice of allocating massive bank credits, under state guidance, to leading industries and conglomerates. The swan song of old-fashioned industrial policy amid, and right after, the Asian crisis was the so-called "big deal"—the government-initiated swap of businesses between major conglomerates with the goal of making each of them focus on their areas of competitive advantage. The "big deal" targeted such industries as semiconductors, train cars, oil refining, power-generating equipment, vessel engines, aircraft, and petrochemicals. For example, the Samsung Group swapped its five industrial divisions and the Hyundai Group did the same with four of its own (ERINA 2005, 58). The number of producers of train cars and power-generating equipment was reduced to just one for each; semiconductors, vessel engines, and aircraft—to two. After the "big deal" the government abstained from any permanent, large-scale intervention at industry level.

In Malaysia, a major change occurred before the crisis. In 1996, the Heavy Industries Corporation of Malaysia (HICOM) was merged with the private conglomerate, Diversified Resources Berhad (DRB), giving birth to the largest *Bumiputra* (Malay people) conglomerate DRB-HICOM. It meant that the policy of creating and promoting a wide range of strategic industries with direct government involvement was eventually dropped.

In China, as a result of the reforms started in the late 1970s and speeded up since 1992, the state has made a major shift from the position of a commander in the planned economy to that of a regulator of market-driven economic activities. In the conventional, socialist-style, planning system every producer gets directives from the state about what, and how much, to produce, whom to sell to, and at what price. This system is no longer in place. In July 1992, the government issued the Rules for Shifting the Operational Mechanism of the Industrial Enterprises Owned by the Whole People. Based on the Enterprise Law, it specified enterprises' 14 rights, including decision-making in production and operation, price-setting for products and labor, selling of products, material purchasing, import and export investment decisions, and disposition of property. State credit allocation plans, based on credit quotas for industries and enterprises, were abolished. In October the same year, the 14th National Congress of the Communist Party of China (CPC) proclaimed that the objective of economic reforms was to establish a socialist market economy and called on state-owned, collectively owned, and other enterprises to enter the market and to compete so that the fittest would survive (China.org 2003).

Most Chinese companies, including state-owned ones, are now operating in a world where prices are set by the market and decisions about production planning, fund-raising, employment, procurement of equipment and materials, selling products, and so on are made by company managers, not the ministry in charge.

Industrial Policy: Still There, But...

Yet, it would be premature to say "Industrial policy, so long!" as in some East Asian states it is retained or has even been restored. For example, in today's China or Indonesia, the state still gets actively involved in the development of leading or promising industries, not making a secret of its intention to rule and guide. However, the concept of industrial policy and the way it is pursued are changing.

Indonesia's Manufacturing Sector Development Policy

In summer 2005, for the first time in the post-Suharto years, Indonesia's Ministry of Industry came out with a long-term National Manufacturing Sector Development Policy. A detailed, 20-year plan, explicitly prioritized 32 industries out of 365 existing in the country, and set targets for each promoted sector with regard to the products it should produce in ten years. The industries designated will enjoy preferential treatment, including fiscal, monetary, and administrative incentives. The government is going to work to expand markets for these industries, channel inward foreign direct investment (FDI), help them to train people, direct and organize university research for their benefit, and build infrastructure tailored to their needs. As of 2005, the 32 prioritized industries produced 78 percent of the country's output in manufacturing and comprised 83 percent of its non-oil and non-gas exports (Hakim 2005). The ministry grouped them into two categories, basic (core and supporting) and future. The target for core industries is to return to the pre-crisis level of competitiveness within five years and to become world-class in the long-term. However, if any of them fail due to "natural competition," government support is to be shifted to other industries.

The Changing Role of Thailand's BOI

In Thailand, the key role in industrial policy is traditionally played by the Board of Investment (BOI), working under the Ministry of Industry. It is authorized to select investment projects—by both domestic and foreign companies—for promotion through tax incentives, income tax holidays of up to eight years, and exemption from import duties for machinery and materials. Projects in the targeted industries have a priority. The BOI has five Incentive Management Divisions responsible for particular industries, conducting project appraisal and monitoring. The list of targeted industries, centered around general machinery, the auto industry, electronics, and steel production, is presented in Figure 3.1. Within every targeted industry, the BOI also specifies particular kinds of products that will be promoted on a preferential basis.

Four other types of priority activities eligible for promotion (designated in 2000 and maybe subject to change) are agriculture and agricultural products, projects directly related to technological and human resource development, infrastructure (public utilities and basic services), and environmental protection and conservation.

While preserving the traditional industrial policy package, the BOI also looks for new roles and approaches. Back in 2001, its then secretary-general, Chakramon Phasukavanich, proclaimed, "The BOI is entering a new era, a knowledge-based age" (*BOI Investment Review* 2001, 1). He argued that not only high-tech sectors, but all industries, can become knowledge-based: for instance,

1. Manufacture of steel casting using induction furnace
2. Manufacture of forged steel parts
3. Manufacture of machinery and equipment
   a. manufacture of molds, dies, and parts
   b. manufacture of jigs and fixtures
   c. manufacture of industrial machinery
      - turning machines
      - drilling machines
      - milling machines
      - grinding machines
      - machine centers
      - gear cutting and finish machines
      - die-sinking electrical discharge machines (EDMs)
      - laser-beam machines
      - plasma and cutting machines
      - electron-beam machines
      - broaching machines
   d. manufacture of parts and equipment for high precision machining processes, namely cutting, milling, turning, grooving, shaving, grinding, polishing, threading
4. Manufacture of sintered products
5. Manufacture or repair of aircraft and aircraft parts
6. Manufacture of vehicle parts
   a. manufacture of anti-lock braking systems (ABS)
   b. manufacture of substrate for catalytic converters
   c. manufacture of electronic fuel injection systems
7. Heat treatment
8. Manufacture of materials for microelectronics
9. Electronic design
10. Software
11. Software parks
12. International distribution centers

Figure 3.1   Board of Investment (BOI) targeted industries in Thailand*
Source: BOI Web site.
*Announced in 2000.

growing rice in a field. With the use of technology, he went on, we have to ask, "How can we improve efficiency as well as the product?" Along with tax incentives for promoted projects, support of cluster creation is becoming increasingly important. Emphasis is put on stimulating growth in supporting industries, most importantly by providing information about subcontracting opportunities and helping buyer firms (mainly foreign) to establish supplier networks. This is the function of the BOI Unit for Industrial Linkage Development (BUILD) within the Investment Facilitation Division. The Marketing Division, for its part, helps domestic companies to establish brands, capitalizing on their national origin and identity.

The Present Stage of Industrial Policy in China

In spite of the visibly increasing role of market mechanisms, China remains a country with one of the most active industrial policies in the region. The government is keen to preserve the option of administering the major sectors directly. In the middle of this decade it articulated policies for two key industries: auto and steel.

The policy for the development of the auto industry was officially announced in June 2004. Its goal is to make China one of the major auto-producing countries in the world within ten years and to turn the auto industry into a pillar of the national economy. One of the most important tasks is the concentration of the production of key parts at domestic companies. To achieve this goal, a new law was enacted in 2005 regulating the imports of eight key auto parts (engines, transmissions, and so on) in order to boost their domestic production. The European Union (EU) and the US filed a complaint to the WTO.

Another goal is to address the issue of excessive production capacity. Entries into the auto industry and production capacity increases are regulated—government permission is needed to establish a new company or build a new plant.

The policy maintains a 50 percent cap on the share of foreign companies in auto-producing firms and limits the number of joint ventures a foreign company can establish in the production of passenger cars, commercial vehicles, and motorcycles to two each (*Sekai Nenkan* 2006, 176).

The steel industry development policy was announced in July 2005. Its major aim was to address the structural problems that had emerged with the remarkable growth of production volumes—China has been the world's largest steel producer since 1996 and its share in global production is about one-third. The number of steel producers has grown significantly but many of them are too small to capitalize on economies of scale and introduce new progressive technologies. In the government's view, the industry has a substantial excess capacity. Other problems are that a significant portion of the machinery and equipment it uses is obsolete, the location of steel mills is inefficient, and the industry has become one of the major air polluters. The four pillars of the announced policy are the rationalization of the location of steel mills, an increase in the level of production concentration, the upgrading of the set of products, and the addressing of environmental problems.

To promote R&D, design, and domestic production of progressive types of equipment, the government will provide subsidies, along with tax rebates and exemptions, for companies launching large-scale projects in these areas. It is calling on steel makers to reduce equipment and technology imports, instructing them to limit imports to advanced equipment which is not produced domestically or produced in quantities insufficient to meet the demand.

Direct administrative involvement sometimes leads to a very special kind of conflict between the government, seeking to prevent the overheating of the economy, put growth under control, and fight pollution, and businessmen striving to expand production as much as they can to take advantage of the enormous market opportunities.

In early 2007, China's top economic planning agency, the National Development and Reform Commission, demanded that the local governments shut down 100 million tons of capacity in the steel industry out of the country's total of almost 500 million. The commission targeted small mills which use more energy per unit of production and cause more pollution. The small mills resisted. Cai Nianguang is a 40-year-old businessman and the owner of a steel mill in Luanxian, Hebei province, some 140 miles from Beijing, which employs about 500 workers and was included in the shut-down list, along with 56 other factories in the province. His view was that "I am a businessman and I talk business only. Industrial policies are always changing, always shifting… My business is good. I sold all my production (200,000 tons) last year and I made money. In such a big market I never worry about competition or sales" (*The Straits Times*, February 22, 2007). Mr. Cai is going to expand, not shut down.

Mr. Cai's mill and the other 56 that the government wants to close are properly registered. Yet, according to local residents, there are many more unregistered plants "hidden away in the Hebei wastelands." And, presumably, steadily increasing their output because demand is there. The government is not that much in control while the free market economy is expanding. Indeed "less government, more market."

New Features of Industrial Policies

Yes, a number of East Asian countries retain industrial policies, but they are different from the industrial policies of yesterday. Today, they are mixed with other policies, boosting competition and encouraging private businesses to go on their own. They don't use protectionism as a major tool. Even when they do resort to this, it is done on a rather limited scale. As time goes by, they put more emphasis on government services (information, consulting, and so on) and coordinating activities than on financial support. They emphasize clustering and networking and target a wide range of small and medium sized firms, rather than prioritizing leading big companies. They are addressing a wider range of tasks than just stimulating the growth of production—for instance, environmental and excessive capacity issues are becoming more important. Finally, they are much more focused on upgrading, technological innovation, and the development of original products and technologies.

An Emphasis on Upgrading and Innovation

A Vector of Change

From initiating industries' creation and expansion to promoting innovation—this is the major vector of change in the governments' role. In this regard too, East Asia is coming closer to Western-style capitalism.

Governments support the development of original products and technologies, encourage cooperation between businesses and academic/research institutions, promote innovative companies, and construct facilities, such as science or technological parks.

These issues are coming to the attention of business communities as well. Sometimes, they openly criticize governments for moving too slowly.

The Malaysia Microchip

One of the most active pro-innovation policies has been launched by the government of Malaysia, emphasizing that Malaysians have to become creators, not mere users of technology.

In February 2007, the government announced the launch of the Malaysia Microchip, the world's smallest microchip with radio technology—a step on the way toward joining the world's leading high-tech chip producers. The size of the smallest version is 0.7x0.7 millimeters and the cost is six cents per unit. R&D in Malaysia, under the agency established to develop and market the product, lasted for more than two years after the government bought the right to design, manufacture, and market the chip from the Japanese firm FEC Inc. in 2003. The development cost is said to have been within the range of US$50–60 million (AFP 2007).

The chip can emit radio waves on multiple frequencies and is detected when embedded in paper documents, objects, or animals. Its first application in Malaysia will be for tagging and identifying original movie versions on DVDs and VCDs. Malaysia's and Hong Kong's international airports are going to use it to track luggage travelling between them making it easier to locate the luggage lost or removed from the plane because the passenger did not show up. The chip will be used for security purposes too.

The Promotion of Innovative Entrepreneurship in China

In China, from the early 1990s, the government greatly increased its effort to nurture domestic entrepreneurs, especially in the science park incubators. The number of domestic, privately owned start-ups (excluding sole proprietorships) grew remarkably, reaching as many as 1.5 million in 1999. Programs supporting high-tech start-ups include research grants and the right to be located in high-tech industrial parks, which also attract state-owned enterprises (SOEs) and foreign companies. To give a boost to high-tech industries, the government doesn't hesitate to encourage competition, including the one between companies with different types of ownership. When developing particular high-tech sectors, it not only promotes SOEs but also leaves room for private companies and even supports them financially. One example is the private software firm Evermore Software LLC. Having successfully developed Evermore Integrated Office software, it joined the ranks of the competitors of Microsoft. The company was launched in August 2003 by the now famous entrepreneur, Gus Tsao, in the southeastern city of Wuxi and the Wuxi Economic Development Group, the investment arm of the local government, provided funding.

Massive Support for Venture Business in South Korea

In South Korea, the government started to drastically increase its support for venture business from the second half of the 1990s. In August 1997, the parliament adopted the Special Venture Business Law, establishing a unique promotion scheme. Its major pillar is the authorization by the government of the status of particular small firms as venture companies. Once such authorization is obtained the firm becomes eligible for massive state support in such areas as funding, technological development, capacity building, access to facilities, and so on. Financial support is provided in the form of investment, credits, and subsidies by the Korea Venture Fund (KVF), the government venture capital company, Tasan Venture, and also by national pension and insurance funds. In addition, authorized companies get priority access to state credit guarantees.

In the period from 1998 to 2001, the amount of public funds, investment, and credit pumped into venture start-ups (companies operating for up to three years) reached 1.6 trillion won. Also, within the same period, the government injected almost 630 billion won into 180 newly established venture capital funds. The outstanding balance of credit guarantees for venture companies hit 8.7 trillion won (ERINA 2005, 108). Critics argued that the government overdid it: the major motive for the start-up could well be getting access to generous public financing and not interest in the business itself.

Along with financial support, the state also builds industrial estates exclusively for venture companies and provides experimental factories and laboratories. In 2000, to coordinate this activity it enacted the system of Special Venture Companies Development Promotion Zones.

Modernizing Agriculture: A New Old Task

An Outline of the Problem

The modernization of agriculture and rural areas is coming close to the top of the economic policy agenda in a number of East Asian countries. It is "a new old" task. Old—because most East Asian economies had been agrarian for centuries. New—because successful industrialization added one more very important dimension to the issue—it has created a large and widening gap between modern industries and the advanced part of the service sector, big cities, high- and middle-income living standards, mostly of urban households, on the one hand and, respectively, the agricultural sector, rural areas and small townships, and low-income living standards, mostly of rural households, on the other. The gap is especially wide in Southeast Asian countries (with the exception of Singapore) and China. In the urban areas, especially in a limited number of major cities, the development policies of the miracle years brought visible results. Rural areas and small townships remain largely underdeveloped.

Singapore and Hong Kong are lucky not to face the problem simply because they don't have rural areas. In Taiwan, a territory of a comparatively small size with an economy centered on industry and services, it is negligible. In other countries the problem is pressing. In China, according to estimates by McKinsey Global Institute, as of 2005, the middle class comprised just 22 percent of the total urban population (Farrell 2006). Here, as well as in Indonesia, the Philippines and, to a smaller extent, in Malaysia and Thailand, the majority of people live in rural areas and adjoining townships and are struggling to make ends meet. The larger the rural, and, respectively, the total population, the more acute and potentially explosive the problem tends to be.

The gist of the problem is that after decades of impressive economic growth, with certain exceptions, such as rice cultivation in Thailand or tropical plantations, East Asia doesn't have an efficient and competitive agricultural sector. Even in Japan and South Korea, though, of course, the urban–rural gap there is not socially explosive, productivity in agriculture is low, its business structure outdated, and its ability to survive without government protection close to zero. In other countries, in spite of the green revolution (improvements in irrigation, infrastructure, the use of fertilizer, and so on) a significant part, if not the majority, of the rural population is still engaged in primitive agriculture, using outdated technologies and production methods.

Japan Tries to Boost Agro-Exports

Up until recently, heavily protected by the state, Japanese farmers (mostly very small-scale) had little to worry about. A variety of subsidies and price support systems was in place. JA (formerly Zennoh), or the National Federation of Agricultural Cooperative Associations, took care of selling their products. Import tariffs on agricultural goods, especially sensitive, were kept high, often prohibitively high. It looked like the Japanese people had reconciled themselves to the fact that domestic agriculture was a low productivity sector which had to be protected because it was not just one of the sectors of the economy but an important element of national culture. Besides, it could hardly be denied that protection was needed to provide food security—meaning both minimum reasonable self-sufficiency levels and quality/safety requirements.

The state willingly protected farmers, both for the reasons mentioned and due to the fact that most rural voters traditionally supported the ruling Liberal Democratic Party.

At this point, Japanese agriculture remains more of a culture, a way of life, than a commercially viable business sector. The vast majority of Japanese farmers have another occupation and for most of them it is more important in terms of income and working time than agricultural activities.

Yet, attitudes and approaches are changing significantly. External pressures are mounting. The number of free trade agreements (FTAs) around the world is rapidly growing. Japan cannot afford to miss the train. However, its Asian and other counterparts, mostly exporters of agricultural products, strongly demand import liberalization.

The government has taken a number of steps to speed up the structural reform of the agricultural sector and facilitate its exports. Among other things, the Koizumi cabinet organized a national conference on agricultural exports where farmers were called upon to push exports of high-quality brand products, such as apples, strawberries, or mandarins. In a number of prefectures (Akita prefecture was a pioneer), local governments and farmers are now working together to promote exports of homemade rice. The prefectural administrations are trying to assist, mostly in sales promotion and market research. Also, the government has begun to ease restrictions on entry into the agricultural sector by large corporations in the areas designated as Special Structural Reform Zones.

Indonesia's Agriculture Revitalization Program

In Indonesia, in 2006, President Susilo Yudhoyono launched a national program to revitalize the agricultural sector—one of the most large-scale undertakings of this kind in the whole region, if not in the world. It has two major goals: first, to increase domestic rice production to provide self-sufficiency; and second, to utilize idle land for biofuel plantations. The government plans to reclaim up to 500,000 hectares of peatland in central Kalimantan (Hudiono 2007).

According to the chief executive of the National Team for Biofuel Development, Al Hilal Hamdi, crops like palm oil, cassava, satropha, and sugarcane could hold the answer to concerns about not only the country's energy security but also unemployment, poverty, the environment, and local unrest (ANTARA News 2007). As of January 2007, foreign firms had signed investment contracts totaling US$12.4 billion and domestic firms US$5 billion. Half of the total amount is to go to Indonesian farmers through domestic banks. Within eight years 5–6 million hectares of land—a territory larger than Denmark and a little smaller than West Virginia—will be planted with biofuel crops. Four million jobs are to be created with incomes above the minimum wage. State enterprises will support the introduction of new crop varieties and better cultivation methods (ANTARA News 2007).

Other New Developments Around the Region

In Malaysia, a Long-term Development Plan, until 2020, fixes agriculture, along with services and tourism, as a major new sector where the government should actively promote upgrading. New emphasis on agriculture is closely interrelated with another important development—the government is changing the focus of the *Bumiputra* support policy—a cornerstone of Malaysia's economic strategy. Since the results of the policy aimed at raising the *Bumiputra's* leverage in manufacturing, commerce, and services have been rather disappointing, in 2007, Prime Minister Abdullah Badawi stated that he "would like to approach the policy through the development of agro-industry because agriculture is familiar to Malays" (*Jakarta Post* 2007). The government has come up with a package to help 10,000 agriculture-based businesspeople. It has also started to promote a *halal* food industry—a new area where Malaysia, one of the most economically successful countries of the Islamic world, is likely to have a sharp competitive edge.

The Chinese government, especially after President Hu Jintao took office in 2003, is shifting the focus of its economic policy from the cities to the countryside, from manufacturing and mining to agriculture. The shift has been confirmed in the 11th Five-Year Plan (2006–10). Rural areas are getting a growing share of fiscal investment, especially in infrastructure. The government is increasing farm subsidies and starting to subsidize medical care for rural residents. In 2005, it eliminated the tax on farm produce and a year later began to abolish countryside school fees.

In Thailand, the state traditionally extends generous financial support to farmers and rural areas in the form of soft credits and grants. It was increased in the 2000s after the economic recovery.

SOEs and GLCs as Leaders in the Market Economy

New Global Players

Most East Asian countries are privatizating SOEs. On the other hand, in China and Southeast Asia, while the overall number of SOEs is declining, the remaining ones often emerge as not only the leaders of their national economies but also powerful global players (the only exception is the Philippines where SOEs are concentrated mostly in infrastructure and utilities). To boost their capital, governments often list them, inviting private investors—domestic and foreign—to take a share. Yet, the state retains the major stake—it is the cornerstone of their policy. Creating, or at least seeking to create, a powerful cohort of globally oriented companies, with the state as a major stakeholder, is one of the region's major economic trends at the dawn of the twenty-first century. Similar developments are taking place in India and Russia.

In China, these companies are still defined as SOEs, in Southeast Asia they are usually called government-linked companies (GLCs).

It would hardly be relevant to define them as "the third sector." This is generally associated with a more-or-less equal partnership between public and private owners while here the government is positioned as the dominant player. Rather, they are "state companies with private capital involved" or "state companies, market-style."

One might argue that companies of this kind are not uncommon in other parts of the world, especially Europe. For instance, the French government has a stake in Renault and the government of Lower Saxony, in Germany, in Volkswagen. Are the Asian countries mentioned not following the same road? In part, the argument is relevant. Yet, at least two important differences exist.

First, European nations have a centuries-long tradition of *laissez-faire*, or free, enterprise. Even when the number of SOEs reached its peak, the private sector played the leading role in their economies. In China and Southeast Asia, there is no deeply rooted, *laissez-faire* ideology and no domestic private sector as strong as in Europe. On the contrary, the state's deep and extensive involvement in business is considered normal. The SOEs and GLCs discussed were initially state-owned, and not nationalized, private companies. Under this condition the stage is set for them to play the leading role in market economies on a much wider scale and over a much longer time span.

Second, in China and Southeast Asia, as well as in a number of the emerging-market countries in other regions, a new model of the state company has appeared—investment holding also called a "sovereign wealth fund" with interests in a wide range of industries—which is actively going global. Europe, and "old developed economies" in general, did not and do not have entities of this kind.

Here, we shall limit ourselves to identifying the major features of East Asia's SOEs and GLCs and describe their latest developments. A more detailed picture of their governance and strategies is presented in the next chapter.

Operating "Almost" Like Private Companies

Today, governments encourage SOEs and GLCs to operate as autonomous business units whose task is to be competitive domestically and globally. It is a big shift. Traditionally, with the exception of Singapore, the mission of SOEs was to contribute to achieving national policy goals, such as creating, developing, or supporting a particular industry, providing jobs, or even financing hospitals, schools, or kindergartens. Profitability was not considered the most important factor.

Today, this basic perception has changed. Governments demand high profitability, managerial efficiency, and company value. Professional managers with work experience in the private sector are appointed to key posts. Many of them have been educated in the West. These managers work under strong administrative and market pressures. They face a real threat of being replaced if they don't achieve the results expected.

More and more often, SOEs are made to compete directly with private firms and, contrary to conventional wisdom, they often win. One of the major reasons is that their management teams are better and that, paradoxically, they work under stronger competitive pressures than managers of private firms. While at a new-style SOE the major criteria for hiring managers is their skills, in a typical private Asian company (naturally, family-owned) top management still consists mostly of family members, relatives, and close friends. Consequently, skill requirements are more lax and, even if the company's performance is poor, replacement is not an option.

The emergence of strong, globally oriented SOEs adds an important new dimension to international competition. As a cohort of powerful SOEs and GLCs enters the ranks of global competitors the level playing field disappears. Though they operate "almost" like private companies, basic differences remain. Unlike private firms, SOEs and GLCs rely on state funding and cannot go bankrupt or be acquired without the government's consent. Also, when they go overseas and seek to acquire large domestic companies in key sectors, national security issues of the host countries may be involved.

Thailand's PTT

Thailand's PTT is a state-owned oil, gas, and petrochemical holding company, which took over the assets of the Petroleum Authority of Thailand in October 2001. It produces 10 percent of the country's GDP. It is the 265th largest company in the world, in terms of market capitalization, at US$19 billion. The target for 2009, is US$28 billion. In 2006, it was one of the 20 most profitable companies in Asia. Now it gets 10 percent of its total revenue from overseas operations and plans to double this share within five years (Shameen 2007, 39–43).

PTT explores, produces, transports, and sells crude and refined oil and natural gas. It is also engaged in gas transmission and processing. It owns refineries, petrochemical plants, and retail gasoline stations both at home and overseas. Oil is explored and produced in the Middle East, Africa, and Southeast Asia. Domestic petroleum production, at little more than 250,000 barrels a day, comprises less than one-quarter of the total produced (Shameen 2007, 39). PTT's exploration and production arm, PTT Exploration and Production (a listed company), is active in Algeria, Egypt, Indonesia, Iran, Oman, and Vietnam.

PTT has used its surplus cash and profits to drastically increase the scale of its operations in the petrochemical and refining businesses as well as to build gas separation plants and extra pipeline capacity.

PTT's strategy, articulated by its CEO, Prasert Bunsumpun, hardly differs from that of a dynamic private company. "Our vision," he says, "is to build the premier Thai multinational, ... a leading regional integrated energy and petrochemical company with a strong base in Thailand and growing international presence." He also stresses PTT's focus on capital efficiency and operational excellence.

The company started from restructuring "the myriad of ... investments in refining, petrochemicals, power generation, and other ventures so as to maximize shareholder value and mitigate risks through integration and diversification as well as generate strong cash flow" (Shameen 2007, 40).

One more important page of PTT's short corporate history turned in 2006, when it purchased a 50 percent controlling stake in the heavily indebted Thai Petrochemical Industry (PTI)—the efficient SOE acquired an ailing private enterprise.

State-Owned Investment and Holding Companies

Another important model of East Asian SOEs or GLCs is the investment and holding company with interests in a wide range of industries—now frequently taking an increasingly global outlook. These entities are often called the government's investment arm or investment vehicle. Such an enterprise is supposed to be profitable and operate on a purely commercial basis.

For the time being, the most powerful company of this kind is Singapore's Temasek Holdings (*Temasek* means Singapore in Malay). It was incorporated in 1974 to manage the government's investments in GLCs (Koh *et al.* 2007, 557). The Ministry of Finance remains its one and only shareholder. It has expanded into a remarkably wide range of industries including telecommunications, media, banking and finance, energy, infrastructure, engineering, pharmaceuticals, and biotechnology. One of the pillars of its strategy is active globalization. As of 2005, it managed a global portfolio of US$103 billion. Inside Singapore, it has shares in the best companies, such as Singapore Airlines (the biggest air company in the world in terms of market capitalization), SingTel, Development Bank of Singapore (the biggest bank in Southeast Asia), and heavy machinery maker, Keppel. Domestic and overseas holdings account for around one half each. Abroad, Temasek has recently acquired shares in such enterprises as the Bank of China, Construction Bank of China, India's ICICI Bank, Indonesia's Bank Danamon, Telekom Malaysia, and Russian telecommunication firm Amtel. It has announced its intention to have one-third of investment in Singapore, one-third in the developed world, and one-third in the developing states.

Malaysia, by comparison, has seven investment and holding state companies of a similar kind. The most powerful one is Khazanah Nasional, incorporated in 1993. Its head is the prime minister. It is investing most actively in the areas of finance, telecommunications, utilities, IT, transportation, and the auto industry. It has stakes in more than 50 companies at home and abroad including leading Malaysian companies, such as Malaysia Airlines, Telekom Malaysia, DRB-HICOM, and Proton as well as foreign companies, such as Japan-based Miyazu Seisakusho, Indonesia's Lippo Bank, and India's Infrastructure Development Finance Corporation (Khazanah Nasional 2008).

In China, the sovereign wealth fund, China Investment Corporation (CIC), established in 2007, has become a symbol of the country's new financial strength. It manages US$200 billion of China's exchange reserves, looking for investment targets worldwide, including such heavyweights as Morgan Stanley (AFP-Jiji 2008).

Concluding Remarks

The Asian crisis visibly accelerated the transformation of the state's role in the region's national economies.

First, East Asia has gone through a drastic change in government–business relations. In the miracle years, the state guided, supported, and protected domestic businesses in general and established close ties with particular industries, companies, conglomerates, families, and clans. Large companies and groups practically had an implicit bailout guarantee. In the wake of the Asian crisis links of this kind had to be severed or at least curtailed.

Second, resource allocation has become more market driven. The governments' role as creators, protectors, and promoters of particular industries has declined.

Third, the promotion of innovation is becoming governments' key role throughout the region. Along with financial incentives, more and more importance is attached to information and consulting services, building infrastructure and facilities, coordinating the activities of companies, research centers, and other parties involved, promoting clusters, and developing the human resource. In this regard, governments in Asia work in an increasingly similar fashion to those in the West.

Fourth, as in the miracle years East Asian states prioritized industrialization and urban development as the backbone of the development process, the gap in incomes and living conditions between urban and rural areas widened, making the situation in many rural areas socially explosive. Today, in most East Asian countries, the modernization of agriculture and rural areas is rapidly climbing up the governments' priority list.

Fifth, in China and Southeast Asia, with the exception of the Philippines, SOEs and GLCs have established themselves as key players and are actively going global. In this regard, the economies mentioned remain different from the West. Governments are betting on these companies to enhance the competitiveness of the national economies. However, they also encourage them to operate as autonomous, self-reliant business entities, competing at full strength domestically and internationally. In many of them, private investors have substantial stakes and managers prioritize profitability and company value.

4

Structural Transformation: Business

Three Big Shifts

The Asian company model is undergoing a fundamental change. This change's scale, range, and depth, especially after the Asian crisis, are so significant that many, though not all, established perceptions and definitions are no longer applicable. We need new ones to adequately portray the present state of things and the direction of change.

East Asian companies cannot rely on massive state support and close interaction with the government in the way they used to. As mentioned, today, the state is pushing their restructuring and reorganization to make them more self-reliant and efficient.

Another big change to the business environment in Asia is a shift from bank loans to equity as the source of financing. Between 1990 and 2005, Asia's capitalization more than doubled. Excluding Japan, it rose almost tenfold. The capitalization of Japan, NIEs, ASEAN 4, China, and India combined reached US\$ 12.2 trillion (Japan's "contribution" was US\$ 7.5 trillion), or almost 30 percent of world capitalization (Purfield 2006).

In 2005, leverages, or corporate debt/equity ratios in, for example, Thailand, South Korea, and Malaysia were 0.70–0.75 (Burton 2007), which is much lower than on the eve of the Asian crisis (see page 19). The close relationship between companies and banks resulting in massive lending, often at much less than arm's length and with the blessing of the state, has become impossible to preserve. In the wake of the Asian crisis banks had to curtail their lending activities and fight with nonperforming loans, and when the fight was over, to strengthen the monitoring of their borrowers, think twice before extending a new loan. It made companies drastically increase equity finance, which increased their dependence on domestic and world capital markets and set the stage for the rise of influence and power of "outside" shareholders who demanded maximization of dividends and company value. (We shall call them "Western-style shareholders.")

Below we will describe the three major trends that are breaking the conventional Asian company model within this new business environment—ownership shift, governance shift, and, last but not least, the shift in the mindset and mode of behavior of the dominant stakeholders themselves. All these result in far-reaching changes in the goals and strategies that Asian companies pursue.

Ownership Shift

The Growing Presence of Western-style Shareholders

One of the major developments is the ownership shift from dominant stake-holders to other, mostly Western-style, investors. In Japan, the process is so intensive that it radically transforms the established ownership pattern. The country is going through a quiet corporate revolution. In most other nations, the transformation of the overall structure of corporate ownership is rather slow. However, two important developments bring about a fundamental change of the *status quo*. First, the Asian crisis marked a starting point for an unprecedented wave of acquisitions of Asian corporations by their foreign, especially Western, counterparts, boosted by progressing globalization and lib-eralization of investment regimes. Second, it also led to the collapse and split of a number of leading Asian conglomerates.

Ownership Structure Change in Japan. Let us start with the overall change of ownership structure and have a look at what is happening in Japan (see Figure 4.1).

We are witnessing a dramatic fall in the share of stock owned by corporations on a long-term basis (stable shareholding), including cross shareholding—a cornerstone of the established corporate system.

From 1990 to 2004, the share of "cross-held," or "mutually held," stock in the total market capitalization declined from almost 20 percent to 7.6 percent. The fall in the share of cross shareholding between banks and nonfinancial corpora-tions was especially rapid.

The share of stock, owned by stable shareholders, decreased from a little less than half of the total to only 24.3 percent. In the case of Japan, stable corporate shareholders are practically identical to dominant stakeholders. They are called "stable" because they hold stock in order to preserve and solidify the business relationship and, basically, abstain from selling it. However, in the 1990s, espe-cially in the second half, they increasingly turned out to be "untrue" to their long-term business partners and did not hesitate to sell their shares when it was deemed necessary to solve their own financial problems.

Stable and cross shareholding have largely ceased to protect companies from a hostile takeover threat the way they used to. New times have come for Japanese managers who are now working under real pressure coming from the possibility of a takeover bid.

The stock released by corporate shareholders is acquired mostly by domestic institutional investors and foreigners. From 1990 to 2005 the combined share of investment and pension trust funds in the total stock ownership went up from about 5 percent to almost 10 percent and the share of trust banks from around 10 percent to almost 20 percent. The share of foreigners increased

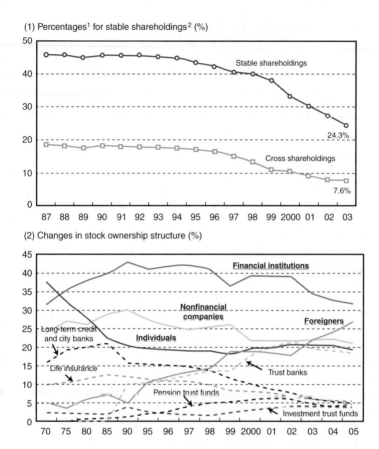

(1) Percentages[1] for stable shareholdings[2] (%)

(2) Changes in stock ownership structure (%)

Notes:
1   A percentage of total outstanding listed shares (total market capitalization) in terms of value.
2   Cross shareholdings are shares that are identified as cross-held under bilateral deals.
    Stable shareholdings include cross shareholdings, financial institutions' shareholdings,
    financial institutions' shares held by nonfinancial companies, and shares held by parent
    firms and affiliates.

Figure 4.1   Changes in Japanese stock ownership structure
Source: Government of Japan, Cabinet Office. "Annual Report on Japanese Economy and Public Finance 2006."

dramatically from about 5 percent to more than one-quarter. In 2005, the total
share of those categories of shareholders combined had reached almost 50
percent. Add about 20 percent owned by individuals, and it will be obvious
that Western-style shareholders, seeking maximization of returns, comprise a
solid majority.

Japan's Leading Shareholders. Who are the leading shareholders in today's
Japan. Surprisingly, at the top of the list, we find not the world-famous corporations and banks, but names still not widely known, even in Japan itself.

The top 30 "chart" for companies listed on the first section of the Tokyo Stock Exchange, as of the end of March 2006, clearly shows that trust banks, managing the stock commissioned by institutional investors, are taking the lead. At number one is Japan Trustee Services Bank, established in 2000 as a joint venture by Daiwa Bank and Sumitomo Trust & Banking Co., with a share of the total market capitalization as high as 5.82 percent. At number two is Master Trust Bank of Japan (their share is 4.96 percent), established by Mitsubishi Trust and Banking Co., Nippon Life Insurance, and several other investors. At number three is State Street Bank and Trust Company—at 2.19 percent. The figures look somewhat sensational—just three trust banks serving institutional investors possess more than 10 percent of the total value of stock. The list of such Western-style shareholders can be continued. Also in the top five there are Nippon Life Insurance (again, an institutional investor) with 1.60 percent and Chase Bank with 1.32 percent. Among the leaders we also find Moxley, a big shareholder of Sony, and Hero, the top shareholder of Toyota. Both are nominees for American depository receipt (ADR) holders (*Nikkei Shimbun*, October 25, 2006).

Though traditional dominant stakeholders, large companies and banks, are also in the list, we can really feel that the winds of change are blowing. In the leading East Asian economy, which created a corporate ownership pattern quite different from Western standards, now corporations belong mostly to the same type of owners as in the West.

What about other Asian economies?

Ownership Structure Change in South Korea. In South Korea, individuals traditionally hold the largest share of corporate stock (in terms of the number of stock), followed by corporate shareholders (see Figure 4.2).

As ordinary South Korean people are not active buyers of corporate stock, the "individuals" are largely conglomerates' (in South Korea they are called *chaebols*) founders and their family members. They are dominant stakeholders. Corporate shareholders (shown in Figure 4.2 as "companies") are largely *chaebol* members. Founders and their families exercise control, either directly or indirectly, through *chaebol* companies in which they have a major stake (including cross shareholdings as the means of control).

Figure 4.2 shows that during 1991–2001 the share of individuals decreased, while the share of corporate shareholders went up. Their combined proportion was practically unchanged: about 60 percent. Presumably, founders and their families came to hold relatively less stock directly, relying more on indirect control mechanisms. By contrast, the share of foreign investors was steadily growing, especially after the Asian crisis. Also, right after the Asian crisis the share of the state (government/public institutions) rose rapidly and then fast growth of the banks' share followed.

In 2004, the share of individuals fell further to 33.8 percent of total corporate stock and the share of companies to 19.0 percent. In contrast, the proportion of banks rose to 18.9 percent, foreigners to 22.0 percent, and the

Structural Transformation: Business   69

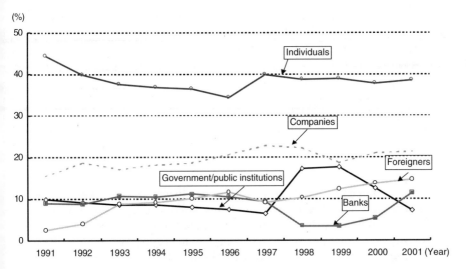

Figure 4.2   Corporate shareholding composition in South Korea

Source: METI, "White Paper on International Economy and Trade 2003," p.92

Note: Banks include other financial institutions. Companies mean nonfinancial companies.

government public institutions to 6.3 percent. In the next three years, individuals and companies partly regained their share: in 2007, they rose to 36.3 percent and 24.6 percent respectively, while the share of banks fell to 15.4 percent, foreigners to 18.8 percent, and the government/public institutions to 4.9 percent (Korea Exchange 2008). Still, the shares of foreigners and banks remain much higher than in the pre-crisis years.

The ownership structure with regard to stock value for the shares of various types of owners in the total amount of stock is quite different to their shares in total market capitalization, or the value of the stock. The proportion of foreign investors started to grow rapidly from the second half of the 1990s, reaching 42.0 percent in 2004 and declining to 32.4 percent in 2007. The big difference, when compared to their share in the total number of stocks, is easy to explain—they target the best South Korean corporations with the highest stock value. On the other hand, the individuals' fraction of total market capitalization is lower than their share of the number of stocks. In 2004, it was 18.0 percent, in 2007 it went up to 21.8 percent. In terms of the value of stock, the combined share of foreigners and banks, in 2007, was as high as 54.2 percent (Korea Exchange 2008).

One of the most important indicators of the degree of the founder families' control is the internal shareholding (this includes stock ownership by the founder family, cross shareholdings by group companies, and the companies' own stock) ratio in the leading 30 *chaebols* (the amount of internally owned stock divided by the total number of stocks of the 30 *chaebol* companies). In the 1990s it was maintained at a 42–44 percent level.

In 1998, the government abolished the regulation imposed four years earlier, which allowed the corporations belonging to the top 30 *chaebols* (excluding financial, insurance, and holding companies) to hold or acquire stocks of other domestic firms only within the limit of 25 percent of their net assets. After that, intragroup acquisitions of stock surged as companies tried to boost their capital in order to meet the government's requirements to reduce the debt-equity ratio. The rise of the internal shareholding ratio continued until December 1999, when it reached the 50.5 percent high (ERINA 2005, 56). At that point the 25 percent limit on the equity investment by the top 30 *chaebol* companies was reimposed. Besides, in 1998, for those firms the Fair Trade Commission banned cross-debt guarantees. Cross shareholding was also prohibited.[1] (However, it is actually maintained through configurations like "firm A owns stock of firm B, B of C, and C of A.") Since 2000, the internal shareholding ratio of the top 30 *chaebols* has begun to fall. In April, 2001, it was 45 percent (METI 2003, 91).

Overall, though the founder families remain the major players, the presence of other, mostly Western-style, shareholders is growing.

Ownership Structure Change in Thailand. As far as Southeast Asia is concerned, some of the most detailed information about corporate ownership change is available on Thailand. Thai scholars. A. Khanthavit, P. Polsiri, and Y. Wiwattanakantang, conducted a comprehensive survey of the ownership structure of all nonfinancial firms listed on the Stock Exchange of Thailand in pre-crisis 1996 and post-crisis 2000 (Khanthavit 2003). The number of firms surveyed was 352 and 322 respectively.

One of their major goals was to identify the controlling shareholders of every corporation. A controlling shareholder is the one who owns, directly or indirectly, 25 percent or more of the company stock. In both years, almost 80 percent of the firms had controlling shareholders.

The results showed that between 1996 and 2000 the share of companies controlled by a single family, or a group of related families, declined from 51.4 percent to 45.7 percent and by a group of unrelated families from 6.0 percent to 5.6 percent. By contrast, the share of companies controlled by foreign investors increased from 13.1 percent to 15.2 percent, domestic financial institutions from 0.6 percent to 1.2 percent (in 2000, companies controlled by institutional investors emerged whereas in 1996, there were none), and the Thai government from 2.3 percent to 2.8 percent.

The proportion of firms with multiple controlling shareholders of different types (for example, a family and a foreign investor) rose significantly from 5.7 percent to 8.7 percent. Within this group the role of single families also decreased. While, in 1996, a single controlling family appeared in 95 percent of firms with multiple controlling shareholders, in 2000, the share went down to 67.9 percent.

Though family-controlled corporations still comprise a majority of Thai listed companies, the transfer of ownership, as well as controlling power, from families to outside shareholders is visible. Especially notable is the fact that the ownership and controlling power of foreign investors is increasing.

A Special Case—Singapore. Some regional economies turn out to be special cases. This applies to Singapore. Here, along with founder families, we find another type of dominant corporate owner—the state, and it shows no intention or readiness to curtail its role in light of the emergence of powerful outsiders as potential alternative corporate owners. In fact, it prefers to act as a shrewd entrepreneur, prioritizing efficiency and profitability.

The state has a stake in many key companies and financial institutions. For instance, Development Bank of Singapore (DBS), the largest bank in Southeast Asia, which accounted for 29 percent of total banking assets in the country in 2004, is publicly listed, but government-controlled.

The government investment arm, Temasek Holdings, controls 22 key firms in various industries as their first-tier companies, the latter having numerous subsidiaries or associate firms, which, in turn, have their own, third-tier subsidiaries, and so on. Many of Temasek's companies are listed on the Stock Exchange, and its major listed corporations account for more than 20 percent of the city-state's total market capitalization (Ramirez 2003).

Similar trends can be traced in Malaysia where a number of government institutions, especially investment company, Khazanah, the Malaysian version of Temasek, are enhancing their role as key corporate owners.

The point, however, is that, to be efficient business organizations, the state investment vehicles have to play the role of Western-style investors—to invest into profitable enterprises and to demand sound management and high returns. As mentioned in the previous chapter, it is not a developmental state intervening in order to correct market-based resource allocation. It is rather an **entrepreneur state** seeking to become a powerful player **within,** not above, the market economy.

Corporate Ownership Structure in China. For China, where the state is the only initial dominant stockholder, the change of its share serves as a key indicator of the speed and depth of ownership transformation. Today, the mode of behavior of the state as a principal owner largely resembles that of principal owners in other Asian countries. It seeks to retain presence and control, but also to make companies competitive—more and more frequently it has to "invite" outside stakeholders, share ownership with them, and to listen to what they say.

Besides state-owned enterprises (SOEs), the National Bureau of Statistics of China defines seven types of company ownership: collective (companies belonging to a workers' collective—this type of ownership is hailed even by orthodox communist ideologists, as collectives are directly controlled by the state), shareholding, private, individual, cooperative or joint-ventured, foreign, and others (Hong Kong, Macau, and other overseas Chinese-invested).

According to Chinese statistics, from 1979 to 2000 the share of SOEs in the gross domestic product (GDP) went down from 56 percent to 29 percent, the share of collective-owned enterprises from 42 percent to 39 percent, and the share of all the other companies rose dramatically from 2 percent to 32 percent (Guo 2003).

According to the International Finance Corporation (IFC) publication, the number of SOEs was reduced from 114,000 in 1996 to 34,000 in

2003 (Garnout 2005, 11). Half of the decline occurred due to privatization (Knowledge@Wharton 2006). In other words, since the latter half of the 1990s we are witnessing a remarkable transfer of ownership from the state to other stakeholders, including private investors.

After the Communist Part of China (CPC) proclaimed the "strategic restructuring" of the state-owned economy at its 15th National Congress in 1997, many local district administrations—especially, but not only, in the coastal areas—moved fast to privatize the local small-scale SOEs which were under their jurisdiction. As well as this, a significant number of small SOEs were reorganized into shareholding cooperatives, which basically means that newly issued shares were distributed among the workers.

Then, privatization started at the municipal level and spread to medium-size SOEs (with about 1,000 employees). Many of them evolved into shareholding companies in which stock was distributed between the state, the employees, and outside investors. According to the Company Law, the state had to have a share of at least a 35 percent in a shareholding company, and in most cases this exceeded 50 percent (Guo 2003, 563).

Finally, since 1997, the listing of large SOEs also accelerated. Initially, they were transformed into limited liability companies, but remained wholly state-owned. In 1999, the selling of state-owned shares began. A model was worked out for leading SOEs to acquire their stock from the state and sell it to designated third parties. The scheme did not work well and, finally, a shift was made to market-based sales to private investors. Among other things, it gave an impetus to the emergence of institutional investors as important owners: in 2000, they acquired about 40 percent of the large SOEs' tradable stock (Imai 2002, 2).

State Regulations. Though the transfer of ownership from the state to other owners is gradually gaining momentum, the state tightly regulates the process. It decides which companies and industries are allowed to introduce a shareholding system and which are not. The central authorities—the National Development and Reforms Commission, the People's Bank of China, and the China Securities Regulatory Commission—approve annual stock issuance plans, fixing the total number of newly issued shares. Then each province is allocated a subquota. Firms wishing to issue shares have to apply to provincial authorities (Guo 2003, 564). The final decision is made by the central authorities. The presence of foreign investors is also restricted. "A" shares, quoted in yuan, are available for Chinese investors only, "B" shares, quoted in US dollars, are available to both domestic and foreign buyers.

Globally Competitive Chinese Companies—the State is Involved. By keeping the ownership transformation process under control, the state itself wants to be a successful company owner.

Those Chinese companies which recently "shook" the business world by their dramatic entries into its leading cohort, are mostly not private companies in the true sense of the word. Even if they do not formally fall into the SOE category, the state preserves indirect control. Haier, a new star in the household-appliance business, is a workers-owned collective. Its chairman, Zhang Ruimin, is a member of the Central Committee of CPC (Crowell 2005). One of the world's biggest PC makers, Lenovo, which acquired IBM's PC department in December 2005, was initially launched by the Chinese Academy of Sciences in 1984. The latter retains a majority stake. In the case of TCL, the electronic giant, Huizhou Municipality owns 25 percent. China has proved that at least some of its companies, directly or indirectly controlled by the state, can be successful and internationally competitive.

Still, Private Owners Are Needed. It is quite obvious that for the ruling elite the most desirable way of reforming SOEs is to make them operate within a market economy and meet its efficiency standards, but without changing the form of ownership. The state is moving to impose harder financial constraints and, as time goes by, it is becoming increasingly difficult for SOEs to rely on budget funds, and, especially, to be bailed out if they have been poorly managed. The government plays the part of a demanding owner requiring self-reliance and profitability (for details see Chapter 7 on China). The above-mentioned examples clearly show that there are companies where this approach works. Yet, all this is not sufficient to solve the efficiency problem of the state sector as a whole—in spite of all the effort, 40 percent of SOEs are losing money (Knowledge@Wharton 2006).

The Chinese regime is not that fond of private investors, or, in other words, outside Western-style shareholders. It would rather distribute shares between insiders (workers and managers) or exploit the "ideologically correct" concept of a workers' collective or cooperative than invite an outside investor.

However, it understands quite well that enhancing the efficiency and competitiveness of a wide range of SOEs is impossible without bringing in private capital, including foreign investors and, basically, does not object to it. In this regard, it is worth recollecting that at the beginning of this decade private Chinese businessmen were allowed to become Communist Party members. Consequently, there emerges a stratum of private owners, buying the stock of state-owned or state-controlled companies. Not only institutional investors but also domestic individual shareholders, hungering for high returns, are becoming increasingly important. Many of them are coming from the ruling elite itself.

With certain modifications, the logic of change, working in other East Asian countries, is starting to work in China too. Ownership is gradually being transferred from a dominant stakeholder—the state—to other owners, not least Western-style shareholders.

Foreign Acquisitions are Booming

One of the major developments in the post-crisis East Asia, accelerating the ownership shift, is the unprecedented wave of stock acquisitions by foreigners, including complete acquisitions of Asian companies by their foreign, especially Western, counterparts.

Acquisitions in South Korea. In a significant number of leading South Korean companies and banks, whose names have symbolized the nation's success in the years of the economic miracle, foreign investors now hold the majority of stocks. As of the end of 2003, in Samsung Electronics, foreign owners' share was 57.3 percent, while intragroup owners held only 15.3 percent. For Hyundai Motors the shares were respectively 51.3 percent and 23.7 percent (ERINA 2005, 74). In the largest South Korean commercial bank, Kookmin, foreign shareholders held 74 percent (ERINA 2005, 68).

From 1998, foreigners were allowed to own business and financial institutions. Samsung Motors was acquired by Renault, Samsung Heavy Industries' construction equipment division by Volvo Construction, and Korea First Bank came under the control of Newbridge Capital of the US.

Acquisitions in Malaysia, Thailand, and Singapore. In Malaysia, acquisitions of equity by foreign investors in post-crisis years provoked a heated debate, and Prime Minister Abdullah Badawi had to publicly dismiss the allegations that they have to be viewed as a new form of colonization. However, the government has called for vigilance so as not to lose shareholding control to foreigners. The biggest acquisition was the purchase by Norway's Telenor of a 61 percent stake in telecommunication firm, DiGi, in 2001.

A number of large-scale acquisitions have taken place in Thailand. For instance, one of the leading producers of integrated curcuits, Alphatech Electronics, was acquired by the American International Group (AIG) and the Swedish firm Ericsson in 1998, which made it possible to restore its solvency. In a major breakthrough, the government allowed foreign investors to own a majority or 100 percent share in Thai financial institutions for up to ten years (after that further offerings have to be limited to local investors). As a result, at the beginning of the 2000s, in four out of 13 major banks foreign investors held a majority stake and 23 out of 28 brokerages were owned by foreign companies (Agami 2002).

On the other hand, Singapore adopts a very tough stance when it comes to control over key domestic companies and banks. The Monetary Authority of Singapore (MAS) requires banks to establish management-nominating committees with only locals as members. The majority of their directors have to be Singapore citizens or permanent residents.

Growing M&A Activities in China. Far-reaching changes are under way in China. For example, it was not allowed to transfer shares owned by the state and state-owned companies to foreign investors, but recently the ban was lifted—though the state has to remain a major shareholder in the companies with a mixed form of ownership. Foreign investors were prohibited from directly acquiring yuan-quoted A-shares but it has now been made possible due to the introduction of the qualified foreign institutional investor scheme in December 2002 (*AsiaPulse News* 2006).

The scheme, earlier implemented in Taiwan and South Korea, enables foreign institutional investors—fund-managing, insurance, and securities companies and commercial banks, approved by the China Securities Regulatory Commission—to invest in China within the quota obtained from the State Administration of Foreign Exchange. To buy the securities, investors have to convert their currencies into yuan. The yield and dividends are converted back into the original currency and repatriated later. A single investor can acquire no more than a 10 percent stake in a single company and a combined share of the eligible investors cannot exceed 20 percent.

Also, leading Chinese companies are increasingly being allowed to be listed overseas.

Foreign Investment in Leading Chinese Banks. A new and remarkable development is the massive sale of stock of leading Chinese banks. In late 2003, the government injected more than US$100 billion of public funds into the major state-owned banks for their recapitalization and bad loan write-downs. Then, it started incorporating them and, finally, invited foreign strategic investors to acquire substantial shares before the banks went public. As a result, acquisitions of the equity of major Chinese banks by foreign investors are among the largest capital transactions in the world.

In 2004, HSBC acquired a 19.9 percent stake in the Bank of Communications for US$2.25 billion. The following year, the Bank of America announced a US$3 billion investment in the China Construction Bank. The consortium led by the Royal Bank of Scotland bought a 19.9 percent stake in the Bank of China for US$2.5 billion and soon another big stake in this bank was bought by Temasek (Anderson 2005). In 2005, Goldman Sachs, American Express, and German insurer Allianz, acquired a 9 percent stake in the Industrial and Commercial Bank of China (Chan-Fishel 2007).

Smaller Chinese institutions, especially city commercial banks, have begun walking along the same road. For instance, Australia and New Zealand Banking Group (ANZ) has agreed to invest in Shanghai Rural Commercial Bank.

Though, unlike other East Asian countries, it is still impossible for a foreign company or institution to fully acquire a big Chinese company or bank, acquisitions of stocks by foreigners are rising at a remarkable speed.

Conglomerates Collapse

Another development, which shook the existing ownership structure, was the collapse and split of a number of major conglomerates in the crisis-hit countries.

Daewoo and Hyundai. The biggest shock was the fiasco of Daewoo. One of the top five South Korean conglomerates, it collapsed under the burden of soaring debts it was unable to control—largely because it had been expanding and making new debts as if there was no tomorrow. The founder, Kim Woo-jung, skipped the country for six years, returning in 2005 to be jailed for fraud. (In December 2007, he was granted amnesty by then President Roh Moon-hyun.) The conglomerate was split into a number of companies focused on particular areas of business and belonging to different owners. Daewoo Motors was put under the control of GM. Daewoo International has become a globally-oriented trading house.

Another cautionary tale is that of the Hyundai Group. After the death of the founder, Chung Ju-yung, the family members failed to agree about how to run the conglomerate together, and it was divided into five groups—Hyundai Motor Company, Hyundai Group, Hyundai Department Store Group, Hyundai Development Company and Hyundai Heavy Industries Group. The names of four out of five clearly show that, unlike classical conglomerates, they are focused on particular industries. Also, Hyundai Electronics, which changed its name to Hynix, and Hyundai Engineering and Construction have become independent companies.

Salim. The story making headlines in Indonesia was the collapse of the Salim group, one of the most famous conglomerates in Southeast Asia, founded by Liem Sioe Liong. On the eve of the Asian crisis the conglomerate was said to have 500 companies in Indonesia itself along with substantial interests in Singapore, Hong Kong, the Philippines, and other countries. Its activities included the production of cars, cement, instant noodles, property development, banking, and telecommunications.

Hit by the Asian crisis, Salim companies found themselves on the verge of a financial catastrophe and the group was virtually disbanded. Its key financial institution, Bank Central Asia, was nationalized. As most of its loans had been extended to Salim companies, they were put under government control. The Indonesian Bank Restructuring Agency (IBRA) took over as many as 107 Salim companies (Desai 2005). Later, some of them were sold to new owners, some went back to Salim, and some remain paralyzed. Key companies, including Bank Central Asia, have been lost forever. The founder himself moved to Singapore. His son, Anthony Salim, started to rebuild the business in his capacity as president of First Pacific Group, based in Hong Kong and bought by his father in the 1990s. It was focused on just two major business areas—consumer food products and telecommunications. Its subsidiary, Indofood has established itself as the biggest producer of instant noodles in the world.

As for Bank Central Asia, the government gradually sold its controlling stake after restructuring the enterprise. Now, 50 percent of its stock is owned by Farindo Investments (Mauritius) Ltd, controlled by the Hartono family.

Foreign capital also acquired Salim's assets. One of its biggest companies, Indocement, came under the control of the HeidelbergCement Group of Germany.

Renong. Malaysia, for its part, experienced the collapse of the Renong Group— the biggest *Bumiputra*-owned conglomerate. It had an investment holding company at the top and more than 100 companies engaged in property development, telecommunications and multimedia, transportation, construction and engineering, and other activities. The group maintained close ties with the politically dominant United Malays National Organization (UMNO). In the late 1990s, Renong faced serious financial troubles. Attempts to list some of its leading companies on the Kuala Lumpur Stock Exchange (KLSE) were unsuccessful.

Halim Saad, Renong's chairman and de facto owner, had a huge personal debt to United Engineers Malaysia (UEM), the core company of the group which was linked with the Renong holding company by mutual shareholding. (Renong had a 38 percent stake in UEM, UEM a 31 percent stake in Renong.) Halim tried to find a way out by obliging UEM to purchase 5.3 billion ringgit worth of Renong's assets and liabilities but the plan did not work (Tselichtchev 2004). In August, 2001, Syarikat Danasaham, a wholly-owned subsidiary of the state-owned investment company Khazanah Nasional, made a conditional voluntary offer to purchase the entire shares and warrants of UEM, including Renong's stake. Having put UEM under its control, Khazanah also became the owner of Renong holding company through the above-mentioned 31 percent stake. Halim was removed from his position as Renong's chairman and replaced by a former Khazanah executive. A new management team was formed, consisting of professionals in accounting, banking and finance, legal services, and so on. It announced that it would work to speed up the listing of the group companies.

The collapse and split of a number of leading conglomerates had very important implications for Asian economies. Their ownership was changed in a revolutionary way—founders were ousted and new owners of a different character emerged. Their failure was a warning to other companies, owned, organized, and run the same way.

Corporate Governance Shift

Governance Matters

In Asia, Governance Means Control from Outside. The ownership shift provides an impetus for improvements in the corporate governance—as outside shareholders increase their share, they demand more control. Furthermore, even in nations and companies where the decline in the share of a dominant stakeholder is insignificant, or where it does not happen at all, pressure to improve corporate governance and prioritize the interests of Western-style shareholders (maximization of the return on capital) is mounting.

As mentioned, in East Asia, corporate governance has a meaning somewhat different from the West. It means the system making it possible for outside shareholders to protect their interests against the dominant shareholders and the managers that those dominant shareholders appoint and control. In other words, a system that provides efficient outside control over a dominant shareholder.

Definitely, despite a fundamental shift in ownership structure, East Asian corporations still often lack effective control, or governance from outside. Yet, corporate governance in the region is significantly improving.

Growing Interest and Initial Steps. In virtually all the major countries of the region we are witnessing an unprecedented rise of interest in "governance from outside" from the business community, policymakers, the mass media, and the general public. In Thailand, then prime minister, Thaksin Shinawatra, even declared 2002 "the year of good corporate governance."

One of the important new trends is the adoption of corporate governance codes—usually nonbinding, but difficult to ignore. In the Philippines, the Securities and Exchange Commission implemented the code in 2002 and required companies to submit their own manuals on corporate governance, which they did the same year. In Malaysia, the KLSE requires companies to disclose in their annual reports a narrative account of how they applied the principles of the code, adopted in 2000, to their structures and processes and on the extent of their compliance. In Singapore, all listed companies are required to present a complete description of their governance practices in their annual reports with specific reference to code provisions. When deviations occur, explanation has to be provided. In Indonesia, a Code of Good Corporate Governance was developed by the National Committee on Corporate Governance, established in 1999, by ministerial decree. It also issued the Code of Good Governance for Banks and guidance for audit committees and independent commissioners.

Outside Directors: A Time for Us?

Listed companies are obliged, or strongly recommended, to appoint outside directors. New laws usually also set the minimum share of outside directors in their total number. Sometimes, they also specify committees or subcommittees, which must consist mostly of outsiders. In short, the stage is being set for outside directors to play a bigger role.

It is a fundamental change, as for most countries the very notion of outside directors is new.

South Korea. For example, in South Korea, until 1998, there were no nonexecutive outside directors and no distinction between directors and officers. Not surprisingly, the boards did not function. Though the law did prescribe formal board meetings, the companies often skipped them and produced fictitious board minutes compiled under the instructions of the chairman's office. Directors, however, did not hesitate to put their personal seals on the minutes as if the meeting had been really held.

The reform of the *chaebols* resulted in the abolition of the institutions of the chairman of the group and the chairman's office. To retain representation rights, a founder was obliged to become a board member and, consequently, to adopt fiduciary duty. For instance, the owner of Hyundai Group, Chung Ju-yung, became a member of the board of Hyundai Construction. In fact, it meant the introduction of the institution of the board of directors in its conventional form. However, there are indications that the measure only had a limited effect. Though owners become board members of particular group companies, in practice they retained control over the whole group, and the chairman's offices were often reanimated under different names.

Since 1998, the appointment of outside directors is required by law. For listed companies with assets exceeding 2 trillion won it became mandatory to raise the share of outside directors to 50 percent or more by the end of 2001 (METI 2003, 47). Also, they are required to establish an auditing committee where outside directors have to comprise not less than two-thirds of all the members, and, when new outside directors are elected, a compensation committee with a share of outside directors of 50 percent or more (ERINA 2005, 47). Committees on managerial strategy, risk management, and remuneration are also mandatory and have to consist mostly of outsiders (ERINA 2005, 66).

As for the banks, after the Asian crisis the newly established Financial Supervisory Commission required them to have a majority of independent directors and strongly encouraged the appointment of outside directors in the position of chairman and key positions in committees in such areas as compensation, risk management, and financial reporting. For instance, the Board of Housing and Commercial Bank (HCB), which before the Asian crisis consisted of six insiders and six quasi-outsiders, drawn largely from its major borrowers, is now dominated by independent directors, including a retail company CEO, an overseas banker, and financial experts (McKinsey 2002, 36).

Southeast Asia and China. In the Philippines, the Code of Corporate Governance sets the minimum share of independent directors at 20 percent or two persons, whichever is less. Their representation on the board's subcommittees was also increased.

In Singapore, until recently, "independent" directors were often family members, politicians, or business associates. The new governance code, effective from 2003, calls for a minimum of one-third of the board to be composed of independent directors and also provides guidance on their relationship with the company.

In Malaysia, the Code of Corporate Governance also recommends that independent directors comprise at least one-third of the board members. It encourages the appointment of committees with clearly stated responsibilities to assist the board, including audit and remuneration committees consisting mostly of nonexecutive directors. According to the KLSE listing requirements, at least two directors or one-third of the board must be independent (World Bank 2005).

In Thailand, according to a survey by McKinsey and the Thai Institute of Directors, which covered 133 leading companies, 68 percent of these firms had 25–50 percent of the board made up of independent directors, though only one firm was found where the latter comprised a majority. Also, 22 percent of the firms had an independent chairman of the board—the percentage is higher than in the US (15 percent), where the roles of chairman and CEO are usually combined (McKinsey 2002, 34–35).

In Indonesia, the role of outside directors is still negligible. Here, under the Company Law, a limited liability company must have a Board of Directors (BOD) responsible for day-to-day management and a Board of Commissioners (BOC) which is supposed to monitor, oversee, and advise the BOD. Both are elected at the general stockholders' meetings. However, in practice, nomination is usually made by management or controlling shareholders.

Though the appointment of independent commissioners is not required by the Company Law, the Jakarta Stock Exchange regulations set their share at not less than one-third of the total number of BOC members. Also, an independent commissioner has to chair the auditing committee (World Bank 2004).

In China, some SOEs try to imitate the private companies' systems. Among other things, they establish boards of directors and make managers accountable to them.

Better Disclosure, More Accountability

Disclosure and accountability rules are becoming stricter while the procedures for shareholders wishing to sue company executives are simplified and their related costs reduced.

In 2004, South Korea adopted securities-related class action litigation, though application of the law was suspended until 2007. Also, in 1998, the minimum share needed to have the right to demand dismissal of a member of the board was reduced from 1 percent to 0.5 percent, and the minimum share for representative legal action from 1 percent to 0.01 percent (METI 2003, 39). Unlike the pre-crisis years, more and more directors and officers are holding liability insurance policies—a clear indication of outside shareholders' growing influence. The latter's presence was especially noticeable in the days of the Daewoo debacle, when, along with banks, suppliers, and former employees, they brought actions against the group companies and their managers.

In Malaysia, the amendment of the Securities Commission Act of 2000 enhanced disclosure obligations on issuers of stock and imposed harsher penalties for false and misleading information in prospectuses. Investors were given the right to pursue civil actions against companies, directors, and their advisors in cases of contravention of the law.

In Indonesia, progress is still comparatively slow. Though class and derivative action lawsuits are allowed, they tend to be too costly for shareholders. In practice, the number of cases is few and shareholders don't win. Also, to file a lawsuit against directors or commissioners, requires the holding of at least 10 percent of total voting shares, which is a higher threshold than in other countries (World Bank 2004).

Grassroots Movements Emerge

A new and remarkable development is the emergence of the grassroots movements seeking to protect the interests of minority shareholders. The most vivid example is South Korea's People's Solidarity for Participatory Democracy (PSPD). Its initial goal was to monitor the actions of the authorities, but since the Asian crisis it has also started to work actively to protect the interests of the minority shareholders of *chaebol* companies who sue corporations and their managers and come out with proposals at the stockholders' meetings.

In Malaysia, the Minority Shareholder Watchdog Group emerged in August 2000 as an independent company representing the biggest domestic institutional funds—the Employee's Provident Fund, Lembaga Tabung Angkatan Tentera (Armed Forces Fund Board), Lembaga Tabung Haji (Pilgrim's Fund

Board), Pertubuhan Keselamatan Sosial, and Permodalan Nasional Berhad. It aims to become a think tank and a resource center for minority shareholders, to protect their interests by monitoring companies for breaches of, and nonadherence to, good governance principles, and by recommending actions against managers when shareholders' interests are harmed. It also seeks to act as a mechanism for collective action for its members by proxy voting on their behalf at the shareholders' general meetings.

The Securities Investors Association of Singapore, an association of small shareholders, educates its members on financial and corporate governance issues. It seeks to attract attention to poor governance practices through the media and at shareholders' meetings.

Difficult Questions Remain

All the changes described put traditional, dominant stakeholders under stronger pressure from outside—not just from the outside shareholders of their own companies but also from society as a whole.

Yet, real change in governance practices and in the balance of power within Asian corporations turns out to be slow and only partial. In practice, dominant stakeholders often do all they can to change as little as possible.

One of the most difficult questions is, "Can a formally independent director be really independent in a company with a highly concentrated ownership?" Or, to go a bit deeper into the matter, "What is the meaning of an independent director in a family-controlled Asian firm (or in a state-controlled Chinese company)?"

Basically, a director is independent if he is not involved in the company management and, thus, presumably, fully committed to exercise genuine control over managers to make sure that the interests of shareholders are protected. However, in a typical family-controlled Asian company (as well as in a Chinese company controlled by the state) the meaning of an independent director is somewhat different. The key point is independence from a dominant stakeholder and protection of the interests of other stakeholders. The problem, however, is that in a company with a highly concentrated ownership an independent director can hardly be appointed without the dominant stakeholder's consent. Logically, it is a trap.

Finding a satisfactory and realistic solution to the problem is not easy. The attitude of a director himself is important—especially his ability to defend the viewpoint he believes to be right even when it goes contrary to the interests and the position of the dominant stakeholder. However, this is hardly sufficient. In addition, at least, the dominant stakeholder himself has to be progressive enough to allow and, maybe, even encourage this kind of independence.

Dominant Shareholders: A New Mentality, a New Mode of Action

The Need to Modernize

Here, we come to our next major point—the changing mentality of the dominant stakeholders themselves.

True, many of them continue to use various techniques to retain control even when their share of ownership is falling. They cling to the old pattern of governance, resisting change.

The fight for control between dominant stakeholders and Western-style investors is one of the major collisions of today's corporate Asia. However, the other side of the coin should not be overlooked.

It would be irrelevant to view the dominant stakeholders as retrogrades trying to preserve the *status quo* by all means. Quite often they are smart and progressive enough to realize the obvious—to survive and win in a rapidly changing and globalizing economy, it is vital to attract an increasing amount of funds from the global capital market. They have to compete for those funds, and to be successful, they have got to establish a positive image in the eyes of the international investment community. Therefore, it becomes imperative to treat outside shareholders as partners, not rivals, in the fight for control. Treating them as partners, in turn, means adapting to their goals—in particular, the maximization of returns.

Maybe, it is the price dominant stakeholders have to pay for remaining in power. However, their own interests are not necessarily hostile to those of outside shareholders. Being the owners, they also benefit from higher dividends and growing company value.

Also, the dominant stakeholders' "progressive wing" has come to understand that the best, if not the only, way to preserve power and wealth in today's world might be the promotion of, not resistance to, the modernization of their companies' governance and management systems so that they meet *de facto* global standards. It implies such basic things as genuine control over management by independent directors and/or auditors, selling nonprofitable business units, focusing on areas of competitive advantage instead of widening the conglomerate empire, differentiating products and services, and competing not only on price, but also on quality, technology, and brand.

To proceed with this kind of modernization, a dominant stakeholder has to rely much more on independent professional managers. He also has to listen attentively to what outside directors are saying and have their opinion reflected in the decisions the company makes.

The latest developments in some Asian companies provide important hints about the ways the founder families' role may evolve. One plausible scenario is their gradual evolution into investors with interests in the conglomerate's companies, exercising large investors' "natural" rights, but, contrary to a conventional Asian conglomerate, not trying to integrate those companies into a single business group under the family's complete control. Also, they would not seek to be directly involved in, and to play the major role in, the decision-making of every company they have a stake in.

In other words, a feasible strategy can be articulated like this: split the conglomerate into a number of focused companies, sell off the uncompetitive ones, retain a stake in the competitive units, and rely on skilled professional managers.

Then, provide good governance so that their activities are properly monitored. All this will help to attract funds from investors around the world.

Some founder families are already taking steps in this direction.

Pioneers of Change

Ayala Group. Ayala Group is the leading conglomerate in the Philippines with interests in banking, mobile telephony, property development, the hotel business, and so on. The owner, Jaime Augusto Zobel de Ayala, who is also chairman of the core company, Ayala Corporation, is said to have openly discussed with members of his family the possibility of splitting the group. Indeed, why do companies in such areas as banking, real estate, and telecommunication have to be run within a single organization, if they, presumably, can be managed more efficiently as specialized separate entities?

Formally, the conglomerate has not been split. However, the major features of a conventional Asian conglomerate seem to be fading. Ayala is not transferring funds between the companies of the group, making more profitable ones support those which earn less. It abstains from actively appointing family members to managerial posts. On the contrary, it operates a "talent bank" of several dozen executives sending some of them to American business schools. It is not engaged in nontransparent transactions, putting an emphasis on cleanliness of business and proper disclosure so as to be attractive to investors worldwide. It issues equity to finance new ventures, such as a mobile telephony company, actively selling shares to Western investors and inviting, for example, Singapore's telephone incumbent to be a partner. Finally, it created a new subsidiary which is run as a Western-style venture fund (*The Economist* 2002).

Hutchison Whampoa. One of the best performing conglomerates in the region, in terms of profits and corporate value, is Hutchison Whampoa of Hong Kong. Its activities include container terminal business, shipping services, manufacturing, retailing, telecommunication, media, energy, finance, and so on. Its success is largely explained by apt and resolute acquisitions and sales of assets by its owner Li Ka Shing. He acts as a shrewd investor, a financial capitalist—not as a conventional conglomerate founder clinging to the idea of a steady expansion of the business empire. For instance, about 66 percent of Hutchison Whampoa's pretax earnings, in 2002, came from profits on asset sales. The most famous were the US$22 billion sale of Orange to Mannesmann and the US$5 billion sale of Voice-Stream Wireless to Deutsche Telekom. To buy VoiceStream originally, Hutchison Whampoa invested US$1 billion: in other words, just one-fifth of the selling price.

An important aspect of its financial strategy is selling companies to their "natural owners" (companies having core competence in the area) at a proper time, which is more than helpful to increase shareholder wealth (Kaye 2003).

Thailand's Hybrid Systems. Some Asian companies are searching for new and original approaches, synthesizing elements of traditional and Western-style corporate models.

Research done by McKinsey in Thailand showed that a number of companies attempt to combine professional management with modified forms of family control (McKinsey 2002). Day-to-day management is delegated to professionals. They may be family members, they may be outsiders. The point is that the former do not have a special career track. However, to preserve the family control, a family forum is established. Its tasks are consensus building, policy setting, and solving family disputes. In the corporate hierarchy such a forum is placed above the board of directors and appoints its members, thus implementing the right of a controlling shareholder.

Another approach is the so-called "private equity solution." The organizational structure of a private equity fund is imitated. Three to five family members are chosen to run the enterprise as if they were general partners. Their responsibility is to create value for the entire family. They are given incentives to meet clearly defined business goals, such as raising of the firm's capitalization, and get performance-based remuneration. Thus, other family issues do not interfere with the business. This approach, however, does not leave much room for outside stakeholders.

A New Mode of Action: Three Features

Ownership shift, governance shift, and the new mentality of dominant stakeholders have given birth to three important and closely interlinked new features, characterizing the new mode of action of today's Asian companies. The first one is prioritizing the maximization of shareholders' returns as a company goal. The second is focusing on core businesses where a company has, or can, develop a competitive advantage. The third is trying to compete internationally—not only on price but also on product differentiation, technology, quality, and brand building.

Prioritizing Returns. Maybe, the most vivid manifestation of the first feature is the sensational growth of dividends Asian companies pay to their stockholders. It marks a really big turnaround, as lucrative dividends have never been a characteristic of the region—massive portfolio investment before the Asian crisis was driven mostly by high returns provided by rising value of stocks.

According to the CLSA Asia-Pacific Markets country head in Singapore, D. Kestel, in the first half of this decade Asian companies' dividend yield (dividend payment as a percentage of the stock price) in Asia, has reached 3.5 percent, while the average for Standard & Poor's 500 was only 1.5 percent.

Focusing on Core Business. Focusing on core business was a natural part of reforming the conglomerates which collapsed under the blows of the Asian crisis. It is also a strategic direction of change for a significant number of companies which managed to get over the crisis and for those who were not hit by it at all. Focusing can be achieved through a sell-off of the units which are not doing well or lack a clear perspective, concentration on one major business activity, or a select group of them, and decentralization of control and the decision-making process meaning that a dominant stakeholder lets companies under his financial wing operate as autonomous units specializing in particular business areas.

Working on Global Competitiveness. Finally, the more profit-oriented and focused Asian companies are increasing their efforts to become really globally competitive. Gone are the days when they could count on the government's protection and massive support to expand their business. Gone are the days when it was enough to compete on cost only. In the globalized economy, where economic barriers between nations are removed, business rules are becoming increasingly standardized, and the free movement of capital eliminates cost advantages for companies of a particular national origin, it becomes very difficult to be competitive and profitable without the development of core technologies, product differentiation, brand building, creation of an effective network of partnerships, and, sometimes, mergers and acquisitions. Japanese and South Korean companies have made it. Today, a cohort of other East Asian firms are trying to address the challenge. Thailand's Charoen Pokphand is successfully establishing an image as "the kitchen of the world," making high-value-added processed foods (Williamson 2004, 2–3). Haier has developed popular world brands of refrigerators and wine coolers. The merger of Sime Darby with two other Malaysian firms, Kumpulan Guthrie and Golden Hope, has given birth to the world's number one palm oil company.

Concluding Remarks

East Asian companies are Westernizing. First, their ownership is shifting from that of dominant stakeholders, with their peculiar set of priorities, to conventional Western-style shareholders. Even when dominant stakeholders remain in control, Asian companies are governed in an increasingly Western way, attaching a greater priority to shareholders' interests. Outside shareholders are becoming part of their power structure—still not dominant, but already impossible to ignore.

Second, East Asian countries have begun to actively introduce the rules and mechanisms of Western-style corporate governance. They are accepting governance principles worked out by the Organization for Economic Co-operation and Development (OECD) as well as standards set by the World Bank and other international organizations. The major reason is simple—growing reliance on equity finance and the changing attitudes of investors, and not only foreign. The emergence and expansion of the middle class in East Asian countries has resulted in an increase in the number of domestic individual shareholders. Some of them buy stock directly, others entrust it to institutional investors. Individual shareholders have started to demand more "corporate democracy," and so does public opinion in general. Today, in broad terms, the image of Asian business tycoons in their own countries is far from being bright. Public opinion favors putting them under more scrutiny because it often suspects them of being engaged in various kinds of unfair practices. Eventually, as time goes by, dominant stakeholders are coming under growing pressure from a maturing civil society they cannot afford to ignore.

Finally, the third aspect of Westernization is that some dominant stakeholders have come to understand that the conflict of interests between them and Western-style shareholders, seeking an emphasis on returns and corporate value, the creation and strengthening of competitive advantages, and the focus on the areas where they exist, is not inevitable.

Westernization means the trend, the direction of change. It does not mean that differences between Asian and Western companies will vanish in the foreseeable future. Asian flavor will remain.

First, most of the changes in ownership, governance, corporate goals, and behavior are rather slow. Conventional, Asian-style dominant stakeholders remain on the playing field and maintain tremendous influence.

Second, the change described is not straightforward. There are backlashes and zigzags. Quite often dominant stakeholders try to revitalize the practices of the "good old days" to resist "undesirable" tendencies. For example, in 2006–07 mutual corporate shareholding in Japan started to grow again due to concern about takeover threats. (Still, restoring its initial scale is out of question—companies cannot ignore the reaction of shareholders and the negative influence on the value of stock.)

Third, certain elements of the conventional, Asian company model may be more than helpful in raising efficiency and competitiveness. Close long-term relations between final product makers and their best suppliers of parts and materials in Japan's auto, electronics, and general machinery industries is a vivid example. Also, cross-border human networks of overseas Chinese may serve as business platforms for information gathering, knowledge accumulation, and the establishment of partnerships strengthening the competitive position of the companies involved.

Yes, some Asian flavor will remain. Yet, there are no forces in sight which can stop Asian companies' Westernization drive. Their transformation will have a number of important implications for the business community in the West. On the one hand, as corporate West and East come to speak a "similar language," the environment for equity investment in Asia, the acquisition of local companies, or business tie-ups is improving. On the other hand, the transformation turns a growing number of Asian firms into stronger players, competing on quality and brand, while still retaining cost advantages.

Endnote

1 From 2002 the government narrowed the circle of companies subjected to those regulations on equity investment, cross shareholding, and cross-credit guarantees, changing it from the top 30 *chaebols* to groups with total assets of 5 trillion won or more (19 *chaebols* at that point). Groups with assets of 2 trillion won to 5 trillion won were subjected only to the regulations on cross shareholding and debt guarantees (ERINA 2005, 71).

5

Structural Transformation: Labor Relations

Overview: Directions of Change and New Challenges

The impact of economic globalization on human resource management (HRM) and employment practices in East Asia is growing day by day, changing previously stable workplace systems and triggering new forms of organization, work, and careers.

In Japan, the recession of the 1990s, coupled with the globalization of most industries, undermined traditional employment practices and accelerated changes that had been under way since the 1980s. In India, the large-scale entry of foreign companies and a shift to a more pro-competition business environment forced local firms to rationalize their HRM practices.

In Southeast Asian countries, the necessity of climbing up the value-added chain makes the upgrading of human capital one of the most urgent tasks. They need much more skilled and knowledgeable workers than their educational institutions can provide and better management to make use of their talent. The same is true for China as today's employers independently determine wages, working hours, and working and living conditions and the *Danwei* (uniformity), control, and stability, traditionally inherent in labor relations at the workplace, is becoming a thing of the past.

Yet, though differences exist, the countries of the region are facing largely similar challenges. Public authorities and companies have to cope with the evolving attitudes of workers toward work in general and their relationship with the workplace in particular, a loss of faith in traditional employment models, and anxieties concerning the impact of the new ones. Above all, despite its huge population, East Asia is suffering from a shortage of skilled labor. Declining birth rates are the region's looming demographic time bomb, pressing it to drastically reshape its employment systems.

To get ready to meet these challenges, East Asian countries are reconsidering HRM concepts, searching for new reward and evaluation systems, working to widen the access to highly skilled human resources, and trying to increase employment flexibility.

Until the Asian crisis, labor markets in the region were mostly tight—sometimes extraordinarily tight, such as in South Korea. In the process of making post-crisis structural reforms practically all major countries introduced systems allowing easier redundancy dismissals and a wider use of nonregular workers (Benson 2004). Having made it easier to lay off workers, the reforms increased the flexibility of labor markets. However, they also resulted in the rise of structural unemployment. While unemployment rates for qualified workers subsequently fell as the East Asian economies recovered, for some categories of the population, especially for the young and the least qualified, they remain high and the number of contingent workers continues to grow (World Bank 2004). In the years to come, Asian countries and companies will face pressure to provide more employment stability.

Like Europe (and probably facing similar difficulties in finding long-term solutions), East Asia is, and will be, increasingly confronted by the problem of internal consistency. How can employment flexibility be combined with commitment of employees? How to create reward differentials, strongly requested by the most dynamic employees and based on objective metrics, while keeping all workers motivated, from core to periphery?

Companies are putting in place HRM rules and systems that are expected to provide a fair performance evaluation and relevant reward, to give freedom to both parties to maintain or sever their work relationship, and to raise human capital efficiency. Yet, they still have to prove that the evaluation and reward systems are fair and convince employees of all categories that "objective" rules and metrics are not just making them interchangeable cogs in a machine, neglecting their attributes as human beings (Caspersz 2006).

Finally, the advent of the knowledge-based economy is turning knowledge workers into a strategic asset. However, Asian managers will have to find an answer to the question of how to accommodate them. As in the US, they appear to be more assertive than other categories of workers, demanding, among other things, better access to strategic information and even participation in decision-making (Debroux 2004).

Evolving Practices and Way of Thinking

In Search of Advanced Methods and Systems

The methods of HRM are rapidly diversifying. The management by objectives (MBO) system, where the roles for individual employees are defined and measurable targets are set on a regular basis, was introduced in most countries of the East Asian region in the 1980s as a method of performance evaluation and career development. It was revised in the 1990s to establish a more direct link between target achievement evaluation and remuneration (Benson 2004).

Since the 1980s, Asian companies have intensified their search for more advanced systems of HRM. These attempts were prompted, in particular, by their growing exposure to international competition. The second reason was the influx of foreign companies. Also, the rise in the number of graduates of European or American universities and business schools—both among current and prospective management personnel—was creating a corporate climate receptive to Western, especially American, standards.

The US as a Model

Contrary to what was expected 15 years ago, the Japanese management style (and, more specifically, HRM practices and work organization) is unlikely to ever become the template in the region. In almost every country in East Asia the number of students wishing to enter American or European companies exceeds those hoping to find a job at a Japanese firm. Japanese companies themselves are changing their practices, both at home and, especially, at their Asian subsidiaries. The management style they adopt is close to the American one in many respects (Jie Yu 2006).

The United States is looked upon as the leader in the fields of both technology and management, and American companies' management patterns are considered by many in the region to be the "best practices."

In general, it is safe to say that Asian companies are attaching greater strategic importance to HRM, though it is not yet clear if they will follow the prescriptive approach based on strategic integration, commitment, flexibility, and quality adopted by large American companies (Legge 1995). HRM concepts are becoming increasingly popular along with the particular techniques associated with them—for instance, flexible labor utilization or the widespread adoption of information and communication technology (ICT)

Less Hierarchy, First Signs of "Impatience with Rule"

Leading Asian firms have a flatter hierarchical structure than ever before. The most successful among them are introducing empowerment schemes (Benson 2004).

However, in East Asia, the room for managers' initiatives and risk-taking remains limited, as most companies still adhere to a set of standardized rules as a norm (Benson 2004). Today, Asian firms are still far from what Storey (1995) called "impatience with rule," or the "can do" outlook associated with the American-style, high-commitment model of HRM (Guest 1995). Nevertheless, a number of leading companies, for example, Samsung Electronics (Umashanker 2005), Matsushita (Khan 2005), and, more recently, Lenovo (Jie Shen 2006), encourage challenging discussions among managers, irrespective of the hierarchical rules, in order to break conformism and create the dynamics of organizational change.

Approaches to Employment and Compensation

With the adoption of HRM concepts employment and compensation practices in East Asia are coming closer to the Western pattern. The most vivid examples include the use of variable and performance-related elements of compensation and flexible work practices.

In the 1990s, Japanese companies made resolute steps to cut, or at least limit, the number of full-time employees, increasing the share of various types of irregular workers, launching early retirement schemes for elderly employees, and offering more job and career opportunities to women. In China, HRM practices are increasingly based on flexible, individual employment contracts. Skills and motivation are becoming the major criteria for selecting recruits, and material rewards, rather than a pledge of job security and social benefits in kind, are used as the major work incentive (Jie Shen 2006). South Korea is shifting from an organizational concept, emphasizing equality and community, toward respect for the individual and market principles (Bae 2004). Nevertheless, the changes described do not result in the visible growth of wage differentials among managers. On the whole, they remain small by Western (especially American) standards (Towers Perrin 2003). In China, despite the strong drive toward labor-market deregulation, the pay system is still influenced by an egalitarian culture (Fang 2004).

The job mobility situation is rather complicated. In Japan, the mobility of managers over 35 years old is growing but remains comparatively low (Debroux 2006). However, in today's South Korea and Southeast Asian countries, a mid-career change of workplace carries almost no negative social image. Most of the newly recruited university graduates here, especially those who have the potential to become managers, anticipate moving to another company in the future.

The Signs of a New HRM System

The Shortage of Skilled Laborers

A large number of East Asian countries have failed to keep up with the demand for human resource.

To cope with the issue is becoming an increasingly urgent task as current favorable demographic trends are unlikely to continue in the long term. Favorable democratic trends mean that a country has a relatively high proportion of the working age and a relatively low proportion of the nonworking age population, or a low dependency ratio, which boosts economic growth. Today, most East Asian countries still have this "demographic window of opportunity," but in the not too distant future it will close. In Japan, it closed already at the beginning of the 1990s. In South Korea, China, and Thailand it will most likely happen within the next ten years. The Philippines, Malaysia, Indonesia, and Vietnam still have about 25–35 years left (Bloom 2004). This scenario poses a big challenge for Asian companies' recruitment, training, and retention practices. They have to maintain their competitive cost advantage while nourishing and attracting talent and offering career opportunities matching those offered elsewhere in the world.

To overcome the shortage of skilled laborers Asian countries adjust their education policies. Thailand, where students traditionally preferred liberal art degrees, is preparing a major policy shift to encourage more students to get science and engineering degrees. Malaysia is seeking to widen the range, and enhance the quality, of education, as well as to improve vocational training. Several new universities were set up in the last 20 years, in both the eastern and western parts of the country. The government is also encouraging foreign universities to establish Malaysian branches.

In Indonesia, the unemployment rate for youngsters under 25 is six to nine times higher than the one for older people (World Bank 2006). The major reason is low learning achievement. Educational institutions remain inadequate and also offer insufficient capacity. Some Asian countries do provide large numbers of college graduates with engineering degrees, but face a supply-demand mismatch. In China and Vietnam, about 80 percent of the new graduates in engineering don't have basic practical skills and need a comprehensive in-house training before being assigned a job (Lynton 2006; Truong Quang 2004).

The deficit of skilled managers is also acute, especially with leadership capabilities in such areas as marketing, sales, and HRM. For East Asia the concept of a manager as a professional with a special degree is still quite new. In North America, there are some 700 schools, accredited by the American Assembly of Collegiate Schools of Business, providing about 150,000 MBA graduates a year. In Western Europe, the figures are about 60 and 25,000, respectively. In Asia, there are only about 20 schools of a comparable standard, with about 10,000 MBA graduates. However, some leading business schools have come to the region. A good example is INSEAD's Singapore campus.

Diversity Management

As time goes by, more and more people in Asia are choosing different lifestyles and working patterns, depending on their preferences, ideals, and personality. Thus, a task of primary importance for Asian companies is the acceptance of diversity management. This implies recognizing individual employees' differences and managing them in a productive way. In Asia, however, employees are generally expected to fit into a uniform corporate culture where individuality can be stifled.

A proactive approach to diversity can simultaneously reinforce competitiveness, help to overcome labor shortages, and open new employment opportunities. This is especially important as decreasing birth rates are expected to cause serious labor shortages and Asian companies will have to change their work organization to accommodate the needs of female and elderly workers, as well as to accept more immigrants. Today, gender discrimination still exists in some countries, but its most blatant manifestations, such as the *de facto* obligation of quitting a job for a married woman or the denial of access to training and career development schemes, are fading away. More and more women now enter the labor market and stay there after getting married and giving birth (Yukongdi 2005).

Recruitment and Promotion

The recruitment and promotion system in South Korea, which used to attach almost as much importance to academic credentials and seniority as Japan, is moving closer to the American pattern, at least in trendsetting companies such as Samsung Electronics and LG. Academic credentials are still important, as are in-house training and promotion. Yet today, companies do not attach priority to recruiting the graduates of the elite universities as much as they used to and also actively search for experienced managers and highly skilled workers in the general labor market. Promotion is based on merit and not on seniority anymore (Bae 2004).

Recruitment and promotion at major companies in Indonesia, the Philippines, and Thailand are rather close to the American system, except that they have a wall dividing executives, mostly members of the founding family, from not only the rank-and-file workers but also employed managers. However, though many top executives still come from founding families and key managerial positions are usually given to relatives, they are supported by an increasing number of selected and promoted salaried managers. For example, in major South Korean companies professional managers without connection with the founding family can be promoted to senior managerial posts, except for the top positions (Bae 2004). The recruitment of foreigners to high-ranking managerial posts is also increasing.

Evaluation and Remuneration

Today, Asian companies are gradually shifting to meritocracy in their HRM and show a stronger interest in objective evaluation of the employees' performances. Among other things they have started to use point-and-ranking systems and feed the evaluation results back to employees. A big challenge is setting credible evaluation standards.

The weight of tenure and age as the criteria for promotion and remuneration is declining all over the region, although they still matter, especially in the case of blue-collar workers and nonmanagerial staff. At the same time, companies are developing new motivation tools. In today's Japan, lower-wage workers are encouraged to take on more risk while being given new opportunities, as companies move away from seniority-based wage increases. A growing number of firms link bonuses to job performance for the majority of their employees (Debroux 2003).

Leading Asian companies utilize salary benchmarking in order to stay competitive and to maintain a level of fairness regarding the wages they pay. The very high cost of young, highly qualified, human resources in some fields (finance, marketing, logistics, and HRM) reflects the demand–supply imbalances in the region, especially in China.

Building Sustainable Labor Relations

Toward a Balanced Psychological Contract, But Not for All

As a result of labor market reforms, career patterns in the region are becoming more diversified. There is a trend toward more contingent types of relationships, driven by the external labor market. Long-term job guarantees as an implicit social contract are fading away. Employees do not perceive Asian companies as benevolent employers any more. However, everywhere in the region, they still expect relevant compensation and promotion opportunities as well as transparency regarding evaluation criteria.

Rousseau (1995) developed a threefold typology of psychological contracts:

1) Relational with high mutual (affective) commitment, high integration and identification, continuity, and stability
2) Transitional with ambiguity, uncertainty, high turnover, termination, and instability
3) Balanced with high member commitment and integration, ongoing development, mutual support, and dynamic

In pre-crisis Asia the seniority-based, relational-type HRM was dominant, albeit with variations from country to country. It shaped various HRM practices such as recruitment, evaluation, training, promotion, pay, and termination (Bae 2004). The Asian model of HRM was widely seen as basically "nonadversarial." Open conflicts leading to actions such as strikes were constrained by culture, ideology, or law (Torrington 1998). Conflict management was handled in a variety of ways, but was largely congruent with the values common for Asian societies, regardless of their political system. The respect for authority, the search for social harmony, and the important role of personal relationships and social connections appear, among other similar examples, in Indonesia's *Pancasila* (Five Principles) emphasizing working in harmony and conflict avoidance; in the Thai concept of *Men pen rai*, reflecting the desire to keep peaceful relationships; or in the National Shared Values in Singapore, reminding people of the need for mutual respect and tolerance (Torrington 1998). Therefore, the transition from a work and business culture putting more emphasis on collectivism (Hofstede 2001) to one based on individualism, is a challenge.

However, the new urban generations, especially the middle class, do not seem to have too many problems with the management culture where promotion, pay, and other organizational benefits are based on individual contributions rather than group characteristics.

Multinationals operating in East Asia are largely blurring the line between local managers and expatriates in terms of reward and career development. The high-commitment type of HRM they introduce for both categories looks quite natural as they often graduate from the same American universities and business schools. Large differentials in compensation (beyond those considered reasonable due to a higher living cost for a foreigner) would be looked upon as discrimination. Domestic companies have no other option but to offer similar packages to recruit and keep the best domestic human resource.

Asian companies are drifting toward a balanced psychological contract. However, it appears to cover only an elite part of their employees.

The Two-Tier System

The two-tier system, treating the working elite and the others very differently, reflects the fact that a new HRM system is seeking to achieve two apparently contradictory objectives. On the one hand, the development of human resource paves the way for an employees–management partnership profitable for both parties. Core employees' participation in decision-making is encouraged and they are delegated rights and responsibilities which influence the company performance (Tomer 2001). On the other hand, companies relentlessly stick to cost-reducing practices, seeking more flexibility. For many employees, rejected from core status, or for those who perceive performance-based systems as a threat to their jobs, it is very difficult to assimilate into the new work culture.

Of course, companies are trying to find ways to motivate all their personnel. Leading local and foreign-affiliated firms develop incentive-based systems bestowing material rewards for both blue- and white-collar workers. Sometimes, it brings positive results.

Labor Market Flexibility

Job-hopping of skilled workers has already become a serious problem in Indonesia, Malaysia, and Thailand. In factories, but also in workplaces such as call centers, the turnover rate is quite high due to the lack of talent development initiatives and attractive career planning systems (Lynton 2006). High labor mobility reduces the companies' motivation to maintain or improve in-house training and education.

A recent survey (World Bank 2006) shows that labor market regulations in East Asia tend to be relatively flexible. Compared with other regions and the Organization for Economic Co-operation and Development (OECD) average, the region has the lowest indices for difficulty in recruiting and laying off, as well as rigidity of hours, recruiting, and laying-off costs.

Management practices emphasizing flexibility can help to attain cost advantage in the short term. However, they may meet strong resistance with negative long-term implications.

Growing flexibility reflects the high job creation potential of labor-intensive service industries, as well as the convenience of part-time employment for those workers who need time to take care of their children. The latter is especially important as Asia's shift to a service economy is accompanied by a rise in the percentage of women in the labor force. This is a positive side.

The problem is not the growing flexibility as such, but a widening gap between different categories of workers and the subsequent feeling of economic and social insecurity it creates. It is liable to cause a backlash against further HRM reforms, especially as no East Asian country has a social safety net comparable to that of the Western European states.

In China, unrest caused by the downsizing of organizations and changing recruitment and retention practices is now more or less contained by the state apparatus, but it is likely to become greater with the growing access of people to information. Indonesia is increasingly plagued by rampant industrial disputes, and so is South Korea in a number of industries.

Providing Relevant Labor Standards

In East Asian countries, there are practically no tripartite forums where inter-dependent social partners—public authorities, labor unions, and companies—work together on labor issues. Also, the role of labor unions in most countries is declining. It forces the region to look for alternative solutions.

One of the options is a thorough implementation of International Labor Organization (ILO) standards. As in Europe, the state, while retreating from direct involvement in companies' management, may go along with a more explicit regulatory framework for labor markets.

In August 2006, the International Finance Corporation (IFC) and the ILO agreed to collaborate in developing a global program for better labor standards in global supply chains. Called the Better Work Program, it will concentrate on a number of sectors, including garments and footwear, plantations, and electronic equipment. The aim is to develop tools for labor standards monitoring and remediation systems. The tools are to be used in developing East Asian countries (along with the Middle East and South Africa) in close consultation with labor authorities and supplemented by capacity building services (Frost 2006).

It is still premature to say whether the region will start working seriously on improving labor standards or whether it will not go beyond mere cosmetic changes. Freedom of association is one of the historical pillars underlying the ILO philosophy. However, multinational companies operating in Asia are not at all enthusiastic about the creation of unions by local workers.

Employee–Management Dialogue

Nevertheless, in a number of Asian companies attempts are made to arrange regular, comprehensive dialogue between the management and all the employees, to reach mutual understanding on the ways of rationalizing and reforming company management.

For example, in LG Electronics and Samsung SDI (known for its digital displays and rechargeable batteries) both managers and employees showed willingness to depart from a traditional, paternalistic management style toward cooperative and participative relations.

At LG Electronics, the cooperation of the union leadership helped to establish a new team production system, based on a labor–management partnership. The company adopted a bottom-up approach with the involvement of frontline employees in the decision-making process. However, the union, though actively participating in collective bargaining and discussions on workplace-related issues, does not have a say on such strategic matters as product development, new investment, or corporate restructuring.

Nonunionized Samsung SDI introduced a lean production mode emphasizing total quality management and Six Sigma.[1] In contrast to LG Electronics, the company has an extensive system of open communications, information sharing, and employee representation. It emphasizes the importance of labor–management cooperation, but stops short of introducing formal systems and mechanisms for employees' participation (Bae 2004).

Concluding Remarks

Labor relations in East Asia are "Westernizing." Conventional practices that limit, modify, and, sometimes, even deny the market-based approach, are becoming more and more difficult to retain. These practices coincide with the perception of the firm as a family and they are typically expressed by the themes of long-term employment, ambiguous evaluation methods, seniority, rigid hierarchy, and the prevalence of groupism over individualism. In today's East Asian companies, labor mobility is growing and personnel reduction and scouting cease to be an exception. Meritocracy is becoming the norm, while seniority is gradually subsiding. Both employees and employers are less and less willing to view the firm as a social institution requiring and deserving some special commitment from its members that goes beyond a clear-cut labor contract. Employees' compensation increasingly depends on their qualifications, assigned job, and working achievement.

Yet, "Westernization" is a gradually developing process which is often painful and meets a lot of resistance. Along with the pressures to "Westernize," strong internal pressures to preserve at least elements of conventional labor relations are also there.

More often than not while pursuing the same goals as in the West, Asian companies use different methods. For example, instead of American-style, massive lay-offs, to cut personnel, Japanese firms launch early voluntary retirement campaigns, with extra benefits for retirees. Various kinds of hybrid approaches also emerge. Sumitomo Corporation has restored a seniority-based wage and promotion system for the first ten years of an employee's tenure but strengthened merit-based evaluation in the years beyond. Southeast Asian conglomerates still prefer to have family members in key managerial positions but are encouraging them to acquire professional skills, get high performance evaluation grades based on objective merit-based criteria, and even to compete with nonfamily members.

Sometimes, traditional Asian approaches help, rather than impede, efficiency and competitiveness. For example, the results of a recent study by the Japanese Government Cabinet Office show that the productivity of an average Japanese worker peaks when he has worked at one and the same company for 13.6 years (Cabinet Office 2006).

Finally, when introducing American-style labor relations, Asia has to address the difficult problems they pose—wide wage gaps and other disparities between workers, low motivation of non-core employees, frustration with tough evaluation criteria, fears of losing the job, and uncertainties about the future. Last but not least, the transformation enhances the threat of higher unemployment.

Endnote

1. The Six Sigma method was originally developed by Motorola. The goal is to identify and eliminate the causes of defects and errors in the production and business processes and to enhance
customer satisfaction. Various quality management methods, including statistical, are used.
A group of people who are experts in these methods is established.

6

Regional Integration and Prospects for the East Asian Community

For almost five postwar decades, regional integration in East Asia was off the agenda. In the 2000s, none of the region's countries can work out its economic strategies outside the context of the integration process. Regional institutions have emerged, and the East Asian Community (EAC) idea is on the table.

The pro-integration drive is down to three major factors. First, economic interdependence in East Asia has been visibly boosted by rising intraregional trade and capital flows, deepening division of labor and production linkages, and an intensifying movement of people, among other things. This process is often called *de facto* integration.

The second factor is a growing sense of crisis about being outpaced by other regions, especially Europe and North America, in terms of the speed and intensity at which regional institutions have been created. Europe has the European Union (EU) and North America has the North American Free Trade Agreement (NAFTA) (not to mention the prospective Free Trade Area Americas (FTAA) which is to include both North and South American countries). Asia has no large-scale regional arrangement of this kind. Thus, apprehensions appear that the two big blocs will set world trade and other international economic rules, while Asian states will be left on the sidelines. They are especially strong in some Association of Southeast Asian Nations (ASEAN) countries, fearing the decline of their international clout.

The third factor is the Asian crisis, which induced East Asian nations to think seriously about the need to address urgent issues as a group and to create the mechanisms that make this possible. The first mechanism was the network of bilateral currency swap arrangements, born as a result of the Chiang Mai initiative of 2000. Then, the notion of working together on a regional scale was applied to a wider range of major issues, including energy and environment, building of infrastructure, and so on.

The core regional cooperation institution—ASEAN Plus Three—(APT—the three are Japan, China, and South Korea) was established in the late 1990s. In 2005, the first formalized East Asian Summit was convened. Discussions of the scenarios for the EAC creation began.

The Interdependence of East Asian Economies

The Nature of Regional Interdependence

Economic interdependence within the East Asian region is growing stronger and deeper. The countries of the region are expanding trade, investment, and other relations with one another much faster than with nations outside the region. Also, intraregional linkages acquire a new depth, because they are prompted by the division of labor within one industry and even one technological chain.

Yet, for a number of reasons, America, Europe, and other nonregional partners remain decisively important for Asian economies. This importance, along with East Asia's diversity, makes it impossible and irrelevant for the region to think of an economic bloc with common import tariffs or other unified rules regulating its members' relations with outsiders. East Asia sticks, and will stick, to the implicit "golden rule": not to push its trade and investment integration beyond Free Trade Agreement (FTA)/Economic Partnership Agreement (EPA) kinds of arrangements. These are open-ended forms of integration: such agreements can be concluded both between East Asian countries themselves and between them and nonregional counterparts.

Trade Interdependence

Table 6.1 presents the data on the share of intraregional trade in East Asia within different groupings. Within East Asia-10 its share is almost 55 percent, which is higher than in NAFTA and a bit lower than in the EU. The most rapidly growing share is within the East Asia-9 group: the four NIEs, ASEAN 4, and China.

Tables 6.2 and 6.3 show the overall composition of exports and imports of the East Asia-9. While the proportion of trade within this group of countries, in both exports and imports, is increasing remarkably, the shares of the US and EU are declining, as well as the shares of East Asia's economic powerhouse, Japan.

On the other hand, for Japan itself, the proportion of trade with its counterparts is on the rise, while the shares of the US and EU are falling (Tables 6.4 and 6.5).

The data brings to light a number of important features of East Asia's intraregional trade. Unlike the US in North America or Germany, France, and other leading economies in Europe, Japan, Asia's leading economic power, is not providing the major market for other regional economies. In a way, Japan's "low import capacity" backfires. It is rooted in the structural barriers posed by its complicated distribution channels and in the legacy of *keiretsu*—Japanese intercompany groups where domestic firms maintain long-term ties with one another, not letting outsiders in (Tselichtchev 2004, 40). Limits on trade with Japan enhance the importance of the markets in the US and Europe.

In East Asia itself, the role of the major importer, as well as exporter, has gone to China. At this point, at least as far as trade is concerned, it has become the region's main integrator. The share of intraregional trade in the total trade of East Asian nations is increasing, first and foremost, because the shares of their

Table 6.1   Shares of intraregional trade in East Asia and other regions (%)*

Region	1980	1990	1995	2000	2006
ASEAN	17.9	18.8	24.0	24.7	27.2
ASEAN+3	30.2	29.4	37.6	37.3	38.3
ASEAN+6	34.6	33.7	40.8	40.5	42.6
East Asia-9	22.7	33.0	39.1	40.6	45.8
East Asia-10	36.8	43.1	51.9	52.1	54.5
EU (old EU-15)	60.7	66.2	64.2	62.3	59.5
EU (new EU-25)	61.5	66.8	66.9	66.3	65.8
NAFTA	33.8	37.9	43.1	48.8	44.3

Source: M. Kawai and G. Wignaraja: "Regionalism as an Engine of Multilateralism: A Case for a Single East Asian FTA." ADB Working Paper Series on Regional Economic Integration. Paper No.14.
*East Asia-10 refers to Japan, the four NIEs, ASEAN 4, and China; East Asia-9 to the same group of countries excluding Japan; ASEAN+3 to all the members of ASEAN plus China, Japan, and South Korea; ASEAN+6 to the previous group of countries plus India, Australia, and New Zealand. The share of intraregional trade means the share of trade within each particular area as part of the total volume of trade of the countries comprising it.

trade with China are increasing. If you exclude China from the equation, the rise is much less impressive (see Table 6.6).

Intra-Industry Trade and East Asian Production Networks

Though Japan plays a relatively modest role in intraregional trade in quantitative terms, it is contributing much to the deepening of the division of labor through the creation of cross-border production networks and technological

Table 6.2   Composition of East Asia's* exports (%)

Export to:	1980	1997	1999	2006
East Asia	22.1	38.7	35.4	42.4
Japan	19.8	11.7	11.3	8.8
EU-15	15.8	13.8	15.2	14.9**
US	20.3	19.9	22.7	16.7
Total	100.0	100.0	100.0	100.0

Source: Ivan Tselichtchev, "Japan-East Asia Economic Relationship: Evolving Pattern." *Management International Review*, Special Issue, 1/2002 Gabler Verlag 2002, p.64; JETRO, Sekai Boeki Toshi Hakusho, 2004, p.393; International Monetary Fund, Direction of Trade Statistics, 2007.
*East Asia: the four NIEs, ASEAN 4, and China.
**EU-25.

Table 6.3 Composition of East Asia's* imports (%)

Import from:	1980	1997	1999	2006
East Asia	22.2	40.2	43.6	49.8
Japan	23.3	18.5	18.9	13.3
EU-15	12.2	13.3	11.8	9.5**
US	16.8	13.4	13.3	8.2
Total	100.0	100.0	100.0	100.0

Source: Ivan Tselichtchev, "Japan-East Asia Economic Relationship: Evolving Pattern." *Management International Review*, Special Issue, 1/2002 Gabler Verlag 2002, p.64; JETRO, Sekai Boeki Toshi Hakusho, 2004, p.393; International Monetary Fund, Direction of Trade Statistics, 2007.
*East Asia: the four NIES, ASEAN 4, and China.
**EU-25.

chains, especially in the electronics and auto industries. During the second half of the 1980s, Japanese companies started a massive transfer of their production sites to other East Asian countries. Mostly, they transferred labor-intensive operations, such as assembly or testing, that did not require advanced technology and highly skilled labor. As time went by, however, they began to produce a much wider spectrum of products overseas, including important parts and components (though usually maintaining the production of key high-value-added items at domestic factories). Also, their ties with local suppliers of intermediate products greatly expanded.

In the 1990s, and especially in the 2000s, companies from the Asian newly industrialized economies (NIEs), particularly South Korea and Taiwan, started to move quickly along the same road, transferring production sites to China and the ASEAN countries and also intensifying the exchange of higher end intermediate products with Japan. Consequently, East Asia as a whole is developing as

Table 6.4 Composition of Japan's exports (%)

Export to:	1980	1997	1999	2006
East Asia	25.2	40.9	35.8	46.4
EU-15	15.2	15.6	17.8	14.5*
US	24.5	28.1	30.7	22.5
Total	100.0	100.0	100.0	100.0

Source: Ivan Tselichtchev, "Japan-East Asia Economic Relationship: Evolving Pattern," *Management International Review*, Special Issue, 1/2002 Gabler Verlag 2002, p.63; JETRO, Sekai Boeki Toshi Hakusho 2004, 2007.
*EU-25.

Table 6.5   Composition of Japan's imports (%)

Import from:	1980	1997	1999	2006
East Asia	22.6	37.3	37.6	42.7
EU-15	5.9	13.3	13.8	10.3*
US	16.8	21.6	21.6	11.8
Total	100.0	100.0	100.0	100.0

Source: Ivan Tselichtchev, "Japan-East Asia Economic Relationship: Evolving Pattern," *Management International Review*, Special Issue, 1/2002 Gabler Verlag 2002, p.63; JETRO, Sekai Boeki Toshi Hakusho 2004, 2007.
*EU-25.

an integrated production platform for electronic goods, auto vehicles, and other machinery products.

However, the majority of final goods are exported to the US, Europe, and other parts of the world. The growth of intra-industry trade and production networks within the region decisively depends on the Western markets.

Table 6.6   Composition of East Asia's* intraregional exports by country/region (%)

Country/region	1985	1990	1995	2000	2005
East Asia	100.0	100.0	100.0	100.0	100.0
Japan	48.7	40.7	33.6	28.9	21.7
NIEs 4	31.3	38.2	40.5	39.9	35.3
Hong Kong	8.3	11.6	13.1	12.2	10.5
Singapore	6.3	7.5	9.0	8.3	7.5
South Korea	8.3	9.6	9.9	10.4	10.3
Taiwan	8.4	9.5	8.5	9.0	6.9
ASEAN 4	12.6	12.2	14.7	16.2	15.3
Indonesia	5.1	3.6	3.4	3.8	3.5
Malaysia	4.2	4.2	5.6	5.9	5.9
Philippines	1.3	1.2	1.3	2.3	1.9
Thailand	2.0	3.3	4.3	4.2	4.0
China	7.5	8.9	11.3	15.1	27.8

Source: H.Hirakawa, K.Ishikawa, A.Ohara, N.Kobayashi, eds."Higashi Azia-no Gurobaruka to Chiiki Togo," Tokyo: Minerva Shobo, 2007, p.223.
*East Asia refers to the East Asia-9.

FDI Interdependence

For the NIEs, the ASEAN 9, and China combined, between 1995 and 2005, the share of foreign direct investment (FDI) from within the region (including Japan) was 48.5 percent as opposed to 28.6 percent for the FDI from the US and the EU (see Table 6.7). However, the high share of intraregional FDI is largely the result of the dominant position of Hong Kong as a direct foreign investor to the major FDI recipient, China.

A closer look shows that for the Asian NIEs the share of FDI from within the region (from Japan, the NIEs, and the ASEAN 9 combined) is comparatively low—from 12.8 percent for Hong Kong to 32.2 percent for Taiwan. Their major foreign investors are based in the US and Europe and also, as we will show in the country chapters in the second part of the book, in the British-ruled tax havens in the Caribbean. However, the ASEAN 9 (ASEAN excluding Singapore) countries, especially Malaysia, Thailand, and Vietnam, receive more FDI from within the region than from outside.

That said, as discussed in the previous chapters, Euro-American capital has been playing a key role in the growing wave of mergers and acquisitions of Asian

Table 6.7   FDI inflows into East Asian countries by source of investment (cumulative amount for 1995–2005) (%)

Country/region	US	EU	Japan	NIEs	ASEAN 9
NIEs 4	16.8	15.8	8.1	5.2	3.9
Hong Kong	5.1	7.4	5.7	5.3	1.8
Singapore	31.7	19.3	8.5	4.0	5.8
South Korea	22.4	40.1	13.3	4.1	7.4
Taiwan	19.9	13.1	15.5	14.2	2.5
ASEAN 9	18.4	29.1	19.1	29.2	4.2
Indonesia	5.7	50.9	3.3	15.0	9.3
Malaysia	27.4	23.4	13.6	22.0	2.1
Philippines	23.4	10.3	23.1	16.9	1.1
Thailand	10.5	10.5	25.1	27.6	0.9
Vietnam	4.8	19.1	14.4	39.2	6.6
China	8.1	8.1	8.6	54.0	1.6
Total for NIEs, ASEAN 9, and China	13.9	14.7	10.5	34.9	3.1

Source: M. Kawai and G. Wignaraja: "Regionalism as an Engine of Multilateralism: A Case for a Single East Asian FTA." ADB Working Paper Series on Regional Economic Integration. Paper No.14.

companies since the Asian crisis. Also, the activities of Western investment funds are on the rise.

East Asia's FTAs

Overview

As of June 2008, 41 FTAs involving the participation of East Asian countries have been concluded (including both agreements under implementation and signed agreements which have not entered the implementation stage). Thirty-one are bilateral and ten are multilateral. (The latter includes agreements between only two parties so long as one of them represents more than one country—for example, the FTA between China and ASEAN.) Fifteen agreements are intraregional and 26 involve at least one non-East Asian country (see Figure 6.1). The data about negotiated and proposed FTAs is presented in Table 6.8. It shows that the free trade area creation process remains very dynamic.

There are four major types of FTAs. Their initial, and most simple, form covers only trade in goods (G). The second type (G+S) includes services as well. The third type adds a number of issues, the inclusion of which was largely initiated by Singapore (Singapore Issues-SI): investment, trade facilitation, rules regarding government procurement, and competition policy. Finally, the fourth type broadens the range of issues even further, embracing cooperation enhancement (CE) measures in the areas of environment, e-commerce, information exchange, small- and medium-sized enterprises (SMEs), and labor standards.

FTAs covering a wider spectrum of issues than just trade in goods, are often called Economic Partnership Agreements (EPAs). The data vividly shows that, as time goes by, FTA upgrading is progressing—agreements of the third and fourth types become more and more frequent.

Table 6.8   FTAs in East Asia* by configuration and geographic orientation

Status	Number of FTAs	Bilateral	Multilateral	Intra-East Asia	Extra-East Asia
Concluded	41	31	10	15	26
Under negotiation	34	25	9	3	31
Proposed/ under study, consultation	29	22	7	5	24
Total	104	78	26	23	81

Source: Asia Regional Integration Center Web site: FTAs by country
*Intra-East Asia FTAs refers to agreements between East Asian countries only, extra-East Asia FTAs to agreements involving at least one East Asian and at least one non-East Asian country.

1. Asia-Pacific Trade Agreement** (G) 1976[+]
2. Laos–Thailand Preferential Trading Arrangement (G) 1991
3. ASEAN FTA (AFTA) (G) 1993
4. Singapore–European Free Trade Association (EFTA) FTA (G+S+SI) 2001
5. Singapore–New Zealand Closer EPA (G+S+SI) 2001
6. Japan–Singapore Economic Agreement for a New Age Partnership (G+S+SI+CE) 2002
7. China–Thailand FTA (G) 2003
8. Singapore–Australia FTA (G+S+SI+CE) 2003
9. China–Hong Kong Closer EPA (G+S) 2004
10. China–Macao Closer EPA (G+S) 2004
11. Taiwan–Panama FTA (G+S+SI) 2004
12. South Korea–Chile FTA(G+S+SI) 2004
13. Singapore–US FTA (G+S+SI+CE) 2004
14. ASEAN–China Comprehensive Economic Partnership Agreement (G+S) 2005
15. China–Chile FTA (G+S) 2005
16. Japan–Mexico EPA (G+S+SI+CE) 2005
17. Singapore–Jordan FTA (G+S+SI+CE) 2005
18. Thailand–Australia FTA (G+S+SI+CE) 2005
19. Thailand–New Zealand Closer EPA (G+S+SI+CE) 2005
20. South Korea–EFTA FTA (G+S+SI) 2005
21. Singapore–India Comprehensive Economic Cooperation Agreement (G+S+SI) 2005
22. ASEAN–(South) Korea Comprehensive Economic Cooperation Agreement (G) 2006
23. Singapore–South Korea FTA (G+S+SI+CE) 2006
24. Singapore–Panama FTA (G+S+SI+CI) 2006
25. Japan–Malaysia EPA (G+S+SI) 2006
26. Japan–Chile Strategic EPA (G+S+SI) 2006
27. Japan–Philippines EPA (G+S+SI+CE) 2006
28. China–Pakistan FTA (G) 2006
29. Taiwan–Guatemala FTA (G+S+SI) 2006
30. Preferential Trade Agreement of Eight Developing Countries[^] (G) 2006
31. Japan–Thailand EPA (G+S+SL+CE) 2007
32. Japan–Brunei EPA (G+S+SI+CE) 2007
33. Trans-Pacific Strategic Economic Partnership Agreement[#] (G+S+SI+CE) 2007
34. South Korea–US FTA (G+S+SI+CE) 2007
35. Japan–Indonesia EPA (G+S+SI+CE) 2007
36. Taiwan–Nicaragua FTA (N/A) 2007
37. Malaysia–Pakistan Closer Economic Partnership Agreement (G+S+SI+CE) 2007
38. ASEAN–Japan Comprehensive Economic Partnership Agreement (G+S+SI+CE) 2008
39. Singapore–Peru Free Trade Agreement (G+S+SI+CE) 2008
40. Taiwan–Honduras–El Salvador FTA (N/A) 2008
41. China–New Zealand FTA (G+S+SI+CE) 2008

Source: M. Kawai and G. Wignaraja: "Regionalism as an Engine of Multilateralism: A Case for a Single East Asian FTA." ADB Working Paper Series on Regional Economic Integration. Paper No.14.: Asia Regional Integration Center Web site: FTAs by country.
*As of June, 2008.
**Initially, the Bangkok Agreement. The signatories are Bangladesh, China, India, Laos, South Korea, and Sri Lanka.
[+]Year of conclusion.
[^]Eight developing countries are Bangladesh, Egypt, Indonesia, Iran, Malaysia, Nigeria, Pakistan, and Turkey. The agreement was signed by all of them, except Bangladesh.
[#]The signatories are Brunei, Chile, New Zealand, and Singapore.

Figure 6.1   East Asian countries' concluded FTAs*

A network of the most important and large-scale FTAs, eventually becoming the backbone of regional integration, is forming around ASEAN in the ASEAN+1 format. ASEAN itself has its own free trade area—AFTA.

AFTA

Since 2003, tariffs on products on the Common Effective Preferential Tariff (CEPT) Scheme inclusive list (IL) began to be brought within the 0–5 percent range. The ASEAN 6 countries (Brunei, Indonesia, Malaysia, the Philippines, Singapore, and Thailand) have already made it apply to more than 99 percent of the products on the IL (ASEAN 2008a). In 2007, they imported 75.7 percent of the IL products from their AFTA counterparts tariff-free (JETRO 2007, 62). Other members (Cambodia, Laos, Myanmar, Vietnam (CLMV)) have included almost 80 percent of their traded products in the IL and for 66 percent of those products tariffs have been brought within the 0–5 percent range (ASEAN 2008a).

The ASEAN 6 will import all products on the IL tariff-free by 2010, others, with exceptions for some items, by 2015 (JETRO 2007, 62).

In November 2004, an agreement was reached on fast-track liberalization in 11 priority integration areas: processing of agricultural products, fisheries, the auto industry, electronics, healthcare, rubber products, wood products, textiles, e-ASEAN (mainly IT products), aviation, and tourism. It was agreed that ASEAN 6 countries would slash import tariffs on goods belonging to the sectors mentioned (the number of the sensitive commodities allowed to be left off the list cannot exceed 15 percent of the total) by January 1, 2007, and the rest of the members by January 1, 2012 (JETRO 2007, 62).

ASEAN–China Comprehensive Economic Partnership Agreement

Talks on the free trade area were started in 2002. An agreement on the liberalization of commodity trade was signed in 2004 and on the service trade in early 2007. In 2005, for the first time, China–ASEAN trade exceeded the US$100 billion mark. In 2006, it climbed to US$160.8 billion (*China Economic Review* 2007). At the final stage of their talks the two sides are negotiating the agreement on mutual investment. The FTA is expected to be fully enacted in 2010.

Since January 2004, both sides have reduced tariffs on the Early Harvest (EH) agricultural and fishery products. Since July 2005, the reduction of nonagricultural goods began in accordance with the commodity trade agreement. Between China and the ASEAN 6, the majority of products put on the normal track are to be traded tariff-free by 2010 (with the exception of no more than 150 items eligible for the grace period that runs until 2012), and by 2012 the normal-track goods trade will be fully liberalized. Trade in goods put on the Sensitive List (no more than 400 items and less than 10 percent of the total imports from the agreement counterpart) and Highly Sensitive List (no more than 40 percent of the sensitive goods or 100 items, whichever is less) will be liberalized gradually, but retaining import tariffs will be possible. Between China and the CLMV group, complete elimination of tariffs for the normal-track group will be postponed until 2018 (JETRO 2007, 63–64).

ASEAN-South Korea Comprehensive Economic Cooperation Agreement

The agreement on trade in goods of the ASEAN-South Korea Comprehensive Economic Cooperation Agreement was concluded in April 2006 and became effective from June 2007. Tariffs on products comprising 90 percent of the two sides' respective imports, in terms of both number and volume, are to be eliminated until 2010 by South Korea and ASEAN 6, by 2016 by Vietnam, and by 2018 by Cambodia, Laos, and Myanmar ("normal track"). Tariffs for goods accounting for the other 7 percent (sensitive goods) are to be reduced to 0–5 percent until 2016, 2017, and 2020 respectively. The remaining 3 percent are highly sensitive products (for example, rice, poultry, fish, garlic, onions). They are eligible for protection through various measures, such as exemption from liberalization and longer tariff reduction periods. The agreement on services and investment was signed in November 2007. Enhanced market access will be provided in such sectors as financial services, adult education, and environmental consultancy. Also, an ASEAN center in Seoul will be established.

ASEAN-Japan Comprehensive Economic Partnership Agreement

This agreement was signed in April 2008 and went into force in December of the same year. It covers trade in goods and services, investment, facilitation measures, and cooperation.

Within ten years, duties for 93 percent of Japan's imports from the ASEAN countries, by value, are to be eliminated. Six major ASEAN members will remove tariffs on 90 percent of their imports from Japan (Kyodo News 2008a). For CLMV, the reduction and elimination schedule will be more gradual. Most tariffs are to be repealed by 2023–2026.

The major exceptions are sensitive (mostly for Japan) agricultural products, such as meat, fish, dairy products, fruit, vegetables, and grain. However, tariffs for most of these products are to be reduced significantly although for rice they will remain unchanged. Most machinery and electronic products are to be traded tariff-free immediately after the enactment. Temporary safeguard measures are allowed.

Japan-China-South Korea Triangle

The pro-integration trend in the Japan–China–South Korea triangle is weak. One of the reasons is complexity in Tokyo's political relations with both Seoul and Beijing. They have been caused by the visits of former prime minister, Junichiro Koizumi, to the Yasukuni Shrine where, along with millions of the World War II dead, war criminals are enshrined (the issue has eventually been resolved, because today's prime minister and other government officials do not go); the Japanese history textbooks issue (in the view of South Korea and China they do not present an adequate picture of what the Japanese did in both countries in the prewar and war years); territorial disputes (over Dokdo/Takeshima island with South Korea and the Senkaku/Diaoyutai Qundao islands with China); differences over fishing rights in the Sea of Japan with South Korea; and drilling rights in the Yellow Sea shelf with China.

Post-Koizumi administrations in Japan, and the Lee Myung-bak administration in South Korea, adopted a more conciliatory stance, emphasizing their desire to build a sound future-oriented relationship. The Chinese administration shares this approach.

China proposed a trilateral FTA with Japan and South Korea back in 2002. The reaction of Tokyo and Seoul was cautious. It was agreed to begin the study of the issue by think tanks. Basically, in the view of the Japanese government, it is necessary to wait and see how China complies with its World Trade Organization (WTO) obligations before considering the FTA opportunities. Apprehensions about violations of intellectual property rights (IPR) are also an impediment. In April 2008, however, the three countries reached an agreement on an "Action Agenda for Improvement of the Business Environment"—effectively a trilateral accord on the investment rules and policies. Talks on the Japan–South Korea FTA have been interrupted since 2004 both by negotiating difficulties (especially on agricultural products) and political tensions. The Lee Myung-bak administration is seeking to strengthen relations with Japan, the FTA issue included. However, unexpectedly strong protests against the resumption of beef imports from the US (due to BSE [mad-cow disease] concerns) in the late spring and summer of 2008, escalating into the protests against the administration's pro-business agenda as a whole, have not only become an obstacle to the ratification of the South Korea–US FTA but are also making the government move more slowly on FTAs in general.

Nevertheless, an FTA between South Korea and China may be the most conceivable first step in Northeast Asia.

East Asia's FTAs as Part of a Global Trend

At the country level, East Asia is experiencing a boom of FTAs, both "internal" between the regional states and "external" between regional states and nonregional counterparts. FTAs are most actively pursued by Singapore, followed by South Korea, China, Japan, and Thailand. Other ASEAN countries rely mostly on the agreements worked out by ASEAN as a whole.

At the time of writing, Singapore is involved in 25 FTAs that are either implemented, negotiated, or studied (excluding arrangements existing or discussed where it is involved as a member of ASEAN or another group of countries), four with counterparts inside, and 21 outside, East Asia. China is involved in 23 FTAs (8 and 15 respectively); South Korea in 22 (8 and 14 respectively); and Japan in 19 (11 and 8 respectively) (Asia Regional Integration Center 2008).

ASEAN also intensively works on FTAs, not only inside East Asia but also with outsiders, negotiating with India (the framework agreement has been signed), the EU, and Australia/New Zealand.

At East Asia's turning point every regional economy finds itself involved in a growing number of FTAs, both within the region and beyond. The FTA boom is opening East Asian economies up to the outside world on a scale never seen before.

Regional Institution Building: ASEAN Plus Three

The EAEC Idea

In the late 1980s, when East Asian economies were booming and Japan seemed to be on the way to becoming "the number one," Malaysian prime minister, Mahathir bin Mohammad, proposed the creation of an East Asian Economic Caucus (EAEC) as a forum to discuss regional economic issues. Also at that time, Malaysia and other Southeast Asian countries strongly urged Japan to "return" to Asia and play the leading role in regional economic cooperation.

Mahathir's proposal failed to get enough support due to very strong opposition from the US. The latter basically opposes the creation of what it sees as a closed regional grouping where it is not a member. Presumably, the fact that the idea came from Mahathir made its opposition especially strong—the Malaysian leader was fond of criticizing American, and praising Asian, capitalism and saw East Asia's integration as a way to raise its clout versus the West.

ASEAN Plus Three

Mahathir's idea was reproduced in a different format. In December 1997, amid the Asian crisis, the ASEAN Plus Three (APT) process was started with the leaders meeting at the sidelines of the informal ASEAN summit in Malaysia. The three were China, Japan, and South Korea. The APT is doing exactly what Mahathir wanted from the EAEC—East Asia's economic issues are discussed by East Asians, with the big powers of the region present and ASEAN playing the key role. Furthermore, it is not only discussing: in a range of areas regional cooperation mechanisms have been created and are already at work.

To begin with, the APT meetings created an opportunity for contacts between the parties involved, which finally resulted in the launch of the region's three major multilateral FTAs in the ASEAN+1 format, as well as a number of bilateral FTAs.

To work out the concept of cooperation, the East Asia Vision Group of eminent persons was established in 1998. It presented its report in 2001. The next step was the establishment of the East Asia Study Group to specify cooperation directions. Its report was submitted to, and endorsed by, the 2002 APT summit in Cambodia. Seventeen short-term and nine medium- and long-term measures were proposed.

At the time of writing, the APT cooperates in 18 areas, which include the economy, monetary and finance issues, tourism, agriculture, environment, energy, information and communications technology (ICT), and also foreign policy and security. In 2003, the APT unit was established within ASEAN to assist the APT co-chairs in coordinating and monitoring the cooperation process (ASEAN 2008b).

Financial Cooperation

APT multilateral cooperation started in the field of finance as a reaction to the Asian crisis. The APT Surveillance Process, established in 1999 and based in the ASEAN Secretariat in Jakarta, is centered on cooperation in monitoring short-term capital flows, developing early warning systems, assessing the region's financial vulnerabilities, and crisis prevention. These issues are covered by the meetings of the finance ministers.

The Chiang Mai Initiative of May 2000 expanded existing ASEAN swap arrangements (ASA) by adding the network of bilateral currency swap and repurchase arrangements (BSAs) which include China, Japan, and South Korea. The aim is to provide short-term currency to countries facing liquidity shortfalls. The ASA scale is US\$1 billion (ASEAN 2008c). The scale of the 16 BSAs combined is US\$75 billion (Hirakawa 2007, 264). It would not have been enough to prevent the liquidity shortage the crisis-hit economies faced in 1997–98.

In late October 2008, in the wake of the global financial turmoil, East Asian leaders agreed to upgrade the scheme from a web of bilateral agreements to a multilateral arrangement worth US\$80 billion (Kyodo News 2008b).

Asian Bond Market Initiative

The Asian Bond Market Initiative, launched by the APT finance ministers in cooperation with the Asian Development Bank (ADB) in August 2003, seeks to provide a better use of Asian savings for investment inside the region. Another aim is to eliminate East Asia's so-called "double mismatch"—its inability to raise funds in its own currencies and a too high dependence on short-term borrowing.

Today, the domestic bond markets of most East Asian countries are small. The major bond issuers are the governments. However, their bonds are mostly bought and held by financial institutions and do not circulate in the market.

The initiative is expected to encourage the issuance of local currency-denominated bonds by governments and financial institutions, promote the creation of asset-backed securities markets, and improve conditions for investors.

An Asian Currency Unit?

The common currency idea was articulated by Mahathir in 1997. He spoke about the Asian yuan. Later, it was referred to by former Chief Secretary of the Administration of Hong Kong, Donald Tsang. Yet, at this point, it is no more than a beautiful dream.

For its part, the ADB has proposed the Asian Currency Unit—a weighted index of currencies for APT countries. It is not a currency, but a currency basket, which would function as a benchmark for regional currency movements and stimulate the coordination and harmonization of monetary policies.

Other Areas of Cooperation

Progress in other areas of APT cooperation is less significant and may be unknown outside the region. Yet, certain important steps have been made in various sectors such as energy, the environment, ICT, agriculture, and social welfare. Ministerial meetings and contacts between government officials, experts, academics, and others help to shape common approaches, study best practices, and, in some cases, provide an impetus for interactions.

For example, the member countries are working to develop the Energy Security Communication System to increase the region's capacity for timely emergency response. In 2003, the first APT Oil Stockpiling Forum was held in Bangkok.

ASEAN countries have received financial and technical assistance from China, Japan, and South Korea to address their social equality issues. At the second Ministerial Meeting for Social Welfare and Development in Hanoi in December 2007 the participants studied the system of community services for handicapped people in Japan, the establishment of committees working for the handicapped in China, and South Korea's law on anti-discrimination against the handicapped.

East Asian Summits

The decision to hold formal East Asian Summits (EASs) was made at the meeting of APT leaders in 2004. At their Laos meeting the following year, the 16 initial participants were determined. The compiling of this list appeared to be a very subtle, complicated, and even controversial issue. An initial proposal about the summits, presented by the East Asia Study Group, presumed participation by the APT states only. However, Japan was pushing for the inclusion of three nonregional countries—India, Australia, and New Zealand. There were two reasons for this. First, it was intended to balance the rapidly increasing role of China in the region in general and in the integration process in particular. Second, in view of its close relationship with the US, Japan had to take into account Washington's opposition to formalizing the summit within the APT group. Adding three, old, Western-style democracies settled the issue, at least for the time being.

Though ASEAN countries and China did not look enthusiastic about the idea, the ASEAN+6 formula was accepted and the first EAS was held in Kuala Lumpur in December 2005.

It was followed by the second EAS in Cebu City, the Philippines, in January 2007. The "Cebu Declaration on East Asia Energy Security" was adopted, where the signatories pledged to find alternatives to conventional fuels and to set individual goals and formulate voluntary action plans for improving energy efficiency.

The summit also agreed to consider a Comprehensive Economic Partnership for East Asia (CEPEA), proposed by Japan (see below).

The third EAS was held in Singapore in November 2007. The major document was the "Singapore Declaration on Climate Change, Energy and Environment." The signatories pledged to formulate voluntary energy efficiency goals by 2009, support cooperation in developing reference benchmarks for environmentally and socially sustainable biofuels, and, where appropriate, to use regional research institutions for this purpose.

The summit agreed to establish the Japan-proposed Economic Research Institute of ASEAN and East Asia to further investigate economic integration between the member countries.

The Creation of the East Asian Community: Dilemmas

Who Will Do It?

It looked like the APT would be a natural core framework to start the EAC building process. First, the community idea itself was articulated by the East Asia Study Group it established. Second, it had already developed a number of regional cooperation mechanisms which could become the community foundation.

However, the emergence of the EASs, with 16 participants, changed the whole plan. Though there was a consensus about the need to work on community-building, the parties involved faced a new dilemma—should the community be created on the basis of the APT or the EASs? The ASEAN countries and China favored the former, Japan and the three non-East Asian participants of the EASs—the latter. The issue dominated the first EAS in Kuala Lumpur in 2005.

Politics are involved. The APT approach explicitly positions ASEAN as the leading community builder (the association itself has set the target of building an EU-style ASEAN community by 2015), while China holds the key as the region's major economic integrator and its rising superpower. In the EAS approach the presence of three, powerful, nonregional players somewhat offsets China's key position and, presumably, reduces the weight of ASEAN. For Japan, it is much easier to work in this format, not only due to the Chinese factor but also because the participation of the three big democracies is vital to get tacit approval from the US and the West in general.

As a result of long and hard negotiations, a compromise formula was found, saying that the APT has to be "the main vehicle" for achieving the community, while the EASs will "play an important role" in it.

Alternative Proposals for a Regionwide Free Trade Area

The EAC needs a regionwide free trade area as its basis. Again, the range of such an area has emerged as an enormously complicated issue. Three major alternative proposals have been made.

East Asia Free Trade Area (EAFTA): ASEAN+3. As mentioned, the idea of the EAFTA covering the APT countries was included in the report of the East Asia Study Group in 2002. After that, China proposed the establishment of an expert study group to conduct a feasibility study. It was created in 2004, following a decision at an APT economic ministers' meeting.

Its report, "Towards an East Asian FTA: Modality and Road Map," was presented at the economic ministers' meeting in August 2006 and then discussed at the Cebu APT summit in January 2007. In the experts' view, the formation of the EAFTA has to be an independent process, but it should take into account all existing and ongoing East Asian FTAs, including those in the ASEAN+1 format, while not necessarily being restricted to them. It should also reflect the Bogor goals[1] set by the Asia-Pacific Economic Cooperation (APEC) and take into consideration the ASEAN economic community's "single market and production base" to be created by 2015. The road map envisages the launch of an independent EAFTA preparation process at the APT summit in 2006; creation in 2007–08 of working groups to do preparatory work for EAFTA negotiations; the start of the negotiations in 2009; and the completion of the EAFTA by 2011 (for CLMV by 2020). Initially, it will be signed by the APT member countries, but other East Asian states and EAS members may join at a later and appropriate time (Zhang 2006).

As a following step, South Korea proposed to conduct a Phase Two study on the details of EAFTA, centered on in-depth, sector-by-sector discussions. The reports are to be presented to the APT meeting of economic ministers in summer 2009.

Comprehensive Economic Partnership for East Asia (CEPEA): ASEAN+6. In 2006, Japan came out with the idea of the Comprehensive Economic Partnership for East Asia (CEPEA) with 16 participants—ASEAN Plus Three plus India, Australia, and New Zealand, and proposed to launch a Two Track study. The proposal was accepted at the second EAS in Cebu in January 2007 and since June of the same year several meetings of the study group have been held under Japan's chair. In November 2007, the interim report was presented to the EAS in Singapore. The final results are to be reported to the fourth EAS in Thailand.

Free Trade Area Asia-Pacific (FTAAP): 21 APEC Economies. FTAAP, pushed by the APEC Business Advisory Council, was formally proposed at the 14th APEC Economic Summit in Hanoi in November 2006. Economic leaders instructed their officials to conduct studies on ways and means of integration within the APEC area, including FTAAP as a long-term prospect, and to report to the Economic Leaders Meeting in November 2007 in Sydney. There it was decided to discuss its feasibility.

The idea is strongly supported by the US. If created, the zone will include not only the APT and EAS countries, but also the United States and other big economies, such as Canada, Russia, and Mexico. As APEC members, Hong Kong and Taiwan would join too. On the other hand, India would be left out.

Compared to the other two proposals, the FTAAP seems to be the most difficult to achieve due to the size of the area it covers and the large number of participants. The chairman of the Japan Economic Foundation, Noboru Hatakeyama, suggests that it may be advisable "to recruit members of the FTA from like-minded economies of the APEC" (Hatakeyama 2008).

Creation of any of these FTAs is going to be a long-term exercise, not only because of the complexity of the issues involved but also due to the fact that

ASEAN prioritizes the establishment of its own economic community and the conclusion of ASEAN+1 agreements.

East Asia's Integration Pattern: A "Do-What-You-Can-Do" Community

We believe that in the medium term—perhaps, around the middle of the next decade, the EAC will be born. It will be a new type of community, reflecting the region's specifics.

The European pattern of community building—from arrangements in particular sectors to a free trade area and then on to a customs union, common market, and economic and monetary union—requires economic, political, cultural, and historical homogeneity. Also, from the 1950s, European integration was driven by strong, and largely unique, political impacts and economic motivations. The former came from the need to counter the Communist threat on the one hand and to accommodate Germany on the other, an approach that had the staunch backing of the United States. The latter was remarkably strong, as the medium- and small-sized European nations needed integration and unity to be competitive against the larger powers—the US, the Soviet Union, and, later, Japan.

In today's East Asia, the initial conditions are quite different. Economic, political, cultural, and historical homogeneity is not there. Common external threats do not exist. Intraregional political and security problems, such as North Korea's nuclear program or cross-strait tensions between China and Taiwan, are addressed within frameworks unrelated to regional community building. Finally, the US is not backing the idea.

Economically too, for the East Asian nations, especially the larger economies, the notion of regional unity is less important than it was (and is) for the Europeans. The reasons are both Asia's enormous intraregional economic gaps and its high dependence on trade and other ties with "outsiders." The concept of the EAC as a bloc standing against other regional blocs is very unlikely to become a guiding principle in spite of some support it has received.

The only viable option for East Asia is to set up a pragmatic, loose, and flexible "do-what-you-can-do" community. It will have a free trade area at its foundation and coordinate policies in selective fields, where all the parties involved believe that such coordination is in their national interest and where it is technically possible.

Endnote

1 The APEC Bogor goals are free and open trade and investment in Asia-Pacific by 2010 for the developed economies, and by 2020 for the developing economies.

Part 2
Nations

7

China: A New Heavyweight

A Few Basics

China has the largest population in the world—1.3 billion people. By territory it runs third after Russia and Canada.

In terms of per-capita gross domestic product (GDP) of the purchasing power parity (PPP) variety, which was US$5,292 in 2007, it still belongs to the group of low-middle-income countries and was ranked ninety-ninth between Samoa and Namibia.

China is very rich in natural resources. Vast cultivated lands are concentrated in its eastern part, grasslands in the north and west, and forests in the northeast and southwest. The country has deposits of most of the fuel and mineral resources known. The major ones include coal, petroleum, natural gas, iron ore, copper, aluminum, tungsten, molybdenum, manganese, tin, lead, zinc, mercury, phosphorus, sulfur, and antimony. The resources of rare metals are the richest in the world. Many deposits are still undeveloped.

China's representative agricultural products are rice (the largest volume of production in the world), wheat, corn, tobacco, soybean, barley, apples, oil seed, cotton, and pork. It produces a uniquely wide variety of teas.

The country has a full set of industries—both mining and manufacturing—and is the world leader, in terms of production volume, for certain major products. The main industries are iron and steel, nonferrous metals, coal, petroleum, electrical and nonelectrical machinery, home electronics, telecommunication equipment, transportation machinery (including production of auto vehicles, locomotives, rail cars, ships, and aircrafts), chemicals and fertilizers, food processing, textiles, and footwear. The defense industry is strong and, in the space development sector, China belongs to the frontrunners.

Leading Chinese companies are becoming increasingly widely known around the world. Representative examples are Lenovo, which joined the ranks of the major computer makers after acquiring the PC business of IBM in 2004, home electronics producer Haier, and TV set maker TCL. In the nonmanufacturing sector, three oil giants—PetroChina, Sinopec (China Petrochemical and Chemical Corporation), and China National Offshore Oil Corporation (CNOOC)—have

117

become big names. In terms of market capitalization, PetroChina now runs first in the world, as of early 2008. Another emerging group of internationally recognized heavyweights is the "Big Four" commercial banks—China Construction Bank, Bank of China, Industrial and Commercial Bank of China, and Agricultural Bank of China.

The People's Republic of China (PRC) consists of 22 provinces (Taiwan is considered the twenty-third, renegade province), five autonomous regions, and four directly controlled municipalities. The gap between the most developed, eastern coastal provinces and the inland areas poses one of the biggest economic and sociopolitical problems. The western region is least developed.

The Chinese cabinet is officially called the State Council. Under the council's jurisdiction, there are 22 ministries, three commissions, and the National Audit Office. A very important role is played by the National Development and Reform Commission, which is responsible for macroeconomic management, formulation of economic and social policy, and structural reforms. Other key economic agencies are the ministries of finance, commerce, industry and information technology, science and technology, land and resources, housing and urban-rural development, transport, railways, and agriculture. This industry-based system of ministries is the legacy of the socialist planned economy.

The legislative body is called the National People's Congress. The Communist Party of China (CPC) is the dominant political force. Its leader is also the country's president. Other political parties, though small-scale, also exist, but they fully recognize the CPC leadership.

Officially, China is a socialist country and its economic system is defined as "the socialist market economy."

Postwar Development

Industrialization Soviet-Style

In 1949, communists under the leadership of Mao Zedong came to power and proclaimed the PRC. They started industrializing Soviet-style with large-scale assistance from the USSR.

The CPC was building an orthodox socialist economy. The private sector was suppressed, though not completely eliminated. Private owners were marginalized when the government announced that it would not protect their property.

The 1st Five-Year Plan covered the period from 1953 to 1957. These years were marked by the speedy growth of the industrial sector, especially heavy industries.

The "Great Leap Forward"

The 2nd Five-Year Plan was compiled along the same lines. Industrialization was the top priority but it was understood that it would take quite some time. However, in 1958, the Maoist leadership announced the "Great Leap Forward" policy, based on a different development concept. Relations with the Soviet

Union deteriorated as China pursued its own path. Mao Zedong's idea was to accelerate the speed of industrialization dramatically and to build a modern industrial economy within a very short period of time, taking advantage of China's enormous and cheap labor resources (and economizing on the imports of machinery). In particular, he dreamed of surpassing the US and the UK in the volume of steel production.

In rural areas, from 1958, the people's communes were set up, while individually cultivated land plots were abolished. Communes consisted of a number of smaller farm collectives and usually included 4,000–5,000 households. Not only all the means of production but even the personal belongings of the members had to be contributed to the commune. The members had absolutely no personal freedom.

The Great Leap Forward continued until 1960 and was a complete failure. Rural mini-plants were technologically inadequate and produced goods of very low value or no value at all—such as steel, made from low-quality iron, which could not be used in any industry. Large factory construction projects were poorly planned and resulted in a huge waste of financial and material resources. Agricultural productivity in the communes was extremely low causing food shortages. Tens of millions of people died from famine.

Amid the economic turmoil Mao Zedong chose to temporarily leave the political arena. He was succeeded by Liu Shaoqi, who represented the pragmatic wing of the CPC leadership. Efforts were made to put the economy back on track by restoring incentives. Individually cultivated plots were allowed again, while the role of the communes decreased. Industrial enterprises got some autonomy regarding production plans, compensation for workers, and so on. Investment in industry was reduced while state support for agriculture expanded. As a result, agricultural production rose and food supplies improved. From 1963, the government started to speed up industrialization again.

The "Cultural Revolution"

A new, big shock came in 1966 with the start of what was called the Great Proletarian Cultural Revolution. It was a political move by Mao Zedong to return to power, ousting Liu Shaoqi and breaking the resistance of the moderate wing within the leadership. The revolution turned out to be an endless series of noisy demonstrations and marches by Mao supporters, mostly students and young workers, carried away by Maoist propaganda. Notable politicians, factory managers, and intellectuals were persecuted and humiliated.

The Cultural Revolution continued until 1969, undermining the established system of economic management and paralyzing the activities of the most educated and well-trained cadres. It disorganized the economy and caused a brisk fall of production.

Back to a "Normal" Planned Economy

As Mao Zedong consolidated his power, suppressing internal opposition, from the early 1970s the country started a return to a "normal," socialist planned economy, gradually putting behind it the political extravaganza of the previous decade. The establishment of diplomatic relations with the US and Japan in 1972 opened the way for more trade with industrially developed countries. Production began to grow and the supply of basic goods improved. Yet, overall the economic situation remained tough.

Mao Zedong died in 1976.

An Historic Shift to Market Reforms

Two years later a new era in China's history began. At the meeting of the Central Committee of the CPC in December 1978, it was decided to launch the openness and development policy, initiated by paramount leader, Deng Xiaoping. From 1978–79 China began gradually to build a market economy.

The reforms started with agriculture. Communes were dismantled and practically ceased to exist by 1984. Instead, a household responsibility system was introduced. A rural household was contracted to cultivate a piece of land and was responsible for supplying a fixed amount of products, specified by the plan quota, to the state at the prices set by the latter. In 1979, state purchasing prices were significantly raised. The remainder could be sold freely in the market. The new policy led to an increase of agricultural production, which solved the food problem within a short period of time.

Also, from the early 1980s the government promoted village and township enterprises—small entrepreneurial units with a rather vague form of ownership. As time went by, various forms of private companies started to develop, outperforming state-owned firms in terms of productivity.

The state-owned enterprises (SOEs) were encouraged to become more self-reliant and profitable, to establish direct ties with their transaction counterparts, and to buy and sell more at recommended, or even freely set, prices, not the prices fixed by the state.

Opening Up for Foreign Capital

The core of the reform policy was the country's opening up for foreign capital. Inward foreign direct investment (FDI) began to play a major role in the growth of production and exports. To attract foreign investors, the government started to establish Special Economic Zones (SEZs), initially in the eastern coastal provinces. In the SEZs, the procedure of examination and approval of foreign-invested projects was simplified, and companies were provided with tax incentives, such as the reduction or elimination of customs duties or income (corporate) tax. SEZs were attached the role of trial parks for the country's modernization with the participation of foreign capital. In reality they became the centers of growth and development.

The first four SEZs were opened in 1980 in Shenzhen, Zhuhai, and Shantou in Guangdong Province and Xiamen in Fujian Province. They were followed by the entire Hainan Province and Pudong area of Shanghai in 1990. From

1984, the government started to establish Economic and Technological Development Zones (ETDZs)—basically, along the same line. The policy priorities for ETDZs were the development of mainly high-tech industries and the building of the export-oriented economy. Between 1984 and 1988, 14 ETDZs were opened (Ministry of Commerce 2003).

Market reforms and the emergence of new types of enterprises quickly led to a dramatic acceleration of economic growth. Between 1978 and 1988 it averaged 10.2 percent a year.

Three Years of Uncertainty and the Acceleration of Reforms

Growth stumbled after the Tiananmen Square massacre of 1989, when the army brutally suppressed a mass pro-democracy demonstration. The tragedy led to a deterioration of relations with industrially developed countries and a squeeze on economic ties with them, investment included. The growth rate fell to 4.1 percent in 1989 and 3.8 percent in 1990. In China itself, the Communist orthodoxy was gaining ground again, causing doubts about the future of the reforms. However, the building of market institutions did not stop. In a very important development, the Shanghai Stock Exchange was opened in 1990 and the Shenzhen Stock Exchange in 1991.

Uncertainty ended in 1992 when Deng Xiaoping, visiting coastal provinces for the Chinese New Year, made it clear that the openness and development policy would be continued and activated. The following year more than 2,000 new economic and trade development zones, both at the national and local level, were opened. Investment in China started to expand at an unprecedented speed, and growth rates reached new heights—14.2 percent in 1992 and 14.0 percent in 1993.

The Marginal Influence of the Asian Crisis and Surfacing Structural Problems

In 1997, the country's GDP growth declined to 9.3 percent, in 1998 to 7.8 percent, and in 1999 further to 7.6 percent (ADB 2008). From 2000, the economy began accelerating again. Basically, China was well protected from the Asian crisis impact because of the inconvertibility of the yuan, huge foreign currency reserves, and a small and immature capital market. There was no massive inflow of speculative short-term capital. The influence of the crisis was indirect—it slowed down the pace of export expansion and temporarily reduced inward FDI. Yet, China felt strong and confident enough to abstain from devaluing the yuan when the currencies of its Asian neighbors were plummeting.

However, at that point, the country was facing deep structural problems of its own, largely resembling those of other Asian economies—in particular, huge nonperforming bank loans, caused mostly by the poor performance of the SOEs, which had been generously supported by the government. On the other hand, moves to reform the SOEs were already leading to massive lay-offs, making the rise in unemployment a major social and political risk.

Structural Reforms

SOE Reform

The following two developments served as important preparatory steps for the reform of the SOEs.

First, slowly but surely, the government reduced the share of their production covered by the direct planning system. Under this system the state was responsible for practically all the aspects of production, including financing, the supply of necessary equipment and intermediate goods, price-setting, and sales.

Second, the SOEs were coming under growing competitive pressure from foreign-affiliated companies, village and township enterprises, and, increasingly, domestic private firms of various types.

The first stage of the reform was launched in 1997, under the strong leadership of Prime Minister Zhu Rongji. Large SOEs were transformed into corporations and part of their stock was sold to private investors. Some of these corporations were listed. However, the state retained the position of the major stakeholder.

By the middle of the 2000s, the transformation of large SOEs into corporations was almost finished. The second stage began. SOEs had to be reorganized, refocused, and turned into entities that were self-reliant and competitive by the standards of the market economy.

The government sought to create a limited number of strong and efficiently managed SOEs, in the strategically important sectors, to act as the backbone of the market economy. The number of SOEs is to be reduced from 159 active at the end of 2006 to 80–100 by 2010 (Institute of Chinese Affairs 2006, 135). The policy aims to turn some of them into competitive global players.

Stock Market Reform

SOE transformation is closely linked with the stock market reform started in 2005. Actually, it is the third attempt—the first two, made respectively in 1998 and 2001, were unsuccessful. The major contents of the reform are simple: nontradable shares owned by the government, which comprised about two-thirds of the total value of stock listed in Shanghai and Shenzhen, were made tradable. The aim was to invigorate the stock market, depressed all through the first half of this decade.

In 2006, almost all listed companies, where the state owns stock, made all their shares tradable. Sales of previously nontradable shares started from June, and there was no lack of buyers. As a result, the capital market was revitalized and stock values surged dramatically. In 2006, the total capitalization of companies, listed in Shanghai and Shenzhen, reached 9.05 trillion yuan—a 2.9 times annual increase. The number of listed firms at the end of the year hit 1,424 (Institute of Chinese Affairs 2006, 137; 141).

The unloading of nontradable shares also paved the way for the market-driven reshuffle of the corporate structure through mergers and acquisitions (M&A), neither initiated nor controlled by the state.

Banking Reform

In the 1980s, direct budgetary financing of SOEs was effectively terminated. Companies were made to borrow from banks and pay the interest. The conventional two-tiered banking system was created. The People's Bank of China became the central bank, or "bank of banks," while loan-related activities were transferred to the Industrial and Commercial Bank of China, China Construction Bank, Agricultural Bank of China, and the Bank of China. The latter bank became responsible for foreign exchange operations.

By the mid-1990s, the government allowed new commercial banks to open as well as foreign banks' subsidiaries. As of 2006, there were twelve major domestic commercial banks—four state-owned (the above-mentioned "Big Four") and eight corporate (Institute of Chinese Affairs 2006, 143).

Until the mid-1990s, state banks continued providing massive loans to SOEs under the government's directives and had no authority to squeeze or terminate credit in case it was commercially nonviable. It was also practically impossible to press enterprises to pay off their overdue debts. Thus, the major banks accumulated enormous nonperforming loans (NPLs).

The situation started to change from the second half of the 1990s with the launch of the SOE reform. Yet, the problem of the NPLs of the four state-owned banks remains difficult (NPLs of other banks are insignificant). While the economy continues to grow fast, providing them enough revenues, the pace of the disposal is still slow. As of the end of 2006, the NPLs of the "Big Four" amounted to 1,054 billion yuan and comprised 9.22 percent of the total amount of their loans outstanding.

In 2003, after the injection of budget funds into the four major banks, in order to increase their capitalization, the China Construction Bank, the Bank of China, and the Industrial and Commercial Bank of China were corporatized and listed.

Present Performance

Aspects of Success

China is the fastest-growing major national economy in the world. Its rapid growth has been practically uninterrupted from the very start of the openness and development era in 1978–79 and has become especially fast since the early 1990s.

Having unveiled the forces of the market, the country aptly capitalizes on its labor resources—unique in scale, very cheap by international standards, diligent, and quick to learn. It also makes the most of an abundance of capital, both domestic—saving rates in China are uniquely high (the ratio of savings to GDP is on the rise and in 2006 it reached 47.3 percent, more than in other major national economy (Fujitsu Research Institute 2008))—and foreign—it has become one of the biggest recipients of FDI in the world.

Global Production Center

China has grown into the global production center for a wide variety of products. It produces one-third of the world's steel and aluminum and half of its cement and flat glass (Kahn 2007). It is the largest producer of cotton clothing, footwear, coal, tungsten, antimony, rice, beer, and toys. It has become the world's number two in the production of auto vehicles and trucks. In 2004, according to the National Development and Reforms Commission, the country had also developed the third-largest manufacturing industry of electronic and information technology (IT) products and grown into the number one producer of program-controlled telephone switches, mobile phone handsets, color TVs, and color monitors, accounting for 30–55 percent of world output (*People's Daily* February 4, 2004).

In mid-2006, China surpassed the US as the world's second-largest exporter of goods and is coming closer to the world leader, Germany. Since 2000, it has more than doubled its share in world merchandise exports to 8.7 percent in 2007.

Leading Financial Power

In a new development, China is emerging as a leading financial power. It has the biggest current account surplus in the world. Its current and capital accounts are both in the black and foreign exchange reserves reached US$95 trillion as of the end of 2008—more than in any other country. The government-affiliated China Investment Corporation (CIC) is the largest wealth fund held by a single nation (*The Daily Yomiuri* 2008).

In April 2006, the government allowed domestic banks, insurance companies, and other Qualified Domestic Institutional Investors to invest in overseas securities.

Investment-Driven Growth

The major driving force of China's growth is the rapid expansion of investment in fixed assets—equipment, factories, and houses. (If you drive through a big Chinese city today, you will be overwhelmed by a myriad of construction sites.) It contributed more than 50 percent of GDP growth in the first half of the 2000s (METI 2006, 114). In relative terms contributions to growth by net exports and private consumption have been rather modest.

Nowadays, China is investing in fixed capital 40 percent more than Japan (IDE-JETRO 2007, 129).

However, the efficiency of investment remains the lowest in the region. In a number of industries—the textile, home electronics, auto, and materials-producing sectors—signs of excess capacity have appeared.

Fighting with Overheating

Excessive investment threatened to overheat the economy. This is associated with rising inflationary pressures due to expanding demand for materials, raw materials, and the labor force, as well as land, office space, houses, and so on.

Table 7.1 Main economic indicators (real annual growth, %)

Indicator	1999	2000	2001	2002	2003	2004	2005	2006	2007
GDP	7.6	8.4	8.3	9.0	10.0	10.1	10.4	11.1	11.9
Agriculture*	2.8	2.4	2.8	2.9	2.5	6.3	5.2	5.0	3.7
Industry*	8.1	9.4	8.4	9.8	12.7	11.1	11.7	13.0	13.4
Services*	9.3	9.7	10.3	10.4	9.5	10.1	10.5	12.1	12.6
Gross fixed capital formation (current prices)	6.9	10.9	11.6	15.6	22.6	21.7	19.0	16.4	16.7
Private consumption (current prices)	6.9	9.4	7.3	6.8	8.1	12.3	11.1	13.5	14.9
Average wage	11.6	12.3	16.0	14.3	13.0	14.1	14.6	14.4	n/a
Unemployment rate (urban areas) (%)	5.8	6.0	6.8	7.7	8.8	8.3	8.4	8.5	8.3
Consumer prices	-1.4	0.4	0.7	-0.8	1.2	3.9	1.8	1.5	4.8
Exports (US$ billions), fob	194.9	249.2	266.1	325.6	438.2	593.3	762.0	968.9	1,218.0
Imports (US$ billions), cif	165.7	225.1	243.6	295.2	412.8	561.2	660.0	791.5	955.8
Average exchange rate (yuan for US$1)	8.2783	8.2785	8.2771	8.2770	8.2770	8.2768	8.1943	7.9734	7.675

Source: ADB: Key Indicators 2008; National Bureau of Statistics: *China Statistical Yearbook 2007.*

*Data for agriculture, industry, and services refers to value added.

Initially, in the Chinese context, rapid expansion of investment and production had a substantial deflationary effect—prices of major goods, such as clothing, transportation machinery, telecommunication equipment, and transportation and telecommunication costs, visibly fell in the first half of the 2000s. Generally, until 2007, consumer price growth rates were very low (see Table 7.1) and 3 percent inflation is fixed by the Chinese government as an alarm line. The other side of the coin, however, is that the rising costs of inputs, especially labor, fuels, and raw materials, made many companies operate at minimal profit margins.

Between 1998 and 2002, the Chinese government was increasing money supply to counter deflationary pressures. Since 2003, monetary policy has been tightened. In March 2006, the government went a step further, designating 11 industries with an excess production capacity (these include steel, aluminum, auto vehicles, cement, coal, and electricity) where new investment projects had to be tightly regulated. In November of the same year, the central government openly criticized the administration of Hebei Province for allowing excessive investment in the steel industry.

One of the major aspects of overheating was an asset bubble resulting from the rise in speculative real-estate transactions and overvalued corporate stock. Concerns about it were exacerbated by the excess liquidity problem, rooted in the huge balance of payments surplus.

To fight the bubble, the government moved to limit speculative transactions in real estate—priority was attached to the construction of smaller and cheaper apartments, which were unlikely to become a target for speculators.

In December 2007, at the annual Central Economic Work Conference—a forum articulating the major directions of economic policy for the coming year—it was decided to shift from "prudent" to "tight" monetary policy, which meant further restrictions on bank loans.

Policy Changes in the Wake of the Global Financial Crisis

In the second half of 2008, as the global financial crisis broke out, a shift was made to a much more proactive fiscal policy and a "moderately easy" monetary policy, both aimed at boosting domestic demand. The Chinese government made it clear that stimulating domestic growth (and not large-scale injections of Chinese money into troubled Western financial institutions) would be the country's most relevant contribution to the world economy in times of turmoil.

In the third quarter, the annual growth rate decreased to 9 percent, and in the fourth-further to 6.8 percent largely due to the negative impact of the global crisis on Chinese exporters, but also because of a slowdown in consumer spending. According to the preliminary data released by the government, the growth rate for the whole of 2008 was 9.0 percent. It is assumed that for today's China an 8 percent annual growth rate represents the critical line—if growth falls below this level, the country may face grave unemployment and other social problems.

However, inflation rates significantly decreased (though for the whole of 2008 the consumer prices' growth reached 5.9 percent), and fighting with overheating and the asset bubble was no longer on the agenda. On the contrary, house prices started to decline.

In major developments, during the September-December period, the central bank cut its key interest rate five times, reducing it from 7.47 percent to 5.31 percent, and lowered bank reserve requirements. Bank lending quotas rose. Taxes on some stock market transactions were eliminated. The government raised the value-added tax refund rates again for the exporters of the low-cost labor intensive products, which had been previously reduced.

In early November, the cabinet compiled an unprecedented two-year economic stimulus package worth 4 trillion yuan (about US$570 billion) to be spent within two years. Specifically, ten major steps to boost growth were announced: expansion of low-income housing construction; an increase in spending on rural infrastructure; the acceleration of transportation network expansion; the improvement of the healthcare system and construction of education facilities; construction of sewage and rubbish treatment facilities preventing water pollution; the enhancement of innovation and industrial restructuring; the rebuilding of areas hit by natural disasters; raising average incomes in rural and urban areas, among other things, by increasing farm subsidies; reform of the value-added tax rules to cut the corporate tax burden by 120 billion yuan (about US$17 billion); and, finally, an increase in the financial support for growth by removing quotas on commercial bank lending (Xinhua 2008).

Three Super-Challenges

Super-Challenge Number One: Natural Resources and Natural Environment

The national economy remains very energy- and resource-intensive. According to the World Bank, industries in China use 20–100 percent more energy per unit of output than those in the US, Japan, and other developed countries. The Chinese government says that the country's energy use per unit of production is 3.4 times the world average (Associated Press 2007). Though it is slowly going down, the pace of the decrease is lagging far behind schedule.

Chinese producers operate under at least a latent threat of shortages of energy, fuel, and raw materials. Both the government and companies are rushing to tap natural resources all around the world, which exerts enormous upward pressure on their world prices, destabilizing the world economy.

As the efficiency of the use of energy and other natural resources remains low while the economy is expanding fast, all kinds of environmental problems, including air pollution, water contamination and shortages, and deforestation, are being exacerbated.

Until now, the national targets set for greenhouse gas emissions have not been met, and, in 2008, China became the number one air polluter in the world. The health of the nation is at stake. According to the Ministry of Health, cancer has become the leading cause of death and the main reason for it is pollution. Ambient air pollution alone results in hundreds of thousands of deaths every year.

Also, nearly 500 million people lack access to safe drinking water (*BBC News* 2007). China has only one-fifth as much water per capita as the US. In particular, the northern part of the country, home to half of its population, suffers from severe water shortages and loses arable land. It faces the threat of turning into the world's biggest desert (Kahn 2007).

To address the environmental problems, the government has moved to shut down heavily polluting coal mines, power plants, and steel mills. It is encouraging the use of clean energy sources, such as solar energy or natural gas, and is tightening environmental regulations in the major cities.

Yet, it is not showing enough capability and political will to work out a resource-saving and environment-friendly model of growth. China opposes any mandatory limits on carbon dioxide emissions. No cost incentives are used to enhance energy efficiency and curb pollution, such as surcharges on energy use above established limits. On the contrary, energy, fuel, and water costs are maintained at an artificially low level—the state continues to subsidize their users, sticking to the "growth first" principle.

Under these conditions it is not surprising that an energy conservation culture or environmentally-conscious behavior of companies or households is not present. Provincial administrations, used to being assessed by the growth rates they have achieved and having close links with local producers, usually resist the anti-pollution measures taken by the central authorities—for example, they reopen factories that the latter has ordered to close. Notably, the move to introduce the "Green GDP" concept[1] and to use it for the assessment of the country's economic performance, endorsed and encouraged personally by President Hu Jintao in 2004, was killed because of resistance from provincial authorities (Kahn 2007).

Super-Challenge Number Two: Employment

The employment problem remains a big headache. First of all, the enormous size of the population makes job creation a very challenging task. Tens of millions of people move from rural areas to cities in search of work and a better life. Second, the restructuring of SOEs results in downsizing and job losses. Third, due to the introduction of better equipment and more up-to-date technologies, as well as the rise in the efficiency of management, the number of workers needed to produce a given amount of goods and services declines.

The official figure for the unemployment rate in urban areas in 2007 was 4.0 percent. However, it is generally recognized that it does not cover all the persons who are really unemployed.

Today, China not only has to create jobs but also to establish a relevant legal framework for protecting workers' basic rights. In this area the country is still lagging far behind recognized international standards. The new Labor Contract Law, effective from January 1, 2008, provides better protection of employees' interests.

Super-Challenge Number Three: Intraregional Gaps

Another very difficult issue China has to work on is a big intraregional imbalance in its economic development. Critically wide gaps exist between urban and rural areas, as well as between coastal and inland provinces. The western part remains underdeveloped. Actually, the Chinese economy consists of various local economies whose stages of economic development are different. China's success remains, first and foremost, the success of the eastern coastal provinces.

Table 7.2 presents data on per-capita GDP in all the provinces, autonomous regions, and directly controlled municipalities. The gap between the leader, Shanghai, and Guizhou Province, where per-capita GDP is the lowest, is almost tenfold. The living standards gap is widening, not narrowing, as in the coastal areas the real disposable income of households and their consumption are growing faster than in the inland ones. Such disparities become a source of tensions. For instance, relatively poor Jiangxi Province, belonging to the central region, neighbors Guangdong, Zhejiang, and Fujian, which are blamed for taking away human resources and capital. Per-capita GDP in Anhui Province, also located in the central part, is only one-third of that of its next-door coastal neighbors—Zhejiang and Jiangsu.

If you look at China's statistical data on regional development, you won't find a single slow-growing area. As of the middle of the 2000s, all the provinces and autonomous regions were growing at an annual rate of around 10 percent. Yet, to catch up, less-developed inland provinces have to grow faster than the coastal ones, but this is not happening.

Foreign-affiliated companies, the most efficient players and leading drivers of growth, are highly concentrated in the eastern coastal area, while in the inland provinces' SOEs—the least efficient players—are prevailing.

A decisive condition for reducing the imbalance is the ability and effort on the part of inland areas to attract more investment, capitalizing on lower labor and other costs. Some signs of change are there, including the transfer of production from the south to the central and western parts of the country. For instance, Ford, Honda, Suzuki, and Yamaha are going inland (Chambers 2005).

Changing Policy Priorities: From Growth to a Harmonious Society

The priorities of the officially proclaimed state economic policy are changing from stimulating economic growth to building a harmonious society. In the 11th Five-Year Plan (2006–10) support for rural areas, improvement of the social security system, and protection of the natural environment are designated as priority areas for the allocation of state funds. For the first time, the government has set mandatory numerical targets to be reached by 2010 for the reduction of energy consumption per unit of GDP. It has to be reduced by 20 percent from the 2005 level (METI 2006, 142).

The Upgrading Game

Growing Labor Costs

China's labor costs are going up. The annual increase of a nominal average wage for all industries between 1999 and 2006 was as high as 13.8 percent

Table 7.2   Per-capita income by province, autonomous region, and directly controlled municipality, 2006 (yuan)

Provinces, administrative regions, and municipalities	Yuan (millions)
Eastern	
Shanghai	56,733
Beijing	49,505
Tianjin	40,961
Zhejiang	31,684
Jiangsu	28,685
Guangdong	28,077
Shandong	23,546
Fujian	21,152
Hebei	16,570
Hainan	12,650
Northeastern	
Liaoning	21,802
Heilongjiang	16,268
Jilin	15,625
Central	
Shanxi	14,106
Henan	13,279
Hubei	13,169
Hunan	11,830
Jiangxi	10,679
Anhui	10,044
Western	
Inner Mongolia Autonomous Region	20,047
Xinjiang Uyghur Autonomous Region	14,871
Chongqing	12,437
Ningxia Hui Autonomous Region	11,784
Shaanxi	11,762
Qinghai	11,753
Sichuan	10,574
Tibet Autonomous Region	10,322
Guangxi Zhuang Autonomous Region	10,240
Yunnan	8,961
Gansu	8,749
Guizhou	5,750

Source: National Bureau of Statistics.

(see Table 7.1). The average monthly wage in 2006 was 1,750 yuan, or about US$230. In Shanghai it was 3,432 yuan (about US$447); in Beijing 3,343 yuan (US$436); in Zhejiang 2,318 yuan (US$ 302); and in Guangdong 2,182 yuan (US$284) (National Bureau of Statistics of China 2007). On average, China retains its low-labor-cost advantage, but as time goes by it becomes smaller in comparison with the ASEAN 4 and other emerging-market countries.

In the major economic centers, labor costs appear to be practically the same or even higher than in Indonesia, the Philippines, and Thailand. For instance, according to the survey by JETRO, based on the data collected by local branches of the Japan Chamber of Commerce and Industry and on the questionnaires sent to particular companies, in 2004, a worker's wage (the wage of a newly employed worker who finished high school) in Shanghai was only a little lower than in Kuala Lumpur and Bangkok, the same as in Manila, and about 30 percent higher than in Jakarta. The wage of an engineer in Shanghai was almost 30 percent higher than in Bangkok, more than 20 percent higher than in Manila, and more than 80 percent higher than in Jakarta (but almost 40 percent lower than in Kuala Lumpur) (METI 2006, 144). In some cities in Fujian and Guangdong provinces, there are deficits of workers in general and skilled workers in particular. According to the Chinese government, in these provinces there was also a shortage of young female workers aged between 18 and 25 (METI 2006, 144).

Developments of this kind put Chinese companies under growing pressure to climb up the value chain.

The Development of Original Products and Technologies

Companies developing original products and technologies get financial support from the state and enjoy preferential treatment as the suppliers of goods for government agencies. The 11th Five-Year Plan sets the target for the ratio of the R&D investment to GDP at 2 percent for 2007 (in 2006 it was 1.4 percent) (IDE-JETRO 2007, 133).

One of the major strategic goals is to strengthen the country's position in the information and communications technology (ICT) industry. In 2006, the long-term strategy of its development was announced. China intends to focus on the R&D of core electronic devices, high-end chips, and ultra-large integrated circuits.

Brand Building

A growing number of domestic companies, both state-owned and private, are developing original products and trying to build their own brands. In 2006, the government made public the list of "model enterprises" engaged in such activities. It consisted of 103 firms (Institute of Chinese Affairs 2006, 148).

A good example is Haier, a home electronics maker. Competing in the medium- and high-price market segments, it has succeeded in branding original products, such as mini-refrigerators (including the model also serving as a PC stand, popular with college students) and wine coolers, which are selling well in the US and Europe.

Today, Chinese companies are trying a new pattern of upgrading: to use the expression of Peter Williamson, they are "buying the brand." A number of big domestic firms have started to actively acquire departments of famous foreign companies, mostly money-losing or at least sold off as non-core businesses, and to form joint ventures with them in order to access their technologies, human resources, sales networks, and, above all, to get the right to use their brands.

Quite often, the units of Western companies the Chinese are buying are barely profitable, if not money-losing. Providing relevant profitability in a very harsh competitive environment turns out to be a big challenge.

A new development deserving attention is the emergence of medium-size private companies led by entrepreneurs with a strategic vision. For example, athletic shoemaker Anta Sports, with its young CEO, Ding Shizhong, inheriting the business from his father, is building the country's first brand of mass-market sports goods.

According to *BusinessWeek* and consulting firm Interbrand, the list of Chinese "serious global players" with recognizable brands, along with Lenovo and Haier, includes the Tsingtao brewery; the state-owned car maker, Chery; and a private telecom equipment maker Huawei. "Contenders," likely to succeed in the near future, along with TCL, are the search engine Baidu, telecom equipment producer ZTE, car makers Geely and Brilliance Auto, and microwave oven and air-conditioner producer Midea (Roberts 2007). Though there have already been some modest achievements, in the short and medium terms the change of China's position and image as, mostly, a supplier of cheap, low-end products for the mass consumer market is unlikely.

Foreign Trade

Since 2002, the annual growth of China's foreign trade turnover has exceeded 20 percent. Its volume of trade is the third largest in the world after Germany and the US.

The Composition of Exports

In 2006, manufactured goods comprised almost 95 percent of total exports. The share of machinery and equipment (including electrical, nonelectric, and transportation machinery) was 47.1 percent. The next most important group of exported products, in terms of volume, is miscellaneous goods (24.6 percent). Other major items include textiles, apparel, steel, chemicals, and rubber products. Basically, China exports almost a full range of manufactured goods.

Exports to Asia comprised 47 percent (Hong Kong 16 percent, Japan 9.5 percent, ASEAN 7.4 percent, and South Korea 4.6 percent), the US 21.0 percent, and the European Union (EU) 18.8 percent.

Foreign-affiliated companies are the major exporters—their share was 58.2 percent. The share of SOEs was 19.7 percent. For the first time they were outperformed by domestic private companies whose share reached 22.1 percent (Institute of Chinese Affairs 2006, 167).

Exports of manufactured products are divided into general exports and exports of processed goods. The former refer to goods which are, so to say, Chinese-made in the true meaning of the word—a substantial part of their value is created inside the country. The latter includes items whose value is created mostly overseas, while Chinese factories are responsible only for a few, mostly final, phases of the production process. Typical examples are electronic products or cars assembled in China from parts delivered from overseas or clothing items designed abroad and made from imported fabrics.

Processing exports are prevailing. In 2006, they comprised 52.7 percent of the total as opposed to 43.0 percent for general exports (JETRO 2007, 159). This means that in the world economy China is still playing the role of an export-processing base for foreign companies rather than of a full-scale producer of internationally competitive products.

In 2006, China's exports of auto vehicles increased by an impressive 30.2 percent and reached 302,000 units—190,000 commercial vehicles and 112,000 passenger cars (Institute of Chinese Affairs 2006, 147). Generally, cars made by domestic companies still don't meet the safety and emission requirements, as well as the quality standards, of developed countries and are exported to the emerging-market states of the Middle East, North Africa, and also Russia. However, cars produced by the joint venture of Honda in Guangzhou are sold in Western Europe.

The Composition of Imports

Manufactured goods accounted for 76.4 percent and primary products for 26.7 percent of the imports total. Due to rising prices for oil, and other natural resources, imports of primary products were expanding faster. Overall, in 2006, machinery and equipment comprised 45.1 percent of the total, petroleum and other energy resources 11.2 percent, chemical products 11.0 percent, and textiles and rubber products also 11.0 percent (Institute of Chinese Affairs 2006, 167).

China is interesting to exporters of practically all manufactured and primary products. Today, it is attracting a lot of attention as a major market for electronic and auto parts as well as various kinds of materials.

The Trade Balance

China's trade surplus is visibly expanding. In 2007, it was 2.7 times larger than that of Japan—the figures were US$262,196 million and US$95,830 million, respectively (ADB 2008). The surplus in trade with the US (US$133,322 million in 2007) is a big political issue. The American side is concerned about the impact on domestic industries, insists that yuan is undervalued, and often raises the issue of China's unfair trade practices.

In trade with the EU it reached US$91,664 million. China became the biggest exporter to its member countries, overtaking the US and putting a number of their industries under very strong competitive pressure. For instance, it commands 40–50 percent of the EU leather shoes market (IDE-JETRO 2007, 134).

However, in its trade with all major East Asian countries, except Singapore, China was in deficit to the tune of about US$70 billion—and this is the usual state of things. In other words, in East Asia, a rapidly growing China creates markets rather than "conquers" them.

The Exchange Rate of the Yuan

As China's overall trade surpluses mount, the US, the EU, and Japan don't hesitate to mention that the yuan is undervalued and that the pace of its appreciation is too slow. China agrees that the exchange rate has to go up but maintains a slow pace to mitigate the negative impact on exporters. Appreciation of the yuan started in July 2005. In May 2006, it passed the 8 yuan for US$1 mark, and, in February 2008, the rate exceeded 7.74 yuan for US$1, or the value of the Hong Kong dollar.

Also, since July 2005, it has been pegged not to the US dollar, but to a basket of major currencies. Chinese authorities have shifted from the direct fixing of the exchange rate to regulating it through market intervention.

Currency control was significantly eased in 2006. Restrictions on foreign currency-denominated current bank accounts for domestic companies were lifted.

Unfair Trade Practices

The yuan exchange-rate policy is not the only target for criticism from China's trading counterparts. The country is often denounced for unfair trade practices because of its inadequate labor standards and working environment. The argument goes like this—Chinese-made products are cost-competitive not least because many people there have to work under conditions that are too harsh, for hours that are too long, and for pay that is too low. Furthermore, some exported goods are made by prison laborers. The above-mentioned new Labor Contract Law was enacted, in part, to address this kind of critique.

Changes in Trade Policy

The policy of a partial value-added tax refund for exporters, one of the major export promotion tools, has been fundamentally reconsidered. From 2006, the government reduced the refund rate for such major export items as steel, non-ferrous metals, cement, plastics, textiles, furniture, wood, and leather products (for many items it was increased again in 2008 to mitigate the blows of the global financial turmoil). However, refund rates were raised for various types of machinery and equipment, some technologically advanced products, and also for processed food. Presumably, the government is trying not only to address the issue of "excessive trade surplus" but also to promote the upgrading of the export structure.

Safety Troubles

Periodically, scandals emerge due to the poor quality of some Chinese-made products and, especially, their failure to meet basic safety requirements. The list of the most recent examples includes poisonous dumplings and pet food, tainted dairy products, unsafe toys containing too much lead, meat and fish products or toothpaste violating basic sanitary norms, and dairy products, beans, and eggs contaminated by the industrial chemical melamine.

Interestingly, in today's world, with China as a world factory, selling non-Chinese goods or not selling Chinese-made ones may work well as a differentiation strategy for a company, especially in the retailing business.

FDI and the Business Environment

Volume and Composition

China is one of the leading recipients of inward FDI in the world (in 2006, the fourth largest after the US, UK, and France). The volumes are shown in Table 7.3.

Since 2004, the pace of FDI growth has begun to slow down. Growing labor and land-use costs, a decrease in value-added tax refunds for many exported products, and the appreciation of the yuan, have worked as inhibitors. Another reason is that FDI in leading manufacturing industries, especially autos and electronics, has passed its cyclical peak as many foreign companies finished a round of production transfer. Having strengthened their engagement with China, they often come to think about diversifying investment. However, in 2007, the increase significantly accelerated again.

The largest amount of FDI came from Hong Kong (32.1 percent of the total in 2006), the UK Virgin Islands (17.9 percent), Japan (7.3 percent), South Korea (6.2 percent), the US (4.6 percent), Singapore (3.6 percent), Taiwan (3.4 percent), the Cayman Islands (3.3 percent), and Germany (3.2 percent). Investment from the UK Virgin Islands and the Cayman Islands, the world's major "tax havens," is made by investors of various national origins.

As far as the targets for FDI are concerned, the share of fully owned foreign subsidiaries is increasing (73.4 percent of the total volume of FDI in 2006), while that of joint ventures and other partnerships with local counterparts is falling.

FDI in manufacturing comprised 57.7 percent of the total. In tertiary industries, the major recipients were the real-estate sector (11.8 percent of the total),

Table 7.3   The amount of inward FDI (US$ millions)*

1996	1997	1998	1999	2000	2001	2002	2003	2004	2005	2006	2007
41,726	45,257	45,463	40,319	40,715	46,878	52,743	53,505	60,630	60,325	63,021	74,800

Source: National Bureau of Statistics.
*Investment by financial institutions is not included.

banking and finance (9.7 percent), leasing and business services (6.1 percent), and transport and telecommunication (2.9 percent) (Institute of Chinese Affairs 2006, 174).

Steps to Improve Conditions for Investors

China's advantages as a place to invest, besides an abundant, diligent, and cheap (though today not as cheap as it used to be) labor force, include a large and rapidly expanding domestic market, economic and political stability, and comparatively good infrastructure.

After joining the WTO, the government opened a number of sectors previously closed to foreign capital such as wholesale and retail trade, banking, brokerage, and insurance. From December 2006, foreign banks were allowed to operate on the same terms as domestic ones (in other words, without any limitations on yuan transactions with local residents) on condition their subsidiaries are registered as local legal persons, not branches.

Tax Incentives

While, until 2008, the headline corporate tax rate in China was 33 percent, foreign-invested companies in the SEZs and EDTZs only had to pay 15 percent. Furthermore, companies were exempt from the tax for two years after they started making profits. Then, for three years, they got a 50 percent reduction. After that it was still possible to get breaks which would keep the rate at just 10 percent. Foreign-invested enterprises, listed in the state-encouraged industrial catalog and established in the central or western regions, or enterprises advanced in technology, got an additional three-year exemption of a halved income. In the ETDZs, and also in the 52 high-tech development zones, companies engaged in manufacturing, and operating in China for ten years or more, enjoyed similar privileges.

In 2007, the government launched a tax reform, which basically eliminated the preferential treatment for foreign-invested companies. It is presented as a step to create a level playing field in accordance with WTO obligations. From 2008, for most companies (both domestic and foreign-owned), a unified 25 percent corporate tax rate has been set, with lower taxation for high-tech industries. For foreign-affiliated companies already operating in China, within a five-year transitional period tax rates will be raised step by step. The companies which had to pay 15 percent, are to be taxed at 18 percent in 2008, 20 percent in 2009, 22 percent in 2010, 24 percent in 2011, and, finally, 25 percent in 2012 (Institute of Chinese Affairs, 2008, 212).

Specifics and Problems

Of course, business people working in China have to know many specifics and tackle a lot of problems. Rules and regulations may change very fast and without a proper prior notice. It is advisable to check in advance whether rights and privileges you are entitled to by law will apply in your particular case. Much may depend on the discretionary judgment of the person in charge, especially in a provincial or municipal administration. Corruption remains a widespread phenomenon.

Sometimes your property may not be properly protected. There have been instances of the assets of foreign investors being usurped by the Chinese side with the backing of the local administration. The mentality of the hosts may also be rather peculiar. For instance, bureaucrats and business counterparts often make you feel that, as they represent a great nation, letting you do business there is a big favor on their part.

One of the biggest problems of China's business environment is the inadequate protection of intellectual property rights (IPR). The notion of IPR itself is not quite in agreement with the traditional culture and mentality. People in China are said to be accustomed to sharing ideas and it is very difficult for them to accept that they have to pay for a trademark, a copyright, or a technology. No other country produces as many fake products and has such a large pirated-goods market. Their production provides jobs for tens of millions of people and involves significant vested interests. China's law leaves certain loopholes for producers or sellers of pirated and counterfeit products.

One more important point to keep in mind is land ownership. In China, all land belongs to the state. A company can rent it from the government—as a rule for 50 years. The rent agreement usually includes clauses allowing for certain rent increases within established time intervals.

A Change in Policy Concept

The middle of the 2000s marked a fundamental change in the concept of government policy toward inward FDI. Emphasis is put not on the quantity but on the quality of the investment. Now, investments contributing to a rise in energy efficiency and preservation of the natural environment, the upgrading of production, the modernization of traditional industries such as textiles and clothing, the development of high-tech sectors, and an up-to-date service industry are attached priority. However, the government intends to severely restrain FDI in low-tech sectors—polluting factories and industries consuming a lot of energy. FDI in such sectors as real estate or the production of steel, cement, and aluminum was also restricted as part of a deflationary macroeconomic policy. In these sectors it is extremely difficult to get authorization for an investment project.

Attitude to Foreign Acquisitions

The prospect of a significant rise in the number of acquisitions of large domestic firms by foreign companies and institutional investors has become a matter of grave concern, especially after the US private equity fund, Carlyle Group, moved to acquire Xugong Construction (an arm of the Xugong Group)—the leading producer of construction machinery, controlling more than half of the domestic market for cranes and road-paving equipment. The group decided to unload the company because of growing competition in the construction machinery sector. In October 2005, it was agreed that Carlyle would get 85 percent of the total amount of stock for US$375 million. However, having studied the details, the Chinese government found it unacceptable. There was opposition in the business community too. Xugong's competitor, Sany Corporation, proposed to purchase the company for a 30 percent higher price. Notably, however, Xugong Group replied that it would prefer a foreign acquirer. The deal was renegotiated twice, and, in 2007, Carlyle agreed to reduce its share to 45 percent. The 55 percent majority stake went to Xuzhou Construction Machinery Group (XCMC), owned by the Xuzhou city government (Chung 2007).

In September 2006, the government moved to tighten the regulations on acquisitions by foreigners. Now, the acquirer has to get an approval from the central authorities if the company targeted belongs to a priority industry (promoted through the industrial policy), possesses an important brand, or if national security matters are involved.

Outward FDI

China's outward FDI is on the rise. In 2006, it exceeded US$16 billion. As many as 16,730 Chinese companies made direct investment in 163 countries and territories around the world (JETRO 2007, 162). Today's China is the thirteenth-largest outward direct investor.

Most of the outward FDI goes to tax havens and Hong Kong. In 2005, the share of the Cayman Islands was 42.1 percent, Hong Kong 27.9 percent, and the UK Virgin Islands 10.0 percent. Among other recipients South Korea is taking the lead (4.8 percent), followed by the US (1.9 percent), Russia (1.7 percent), Australia (1.6 percent), and Germany (1.0 percent) (JETRO 2007, 166).

Africa is also considered an important destination. China has come up with a new strategy: along with FDI into natural resources, it promotes direct investment into the infrastructure of the recipient countries and the development of their local industries. Mutual benefit is a key phrase—China gets access to the region's natural resources, while contributing to its economic development and a rise in living standards.

In a new development, the government has started to promote the construction of Chinese industrial zones in developing countries. For this purpose it allocates budget funds, though the companies themselves, both Chinese and local, are expected to provide the major part of the financing.

Concluding Remarks

China has established itself as one of the world's leading economic powers. It has become Asia's largest trading nation—both as exporter and importer. Its GDP, calculated on the PPP basis, is also the largest in the region. It attracts more foreign capital than any other Asian country and is becoming an important outward investor. Its trade surplus and foreign currency reserves are the largest in the world. It leads, in terms of volumes, in the production of many manufacturing and agricultural goods.

As a new regional, and also global, economic leader China has a number of important distinctive features. It is providing a critical mass of cheap products for everyday use all around Asia and the globe. Wherever we live, our life today is unthinkable without goods made in China. Even if China loses its cost advantages in relation to Indonesia, the Philippines, or even Thailand—as it is already beginning to do—it will still remain world factory number one merely due to its size.

However, a brand new story has started—labor, fuel, raw materials, and other costs, in today's China, are noticeably increasing. Food prices, from mid-2007 till late 2008 behaved like crazy, amplifying inflationary pressures.

As "world factory number one," for the time being, China as a whole can "afford" rising costs without losing world market share, though for particular domestic companies the game is tough. Chinese mass-produced goods will remain relatively cheap but not as cheap as they used to be. Gone are the days when China's emergence as the world's factory was bringing down prices worldwide. Now it is starting to push them up, "contributing" to global inflation.

It may seem that, having no competitors of a comparable size, China can comfortably stay in the low-cost and low-value-added products segment. However, it is not so. The challenge comes from within China itself. Hyperexpansion of low-end manufacturing critically exacerbates environmental, energy, and natural resource problems.

China's impressive achievements in space development, where it has become the first and, at this point, the only country after the pioneers, the US and Russia, to successfully achieve manned spaceflight, show that it is already capable of joining the world leaders in particular high-tech sectors.

Yet, at this point, upgrading of the economy as a whole is slow. Today's China is among the leaders in terms of the volume of industrial production, scale of foreign trade, size of the domestic market, and financial might, but, unlike the economies which emerged as new world leaders in the past, it is not the frontrunner in the fields of technology and product development. This latter fact weakens China's competitive pressure in global markets and opens significant business opportunities for other players. Its economic rise is creating markets for companies from various parts of the world and, especially, from the neighboring East Asian states, most of all for producers of high-end capital and consumer goods from machinery, equipment, and electronic parts to cosmetics and furniture.

However, as East Asia's growth today is largely China-led, regional economies are becoming China's "hostages." The more they depend on their Chinese links, the heavier will be the blow they suffer if the Chinese economy goes wrong.

China's ability to preserve social and political stability in the medium and long term is an especially thorny issue. As it seeks to combine the Communist Party's political dominance with the market, or capitalist (irrespective of all the "socialist market economy" rhetoric) economic system, it has to address two different kinds of social conflicts at one and the same time.

The first one is the "classic" capitalist conflict between the haves and have-nots. While the upper and middle class are expanding and their living standards are rising fast, hundreds of millions of Chinese are still struggling to earn the minimum necessary to satisfy their basic needs.

The second one, by contrast, is the conflict between the party and state elite on the one hand and the people it rules on the other.

In a society with no civilian control, and without a system of checks and balances, the ruling elite often thinks and acts with disdain and disrespect for the ordinary population.

More often than not the ruling elite and big business collude. Political bosses, especially at the provincial and local level, maintain close ties with such businesses as construction firms, property developers, and large manufacturers. For example, when a new chemical factory is built where local rulers have a stake neither businessmen nor authorities think too much about how it will influence agriculture in the surrounding areas and don't hesitate to seize the land that farmers are cultivating. Similarly, when a property development project is launched, the houses of the poor may be easily demolished if they stand in the way.

According to state media reports, from September 15, 2007, to January 15, 2008, the Chinese authorities uncovered 31,700 cases of illegal land grabs. Illegally seized land amounted 224,000 hectares. Local authorities and businessmen colluded to make way for lucrative development, kicking people out of their homes or off their land for little or no compensation. According to Xinhua, in 2007, the amount of illegally grabbed land was 68 percent more than in 2006. The Ministry of Public Security reports that in 2005 there were 87,000 protests across the country (50 percent more than a year earlier), many of them over land grabs (*Sino Daily* 2008).

As the two conflicts overlap and amplify one another, as hundreds of millions of people remain poor, as pollution threatens the very basis of the living environment, the scenario of a simultaneous escalation of massive riots in many regions, driving the country into widespread political turmoil and paralyzing economic activity, does not look improbable.

It is often argued that, as an economy develops, pressures to change a dictatorial regime or a system based on one-party rule grow, because a more affluent society requires more freedom and pluralism. For some East Asian countries and territories this is true. South Korea and Taiwan have made a genuine shift to parliamentary democracy. Indonesia has stepped out along the same road. However, a different pattern also exists. We can call it quasi-democracy (or quasi-dictatorship). It is a system which is formally democratic and pluralistic, but where in reality just one party, or political force, has a monopoly on power, while the activities of the opposition are constrained in various ways. This pattern, though deplorable from the viewpoint of those who care about real democracy, may not be detrimental for economic growth. Presumably, China can also evolve in this direction. (Today, along with the CPC, eight other political parties exist, though they are small and fully recognize Communist rule.)

However, to preserve its power in any form, the Communist regime has to be able to restrain power abuse in its own name. If it fails, the consequences may be fatal. The experiences of the Soviet Union and Eastern Europe, in the late 1980s–early 1990s provide a good example of where the conflict between the "almighty" Communist ruling elite and the people can go.

Today, the Chinese leadership does not show enough ability to curb power abuse by those who represent it in the provinces, cities, wards, towns, and villages, though it says that it wants to do it. Paradoxically, China's problem may not be that the power of the Communist leaders in Beijing is too strong, but that it is too weak.

Endnote

1 The idea of the "Green GDP" concept was simple: deduct the calculated damage to the environment and people's health from the real GDP growth rate—for instance, in 2005 real GDP grew by 10 percent but the damage was assessed at around 3 percent of GDP, so the adjusted GDP growth was 7 percent.

8

Hong Kong: Ten Years with China

A Few Basics

Hong Kong is strategically located in the very center of East Asia. It is one of the most densely populated places in the world—6.9 million people in 2006 (see Figure 8.1) living on about 420 square miles.

The territory has always been looked upon as the model of freewheeling capitalism due to minimal government involvement in business activities, low taxes, free trade-oriented policies, and zero customs duties.

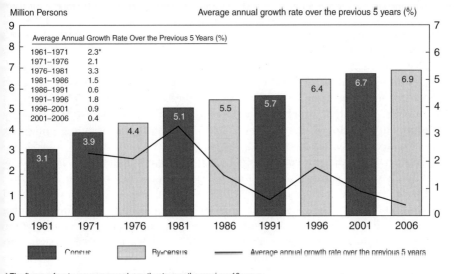

* The figure refers to average annual growth rate over the previous 10 years.

Figure 8.1   Population and average annual growth rate of Hong Kong, 1961–2006

Source: "2006 Population by Census—Graphic Guide," Department of Census and Statistics, The Government of Hong Kong SAR, 2007.

Of course, the "positive noninterventionism" stance does not mean that the authorities always stay aloof. They have launched large-scale public housing programs, extended student loans, and provided export credit insurance, among other things. The government also regulates economic activities in public utilities, transport, banking, and finance. However, Hong Kong's policy is to keep the public sector small and governmental interference minimal. In 2006, government spending equated to only 17 percent of gross domestic product (GDP), far below the 40 percent average of the Organization for Economic Co-operation and Development (OECD) countries (*The Economist* 2007).

As a territory, Hong Kong is not ranked in the International Monetary Fund (IMF) list of countries by size of GDP and per-capita GDP. If it were included in the ranking, it would be the 37th largest economy in the world. As for per-capita GDP (purchasing power parity (PPP)), it is only slightly lower than in the US, higher than in all the other G7 countries, and the second highest in East Asia after Brunei.

Today's Hong Kong is a diversified service economy. The leading sectors are foreign trade, banking and finance, transportation and logistics, telecommunications, hotels, catering and tourism, consulting, and other business services. The role of manufacturing has been rapidly declining with the relocation of production sites to mainland China. Its share of GDP in 2006 was only 3.2 percent, while 91.2 percent was accounted for by services. There is virtually no agriculture and no natural resources.

As of June 2008, foreign and domestic trade, catering, and hotels provided 43.0 percent of total employment; finance, insurance, real estate, and business services 21.3 percent; community, social, and personal services 19.4 percent; transport, storage, and communications 7.9 percent; and manufacturing 6.1 percent (Census and Statistics Department 2008a).

Hong Kong is home to a number of large, internationally known conglomerates and companies. A good example is Cheung Kong Group. One of Asia's most famous entrepreneurs, Li Ka Shing, is the chairman of its core company, Hutchison Whampoa, which is perennially on the Fortune 500 list. It is strongly positioned in seaport management, telecommunications, retailing, property development, and infrastructure.

Another large and powerful conglomerate is Hopewell Holdings, founded by Gordon Wu and active in a wide range of businesses, including infrastructure, property, hotels, catering, and construction. Li & Fung is a well-known global trading company managing supply chains for high-volume and time-sensitive consumer goods. VTech is an important contract manufacturer of electronic products. Varitronic Systems produces original, visual-learning tools designed to help teachers, students, administrators, and others.

Hong Kong's major economic agencies are the Commerce and Economic Development Bureau, the Financial Services and Treasury Bureau, the Labor and Welfare Bureau, and the Hong Kong Monetary Authority (the central bank).

The currency, the Hong Kong dollar, is pegged to the US dollar.

An Historical Perspective

Under British Rule

The British unofficial occupation of Hong Kong and Canton (now Guangzhou) began in the seventeenth century. In the nineteenth century, the territory was formally ceded to the United Kingdom. The island of Hong Kong became a British colony in 1843, and the peninsula of Kowloon, another major part of the territory—in 1860. Hong Kong was deeply involved in commerce activities within the British Empire as part of the colonial network of ports, which expanded rapidly during the nineteenth century. It was also strategically important as the British military and naval base in the Far East. Economically, it developed mainly as the center of intermediary trade between China and the rest of the world.

During the Cold War the territory flourished as a free port. Following the establishment of the People's Republic of China (PRC) in 1949, the Chinese authorities strongly opposed the notion of an independent Hong Kong. Relations between the Communist regime and the British government were very tense. The border with China was sealed in 1950.

In 1972, China joined the United Nations and reasserted its claim to Hong Kong as part of its territory. Sino-British negotiations ensued and the Joint Declaration, signed in 1984 and ratified in June 1985, agreed the handover of sovereignty, from the UK to China on July 1, 1997. The declaration also provided Hong Kong with the status of a Special Administrative Region (SAR) within the PRC.

Special Administrative Region (SAR)

Hong Kong has never been an independent entity. Its decolonization was not a preparation for independence but a reintegration within another sovereign state. Until recently, there were no moves to hold free elections or establish a system of self-government. The constitution of Hong Kong—the document known as "The Basic Law"—was adopted by the PRC at the 7th National People's Congress in 1990. It guarantees the maintenance of the existing system for at least 50 years. Under the Basic Law, Hong Kong has maintained a large degree of autonomy from the PRC—it has its own currency and border control with the mainland is retained. The only areas where the PRC is completely in charge are those of defense and foreign policy.

Before the democratic reforms of the mid-1980s, Hong Kong was an "administrative state" (Common 2001). Its governors were British senior civil servants. (Only the last one, Chris Patten, was a politician.) Bureaucracy was the repository of centralized state power with no demarcation between politics and administration. Since 1997, the SAR government has remained the dominant political institution. The scope for political participation is relatively limited.

In March 2007, almost ten years after reintegration, the candidate supported by the PRC, Donald Tsang (formerly Hong Kong's senior civil servant), was easily re-elected for the post of chief executive by the 800 members of the Election Committee. The latter represent "functional constituencies," that is, professional, commercial, and other interest groups. His re-election was followed by its approbation by the PRC.

So far, there is no accountable government checked and balanced by a representative legislature. The ultimate aim of direct, universal, suffrage-based election of both the Legislative Council (LegCo) and the chief executive, promised by the basic law, is still far away.

Still, far-reaching change has started. Until 1985, all LegCo members were appointed by the governor. In 1991, for the first time, 18 members out of the 60 were elected directly. In 2000, the number increased to 24, and, in 2004 and 2008, to 30 (the other 30 are elected by functional constituencies—professionals and businessmen). In 2007, the present chief executive, Donald Tsang, supported by the PRC, won by a landslide, but, unlike the previous elections of 2002 and 2005, there was a competitor who received the support of more than 100 members of the Election Committee (out of 800), which is the number required to participate in the contest.

Postwar Development

The defeat of the Kuomintang, in 1949, was a very significant development for Hong Kong. About one million Chinese fled to the territory from the mainland, including those with capital and expertise in manufacturing and other business. (About 50 percent of today's Hong Kong citizens are descendants of those post-1949 migrants.)

At the end of the 1970s, Deng Xiaoping's openness and development policy served as a catalyst for another major transformation of the Hong Kong economy. Local entrepreneurs were quick to seize the opportunities for trade and investment brought about by China's reforms and started to build a vast manufacturing empire in the Pearl River Delta. It was a reverse transformation—production sites were relocated to the mainland, while Hong Kong started to evolve into a diversified service economy.

The strengths of Hong Kong's manufacturing and trading companies are speedy market development and flexibility. Without significant support from the state they entered the right market niches at the right time. Coming out with new designs or product configurations, Hong Kong's producers of electronics, toys, garments, and watches were targeting niche markets that are time sensitive and influenced by fashion cycles. They were able to shift production at a high speed in order to succeed.

Present Performance

Three Crises

Though the territory was not hit by the Asian crisis as severely as South Korea and the ASEAN 4, speculative pressure on the HK dollar posed a big problem. Also, when regional demand collapsed, Hong Kong fell into a recession.

Unemployment dramatically increased. In 1999–2000, the economy rebounded, reaching a 10 percent growth rate.

However, at the beginning of the 2000s another crisis came with the burst of the speculative asset (especially real estate) bubble. In 2001, the growth rate was only 0.5 percent.

The third crisis was caused by the SARS outbreak in 2003. At its lowest point, traffic at Hong Kong International Airport dropped by 70 percent. The number of foreign visitors abruptly declined, and Hong Kong citizens themselves were restraining their outdoor activities in order to avoid contamination. All this exerted negative influence on a wide range of service industries.

From 1998 until 2004, the Hong Kong economy was in deflation (see Table 8.1).

The Acceleration of Growth

To stimulate economic activities in the territory, the PRC authorities took two important steps. First, the newly established Individual Visitor Scheme (IVS) allowed Chinese citizens to obtain individual visas, valid for seven days, to sojourn in Hong Kong. (Previously visas were issued only for businessmen and tourist groups.) As a result, in the first four months after its enactment, about 450,000 Chinese tourists entered Hong Kong, strongly contributing to the recovery of local businesses (Census and Statistics Department 2006).

Table 8.1   Main economic indicators (real annual growth, %)[*]

Indicator	1999	2000	2001	2002	2003	2004	2005	2006	2007
GDP	2.6	8.0	0.5	1.8	3.0	8.5	7.1	7.0	6.4
Industry[**]	n/a	n/a	−4.1	−3.7	−4.9	−2.0	−1.1	−2.0	−0.8
Services[**]	n/a	n/a	1.7	2.7	4.3	9.9	7.5	7.1	7.5
Private consumption	1.2	5.1	1.8	−0.9	−1.3	7.0	3.0	6.0	7.8
Gross domestic capital formation	−16.0	16.3	−2.8	−1.6	1.9	1.7	−0.1	8.3	9.8
Consumer prices	−4.0	−3.8	−1.6	−3.1	−2.5	−0.4	0.9	2.1	2.0
Average wage	−0.3	1.4	1.9	−1.1	−1.8	−0.6	3.5	2.4	3.9
Unemployment rate (%)	6.2	4.9	5.1	7.3	7.9	6.8	5.6	4.8	4.0
Exports (HK$ billions), fob	1,349	1,573	1,481	1,561	1,742	2,019	2,250	2,461	2,688
Imports (HK$ billions), cif	1,393	1,658	1,568	1,619	1,806	2,111	2,329	2,600	2,868
Average exchange rate (HK$ per US$1)	7.76	7.79	7.80	7.80	7.79	7.79	7.78	7.77	7.78

Source: ADB; Key Indicators 2008; World Bank Country Indicators; Census and Statistics Department, Government of Hong Kong SAR, Web Portal.
[*]Calendar year (fiscal year in Hong Kong begins April 1)
[**]Data for industry and services refers to value added.

The second step was the signing of a free trade agreement (FTA) between Hong Kong and the PRC, called the Closer Economic Partnership Agreement (CEPA). It gave Hong Kong companies privileged access to the Chinese market in 44 cities encompassing a total population of 200 million. According to estimates, by February 2006, it had helped to create 29,000 jobs.

After 2004, a wave of high growth began, boosted mostly by private consumption and robust exports. This was led by services, especially finance, and domestic and foreign trade.

In 2007, growth slowed down a little, while inflationary pressures caused by rising oil and food prices, as well as the HK dollar depreciation against the yuan (making imports from China more expensive), increased. In 2008, in the wake of the global financial turmoil the economy slid into recession. On an annual basis, GDP fell by 1.4 percent in the second quarter and by 0.5 percent in the third quarter. The slump continues into early 2009. From January to October 2008, the benchmark Hang Seng stock index dropped by 58 percent. Exporters suffered a blow, consumers became more cautious, and the unemployment rate began to climb after hitting a decade low in September. In October–December it was 4.1 percent.

Steps were taken to restore confidence and stimulate growth. The government guaranteed all the bank deposits, while the Hong Kong Monetary Authority reduced its base rate to a half-century low of 1.5 perccent and promised to inject liquidity into the market whenever necessary. It also accelerated the implementation of infrastructure projects to create jobs. To find ways to fight the credit crisis a special task force was formed, with Chief Executive Donald Tsang as its head.

Closer Integration with the Mainland

In the 2006–10 Five-Year Economic Plan the Chinese government, for the first time, articulated the policy of actively using Hong Kong's strength in finance and distribution to boost economic development in the mainland. Hong Kong's banks were the first place outside the mainland to offer financial services in renminbi.

Capital overlap at the corporate level is also increasing. For example, in 2006, Swire, one of the oldest Hong Kong businesses, acquired 100 percent of China's airline company Dragonair and doubled its share in Air China from 10 percent to 20 percent. On the other hand, it reduced its share in Cathay Pacific, while Air China acquired 17.5 percent of its stock (*The Economist* 2007).

Independent-minded Hong Kong citizens are concerned that growing economic integration may erode the "one country-two systems" framework. After the reversion of the British crown colony to Chinese sovereignty and control many Hong Kong residents migrated to Canada, Australia, and elsewhere. Later, attracted by business opportunities and feeling secure with the Western countries' passports they had obtained, they began to come back. Since 1997, the expatriate, especially British, population—both businessmen and former civil servants— has substantially declined. However, the mainland Chinese immigrant population has significantly increased. Hong Kong citizens are generally unhappy with this change as they consider themselves "Hong Kongese" and not "Chinese." Despite growing economic integration they want Hong Kong to retain its uniqueness, as a privileged place where the world and China meet together.

An important opportunity for Hong Kong is to leverage its role as the PRC's strategic partner and as an interface with the rest of the world. It can develop as China's platform for technology transfer and intellectual property rights (IPR) trading, as the mainland does not have a conceptual, legal, and management framework in this area.

A Weakening Role as Trade Intermediary

Such a shift is especially important because Hong Kong's traditional trade intermediary role is declining. Though, since 1996, the absolute volume of intermediary trade has doubled, today, it only intermediates 20 percent of China's trade as opposed to 60 percent in the 1980s (*The Economist* 2007). In 2006, Shanghai overtook Hong Kong in terms of the number of containers handled. Shenzhen may do too within a few years (*People's Daily* 2008).

Other developments are likely to further diminish the territory's role as a re-export hub. Today, Xiamen, Beijing, and Shanghai provide most of the air cargo flow for the PRC. Expanding direct links between these cities and the US, Europe, and Southeast Asia will mean a reduction in their trade through Hong Kong.

Though the Pearl River Delta remains one of the top manufacturing regions in the PRC—especially regarding goods transported by air (electronics, pharmaceuticals, perishables)—producers have started to relocate their factories to central and western China. For its part, the delta area is shifting its competitive advantage to trade and logistical support, becoming Hong Kong's direct competitor.

The Tourism Industry Under Pressure

Tourism is one of the pillars of the Hong Kong economy. With more than 25 million tourists a year the industry is booming. In 2006, it provided revenues of US$15.3 billion (Hong Kong Tourism Board 2007). The territory is one of the world's top ten tourist destinations, and the United Nations World Tourism Organization (UNWTO) predicts that by 2020 it will be in the top five. However, look deeper at the situation in the industry and you will find a lot of structural weaknesses. The number of tourists coming from China is rapidly rising, while the number of other tourists is rising at a much slower pace. Between 2003 and 2006, the average length of stay of a tourist decreased and so did the number of visitors coming for business purposes. Visitors' spending on per-capita overnight and per-diem, same-day purpose bases either remained flat or decreased. Expenditure on shopping and entertainment dropped (Hong Kong Tourism Board 2007).

One of the major reasons is growing competition from the mainland. For example, a joint venture between Shenzhen Sanguo (Three Kingdoms) Culture City Industrial Development and Canada-based Bedford International Financial Group is planning a US$3 billion theme park called China Today on Shenzhen's eastern shore, which is expected to open in 2010.

Weakness in R&D

Hong Kong's weak point is a relatively low capacity to create new knowledge and to develop high-value-added products and services. While Singapore, South Korea, and Taiwan are persistently promoting knowledge-intensive industries, Hong Kong is doing very little in this respect.

Phase I of the Cyberport project, Hong Kong's science park, was not inaugurated until 2004, long after South Korea, Taiwan, and leading Chinese cities. It is a US$2 billion information technology (IT) flagship scheme aimed at making Hong Kong the leading IT hub of the Asia-Pacific region. It won the Intelligent Building of the Year Award in 2004 and 2005, and has since developed into a 60-acre site hosting about 100 IT companies and two university programs (Fong 2008).

Hong Kong universities have first class researchers, but academia-business links are weak. The government's support of R&D is small-scale. In 2004, just 0.03 percent of GDP was spent on applied R&D and related activities by the Innovation and Technology Commission. The Applied Science and Technology Research Institute (ASTRI) was only established in 2001 (Baark 2006).

Overall, Hong Kong is spending no more on R&D than 0.6 percent of its GDP, while the standard for countries with similar per-capita GDP is 1.5–3 percent (Baark 2006).

A Cohort of Technology-Intensive Companies

The list of companies active in the IT sector is not long. Examples include Johnson Electric, VTech, Gold Peak, and Varitronix.

Several firms have succeeded in global markets with original, high-tech products. For example, OOCL, one of the world's largest container, transportation, logistics, and terminal companies, is a recognized global brand. In the early 1990s it developed an IT platform, the Cargosmart system, for managing its global container fleets, which significantly raised its global competitiveness. The system is one of the most advanced portal and integration providers for ocean containers in the transportation industry.

Structural Unemployment and Disneyland

While the knowledge economy lacks dynamism, to boost growth, the territory relies on such mass-volume/low-margin undertakings such as the Disneyland project, the second in Asia after Japan. The venture with Disney to form Hong Kong International Theme Parks Limited, in 1999, was a major departure for the Hong Kong authorities from their noninterventionist stance. Job creation was the main objective.

One-third of Hong Kong's workforce has an educational attainment of only lower secondary or below. For them focusing the territory's economy on core service industries, requiring high skills, resulted in job destruction. In this regard, the Disneyland scheme was important to curb structural unemployment.

Frustration

Despite rapid economic growth, many Hong Kong residents are ambivalent about their lives. They see increasing numbers of affluent Chinese tourists who clearly have much higher purchasing power than before, and often higher than their own. Many Hong Kong workers have not had a wage increase for the last ten years or so.

In terms of per-capita GDP, Hong Kong is one of the wealthiest places in the world but, for a very significant portion of its citizens, living conditions remain tough. Between 1991 and 2001, the Gini coefficient (measuring income gaps), already one of the highest in the developed world, was rising even further at a surprisingly high speed. Now, it stands at 43.4 (UNDP 2008).

Generally, a higher coefficient reflects the shift of the Hong Kong economy toward high-value-added industries and services. Unemployment, underemployment, and pay cuts were more common among low-income people than the higher income ones during the economic downturn at the beginning of the decade.

However, as the economy has rebounded since 2003, employment opportunities for lower skilled workers have expanded and the earnings of many low-income families, though not all of them, have also increased. Besides, it has to be taken into account that for the low-income households the government provides various services in education, healthcare, and housing.

Foreign Trade

Hong Kong is the world's tenth-largest exporter of services. In 2006, the total value of trade in goods and services, including re-exports, equaled 400 percent of the GDP (Census and Statistics Department 2008b).

The territory is the eleventh-largest international trade center and the thirteenth-largest banking center in the world. It is one of Asia's most important logistic hubs. It handles one of the world's largest volumes of airport cargo and has the third-largest container port.

The Composition of Exports

Hong Kong's exports are divided into domestic exports and re-exports. The latter prevail—the amounts, in 2007, were respectively HK$109.1 billion and HK$2,578.4 billion.

The main sectors for domestic exports are apparel and clothing accessories (35.7 percent); jewelry and precious and semi-precious materials (8.0 percent); and electrical machinery and parts (7.2 percent). The main destinations for domestic exports are mainland China (37.2 percent) and the US (21.9 percent). Other major export markets are the UK (5.3 percent), Taiwan (3.7 percent), and Singapore (2.7 percent).

For re-exports the share of mainland China is higher at 49.1 percent as opposed to 13.4 percent for the US and 4.5 percent for Japan.

Ties with the PRC have been reinforced by the CEPA. Exports to China are expanding faster than to any other country. Exports to Asian emerging markets such as India, Indonesia, Malaysia, Thailand, and Vietnam have also grown rapidly in the latter half of the 2000s, although their share remains low.

Hong Kong is also a big exporter of services—especially trading, transportation, travel, and finance.

The Composition of Imports

Merchandise imports are divided into retained imports and goods imported for re-export. In 2007, the amounts were HK$727.9 billion and HK$2,140.1 billion, respectively.

Imports from mainland China comprised 46.4 percent of the total, Japan 10.0 percent, Taiwan 7.2 percent, the European Union (EU) 7.1 percent. Singapore 6.8 percent, and the US 4.8 percent.

Out of all the imports 38.3 percent were accounted for by raw materials and semi-manufactures, 26.6 percent by consumer goods, and 24.4 percent by capital goods. The shares of fuel and foodstuffs were comparatively low—3.1 percent and 2.7 percent, respectively.

FDI and the Business Environment

Hong Kong is one of the most open economies in the world with a business friendly regulatory environment. Access to sophisticated business information is about the best in the region. Also, it has a very convenient location, adjacent to the most economically dynamic provinces of China and close to both Singapore and Tokyo.

It is a center for merger and acquisition (M&A) activities and hosts many investment companies. Thousands of multinational corporations (MNCs) have also chosen it as a location for their Asian regional headquarters. Hong Kong's advantages for such companies include financial expertise and a high level of investor protection through corporate governance.

Chinese companies began raising capital on Hong Kong's stock market in 1987 and this amounted to US$140 billion in the first ten years. The scale of initial public offerings (IPOs) increased in the second half of the 1990s. Largely due to this activity, in 2006, the Hong Kong Stock Exchange overtook New York, in terms of the value of IPOs (US$40 billion), and became the second largest in the world after London (Hong Kong Monetary Authority 2006).

Inward foreign direct investment (FDI) has been growing rapidly since 2005 (see Table 8.2).

Statistically, mainland China is by far the biggest direct investor in Hong Kong. In 2006, its share was 31.1 percent of the total. It was followed by the British Virgin Islands (22.5 percent), the US (14.7 percent), Netherlands (8.0 percent), Bermuda (6.8 percent), Japan (5.4 percent), and the UK (5.1 percent) (Census and Statistics Department 2008a).

Table 8.2   Inward and outward FDI (HK$billions)

Direction	2002	2003	2004	2005	2006
Inward	75.5	106.3	265.1	261.5	350.0
Outward	136.2	42.9	356.1	211.5	349.4

Source: Census and Statistics Department, Hong Kong.

However, the data on FDI from China may be quite deceptive. There is a lot of "round-tripping"—up until 2008, many Chinese companies invested in the mainland through Hong Kong entities to become eligible for tax incentives extended to foreign-owned firms.

Inward investment is highly concentrated in the leading service sectors. In 2007, investment holdings, real estate, and business services accounted for 41.5 percent of the total. The share of banks and other financial institutions was 25.2 percent; wholesale, retail, and the import/export trade 20.9 percent; transport and related services 5.7 percent; and manufacturing 3.1 percent.

As for outward FDI, in 2006, investment holdings, real estate, and business services accounted for 62.6 percent, banks and other financial institutions 17.7 percent, transport and related services 9.4 percent, and manufacturing 4.4 percent. The mainland absorbed 47.7 percent of the total. It was followed by the UK Virgin Islands (22.3 percent), Japan (9.9 percent), and India (8.9 percent) (Census and Statistics Department 2008a).

The Pearl River Delta region remains the major target. There, Hong Kong companies employ more than 11 million people and provide two-thirds of all FDI. In industries such as garments and electronics they actively transfer technologies and expertise.

At present, however, facing higher labor costs, environmental problems, and logistic bottlenecks, Hong Kong firms are moving more and more to the Chinese hinterland.

Concluding Remarks

Hong Kong remains one of the most vibrant global business locations in the world. Its companies are enhancing the quality, reliability, and inventiveness of business solutions in both low-technology sectors, such as textiles, garments, or watches, and high-value-added services. Despite high labor costs, many Hong Kong service companies remain competitive in the region and in the world.

However, Hong Kong is lagging behind its neighbors in the knowledge creation and development of more R&D-intensive products and services.

The risk of losing uniqueness and becoming "just another big Chinese city" is real. To address it, Hong Kong has to enhance its own technological capabilities, differentiating itself from rising Chinese firms in terms of the menu and quality of services and products.

9

Taiwan: A Center of Advanced Manufacturing

A Few Basics

In 1895, Taiwan (Formosa) was placed under Japanese colonial rule and it was not until 1945 that the island was returned to China. In 1927, civil war broke out on mainland China between the ruling Kuomintang (KMT) regime of Chiang Kai-shek and the Communists. In 1949, the KMT lost and the administration fled to Taiwan, continuing to claim that it was the only legitimate government of China.

Initially, the US and other major industrially developed countries maintained diplomatic relations with the Taiwanese administration, which also represented China at the United Nations (UN). However, in the early 1970s they started to normalize relations with mainland China and sever official diplomatic ties with Taipei, though preserving economic and other links, along with commitments to protect it in case of emergency. The seat at the UN was lost in 1971.

In terms of nominal gross domestic product (GDP), in 2007, Taiwan was ranked twenty-fourth on the International Monetary Fund (IMF) list. By per-capita GDP (purchasing power parity (PPP)) it was twenty-eighth—between Italy and Spain. The territory is one of the world's largest foreign exchange reserves holders—US$290 billion as of May 2008.

Taiwan has a developed economy with a wide range of heavy and light industries. The leading sectors are the production of PCs, semiconductors, and other electronic products, chemicals and the petrochemical industry, oil refining, and the production of steel, nonferrous metals, and metal products.

The agricultural sector is small, but Taiwan is known as a producer and exporter of tea, bananas, and a few other products.

In 2007, the share of agriculture as part of total employment was 5.3 percent, industry 27.6 percent, and other sectors, mostly services, 67.1 percent. Their shares in GDP were 1.5 percent, 28.3 percent, and 70.2 percent, respectively (ADB 2008).

Mineral resources are limited to small deposits of coal, natural gas, limestone, and marble.

Some Taiwanese companies, especially from the electronics and semiconductors sector have established very strong positions in the world market. Taiwan Semiconductor Manufacturing Company (TSMC) and United Microelectronics Corporation (UMC) are the largest wafer foundries (wafer fabrication companies) in the world. The PC maker, Acer, has built an internationally recognized brand and entered the list of the top five producers.

In Taiwan, large conglomerates play a much smaller role than in other East Asian economies. However, a cohort of powerful family-owned business empires exists and their activities are spread over heavy and light industries, as well as a variety of services. Leading groups, though, are more focused on core business areas than other Asian conglomerates. Probably the most widely known group is Formosa (Taiwan) Plastics. Its main business area is petrochemicals and plastics, but it also has a strong position in the fiber and textiles industry, electronic materials, machinery, and transportation sectors.

The major economic agencies in Taiwan are the Ministry of Economic Affairs and the Ministry of Finance.

Taiwan's national currency is New Taiwan Dollar (NTD). New dollars began to be issued in 1949 to curb high inflation.

Today's Taiwan is a parliamentary democracy. At present the ruling party is the KMT and its main opponent is the Democratic Progressive Party (DPP).

Postwar Development

The Beginnings

Taiwan's postwar development is one of Asia's most remarkable success stories. In 1958, its per-capita GNP was just US$130—less than in Myanmar (Watanabe 1995, 57).

In the colonial years, industry was under Japanese control while the Taiwanese were engaged mostly in agriculture. The only developed local industry was sugar-making. Factories built by the Japanese in such sectors as fertilizers, cement, textiles, paper, aluminum, steel, and petrochemicals suffered heavy damage during World War II.

On the positive side, the island's economy got a boost from large-scale migration from the mainland after the Communist takeover. Many immigrants were experienced entrepreneurs who brought with them their capital and expertise.

"Development Dictatorship"

In 1948, the so-called "Temporary Provisions Effective During the Period of Communist Rebellion" (essentially, a state of emergency) were introduced, suspending democratic freedoms and banning political opposition. After the KMT's arrival in 1949 these provisions effectively applied to Taiwan only. The island became a "development dictatorship."

In the Korean War years (1950–53) the territory was provided with large-scale aid from the US. A mutual defense treaty was signed in 1954.

From 1953, the administration worked out four-year economic plans, which were successfully realized. From the 1970s, they were changed to looser, six-year plans centered on public works.

Export-Led Growth

In the latter half of the 1950s, Taiwan shifted from import substitution to export promotion. A single exchange rate for the currency was introduced in 1960 and kept at a low level. High import tariffs were imposed to protect domestic industries but from the mid-1950s the government paid back up to half of the custom fees for raw materials used in the production of exported goods (Watanabe 1995, 60).

Export processing zones (EPZs) were established which allowed the import of equipment, materials, and raw materials duty free. They attracted many manufacturing companies, both domestic and foreign (especially Japanese).

Tax incentives, introduced in the early 1960s, included corporate tax exemptions for companies investing in particular industries and duty-free imports of important equipment. Japanese, US, and other foreign-affiliated companies became the leading players in the national economy.

In 1965, US aid was stopped. However, Japan extended large-scale yen loans. For several decades, the GDP annual growth rate exceeded 10 percent. Initially, growth was mostly led by textiles and other export-oriented, labor-intensive industries. In the mid-1970s, the territory's trade balance went into the black.

Corporate Structure

The administration nationalized financial institutions and companies owned by the Japanese in the colonial era (railways, electric power plants, oil, steel, and aluminum companies). In the 1950s, the nationalized sector provided about half the industrial production. For decades, state-owned companies dominated in the heavy industry and financial sectors. However, as export-led industrialization got under way, their role significantly declined—the major exporters were not state-owned, but private firms, largely small- and medium-sized enterprises (SMEs).

The Need For Upgrading

From the late 1960s, in the wake of rapid industrial growth, labor shortages emerged. Migration from the mainland stopped. The inflow of people from rural areas was too small to provide enough workers and upward pressure on wages increased.

The upgrading of exported products became an urgent task. In the 1950s, Taiwan's major exports were agricultural products such as sugarcane, tea, and bananas. At the initial stage of its export-oriented growth it also exported textiles, leather goods, and timber. From the second half of the 1960s, the territory became an exporter of electronic products as well, with foreign-affiliated companies taking the lead. In 1974, the government began a heavy industrialization policy with steel, shipbuilding, oil refining, and petrochemicals as the major targeted sectors. The move was largely driven by the desire to catch up with South Korea.

The administration of President Chiang Ching-kuo (term of office 1978–88) launched ten large construction projects—among them were the building of airports, highways, harbors, petroleum plants, iron works, and nuclear power stations.

In the 1980s, structural upgrading continued, resulting in the increasing presence of technology-intensive sectors in both production and exports. Taiwanese companies emerged as leaders in large-scale wafer fabrication.

By the mid-1980s, in terms of per-capita GDP, Taiwan was no longer a developing economy. On the negative side, during the second half of the decade an asset bubble emerged. Real estate prices soared, speculative transactions reached an unprecedented scale, and powerful mafia groups appeared.

Liberalization and Democratization

Between 1984 and 1989, foreign trade liberalization was carried out—the average import tariff was reduced from 30.9 percent to below 10 percent (Watanabe 1995, 67). The administration shifted to selective regulation of imports from countries which had a large surplus in trade with Taiwan, especially Japan.

In 1987, the Temporary Provisions, brought in by the KMT in 1948, were lifted. Opposition parties started to emerge, the mass media were allowed a free hand, and labor unions were legalized.

President Chiang appointed local Taiwanese to important public posts (previously occupied by officials born on the mainland) to boost popular support for his administration. After his death in 1988, the presidency went to Lee Teng-hui—the first Taiwan-born leader.

In the 1990s, the liberalization of foreign direct investment (FDI) in service industries began. Restrictions on outward FDI were also eased.

New Relations with China

Also, in the 1990s, controls on ties with the mainland were relaxed and large-scale trade and investment connections were established through third-party territories, especially Hong Kong. China became the second most important export market after the US.

However, in the middle of the decade cross-strait political tensions increased. In 1996, Lee Teng-hui became the first president to be elected by direct popular vote (before that the president was elected by the Legislative Yuan (national assembly)). China accused him of "splitting the motherland" and, several days before the elections, conducted a series of military exercises right in front of Taiwan. This disrupted trade and shipping and led to a temporary fall in stock prices. However, inside Taiwan support for Lee and his policies grew stronger.

The Effect of the Asian Crisis

The Taiwanese economy was not strongly affected by the Asian crisis, largely because banks were sticking to a conservative lending policy, and a highly competitive economic environment did not allow companies to forget about financial discipline. In 1998, the economy grew by 4.5 percent—down from 6.6 percent in 1997 (ADB 2008).

Still, from June 1997, the Central Bank of China (Taiwan's central bank) spent US$7 billion to maintain the NT$28.6 for US$1 exchange rate before freeing the currency in October. Between June 1997 and the first week of January 1998 it dropped by 19 percent (Chen 1998).

Structural Reforms

The dominance of state companies in a number of major, especially heavy, industries and the financial sector is a key feature of the postwar Taiwanese economy. The state inherited companies, owned by the Japanese during the colonial period, and also expanded into new fields. However, as the private sector developed and democratization progressed, the ruling elite recognized the need for a more liberal market economy with wider room for private initiative.

In 1989, the government submitted to the legislature a list of the first 22 companies and financial institutions to be privatized. As the plan met resistance from various interest groups, in 1996 the president proclaimed privatization a national priority. By 1998, fifteen companies in key sectors went private. Then, until 2005, nine banks were privatized and, at present, four state-owned banks remain, accounting for 16 percent of total bank assets (Heritage Foundation 2008). The privatization of the telecommunication company, Chunghwa, was also completed in 2005.

In the late 1980s, the government started to issue licenses for newly established insurance companies and since 1991, for private banks.

Present Performance

The Picture of Taiwan's Growth

The Taiwanese economy grew fast in 1999–2000, but in 2001 GDP fell, mainly because of the world information technology (IT) recession (see Table 9.1). An export-driven recovery started in 2002, but growth rates were relatively low by Asian standards. Private consumption is sluggish—largely because wages are rising at a slow pace. In 2001–2003, the economy was in deflation.

The Nonperforming Loans Problem and the Household Debt Crisis

The nonperforming loans (NPL) problem in Taiwan became a headache, not during the Asian crisis years, but at the beginning of the 2000s, largely because bank lending was biased toward the real-estate sector, while the latter entered a recession. Cleaning up bad loans became the first priority for the administration of President Chen Shui-bian, the leader of the Democratic Progressive

Table 9.1   Main economic indicators (real annual growth, %)

Indicator	1999	2000	2001	2002	2003	2004	2005	2006	2007
GDP	5.7	5.8	−2.2	4.6	3.5	6.2	4.2	4.9	5.7
Industry*	5.4	5.8	−7.5	7.3	4.0	8.9	6.3	7.0	9.2
Services*	6.1	5.8	0.6	3.4	3.3	4.9	3.7	4.1	4.5
Gross domestic capital formation	0.2	3.9	−22.2	3.2	4.0	24.7	−1.7	0.7	2.0
Private consumption	5.5	4.6	0.7	2.6	1.5	4.5	3.0	1.8	2.6
Consumer prices	0.2	1.3	−0.0	−0.2	−0.3	1.6	2.3	0.6	1.8
Unemployment rate (%)	2.9	3.0	4.6	5.2	5.0	4.4	4.1	3.9	3.9
Average earnings of employees in manufacturing	3.7	3.2	−1.3	−0.1	2.6	2.6	2.8	1.3	1.7
Exports (US$ billions), fob	123.7	152.0	126.3	135.3	150.6	182.4	198.4	224.0	246.7
Imports (US$ billions), cif	111.2	140.7	108.0	113.2	128.0	168.8	182.6	202.7	219.3
Average exchange rate (NT$ per US$1)	32.3	31.2	33.8	34.6	34.4	33.4	32.2	32.5	32.8

Source: ADB: Key Indicators 2008; Ministry of Economic Affairs; Chung Hua Institute for Economic Research, "Major Economic Indicators of Taiwan."
*Data for industry and services refers to value added.

Party (in office from 2000 to 2008). The NPL ratio dropped from its peak of 8.0 percent in the first quarter of 2001 to 3.8 percent in June 2004 (Huang 2004).

Another headache was a severe credit card and cash card crisis, which escalated in 2004–05. It hit both the financial sector and curtailed private consumption. As consumer loans were reaching unprecedented heights, overdue credit card debt in 2004 rose to NT$452 billion (about US$13.2 billion) and cash card debt to NT$193.5 billion (about US$5.6 billion) (Ridley 2004). A cash card is a new form of short-term loan targeting the subprime market. To capture market share at the early stage of the new business, large Taiwanese banks rushed to increase transactions without proper screening of borrowers.

The Collapse of a Conglomerate

In early 2007, a new shock came with the collapse of the Rebar conglomerate. It exposed weaknesses in the financial regulation system. Two of the group's companies—China Rebar (engaged in insurance, finance, broadband, and TV shopping businesses) and Chia Hsin Food and Synthetic Fiber—filed for bankruptcy. The founder, Wang You-theng, fled from the island. The government took over the group's financial institutions—the Chinese Bank and the Great Chinese Bills Finance Corporation—and guaranteed depositors' bank accounts (Yin 2007). To make things worse, simultaneously, it had to take over another ailing financial institution—the Enterprise Bank of Hualien.

However, in 2007, the economy grew by 5.7 percent, driven by robust exports. The growth of both private consumption and capital investment also accelerated.

The Impact of the Global Financial Turmoil

In the second half of 2008, the situation worsened under the blows of the global financial turmoil. In the third quarter (July–September), the economy contracted by 1.02 percent year-on-year, and by the end of the year, the situation worsened due to the unprecedented fall in exports (by 42 percent year-on-year in December). Since the third quarter private consumption also began to fall. In September, unemployment rose to a four-year high of 4.27 percent. High-tech manufacturers, airlines, and financial companies began to consider downsizing and salary cuts. In early 2009, the government unveiled a NT$320 billion (US$9.5 billion) plan to create jobs (Reuters 2009).

The major risk for Taiwan is that declining exports and unemployment are likely to further squeeze household incomes, making it difficult for many families to pay back their mortgages.

Yet, Taiwan's banks appeared to be largely "insulated" from the turmoil due to their still low degree of internationalization and tough government regulations (AFP 2008). (For instance, they are required to maintain their loan/deposit ratio at around 80 percent, as opposed to 400 percent in some European banks.) The losses of the domestic banking sector and its exposure to troubled Western financial institutions were marginal.

To boost the economy, the central bank cut reserve requirements and extended repurchase agreements[1] with financial institutions to provide ample liquidity. It also guaranteed all domestic deposits. The discount rate was cut six times, reaching just 1.5 percent in January 2009. In the same month, the government started to hand out shopping vouchers to each citizen, NT$3,600 (about US$107) worth per person. Spending on infrastructure was also increased.

Leadership in Electronics Manufacturing

One of the major sources of strength of the Taiwanese economy is a uniquely sharp competitive edge in contract electronic manufacturing. Taiwanese firms command key manufacturing technologies and are developing remarkable engineering capabilities. Taiwan is the largest manufacturer of such products as notebook PCs, routers, and cable modems. Quanta Computer is the top global maker of notebook PCs and a key supplier for Dell and Hewlett-Packard. ASUSTeK Computer produces i-Pods and Mac minis for Apple on a massive scale at its Chinese factories.

Taiwan is also a leader in the production of thin-film-transistor liquid crystal display (TFT-LCD) panels. Its largest manufacturer, AU Optronics, after merging with Quanta Display in 2006, became number one with a 20 percent share of the global market. Its panels are supplied to major LCD makers from Apple to Taiwan's BenQ Corporation.

Today, the island's electronics manufacturers are moving further up the value chain. Often they are commissioned to perform not only manufacturing, but also product design, thus upgrading their status from purely original equipment manufacturing (OEM) to, additionally, original design manufacturing (OEM/ODM) companies. Notably, in April 2007, Quanta announced a large-scale partnership with the Massachusetts Institute of Technology (MIT), including the development of a US$100 dollar PC for children (ARC Report Taiwan 2008, 68).

Brand Building

The next natural step and also great challenge for Taiwanese firms is the development of their own globally recognized brands. In 1990, the government adopted its first five-year plan to up the international image of Taiwan-made products through brand-building promotion. In December the same year, a system of special loans for brand builders was enacted. In the 1990s, they were extended to 67 firms (ARC Report Taiwan 2007, 112). Acer became the first Taiwanese company to shift from OEM to producing and selling under its own brand.

In 2001, Acer CM (initially Acer Peripherals)—its arm producing consumer electronics, computing, and communication devices (LCD monitors and TVs, digital projectors and cameras, computer keyboards, and smartphones)—spun-off, changed its name to BenQ and launched the BenQ brand. (The first three letters reflect the company's vision of "bringing enjoyment" to life.) Other companies followed. In other sectors, for instance, to sell its branded products, the leather footwear firm LaNew has opened the first store in Ginza in the very heart of Tokyo.

In 2005, the government adopted a new brand development plan which includes measures to raise brand consciousness, establish platforms for knowledge exchange, promote venture capital, create a guidance/consulting system for brand management, and provide human resources (ARC Report Taiwan 2007, 112).

In a new development, increasingly often overseas companies, commissioning production from Taiwanese makers, offer them their brands too, for purchase. The buying of prominent foreign brands is supported by government loans and credit guarantees.

Science Parks

Science parks are created and actively promoted by the government. The major science parks are Hsinchu, Central Taiwan, and Southern Taiwan. Their business is booming.

At the end of August 2007, the number of companies in these three science parks exceeded 600 and the number of workers had reached 185,000 (excluding foreign workers). Integrated circuit (IC) manufacturing is the largest industry in the parks, followed by opto-electronics.

Development Strategies

China's entry into the World Trade Organization (WTO), in 2001, caused a lot of concern in Taiwan—mainly because domestic businesses working with mainland China were apprehensive of rising competitive pressures. Taiwan itself became a WTO member in January 2002.

The government announced a development plan for 2002–07, the aim of which was to address new globalization challenges. Later it was integrated into the economic Development Vision for 2015, covered later in this section. The plan was called "Challenge 2008." The target was to maintain the average growth rate at 5 percent and unemployment at below 4 percent (both tasks were under-fulfilled). Also, the territory was challenged to produce at least 15 products or technologies that would be the best in the world.

The "two trillion and twin stars industry plan," the integral part of Challenge 2008, targeted semiconductor manufacturing and the production of flat-panel displays (FPDs), seeking to make them both NT$1 trillion (around US$30 billion) industries (JETRO 2007, 177). The digital content industry and biotechnology were designated as two "star industries" for the future (ARC Report Taiwan 2007, 106). The biotechnology promotion policy was largely centered on biotechnology-pharmaceuticals and biotechnology-electronic materials linkages in R&D and production.

The plan also targeted "new traditional industries," such high-tech spinning, health food, skincare products, high-end materials, chemicals for opto-electronics, light metals, and so on. Companies that had shifted their production to China and other places, but were willing to return to Taiwan, were promised low-interest loans of up to NT$200 billion and other incentives.

In 2006, the government announced the Development Vision for 2015, a three-stage development plan, and its first stage—the Three Year Sprint Program for 2007–09—consisted of five packages: industrial development, financial markets, industrial manpower, public construction, and social welfare. The core planning theme was "big investment-big warmth," the latter meaning caring about the disadvantaged (Council for Economic Development and Planning 2007).

After the KMT returned to power in early 2008, the new president, Ma Ying-jeou, articulated a vision of his own, known as "633." This targeted an economic growth rate, up to 2016, of 6 percent, an unemployment rate of 3 percent, and a per-capita GDP in 2016 of US$30,000.

Deepening Ties with the Mainland

Expanding ties with mainland China holds the key to growth. To give just one example, today the government is counting on the mainland's strong demand for its TFT-LCD panels as a major boost for the national economy because China is becoming the world's biggest manufacturer of products where TFT-LCD screens are applied (Government Information Office 2008).

Most of the factories of the big Taiwanese electronic manufacturers are located on the mainland. According to estimates, the share of Taiwanese-owned firms in

China's exports of electronic hardware lies somewhere between 40 percent and 80 percent (Einhorn 2005). In 2000–08, under President Chen of the DPP, the relationship with Beijing went through a difficult period, as his administration was openly pushing the idea of statehood for the island.

In the presidential election, held in 2007, the DPP lost and the KMT was brought back to power. Its candidate, Ma Ying-jeou, became the new president, pledging to make the economy his first priority and to be realistic and pragmatic in his approach to China.

Today, issues related to economic links with mainland China, especially in the areas of transportation and tourism, are at the top of the government's agenda. As a first big step, the administration has focused on opening the island to more Chinese tourists and expanding the number of charter flights, initially limited only to the four Chinese national holidays.

In June 2008, as a result of the first formal talks since 1999, Beijing and Taipei agreed to allow 36 cross-strait charter flights, shared equally between Chinese and Taiwanese airlines and to permit up to 3,000 Chinese tourists to visit Taiwan for up to ten days (Associated Press 2008).

The regulations on Taiwanese investment in mainland China are also gradually being eased. Since March 2004, investment of up to US$200,000 is practically free, provided the necessary documents are submitted to the authorities. However, the company has to report to the authorities within six months after the investment was made.

Investments of up to US$20 million are a subject for a simplified examination, and those beyond this level for a full-scale examination by the Investment Commission.

Since August 2002, it has become possible to invest in mainland China directly, not through a third-party territory. The government intends to relax the cap on investment, which is now 40 percent of the company's net worth, and to allow a moderate inflow of Chinese investment in the island (*Sino Daily* 2008).

On the other hand, it bans investment in a range of sectors where security or technology leak issues are involved, including ten kinds of electronic devices and 23 pharmaceutical, agriculture, service (postal services, finance services, and information and communications design), and infrastructure items (ARC Report Taiwan 2007, 136).

Foreign Trade

Naturally, Taiwan's major exports are electronic and electrical products. In 2006, their share reached 49.8 percent, greatly exceeding that of any other group of products. Other exports cover a wide range of sectors. Steel and metal products followed with 10.7 percent, precision machinery 8.2 percent, plastics 7.1 percent, textiles 5.3 percent, and chemicals and mineral products with 5.0 percent each.

Mainland China is Taiwan's major export market. However, as Taiwanese companies are not allowed to sell to the mainland directly, most of their exports go through Hong Kong. Statistical data is based on the government's estimates of the volume of Taiwan–China trade. (Also, the Taiwanese call their trade with the mainland not "foreign," but "cross-strait.")

In 2006, the share of mainland China in total exports was estimated at 23.1 percent. Hong Kong followed with 16.7 percent. Effectively, about 40 percent of Taiwan's exports went to the greater China area. Other important export markets were the US (14.4 percent), Japan (7.7 percent), Singapore (4.1 percent), and Malaysia and Germany (2.2 percent each).

Electronic and electrical products were also the major imports (35.8 percent). The share of crude oil and other mineral products was 19.2 percent, steel and metal products 11.4 percent, chemicals 11.1 percent, precision machinery 6.1 percent, and agricultural and fishery products 3.5 percent (JETRO 2007, 175–176).

The leading exporters to the Taiwanese market were Japan (22.8 percent), China (12.2 percent), the US (11.2 percent), South Korea (7.4 percent), Germany (3.0 percent), Malaysia (3.0 percent), and Singapore (2.5 percent) (ADB 2007).

Taiwan faces enormous difficulties in concluding free trade agreements (FTAs). It has diplomatic relations with 23 small countries, which appear to be the only feasible partners for such arrangements.

FDI and the Business Environment

The Composition of Inward FDI

In 2006, the biggest direct investor in Taiwan was the Netherlands (38.8 percent of the total on the notification basis). The share of Japan was 11.1 percent, UK 10.8 percent, Singapore 6.8 percent, and the US 6.3 percent. Overall, 53.8 percent of foreign direct investment (FDI) came from Europe and 22.0 percent from Asia.

The order of the leading investors varies a lot from year to year (for example, in 2005 the largest amount of FDI came from the US, and Japan was second). In 2006, the Netherlands' high share stemmed from a large-scale investment by Philips in the shares of TSMC and for the UK from the acquisition of Hsinchu International Commercial Bank by Standard Chartered.

In 2006, manufacturing received 51.7 percent of total FDI and almost all of it (47.7 percent) went into the electrical and electronic industry. In the service sector, the major recipient was finance and insurance (33.0 percent). The share for wholesale and retail trade stayed at 6.1 percent (JETRO 2007, 177).

The Conditions for Investing

Taiwan prohibits or limits FDI in a number of industries put on the so-called "negative list." Companies with foreign ownership below 33 percent are exempt from its limitations and receive the same regulatory treatment as domestic firms. As time goes by, some industries are removed from the list, and others are transferred from the prohibited entry to the limited entry category.

The list of industries closed to foreign capital is not long. It includes forestry, various kinds of chemicals, weaponry, land transportation, postal services, radio and TV broadcasting, and the leisure industry. Sectors where foreign entry is restricted include agriculture and fisheries, the production of alcoholic beverages, the production of several kinds of chemicals, finance and insurance, telecommunications, electricity transmission and distribution, water supply, and legal services (US Department of State 2007).

In the sectors not included on the negative list, FDI is authorized without any restrictions or additional conditions. Investment from mainland China is not permitted with the exception of the real-estate sector (ARC Report Taiwan 2007, 135).

The top corporate tax rate in Taiwan is comparatively low at 25 percent while the top income tax rate is 40 percent.

Property rights are protected by the judiciary. Intellectual property rights (IPR) protection is improving (Heritage Foundation 2008).

The flexibility of the labor market is low. Though the nonsalary cost of employing a new worker is insignificant, firing is relatively costly and burdensome (Heritage Foundation 2008). High-tech industries are fighting with labor shortages. Wage levels are rather high. As of 2006, the average monthly wage in manufacturing was NT$43,958 (US$1,353) (US Department of State 2007).

Incentives for investors include accelerated depreciation and tax credits when investing in an emerging, or a strategically important, industry, pollution control facilities, production automation, and energy conservation. Equipment for R&D purposes can be imported duty free.

Science-based industrial parks and EPZs have a simplified procedure of application and approval. In the EPZs, located all around the island, import duties, commodity tax, and business tax are exempted on machinery, raw materials, fuels, materials, semi-finished products, and musters imported.

The government agency in charge of FDI is the Investment Commission of the Ministry of Economic Affairs.

The Composition of Outward FDI

A remarkable rise in Taiwan's outward FDI took place in 2006 (see Table 9.2). China absorbs about 60 percent of the territory's outbound investment.

Among other destinations, the biggest recipients, in 2006, were the Cayman Islands and other UK-ruled tax havens in the Caribbean (42.2 percent of the total excluding China). The share of Singapore was 18.7 percent, the US 11.2 percent, and Vietnam 2.9 percent. Major moves affecting the figures include UMC making a big investment in its subsidiary in Singapore and BenQ doing similarly in the Netherlands.

Overall, the electrical and electronic industry accounted for 23.7 percent of total FDI and the chemical industry 6.6 percent. In the nonmanufacturing sector the major recipients of Taiwan's FDI were the finance and insurance (49.9 percent) and wholesale and retail trade (11.1 percent) sectors (JETRO 2007, 178).

According to a survey of domestic companies with overseas (including China) operations, conducted by the Ministry of Economic Affairs in April–March 2006,

Table 9.2   Inward and outward FDI (approval basis, US$millions)

Direction	1999	2000	2001	2002	2003	2004	2005	2006	2007
Inward FDI	4,231	7,608	5,129	3,372	3,576	3,952	4,228	13,969	15,361
Outward FDI (China excluded)	3,269.0	5,077.1	4,391.7	3,370.0	3,968.6	3,382.0	2,447.4	4,315.4	6,470.0
Outward FDI to China	2,034.6	1,252.8	2,607.1	2,784.1	6,723.1	7,698.8	6,940.4	7,642.3	9,970.5

Source: Ministry of Economic Affairs.

more than 80 percent of the respondents were doing business in mainland China, 22 percent in the ASEAN states, and 17 percent in the US (ARC Report Taiwan 2007, 37).

Concluding Remarks

The key issue for Taiwan's economic future is its relations with China. Rapid growth on the mainland opens remarkable business opportunities—even more so because, in spite of China's progress, Taiwanese companies retain strong advantages in technology, product design, marketing, management know-how, and access to international distribution channels. Economic relations between China and Taiwan are much more complementary than competitive. Finding a relevant political formula for the relationship with Beijing holds the key. Perhaps, it can be "mutual nondenial."

However, the economic future of the territory should not, and will not, entirely depend on its supporting role for the booming mainland. Taiwan's economy is globally oriented, and its companies have proved their ability to lead in the world markets of key products.

Endnote

1 Repurchase agreement allows a borrower to use a financial security as collateral for a cash loan at a fixed interest rate. The borrower agrees to immediately sell a security to the lender and has to buy it back at a specified later date, at a predetermined price. The difference between the latter and the spot market price is the interest on the loan and the day of buying back is its maturity date.

10

South Korea Reformed: Challenges for a Newly Developed Nation

A Few Basics

South Korea is a mid-sized country with a population of 48.3 million people. In 2007, it was the thirteenth-largest economy in the world in terms of nominal gross domestic product (GDP)—after India and above Australia—and ranked thirty-fifth by per-capita GDP (purchasing power parity (PPP))—between the Bahamas and the Czech Republic and also ahead of Portugal.

The country is divided into nine provinces and seven metropolitan cities. Economic activities are mainly concentrated around two the major cities—the Seoul metropolitan area in the northwest and one of Asia's major seaports, Busan, on the southeast coast. The population of the Seoul metropolitan area, neighboring Gyeonggi Province, and the Busan metropolitan area comprises 50 percent of South Korea's total.

Today's South Korea is an industrially developed country. It was the second Asian nation, after Japan, to join the Organization for Economic Co-operation and Development (OECD), gaining membership in 1996.

In 2006, agriculture accounted for 2.9 percent of the country's GDP, industry 35.2 percent, and services 61.9 percent. The share of agriculture in the total number of persons employed was 7.4 percent, manufacturing 17.4 percent, and other industries (mostly services) 74.3 percent (ADB 2007).

South Korea has almost the full set of heavy and light manufacturing industries. The most internationally competitive among them are transportation machinery (especially the production of auto vehicles and shipbuilding) and the electronics industry (the production of semiconductors, telecommunication equipment, audio-visual products, computers, and so on). It is also a big producer of steel, chemical, and petrochemical products.

The country has virtually no important natural resources. Agricultural production is small-scale and internationally noncompetitive.

The leading South Korean conglomerates, called *chaebols*, are Samsung, Hyundai, LG, and SK. Their major member companies have grown into heavyweight global players and have established internationally recognized brands—mostly as producers of electronic products, autos, and vessels.

South Korea's major economic agencies include the Ministry of Strategy and Finance (formerly the Ministry of Economy and Finance); the Ministry of Knowledge Economy; the Ministry of Foreign Affairs and Trade; the Ministry of Education, Science, and Technology; the Ministry of Land, Transport and Maritime Affairs; and the Ministry of Food, Agriculture, Forestry, and Fisheries.

From 1961 to 1993, South Korea was ruled by the military. Having started a democratization process in the early 1990s, it succeeded in creating a genuine parliamentary democratic system with two major political parties—the Grand National Party (the ruling party at the time of writing) and the United New Democratic Party (opposition party)—at its core.

Postwar Development

The Late 1940s and the 1950s

Korea was divided into North and South back in 1948. At that time, the North was more industrialized and the South was mostly agrarian—farmers comprised 90 percent of the population, most of them cultivating tiny lots of land (Watanabe 1995, 35). The division was a big blow for the South because, among other things, it completely depended on the North for supplies of electricity.

The Korean War, which lasted from 1950 to 1953, had a devastating effect on the national economy. The country faced shortages of basic consumer goods. Infrastructural facilities were in critical condition. Budget deficits soared. Until the early 1960s the national economy was kept going, first and foremost, due to large-scale American aid.

When, in the late 1950s, the aid was reduced, the economic situation deteriorated. Production fell rapidly and inflation and unemployment rose. In 1961, the military, led by General Park Chung-hee, seized power and governed the country for the next three decades.

Development Dictatorship and Export-Oriented Industrialization

The South Korean military regime turned out to be probably the most successful development dictatorship ever. The real growth rate of the GDP averaged 8.7 percent during the period 1962–73, 7.1 percent in 1974–82, and 9.1 percent in 1983–92. The average growth of production in manufacturing was, respectively, 18.9 percent, 12.7 percent, and 11.8 percent (Lee 1997). It was the highest in the region.

Having put economic modernization and poverty alleviation at the top of its political agenda, the Park regime showed a very strong commitment to fostering industrial development, using all the power it had at its disposal. From 1962, the government started to compile five-year development plans articulating its economic targets, policies, and priorities. The Economic Planning Board was established as a powerful agency that played a key role in selecting priority industries and allocating funds. (In 1994, it was merged with the Ministry of Finance to become what is now the Ministry of Strategy and Finance.) Domestic banks were nationalized in 1961 and guided to extend large-scale loans to sectors and companies which were in the vanguard of industrialization. (During 1981–83 they were reprivatized, but even after that the government retained substantial control over their activities.) Large public enterprises were set up, not only in the infrastructure-related industries but also in manufacturing. A good example is the Pohang Iron and Steel Company (POSCO).

From the outset, the domestic market was too small for steadily expanding industries, so the Park government pursued export-oriented industrialization. To support the exporters, it set a single exchange rate for the won (fixing it at a low level); provided tax incentives, subsidies, and low-interest loans; and introduced the export-import link—successful exporters were allocated limited foreign exchange on a preferential basis so that they could import "precious" foreign equipment and materials. The Economic Planning Board set export targets for companies.

In the early and mid-1960s, industrial growth was led by light industries, producing foodstuffs, textile products, and footwear. From the end of the decade, the government started to promote the creation of heavy industries. It provided large-scale financing for the construction of a number of big production facilities, such as a petrochemical complex in Ulsan and a steel mill in Pohang. It encouraged *chaebols* to take over factories it built and extended generous support to those who did. When, in 1978, Daewoo took over the Okpo Shipyard at the government's request, the latter provided all the financing needed to complete the shipyard and also assisted in building a large-scale machine industry complex in the surrounding area (Haggard 2003, 153).

Officially, the heavy industrialization policy was proclaimed in 1973. A target was set for the share of heavy industry products in total exports to hit 50 percent by 1980. In reality it reached 47 percent (Watanabe 1995, 38).

Petrochemicals, steel and nonferrous metals, shipbuilding, electric machinery and electronics, and the production of auto vehicles were designated as "important industries." They were protected from foreign competition by high import tariffs and quotas

In the late 1970s, South Korea's per-capita GDP exceeded US$1,000 for the first time and it became a middle-income country (Watanabe 1995, 38).

Structural Problems

However, the economy faced a number of structural problems. It was dominated by large companies, especially those belonging to the 30 leading *chaebols*, while small- and medium-sized enterprises (SMEs) remained underdeveloped. They were in a very disadvantageous position regarding access to financial and other resources.

Unlike Japan, South Korea did not succeed in creating a pool of efficient SMEs supplying leading producers with parts and materials. Thus, major companies in the automotive or electronics industry were highly dependent on imports of key intermediate products, as well as equipment. Consequently, in spite of a remarkable export drive, the current balance of payments remained mostly in the red and foreign debt surged.

Besides, like Japan ten years earlier, South Korean society began to realize that industrial growth was "not everything" and that it was high time to think seriously about environmental issues, overpopulated cities, traffic jams, and better social protection for the poor and the elderly.

The 1980s

In 1979, President Park was assassinated. His successor Chun Doo-hwan articulated a new national goal—to become a developed nation by 1990. His economic policy doctrine put more emphasis on sustainable development and social welfare. Also, the new administration intended to limit government involvement in economic activities.

The early 1980s were a rather difficult period for the South Korean economy, largely because of the second oil shock of 1979–80. Growth in 1980 was negative, while inflation hit 28.8 percent (Watanabe 1995, 39). However, in the latter half of the 1980s, growth accelerated again, boosted by a simultaneous fall in the exchange rate of won, world oil prices, and global interest rates.

In June 1987, the government issued the Declaration for Democratization, promising the election of the president by a direct popular vote. It was clear that a transition to civilian rule and democracy was near. The voice of labor unions grew stronger, which exerted an upward pressure on wages.

Rising costs, along with the appreciation of the won, started to adversely affect exports, especially as price competition from the Association of Southeast Asian Nations (ASEAN) and other low-cost economies became fiercer than ever before. The upgrading of production, product differentiation, and competing on quality became an urgent task.

The 1990s

In the early 1990s, the share of the machinery sector (auto industry, computers, audio-visual products, semiconductors, and general machinery) in total industrial production began to increase significantly. However, domestic companies were incapable of producing many key parts and did not command core technologies such as thermal or high-precision metal processing. Therefore, the high dependency on imports remained.

More positively, rising household incomes and the expansion of the middle class enhanced the role of domestic demand as a growth driver.

With the parliamentary and presidential elections of 1993 the country made the transition to democracy. The administration of Kim Young-sam, the first democratically elected president since the start of the high-growth story, emphasized the notions of efficiency and fairness and pledged to accelerate a shift to a high-value-added economy.

In the mid-1990s, growth remained strong. However, structural deficiencies, especially the dominance of a limited number of leading *chaebols*, the extremely high dependency on debt financing, excessive diversification, reliance on government back-up, and poor corporate governance were left virtually unchanged. As a result, South Korea became the only Asian newly industrialized economy (NIE) to be severely hit by the Asian crisis.

Structural Reforms

South Korea's structural reforms in all the major areas—disposal of nonperforming loans (NPLs), transformation of company management, reorganization of conglomerates and banks, the strengthening of supervision and prudential regulation, liquidation of ailing companies and financial institutions, the creation of a sound framework for genuine corporate governance, and opening up the economy for foreign direct, and portfolio, investors—were the most wide-ranging, far-reaching, and persistent among all the crisis-hit economies (see Chapter 4). As a result, post-crisis South Korea emerged drastically reformed and full of growth energy.

A Case in Point: Reorganizing Daewoo

One of the best examples is the restructuring of the Daewoo Group carried out by the Korean Asset Management Corporation (Kamco)—an institution established to dispose bad debts and restructure troubled banks and companies—together with the Korea Development Bank (KDB). The conglomerate was split into independent companies and these were then focused on their core business areas. These companies also underwent extensive restructuring, including large personnel cuts. For instance, Daewoo Electronics cut its workforce by one-third and Daewoo International by 15 percent. Creditors agreed to write-off about US$49 million of debts or to swap debts into equity (Kim 2005).

Initially, Kamco and KDB became the major shareholders of the reorganized companies but as the latter were getting back on track they sold off their shares to private investors. A number of the conglomerate's former member companies have become dynamic international players and some of them have even joined the ranks of world leaders in their business areas.

Daewoo Corporation, formerly the trading unit of the conglomerate, was split into two independent companies—Daewoo Trading and Daewoo Engineering and Construction. The latter became one of the most profitable construction companies in the country. In 2006, it was acquired by Kumho Asiana Group, a division of Korea Kumho Petrochemical.

Daewoo Heavy Industries was divided into shipbuilding and heavy equipment producing companies. In the middle of this decade the latter, Daewoo Heavy Industries and Machinery, rose to the position of the world's number five maker of construction equipment. Kamco and KDB sold their shares in the company to a private consortium led by Doosan Heavy Industry and Construction, and the firm's name was changed to Doosan Infacore.

Daewoo Shipbuilding and Marine Industry, where at the time of writing KDB remains the biggest shareholder, is one of the world's leading shipbuilders

GM bought a controlling share in Daewoo Motors and the company made a new start under the name of GM Daewoo Auto and Technology in 2002.

Daewoo International, formerly the foreign trade arm of the conglomerate, evolved into a global trading company especially active in three areas—mediation between buyers and sellers in various parts of the world, organization of international business projects, and the development of energy and other natural resources.

The Transformation of the Corporate Sector

By the beginning of the 2000s, the banks had mostly disposed of their NPLs. Their management and supervision had significantly improved. Corporations strove to sell non-core units and affiliates and to focus on their areas of competitive advantage. The top four *chaebols* reduced the total number of their affiliates by one-third. The excessive capacity problem—a product of the "borrowing too much–diversifying too wide" mode of behavior in the pre-crisis years, was mostly resolved.

Also, the issue of corporate transparency became the focus of attention. Consolidated financial statements meeting international standards started to be introduced from 2000. However, the drive for transparency in post-crisis South Korea was accompanied by bribery and corruption scandals involving the leading and most famous conglomerates and top businessmen.

Capital Market Reform

South Korea is seeking to become the regional financial hub. In this regard, one of the most important developments in the later 2000s is the launch of the capital market reform. At present, South Korea's capital markets remain underdeveloped, posing an impediment for growth. Market capitalization in South Korea, US$717.6 billion, comprised only 90.5 percent of the GDP versus 165.1 percent in Japan, 155.1 percent in the US, 270.0 percent in Singapore, and 137.5 percent in Taiwan (Purfield 2006). South Korean securities companies are relatively small and weak.

Big changes are expected to take place with the enactment of The Financial Investment Services and Capital Market Act (Capital Market Consolidation Act). It was adopted in July 2007, and is to go into effect in 2009. Business barriers separating banking, securities, and insurance sectors will be eliminated.

Also, at present, different regulations are applied to the same financial service (such as advisory, trust, and so on) if it is provided by different kinds of institutions—securities, asset-management, future, real-estate investment, or trust companies. Each type of institution can only be engaged in a limited set of particular financial functions.

The act will eliminate those barriers too. All the institutions mentioned are to be categorized as financial investment companies (FICs), and the same financial service will be subject to the same regulations.

The major economic effect expected is the transformation of security broker-ages into integrated investment banks.

Present Performance

Growth is Fast But Uneven

South Korea's economic growth after the Asian crisis was dynamic, but very uneven—the yearly fluctuations were probably the greatest among all the major regional economies. In 1999 and 2000, the economy rebounded at a surprisingly high speed. Annual growth rates hit 11 percent and 8.5 percent, respectively, causing concerns about overheating. However, in 2001, the slow-down in the world economy, most of all in the information technology (IT) sector, adversely affected the country's exports, and growth slowed to just under 4 percent (see Table10.1).

The government moved to stimulate domestic demand, especially consump-tion by households, and growth rates rose again, but only for a short while. In a way, consumers started to behave like companies before the Asian crisis—borrowing too actively (banks, having gotten over the NPL problem, were more than willing to lend) and buying too much. Household debts reached critical lev-els with a growing number of borrowers unable to pay them back.

Then, in 2004–07, due to a rapid expansion of exports, growth accelerated again and was maintained within the 4–5 percent range. Though quite decent by international standards (especially for developed countries), such rates caused a lot of dissatisfaction in the business community, mass media, and general pub-lic—largely because consumption remained weak and too many households did not feel the benefits of this growth.

In 2006–07, household consumption recovered. Capital investment growth also accelerated and unemployment fell significantly. On the other hand, the role of net exports as a growth driver started to decline. Though exports continued to rise steadily, in spite of the appreciation of the won, from 2005, imports expanded faster because of soaring prices for imported oil and other natural resources.

Concerns About Capital Outflow

In 2006, for the first time since 1997, outward foreign direct investment (FDI) was significantly larger than inward—net outflow was US$4,540 million. In 2007, it went further up to US$13,697 million (ADB 2008). However, at this point, no visible sign of the hollowing-out of domestic industries is in sight. Like their Japanese counterparts, South Korean firms have started to move actively to China and Vietnam, seeking lower production costs and more flex-ible labor markets, but they continue to produce high-value-added items at home.

The net outflow in the portfolio investment sector is much bigger. It started in 2005 and, in 2006, reached US$22,746 million (ADB 2008). The major reason is

Table 10.1   Main economic indicators (real annual growth, %)

Indicator	1999	2000	2001	2002	2003	2004	2005	2006	2007
GDP	9.5	8.5	3.8	7.0	3.1	4.7	4.0	5.1	5.0
Agriculture*	5.9	1.2	1.1	−3.5	−5.3	9.2	0.7	−1.5	1.1
Industry*	12.2	11.7	3.1	6.4	6.1	8.6	5.7	6.6	5.5
Services*	6.6	6.1	4.8	7.8	1.6	1.9	3.4	4.2	4.8
Gross domestic capital formation	24.1	10.7	−0.0	5.9	2.5	4.8	2.1	3.8	2.5
Private consumption	11.5	8.4	4.9	7.9	−1.2	−0.3	3.6	4.5	4.5
Wages (average for all occupations)	5.5	8.5	6.0	10.0	7.7	6.0	10.7	7.4	n/a
Consumer prices	0.8	2.3	4.1	2.8	3.5	3.6	2.8	2.2	2.5
Unemployment rate (%)	6.3	4.1	4.0	3.3	3.6	3.7	3.7	3.5	3.2
Exports (US$ billions), fob	143.7	172.3	150.4	162.5	193.8	253.8	284.4	325.5	371.5
Imports (US$ billions), cif	119.8	160.5	141.1	152.1	178.8	224.5	261.2	309.4	356.8
Average exchange rate (won per US$1)	1,188.8	1,131.0	1,291.0	1,251.1	1,191.6	1,145.3	1,024.1	954.8	929.3

Source: ADB: "Key Indicators 2008;" *Korea Statistical Yearbook*. 2007.
*Data for agriculture, industry, and services refers to value added

the increase in purchases of foreign assets by individuals, boosted by weakening government regulations.

Good Macroeconomic Performance and Mounting Social Problems

The main economic indicators (see Table 10.1) show that, until 2007, the post-crisis South Korean economy was in a good shape. Inflation and unemployment were low. From 2002 until 2007 the won was rapidly appreciating against the US dollar. Yet, as mentioned, exports were steadily growing—a very important signal that South Korean companies had become capable of differentiating their products and competing on quality.

The trade and current account balances during 1998–2007 were permanently in the black. Foreign currency reserves went up from US$20.4 billion at the end of 1997 to US$262.2 billion at the end of 2007 (ADB 2008).

Nevertheless, the perceptions of many South Koreans about the economic situation were largely negative. Most people's everyday living standards remained modest—compared to the "old developed economies" of the West—and, generally, they didn't feel affluent.

Also, there was a widespread perception that the economic policy of President Roh Moon-hyun's administration (2003–08) was a failure.

What exactly went wrong? Besides the above-mentioned real-estate price hike, the list of factors looks like this: income gaps between high- and low-income households increased; the growth rates of employment and households' consumption fell to half of their previous levels; wage growth slowed down; and it became extremely difficult for young people to find jobs, especially well-paid jobs.

Besides, the government had launched a number of ambitious, but controversial, national projects which have either stumbled (like the relocation of the capital to Chungcheong region) or turned out to be very costly.

Yet, the roots of the problems mentioned lie deeper than the failures of one particular administration. Many of them look like a "by-product" of the post-crisis structural change—a step closer to Anglo-Saxon-style capitalism.

The new president, Lee Myung-bak, the leader of the Grand National Party and a former business executive at Hyundai Construction, has announced the "South Korea 7-4-7" strategy. The figures mean economic growth of 7 percent for ten consecutive years to increase per-capita national income to US$40,000 by 2017 and to make the national economy the seventh largest in the world (Hirano 2007).

However, the start of Lee Myung-bak's term turned out to be controversial due to massive rallies against the resumption of imports of US beef (due to concerns about "mad cow disease"). The president apologized twice for the way the matter was handled. The "beef riots" have subsequently escalated into growing public discontent against the new leader's pro-business stance (in other words, the intention to pursue deregulation, privatization, corporate tax cuts, and so on) as a whole.

The Impact of the Global Financial Turmoil

South Korean banks have been strongly exposed to the global credit crunch of late 2008. Substantial difficulties have emerged in rolling over foreign currency loans, which were used largely for the forward covering of companies' export deals.

Liquidity constraints in the banking sector squeezed domestic lending adversely affecting the real-estate sector. The government decided to guarantee US$100 billion of the banks' debt. The authorities increased the US dollar supply to the banking sector, mainly through the currency swap deals of the Export-Import Bank of Korea.

In 2008, the won became the worst-performing currency in Asia, depreciating by 28 percent against the US dollar between January and early November. Consequently, inflationary pressures remained strong in spite of the plunge in oil and other commodity prices.

In the fourth quarter (October–December), the economy shrank by a shocking 5.6 percent against the previous quarter and by 3.4 percent year-on-year, according to the preliminary figures from the Bank of Korea. Private consumption plunged by 4.8 percent and facility investment—by 16.9 percent. Exports continued to decline, and in January 2009, registered a record year-on-year fall of 32.8 percent (*The China Post* 2009). The danger of sliding into a recession became real.

The key Korean Composite Stock Price Index (KOSPI) lost more than half of its value within the same period. Export growth slowed down and consumers began to severely restrain their spending. In addition, the consumer debt problem worsened.

In late October-early November 2008, the Bank of Korea implemented its largest ever interest rate cuts bringing the rate down from 5.0 percent to 4.0 percent. It also pledged, for the first time, to purchase commercial banks' bonds in order to inject more cash into the financial sector.

The government unveiled a stimulus package, consisting of additional spending and tax cuts, especially for small businesses and low income earners. In January 2009, extra spending was announced. One of the major projects, a "Green New Deal," is aimed at reducing the effects of floods and droughts along main rivers. Its scale is 14 trillion won (US$10.3 billion) (AFP 2009).

Seeking to Lead in Technology

One of the main features of post-crisis economic development is a growing emphasis on the development and introduction of high technology by both the government and business. The goal is to establish a strong position among the world leaders in a number of major technological fields.

The government has come up with a plan to make South Korea the world's leading IT nation by the beginning of the 2010s and has started allocating substantial public funds to upgrade infrastructure and develop key technologies. One example is the development of the WiBro—a mobile version of regular broadband technology, commercialized in 2006.

Also, a very ambitious goal has been set to become the world's number one robotics nation by 2025. South Korea is focusing on service robots and aims to install a robot in every household by 2020 (Lovgren 2006). The government is starting to invest in this sector too. Other areas on the priority list are biotechnology and nanotechnology.

Several leading South Korean companies have strengthened their positions as world leaders in particular markets. In 2007, Samsung Electronics surpassed Motorola to become the world's number two producer of mobile phones after Nokia (Mehta 2007). It is already dominating the slider mobile-phone market. In the global semiconductors market, Samsung

Semiconductors runs second after Intel with a share of 7.6 percent in 2006, and in the same year, Hynix, steadily enhancing its presence, entered the top ten at number seven, with a share of 3.0 percent (*Evertiq* 2007). South Korean shipbuilding companies held the top five (Hyundai Heavy Industries, Samsung Heavy Industries, Daewoo Shipbuilding and Marine Engineering, Hyundai Mipo Dockyard, and Hyundai Samho) and seven out of the top ten positions, in terms of backlog orders received (*The Chosun Ilbo* 2006).

The Service Industry and "Soft Power"

Achievements in the service industry remain less impressive than in manufacturing. A wide range of sectors have much room for growth and a rise in the quality of services. However, in recent years, the country has started to strengthen its "soft power" too. This especially applies to South Korean television dramas, such as *Winter Sonata*—a sensation that became a popular brand in Asia, from Myanmar to Uzbekistan. A touching love story, *Winter Sonata* opened a new page in relations between South Korea and Japan, starting a "Korean-style" boom in the Japanese market and providing an unprecedented impetus for human and business contacts.

Ties With the North

An issue of special importance is the relationship with North Korea. On the one hand, the militarized North, with its nuclear ambitions and unpredictability of action, is looked upon as a threat—perhaps the major threat to national security and stability. On the other, in recent years, South Korea's policy stance toward the North—the "Sunshine policy" of the United New Democratic Party— was mostly conciliatory. It paved the way for two North–South summit meetings in Pyongyang in 2001 and 2007 and created a better environment for expanding economic links (see Chapter 17).

As the Grand National Party came to power and the Lee Myung-bak administration started its term, North–South relations deteriorated. The new president emphasized the conditionality of economic assistance, linking it to the North's readiness to change, and made clear that aid had to be asked for. The North responded with harsh criticism. The South proposed to resume the dialogue, but bilateral relations suffered a new setback in July 2008, when a South Korean tourist was killed by a North Korean soldier at the Mount Kumgang resort when she allegedly entered a restricted area.

Foreign Trade

The Composition of Exports

South Korea is one of the world's leading exporters of electrical and electronic products. The latter accounted for 37.1 percent of the country's total exports in 2006. It has established an especially strong position as a producer of semiconductors, mostly dynamic random access memory (DRAM). In a recent development it has become a major exporter of NAND flash memory chips, used in digital cameras and MP3 players. Other key electronic products exported include mobile phones, liquid crystal displays (LCDs), personal computers (PCs), television sets, and audio-visual products.

Transportation machinery comprised 20.7 percent of total exports, including 9.4 percent for passenger cars and 6.8 percent for vessels (JETRO 2007, 183). South Korea was the only emerging-market country—not only in Asia, but also globally—which managed to join the ranks of the world's major exporters of cars. As far as vessels are concerned, it is the number one producer and exporter in the world. Other major export items are petrochemical, petroleum, and steel products.

The US used to be the most important export market but, in this decade, the situation has changed—China has become market number one with 21.3 percent of total exports in 2006.

The US absorbed 13.3 percent of the country's exports, Japan 8.2 percent, Hong Kong 5.8 percent, Taiwan 4.0 percent, Germany 3.1 percent, Singapore 2.9 percent, the UK 1.7 percent, and Malaysia 1.6 percent (Korea National Statistical Office 2007).

The Composition of Imports

As far as imports are concerned, almost one-third is accounted for by natural resources, mainly crude oil (18.1 percent). The share of electrical and electronic products is 22.5 percent, including 11.5 percent for electronic parts (JETRO 2007, 183). Other major items are general machinery and chemical products.

During 1999–2007, South Korea was maintaining the surplus of its trade balance and of the current account as a whole. Importantly, its exports of electronic and nonelectrical machinery products significantly exceed imports.

In 2006, imports from Japan accounted for 16.8 percent of the total, China 15.7 percent, the US 10.9 percent, the United Arab Emirates 4.2 percent, Germany 3.7 percent, Taiwan 3.0 percent, Indonesia 2.8 percent, and Malaysia 2.3 percent (Korea National Statistical Office 2007).

South Korea's average import tariff was 9.3 percent as of 2005. Yet, prohibitive tariffs for a number of goods, especially agricultural, are retained. Nontransparent and restrictive regulations and standards may also pose a problem (Heritage Foundation 2008).

FDI and the Business Environment

A Changing Attitude

From the beginning of postwar growth and up to the Asian crisis, South Korea took a more than cautious attitude toward inward FDI and its volume

Table 10.2   Inward and outward FDI (arrival and departure basis, US$ millions)

Direction	1999	2000	2001	2002	2003	2004	2005	2006
Inward FDI	11,001	10,267	5,083	3,806	5,131	9,265	9,669	9,055
Outward FDI	3,329	5,070	5,152	3,689	4,048	5,980	6,858	11,194

Source: World Economic Information Services: "ARC Report. Republic of Korea." 2005–07; Export-Import Bank of Korea.

was relatively small. Not any more. In the two post-crisis years inward FDI significantly increased, exceeding US$10 billion (see Table 10.2). In 2001–03, its level was low but, since 2004, it has recovered, approaching the US$10 billion mark again.

The Foreign Investment Promotion Act was enacted in 1998 and between that year and 2006 the total amount of inward FDI reached US$1.21 billion—4.1 times as much as in the period from 1962 to 1997 (Invest Korea 2008a).

Yet, the presence of foreign-affiliated companies in the national economy is still rather limited. In 2005, their share in the total number of persons employed was 7.0 percent, in sales in the manufacturing industry 13.9 percent, and in exports 13.7 percent (Invest Korea 2008a).

Composition

On the notification basis, the total amount of inward FDI in 2006 was US$11,233 million. Out of this total 37.8 percent went into manufacturing with the electrical and electronic industry taking the lion's share (16.0 percent). It was followed by the chemical industry (6.8 percent). The share of services was 59.0 percent, with banking and finance leading (26.9 percent), followed by hotels and catering (9.9 percent).

Japan was the biggest direct investor with a share of 18.8 percent, followed by the US (15.2 percent), France (10.5 percent), the Netherlands (7.1 percent), and the UK (6.3 percent) (Korea National Statistical Office 2007).

Investment Promotion

The major motive for investing in South Korea is getting better access to the local market for goods and services.

The government is working to improve the investment environment. On the positive side, the number of business areas closed for foreign investors is insignificant—they include electric power, the media, and some areas of agriculture. Post-crisis deregulation and liberalization in the financial sector has opened up new business opportunities. The top corporate tax rate is also comparatively low at 25 percent.

The key institution responsible for promoting foreign investment is the Korean Trade-Investment Promotion Agency (KOTRA). One of its departments, named Invest Korea, specifically promotes investment.

Invest Korea Plaza, opened in 2006, has become the state incubator, working exclusively with foreign companies. It provides office space and consults foreign companies on a wide range of issues from investment opportunities to Korean business culture and everyday life.

Foreign companies, investing in high-tech industries or industrial support services, can get a five-year tax holiday and a 50 percent reduction for two more years (Korea.net 2008). If they invest more than US$10 million in these areas a cash grant from the government can be provided. Also, companies investing in the R&D sector, and having ten or more employees as R&D staff, are eligible for government subsidies (Invest Korea 2008b).

Three free economic zones (FEZs) are in operation—Busan/Jinhae, Incheon, and Gwangyang Bay. Three more are being developed in the western coastal area, North Jeolla Province, and Daegu. In these zones foreign investors are exempt from paying income tax and corporate tax for three years, and then taxes are reduced by half for the next two years. A flat 17 percent income tax will apply thereafter.

The list of leading companies successfully operating in South Korea includes Texas Instruments, Volvo, Sony, Yahoo!, and Agfa. The joint venture between Corning Inc. of the US and Samsung Electronics, established in 1973, is known for a number of important technological breakthroughs.

Problems

The biggest problem with South Korea's investment environment is an inflexible labor market. Labor laws and established practices make it extremely difficult for companies to lay off workers. Before the Asian crisis, a company was permitted to start layoffs only if it had been in the red for quite a long period of time or had gone bankrupt. After the crisis, it became possible to resort to layoffs due to the "imperative needs of management." The minimum notification period before a layoff was reduced from 60 to 30 days. Yet, companies are still required to avoid layoffs and to consult workers whenever possible. In reality, layoffs remain extremely difficult to undertake.

Layoffs aside, relations with local personnel may well pose various problems for a foreign businessman working in South Korea. It may be not so easy to find a common approach to issues under discussion. By and large, the ability to communicate in English remains low. As a foreigner, one may be treated with suspicion, and, when opinions differ, local counterparts may decide to do things their own way, showing no inclination to seek a mutually acceptable solution. Also, strict compliance with the terms of a contract is not necessarily an established norm. In addition, administrative regulations may be nontransparent and difficult to understand.

Though, generally, South Korea has good infrastructure, the density of railroads is surprisingly low. Consequently, the burden on the road system, with regard to the transportation of both passengers and goods, is very heavy and traffic jams are often a nightmare.

It is advisable to remember that South Korea has become a high-cost economy. Its housing, transportation, telecommunications, and energy costs are high by any international standards. Labor costs are rising fast and already differ little from those in the "old developed economies."

In other words, remember that, if you choose to do business in South Korea, your goal should be not economizing on cost but getting or expanding access to a promising domestic market, skilled human resources, and, maybe, the progressive technology that local firms possess.

The Government Vision

The government's FDI Vision 2015 underlines the need to do more to boost inward FDI so as to increase its contribution to growth, job creation, and upgrading. It is considered indispensable in order to make South Korea an open economy and a northeast Asian economic hub. The strategy is to attract FDI in the four most promising major industries—parts manufacturing, R&D, logistics, and knowledge-based services.

The target is to increase the contribution of foreign companies to employment from 6.2 percent in 2004 to 16 percent in 2015 and to sales in manufacturing from 14.5 percent to 24 percent, respectively. The targeted share in corporate R&D investment is 20 percent (Ministry of Finance and Economy 2006).

Outward FDI

Outward FDI from South Korea is also on the rise. In 2006, it reached US$18,549 million on the notification basis and US$11,194 million on the departure basis as opposed to US$9,204 million and US$6,858 million in 2005, respectively (ARC Report Republic of Korea 2007). FDI in manufacturing comprised 47.2 percent of the total (departure basis) with the electronic and auto industries as the lead recipients (JETRO 2007, 185). In 2006, 30.8 percent of total FDI went to China and 16.3 percent to the US. Recently, South Korean companies have been increasing their presence in Hong Kong, Vietnam, Canada, and Eastern and Central Europe.

Concluding Remarks

South Korea has achieved enormous economic success as an emerging-market country. The time has now come to show its strength as a developed economy. The post-crisis years were marked by an unprecedented emphasis on technology and the upgrading of production on the parts of the government, business, and society as a whole. Today, the country belongs to the cohort of leading IT nations.

South Korean companies have established themselves among the world's major producers of semiconductors, mobile phones, LCDs, flat-screen TVs, and PCs. The country is an indisputable world leader in the shipbuilding industry. It is the only newly developed nation in which domestic auto producers have a strong position in the world market.

Yet, a substantial gap remains between a group of major companies, belonging to or originating from the *chaebols*, and the rest of the economy.

Another important matter for concern is the geo-economic factor—the country is "squeezed" in between the two economic giants of China and Japan. It is feared that, with such neighbors, South Korea's position may become overshadowed in spite of its potential.

Paradoxically, such a sense of crisis may be of good service to the national economy as it will stimulate an effort to upgrade products and services in order to differentiate them from "made in China" and to discover global market segments where South Korean companies can be stronger than the Japanese.

Finally, the time is ripe to approach the issues of quality and upgrading from a broad perspective. It is necessary to put more emphasis on housing and the creation of modern and convenient residential zones, the protection of the natural environment, the improvement of leisure and recreation facilities, better quality of services, and so on. Today, buying a house, and living, working, and educating children in the US or Europe is a cherished dream for many South Koreans and a natural choice for those who can afford it. The task of building a developed economy will be solved completely and entirely when such a perception changes.

11

Singapore: Globalized, Entrepreneurial, Diversified

A Few Basics

Singapore is a highly developed city-state. Its population, as of June 2008, was 4.84 million. With a gross domestic product (GDP) of US$161,349 million in 2007 it belongs to the top 45 economies in the world, in spite of its very small size. In terms of per-capita GDP, on the purchasing power parity (PPP) basis, it is among the world's leaders—in 2007, it was at number five, below Brunei and above the United States.

In its *World Competitiveness Yearbook 2008,* The International Institute for Management Development ranked it second and the World Economic Forum (WEF) in its Global Competitiveness Index for 2008–09 fifth.

There are three major types of Singapore-based companies. Foreign-affiliated firms are the strongest players, in terms of capital and production capacity. They are also the biggest exporters. As of 2003, wholly owned or majority-owned foreign firms accounted for 71 percent of net fixed assets in the manufacturing sector, 73 percent of its value added, and 44 percent of employment (Koh 2007, 168).

The second group is comprised of several hundred state-owned, or government-linked, companies (GLCs). Most of them are controlled by the state holding company, Temasek. Many GLCs are listed and are actively attracting capital from private investors across the world. Some of them have grown into large global players. The most well known GLCs include Singapore Airlines (the largest air company in the world in terms of capitalization), Development Bank of Singapore (DBS; the largest bank in Southeast Asia), SMRT (the city light railway network), SingTel (telecommunications), Singapore Power (public utilities), CapitaLand (property development), PSA International (the management and operation of seaports), Neptune Orient Lines (shipping), Singapore Press Holdings (publishing), and Keppel Corporation (famous as the world's leading producer of jack-up rigs for the oil industry and engaged in the production and repair of ships and offshore structures, property development, power generation, and the infrastructure business).

Finally, the third group is represented by domestic private businesses, mostly small- and medium-sized enterprises (SMEs). SMEs comprised 90 percent of the total number of companies, employed more than half of all workers, and produced 40 percent of the country's GDP as of 2004 (Koh 2007, 507). Generally, they are considered to be relatively weak and inefficient. However, a pool of strong private firms also exists. One of the most representative examples is the Oversea-Chinese Banking Corporation (OCBC) Group with one of the country's largest banks at its core.

Singapore's leading manufacturing industries are electronics (which attracts about half of inward foreign direct investment (FDI) and comprises half of non-oil exports), general machinery (especially the production of oil-drilling equipment and various kinds of machine tools), oil refining, petrochemicals, shipbuilding (including repair), pharmaceuticals, and biomedical products. It has a highly developed and diversified tertiary industry, led by such sectors as banking and finance, telecommunications, logistics, and hotels and catering. The tourist industry is also very important.

In 2007, manufacturing comprised 24.1 percent of the GDP, construction 3.8 percent, and services 65.9 percent. As for the particular service sectors, the share of wholesale and retail trade was 16.2 percent, financial services 12.4 percent, business services 12.5 percent, and transport and storage 9.4 percent.

The breakdown of employment by industry as of June 2007 was as follows: manufacturing 17.0 percent; construction 5.6 percent; community, social, and personal services 20.8 percent; wholesale and retail trade 15.3 percent; real estate, rental, and business services 12.4 percent; transportation and storage 9.9 percent; hotels and restaurants 6.8 percent; information and communication 4.9 percent; and other industries 1.1 percent (Singapore Department of Statistics 2008a). The city-state has practically no agriculture as well as no mineral resources of its own.

Singapore is a republic and, formally, a parliamentary democracy. The dominant political force is the People's Action Party (PAP), which has no rivals of comparable strength.

The country's key economic agency is the Economic Development Board (EDB), which was established in 1961. It plays a major role in articulating and implementing economic development policy, including the attraction of foreign investment. Since the mid-1960s it has initiated capital-intensive projects in the oil-refining and shipbuilding industries with the co-participation of the private sector and, since the 1970s, has launched a promotion policy for the electronics industry. From the 1980s, to present, it supports knowledge-intensive activities and clusters in the electronics, petrochemical, and engineering sectors and also promotes the biomedical industry.

International Enterprise Singapore is another important agency responsible for developing the capabilities, connections, and access to capital of both domestic and foreign-affiliated companies to foster their internationalization. It is also helping SMEs to develop partnerships with foreign businesses and expand overseas.

The National Wages Council (NWC) is a tripartite body of employees, trade unions, and officials. It was formed in 1972. It sets wage guidelines reflecting the country's macroeconomic conditions. Its recommendations are not mandatory, but in practice they are followed.

Tripartism, or cooperation between trade unions, employees, and government, is attached a high priority. The National Trade Unions Congress (NTUC) covers almost 99 percent of the organized labor and has a close relationship with the PAP.

The Central Provident Fund (CPF) is the core of the social security system. Contributions to the fund are mandatory for all the employees. From 1968, the use of CPF funds was liberalized for approved purposes, especially for housing finance (Koh 2007).

The Housing Development Board (HDB), under the Ministry of National Development, is responsible for the construction, rental, and sale of public housing units. About 83 percent of Singaporeans live in HDB homes (Koh 2007, 241). Contributors to the CPF are allowed to use money in their accounts to buy apartments from the HDB—a unique scheme that has proved to be instrumental in providing adequate housing for the vast majority of Singaporeans. However, as a result, many of them retire without enough savings.

Postwar Development

An Historical Perspective

Until the early nineteenth century, Singapore was an ordinary Malay village. In 1819, Stamford Raffles, then the Governor Lieutenant-General of Bencoolen (now Bengkulu on the island of Sumatra in Indonesia), established a settlement and a free trade port on the island of Singapura (the "Lion City" in Malay)— partly in order to offset the growing Dutch influence in Southeast Asia. He is considered to be the founder of colonial Singapore.

The village became the center of intermediary trade for the East India Company. It was administered jointly by the British and Malays until 1824, when the latter ceded it to the company and its heirs. The company held it until its own dissolution in 1858. After that it was administered by the Indian Office of the British Government.

Singapore largely capitalized on its location—an excellent harbor in the very center of Southeast Asia. It imported primary goods from the countries of the region and re-exported them to the rest of the world.

Independence and Merger with Malaysia

After World War II, the pro-independence trend gained strength across the region. Singapore achieved self-government in 1959. The PAP, under the leadership of Lee Kuan Yew, emerged as the leading political force. Lee Kuan Yew was Singapore's prime minister from 1959 to 1990, when he stepped down and became Senior Minister, which is a nonexecutive cabinet position. From 2004 to the present, he has held the post of Minister Mentor, which has been created specially for him in recognition of his outstanding role as the national leader. (His son, Lee Hsien Loong, is the present prime minister.) Also in 1959, after a landslide victory in the parliamentary elections, the PAP formed the country's first autonomous government. In 1963, as a result of a government-initiated referendum, Singapore merged with Malaysia and thus gained independence.

At that point, the major sectors of the national economy were intermediary trade and related services. As they did not provide enough jobs, the government launched an industrialization policy. Initially, it sought to pursue import substitution and sell manufactured products to the Malaysian market.

However, the strategy did not work, mainly because the merger itself was unsuccessful. For the United Malays National Organization (UMNO), Malaysia's dominant political organization, the PAP turned out to be a rival and rather a dangerous one too as it was well-organized, had a strong leader, and articulated fundamentally different concepts. While UMNO viewed Malaysia as an extension of the old Malaya and advocated preferential treatment for the indigenous Malays, the PAP was promoting the principle of meritocracy within a multiethnic state, emphasizing the notion of Malaysian—not just Malay—people.

In 1965, Singapore was separated from Malaysia in order, in the words of then Malaysian prime minister, Tunku Abdul Rahman, "to save the rest of the body from gangrene" (Watanabe 2003, 87). Separation marked the start of Singapore's history as an independent city-state.

Export-Led Industrialization

In the mid-1960s Singapore embarked on a policy of export-led industrialization. Initially, the pivotal role was played by labor-intensive industries, such as the production of transistors, textiles, and leather products made by local enterprises. Between 1966 and 1973, the Singapore economy registered double-digit growth every year, and the average growth rate for the period was 12.6 percent (Singapore Department of Statistics 2008b). The annual growth of exports between 1965 and 1974 averaged 19 percent (Koh 2007, 187).

In the second half of the 1960s, the national economy suffered a blow caused by the closure of British military bases and the withdrawal of British troops—bases-related production comprised 20 percent of the gross national product (GNP). Unemployment, at that time, was around 10 percent and living conditions were more than tough (Watanabe 2003, 85).

Under these conditions, the government adopted the strategy of export-oriented industrialization driven by FDI in heavy industries. Singapore was one of the few developing nations which allowed companies with 100 percent foreign ownership. To promote inward FDI, the government introduced strong tax incentives and actively developed infrastructure.

The strategy worked. The foreign-affiliated companies came to dominate both production and exports, becoming the locomotives of industrial growth. The shipbuilding, oil refining, and electronics sectors led the industrialization drive.

Along with attracting foreign capital, the government created state-owned companies, both in tertiary industry and manufacturing, such as Singapore Airlines, DBS, and Sembawang Shipyard.

Domestic private companies—overseas Chinese conglomerates and SMEs—were mostly active in trade and services. Their role in the industrialization process was smaller.

Climbing Up the Value Chain

In the wake of the world economic slowdown, caused by the first oil shock, the growth of the Singapore economy fell to 6.1 percent in 1974 and further, to 4.1 percent, in 1975. In the latter half of the 1970s it accelerated and the average growth during 1974–84 was 7.8 percent (Singapore Department of Statistics 2008b).

In the 1970s, especially in the latter half, as the country reached almost full employment, the government started to promote a shift from labor-intensive to capital- and technology-intensive industries. For instance, production of computer peripherals was designated as a priority industry (Koh 2007, 251). From the early 1980s the emphasis was put on promoting R&D, engineering design, and computer software.

From 1979, to encourage companies to climb up the value chain, the NWC initiated wage increases of about 20 percent for three years in a row.

Growth Acceleration After Interruption

In the first half of the 1980s, the Singapore economy faced problems caused by the second oil shock and a decline in exports due to the world economic slump. Growth was interrupted in 1985 when, for the first time ever, the city-state's GDP decreased (by 1.4 percent).

In this situation the government froze wages and reduced income and corporate tax rates. Special tax incentives were introduced for foreign companies choosing Singapore as a location for their regional headquarters. Also, a policy shift was made from industrialization to the promotion of both manufacturing and tertiary industries, especially finance, transportation, logistics, and services.

In the 1980s, the city-state succeeded in attracting most of the major electronics multinationals, thus becoming an important production platform for computers and hard disk drives.

From the second half of the 1980s, the Singapore economy noticeably accelerated and, between 1987 and 1997, growth rates averaged 9.2 percent per annum (Singapore Department of Statistics 2008b).

In the 1990s, the role and share of the electronics industry, especially disk drives and personal computers, increased further in terms of both production and exports. In the second half of the decade, several wafer fabrication plants had come into operation too. Also, the biomedical industry was first targeted as a priority sector.

On the financial front, heavy investment, by both foreign and local capital, in property and stock in the first half of the decade led to a surge of asset prices, resulting in a financial bubble. Stock and property prices peaked in 1996 and had begun to decline before the Asian crisis.

The Asian Crisis—A Marginal Influence

Generally, the influence of the Asian crisis on the national economy was marginal. Still, in 1998, GDP fell by 1.4 percent and stock prices plunged by over 60 percent from their peak. The management of banks remained healthy, though they had to fight with nonperforming loans (NPLs), mainly to clients in the crisis-hit countries. Their capital adequacy ratio remained above the 12 percent minimum set by the Monetary Authority of Singapore (MAS), which itself is 1.5 times higher than the 8 percent Bank for International Settlements (BIS) standard (Chia 2000).

Structural Features

The Key Role of the Bureaucracy

Unlike most other East Asian economies, Singapore faced no structural crisis and did not have to undertake painful reforms, drastically revamping the economic system. Evolutionary structural changes in the national economy are aimed at further improving and polishing the system already in place.

In a way, Singapore's economic and national governance system is unique. Its core is a very efficient, noncorrupt, and business-oriented government bureaucracy, whose key priority is to make a tiny city-state highly competitive in the global economic arena. Singapore is known for the high salaries of government officials and ministerial staff, and the country's prime minister earns significantly more than, say, the president of the US or the prime minister of Japan. When, in 2007, some debate arose, Minister Mentor Lee Kuan Yew dismissed the counterarguments as absolutely irrelevant, emphasizing that well-paid bureaucracy and government officials were a prerequisite of efficient and corruption-free national governance, which in turn was indispensable for the country's economic success and its citizens' well-being. To those who doubted it the Minister Mentor recommended taking a look around and seeing what was happening in neighboring countries. The debate faded within a short period.

The Transformation of GLCs

The major structural strengths of the Singaporean economy are the predominance of foreign-affiliated companies, mainly the subsidiaries of leading multinational companies (MNCs), and the existence of efficient GLCs. In the 1980s and 1990s, the latter expanded and diversified their operations, becoming active overseas.

There were calls, both in the political establishment and business community, to reduce the role of GLCs, proceed with their privatization, and rely more on the private sector. A number of GLCs, such as Singapore Airlines, DBS, and Singtel, were divested through limited initial public offerings (IPOs). The government is basically positive to attracting private investment on a limited scale to boost GLC strength. However, the major policy direction is to further raise the GLCs' efficiency, competitiveness, and company value.

The government-linked companies are directly involved in global competition and have become increasingly active as international investors and players in the cross-border mergers and acquisitions (M&A) game. They recruit professional managers on a meritocracy basis and actively search for talent all around the world.

Nurturing Domestic Private Businesses, Especially Technology Start-Ups

Today, the main policy seeking to change the economic structure of Singapore is that of nurturing stronger local private businesses, especially SMEs, in technologically advanced sectors such as information technology (IT) and the biomedical industry. One of the first priorities of this policy is the support of business start-ups.

In 2000, an SME ten-year plan was formulated. Its three major goals were to groom innovative, high growth SMEs, to develop productive SME sectors in service industries, and to create a knowledge-based, pro-enterprise environment (SPRING Singapore 2000).

The EDB and the Standards, Productivity, and Innovation Board (SPRING Singapore), the agency for enterprise development, are launching a wide variety of SME and start-up support schemes in the areas of financing, capacity building, and networking.

At present, it is still premature to say that SMEs in general, and venture-style, high-tech entrepreneurs in particular, have become a noticeable driving force for the country's economic growth. The effect remains to be seen in the future. Yet, certain positive shifts are already apparent. As of early 2008, the city-state had about 150 venture-capital firms managing some S\$19 million in funds (Biomed Singapore 2008).

Present Performance

A Picture of Singapore's Growth

The decisive factor upon which the growth of the Singapore economy depends is exports. In the manufacturing sector exports comprise two-thirds of production volume. The share of net exports of goods and services in GDP increased from 15 percent in 1996 to 32 percent in 2006.

The 40 percent share of private consumption is lower than in most other economies with bigger domestic markets. From the beginning of the 2000s it has been gradually declining.

The share of gross fixed-capital formation has also declined from 33.8 percent in 1995 to 29.9 percent in 2007 (ADB 2008). However, the efficiency of investment is rising—the increment in gross capital formation needed to generate every 1 percent increment of GDP is becoming smaller. Also, it has to be taken into account that, to attract companies and talent from all around the world and to further strengthen the image of Singapore as a city with a unique business and living environment, the government is actively investing in the development and upgrading of infrastructure, which also boosts growth.

The post-crisis recovery of the Singapore economy was quick, but short. In 2000, the growth rate hit 10 percent, but in 2001, in the wake of the IT slump and a slowdown in the US and Europe, exports fell and GDP declined by 2.3 percent. In the following two years, growth, by the standards of Singapore, remained low.

However, in 2004–07, exports were expanding rapidly again and the economy accelerated (see Table 11.1). Another important driver of growth, gross fixed-capital formation, which fell noticeably in 2001–03, rebounded too. Private consumption also went up, but the small size of the population inevitably limited its contribution to growth.

The city-state has made significant steps to strengthen its position as an important financial power, not only on a regional but also on a global scale. This drive is led by the government's investment arms—Temasek and the Government of Singapore Investment Corporation (GIC).

The Impact of the Global Financial Turmoil

In 2008, in the wake of the global financial turmoil, the Singapore economy slowed down, first and foremost because of a slump in exports. Technically, it entered a recession as GDP declined for two quarters in a row (the second and third). In the fourth quarter it shrank dramatically 17.0 percent on a quarter-to-quarter and 3.7 percent on a year-to-year basis. The growth rate for the whole of 2008 was only 1.2 percent. Signs of deflation appeared. The key Straits Times Index (STI) fell almost 55 percent between the beginning of the year and the end of October (Wijaya 2008). Unemployment began to rise. DBS announced the cut of 900 jobs, or 6 percent of its workforce. House prices fell.

The government's S\$20.5 billion Resilience Package for 2009 consists of five components: job creation; stimulation of bank lending (the government is to extend capital to share risks with banks); enhancing business cash-flow and competitiveness (through tax measures and grants); supporting families; and building a home for the future (infrastructure spending and expanded provisions for education and healthcare (Singapore Budget 2009)).

The direct exposure of Singapore financial institutions to subprime mortgages was small. However, it was feared that acquisitions by Temasek and GLCs of significant stakes in a number of troubled Western investment banks (such as Merrill Lynch) could adversely affect activities in the financial sector. The government pledged to shift to an expansionary fiscal policy.

The Goals of Economic Policy

In December 2001, the government established the Economic Review Committee (ERC) to comprehensively examine the status of the national economy and articulate the goals of economic policy. In February 2003, it came out with a report containing three major recommendations. Singapore, it said, had to be remade into: first, a globalized economy, positioned as a key node in

Table 11.1 Main economic indicators (real annual growth, %)*

Indicator	1999	2000	2001	2002	2003	2004	2005	2006	2007
GDP	7.2	10.1	-2.3	4.0	3.5	9.0	7.3	8.2	7.7
Industry**	7.7	12.0	-9.0	4.0	1.2	10.5	8.1	10.5	7.3
Services**	6.5	8.2	2.0	3.9	4.3	7.8	6.7	7.2	7.8
Gross domestic capital formation	10.4	24.1	-22.4	-4.9	-30.7	48.1	-1.0	15.2	21.4
Private consumption	9.1	14.9	4.7	4.9	0.9	5.2	3.9	3.3	4.6
Nominal wages (average monthly earnings of CPF contributors)	2.7	8.9	2.3	0.8	1.7	3.6	3.5	3.2	6.2
Consumer prices	0.0	1.3	1.0	-0.4	0.5	1.7	0.5	1.0	2.1
Unemployment rate (%)+	3.6	4.4	2.7	4.2	4.5	4.4	4.2	3.4	2.9
Exports (US$ millions),^ fob	114,628	137,953	121,687	125,043	144,128	198,562	229,832	271,603	298,976
Imports (US$ millions),^ cif	111,001	134,676	115,919	116,337	127,897	163,820	200,187	238,478	262,743
Average exchange rate (S$ 1 per US$ 1)	1.70	1.72	1.79	1.79	1.74	1.69	1.66	1.59	1.51

Source: Singapore Department of Statistics (Singstat), ADB: Key Indicators 2008

*Calendar year (fiscal year in Singapore begins April 1)

**Data for industry and services refers to value added

+As of June

^Data for 1999–2002 does not include Indonesia

the global network and linked to all the major economies; second, a creative and entrepreneurial nation willing to take risks to create fresh businesses and flag new paths to success; and third, a diversified economy, powered by the twin engines of manufacturing and services, where vibrant domestic companies complement MNCs and new start-ups co-exist with traditional businesses exploiting new and innovative ideas (Ministry of Trade and Industry 2003).

Consequently, building a globalized, entrepreneurial, and diversified economy are now the major goals of government policy. The five key strategies to achieve the goals are: first, expanding external ties through the World Trade Organization (WTO) framework, regional cooperation, and bilateral free trade agreements (FTAs); second, maintaining competitiveness and flexibility by keeping taxes low, the labor market and wages flexible, and the prices of production factors competitive; third, promoting entrepreneurship and domestic companies; fourth, promoting the growth of both manufacturing and services through improving cost competitiveness, raising skills, and developing new capabilities and industries; and fifth, developing human capital by actively investing in education and training and welcoming global talent. The growth rate targeted for the medium term is 4–6 percent a year (Ministry of Trade and Industry 2003).

A Knowledge-Based Economy

The key phrase Singaporeans use to define their national economic strategy is the creation of the "knowledge-based economy."

Perhaps, one of the most vivid examples of progress in this direction is the development of the One-North area—a cluster of research and educational institutions and high-tech companies whose major hubs are Fusionopolis (information and communication technology (ICT) and media) and Biopolis (biomedicine).

The promotion of the ICT industry remains the number one priority and some local companies have attracted attention by the successful development of technologies and new services. For instance, in mobile telephony the firm, Bubble Motion, has become known for its BubbleTALK™ application that makes it possible for mobile users to send a voice recording through a text message.

In tandem—the other important development—the biomedical sector has started to be promoted as a new leading industry. The government has invested hundreds of millions of Singapore dollars in building the infrastructure and funding R&D. It actively supports cooperation between research centers and producers and between the public and private sectors.

Biopolis, an international biomedical R&D center, provides space for R&D along with opportunities for collaboration between research centers and companies, as well as among researchers and businessmen. Also, Singapore is developing a cutting edge in contract biologics manufacturing.

From the Lower Half to the Top Half of the First World

In his speech at a Chinese New Year Dinner in February 2007, Minister Mentor Lee Kuan Yew articulated a new development paradigm for the city-state. The key point is simple. Singapore can, and has to, move from the lower half to the top half of the First World in the next 10–20 years.

Singapore's landscape, he said, will be transformed by incorporating the best features of the world's top cities—Paris's al fresco buzz, London's cosmopolitan mix, and New York's arts and business charm. But it will come with a tropical twist—lots of water and greenery.

The "Making of the City"

Singapore may look like a beautiful dream of paradise on earth but it is not. It reflects Singapore's reality: the "making of the city" has become a key strategic industry, a major element of the national strategy. Very few countries or cities would prioritize it to that extent.

For Singapore, city-making has a special meaning. It is not just about solving the problems of a big city or addressing the challenges it faces. It is an "aggressive" policy of making it: uniquely beautiful in terms of architecture, scenery, and design; uniquely orderly and well governed; and uniquely friendly to its residents and visitors. This stance is strategically important in purely economic terms—to attract capital and talent from around the world. (It would be safe to say that Singapore remains the only country in Asia that has managed to create living and working conditions for people from the developed world better than in their own countries.) That is not to say that a good living environment doesn't help Singaporeans themselves "feel good" and work well too.

The strategy of creating a super-city, as well as political will to do it, are definitely present and so is a *de facto* national consensus about the importance of this task. It serves as an excellent tool to unite the nation, provide political and social stability under PAP rule, and boost economic development.

Problems

Very rapid building of a knowledge economy brings its own problems. The upgrading of production and higher wages for skilled laborers, along with the growing inflow of wealthy foreigners, naturally, exerts strong upward pressure on prices. High demand for office, factory, and living space on a very small territory leads to asset inflation.

Singapore has become a high-cost city, which poses new problems for the households not directly involved in the new economy, especially low-income families.

The average monthly income of a Singaporean household with at least one working member in 2007 was S$6,830. The average income from work for the top 10 percent of earners was S$20,240 as opposed to only S$1,210 for the bottom 10 percent. The gap is widening as the incomes of high earners are growing much faster (Chew 2008).

The government is introducing various support schemes for low-income families, trying to make up for the rise in living costs. It is also moving to create more reliable social safety nets. However, Singapore firmly sticks to the basic principle of citizens' self-responsibility. Pension payments, for example, depend on the outstanding balance on each beneficiary's account at the CPF—there is no pooling of funds based on the premise of mutual support.

Foreign Trade

The city-state is one of the leaders in international trade liberalization. Its imports are mostly tariff-free. Duties are imposed only on a few consumer items, such as cars, perfume, liquor, and tobacco (Koh 2007, 168). It has also adopted a very active stance regarding bilateral and multilateral FTAs with both Asian and non-Asian countries.

The volume of Singapore's foreign trade is three times greater than its GDP. As one of the major international trade centers it is widely engaged in re-export operations, which are approximately the same in scale as domestic exports. Also, it is one of the major oil-trading centers.

The Composition of Exports

In 2007, the country's total exports amounted to S$450,628 million. Re-exports were S$204,181 million. Out of total exports, 69.7 percent went to Asia, and Malaysia remains the major export market (a remarkable 12.9 percent of the export total for 2007). The US used to be the second-largest market but, in 2006, for the first time, it was overtaken by Hong Kong (in 2007, the shares were 8.8 percent and 10.5 percent respectively), and in 2007, also by Indonesia (9.8 percent) and China (9.7 percent). Other major markets are Japan (5.5 percent) and Thailand (4.1 percent). Exports to Europe comprised 11.9 percent of the total.

The composition of domestic exports by product is as follows. The share of petroleum and products was 26.6 percent of the total. Electronic products comprised about 30.4 percent of all domestic exports and 41.4 percent of non-oil domestic exports. Among electronic products themselves, the major export items are integrated circuits (9.5 percent of all domestic exports), parts for PCs (6.6 percent), disk drives (4.1 percent), telecommunication equipment (3.1 percent), and consumer electronics (2.1 percent). The share of machinery and equipment other than electronics was 10.3 percent.

Another important group of exported products is chemicals and chemical products (19.2 percent of all domestic exports). The role of medical products, which are included in this group, is increasing. Their share was 3.4 percent.

The Composition of Imports

Imports, in 2007, reached S$395,980 million. The share of Asia was 69.8 percent, Europe 14.3 percent, and the US 12.3 percent. On a country basis, Malaysia was the major exporter to Singapore (13.1 percent), followed by the US (12.3 percent), China (12.1 percent), Japan (8.2 percent), Taiwan (5.9 percent), Indonesia (5.6 percent), and South Korea (4.9 percent).

Machinery and equipment comprised 52.6 percent of the total imports, including 34.3 percent for electronic products. The next most important items were petroleum and products (20.0 percent), chemicals (6.0 percent), iron and steel (2.2 percent), and nonferrous metals (1.9 percent). Also, Singapore is very highly dependent on imported foodstuffs and consumer goods (Singapore Department of Statistics 2008c).

FDI and the Business Environment

The business environment is generally very favorable. The legal system is sound, regulations are relatively few, and transparency is high. Registration procedures are simple. Bureaucracy is efficient and noncorrupt. Income and corporate taxes are low. Both have been progressively reduced since the 1980s. In 2007, the maximum personal income tax and corporate income tax rates were both only 20 percent.

Various kinds of tax incentives for corporations are available. The pioneer tax incentive, or a full corporate tax exemption for a set period, is applied to strategically important projects in desirable industries. The development expansion incentive, or preferential tax rate for a set period on all qualifying profits above a predetermined base, is given to companies moving into higher value-added activities, if their projects are considered to generate significant economic spin-offs for Singapore. Investment allowance on equipment cost, incurred within a set period, is extended to investment expected to raise efficiency of resource utilization or introduce new technology into existing industries.

Infrastructure—roads, telecommunication systems, the airport and seaports, transportation, and storage facilities—is excellent, and so is the living environment.

The country is very politically stable. As mentioned, there are practically no labor conflicts. The labor market is flexible. However, labor costs, especially compensation for skilled personnel, are noticeably going up. Land, utilities, and other costs have also become high by any international standards.

Overall, Singapore is an attractive place to invest in R&D and the production of high-value-added products for Southeast Asian, Chinese, and global markets or to establish a regional headquarters for Southeast Asia and, maybe, the whole of the Asian continent. Also, the advantage of doing business in Singapore, one of the most modern global cities in the world, is the availability of highly skilled human resources, both local and foreign.

The volume of FDI in Singapore is shown in Table 11.2. The ability to attract more than S$40 billion (almost US$30 billion) of FDI annually is extraordinary for a country of such a small size. At the same time, Singapore companies have become important direct investors in Asia and are increasing their global presence.

As of the end of 2006, the stock of inward FDI was S$364 billion. From the mid-1990s, Europe overtook Asia and became its largest source. Its share in FDI stock

Table 11.2   Inward and outward FDI* (S$ millions)

Direction	2001	2002	2003	2004	2005	2006
Outward	33,797.4	15,027.0	6,476.0	26,170.2	22,330.4	24,193.5
Inward	25,452.8	13,694.6	16,036.3	30,633.8	47,001.9	40,114.0

Source: Singapore Department of Statistics (Singstat).
*Net flow.

reached 47.2 percent with the UK as the major investor (15.1 percent), followed by the Netherlands (13.3 percent). The share of Asia was 22.4 percent (including 12.4 percent for Japan) and of the US 10.2 percent. Most inward FDI goes into financial and insurance services (38.7 percent of the total stock), manufacturing (29.9 percent), wholesale and retail trade and hotels and restaurants (18.2 percent), and transport and storage (6.2 percent).

Outward FDI stock, as of the end of 2006, was S$226 billion. Most of Singapore's FDI goes to Asia (49.4 percent)—especially to China (13.6 percent of the total), Malaysia (7.7 percent), Indonesia (7.3 percent), and Hong Kong (6.2 percent). The share for South and Central America and the Caribbean was 23.0 percent, Europe 11.5 percent (with the UK as the major destination), and the US 3.8 percent. The major targets for outward FDI are the financial and insurance services sector (53.4 percent), manufacturing (31.6 percent), wholesale and retail trade and hotels and restaurants (18.0 percent), and ICT (5.8 percent) (Singapore Department of Statistics 2006).

Concluding Remarks

Singapore is strengthening its position as Asia's major, and Southeast Asia's number one, financial and trading center. It is Asia's major logistics and transportation hub—both Changi International Airport and Singapore seaport are among world leaders in terms of cargo and passenger turnover. In the 2000s, Singapore has made significant progress toward becoming the center of high-value-added manufacturing, R&D, and education.

The Singapore economy is in good shape. It is highly developed and well balanced—both the service sector and manufacturing are strong. It attracts a lot of FDI. The environment for business appears to be one of the best in the world.

The city-state has proved to be uniquely successful in making GLCs efficient by the standards of the market economy. The government neither controls them in a bureaucratic way nor provides a shelter for them from market competition. It has rather adopted the role of a demanding owner, encouraging company management to raise profitability and global competitiveness. Generally, GLCs are more efficient and competitive than the domestic private sector. The leading Singaporean firms, especially GLCs, are steadily moving up the value chain and becoming important international players. The strongest domestic companies are concentrated in the tertiary sector.

Currently, domestic private businesses remain significantly weaker than foreign-affiliated companies and GLCs. The city-state still does not have a pool of dynamic SMEs and venture business is just starting to emerge as a noticeable player.

The decisive factor in upgrading of Singapore's economy is the country's ability to attract highly skilled human resources from overseas. Domestic human resources are insufficient—and not only because the population of the city-state is too small. In spite of all the progress achieved in recent years, educational institutions do not provide the number of skilled, especially knowledge, workers required. The mismatch between workers' skills and employers' demands has become a major headache.

Singapore's intrinsic problems—small size, the absence of an agricultural sector, and the lack of natural resources, including such basic ones as water—give it, in the words of Chia Siow Yue, "a perpetual threat of vulnerability" (Chia 2000). The decisive role of exports as a driver of economic growth (Singapore cannot make up for export slowdowns by the expansion of the domestic demand like bigger countries do) and a very high dependency on imports of not only food, fuels, and raw materials, but also manufacturing goods, makes this vulnerability even more acute.

Another of Singapore's problems is its location amid countries which are much bigger in size but are further behind in their economic development. They tend to look at the city-state with mixed feelings of envy toward its success and wealth and apprehension that it will dominate the region economically and financially.

On the other hand, Singapore is successfully developing good economy-centered bilateral relations with all the major economic players around the world. It is one of the world leaders regarding the number of FTAs concluded. Interestingly, it is also the only country in the region showing no signs of apprehension about China's economic rise, seeing it only as a big opportunity.

When you think about today's Asian economy, the first idea to cross your mind would be, probably, the emergence of giants—China and India—as new economic superpowers. However, don't forget about tiny Singapore. Its position as Asia's leader in terms of quality of economic growth and, furthermore, quality of life is becoming more and more significant.

12

Malaysia: Developed by 2020?

A Few Basics

Malaysia is a federation with a population of 25 million people, consisting of 13 states (nine sultanates and four states) and one federal territory (with three components—the capital city of Kuala Lumpur, the administrative capital of Putrajaya, and Labuan). Its western part (40 percent of its territory), where 83 percent of the population live, is located on the Malay Peninsula bordering Thailand. The eastern part (60 percent of its territory), consisting of the states of Sabah and Sarawak, is situated on the island of Borneo.

In 1948, the British territories on the peninsula formed the Federation of Malaya, which became independent in August 1957. Malaysia was formed in 1963 when the former British colonies of Singapore, Sabah, and Sarawak joined the Federation. Singapore seceded in 1965.

By nominal gross domestic product (GDP), in 2007, Malaysia was ranked thirty-eighth in the world. In terms of per-capita GDP (purchasing power parity (PPP)) it was fifty-sixth, below Chile and above Argentina.

The country is rich in natural resources. The most well known are oil, natural gas, tin, natural rubber, and timber. It is a net exporter of energy resources. Also, Malaysia accounts for more than half of the world's production of palm oil. Other important primary products are sugarcane and cocoa.

The major manufacturing industry is electronics, including computers and parts (especially integrated circuits), and home electronic appliances. This sector is dominated by foreign-affiliated companies. Other important exporting industries are oil refining, chemicals and petrochemicals, and textiles. Food, paper, auto, and other manufacturing industries are producing mostly for the domestic market.

In 2006, the share of agriculture in the GDP was 8.7 percent, industry 49.9 percent, and services 43.5 percent. The shares in the total number of persons employed were 14.6 percent for agriculture, 20.3 percent for manufacturing, 0.4 percent for mining, and 64.7 percent for services (ADB 2007).

Probably, Malaysia's most internationally famous company is the state-owned, oil-and-gas firm, Petronas. It is ranked among the Fortune 500 and has business interests in more than 30 countries. Its activities include oil exploration and refining, the marketing and distribution of petroleum products, gas processing and liquefaction, and petrochemicals, as well as well as automotive engineering and property investment.

There is a cohort of powerful conglomerates—mostly, but not only, overseas Chinese. The richest Malaysian tycoon is Hong Kong-based international businessman, Robert Kuok, chairman of Kuok Group and Kerry Group. His interest in Malaysia, Kuok Brothers, is led by nephew, Chye Kuok, and its activities include the palm oil and grain business, finance and insurance, transportation services, and hotels.

YTL Corporation is an old family business run by five brothers and engaged in construction and infrastructure, manufacturing, hotels, and resorts. The IOI Group, known mostly for its food and drinks products, includes one of the best-performing plantation companies. It has also set up the largest palm-oil refinery in Europe. AirAsia, the brainchild of the business star, Tony Fernandes, is a world-famous budget airline. Maybank is one of Southeast Asia's biggest financial institutions. Another symbol of successful Malaysian business is the Sime Darby conglomerate, which is involved in 20 countries and engaged in plantations, property development, auto dealerships, engineering, infrastructure, and utilities.

Malaysia's major economic agency is the Ministry of International Trade and Industry (MITI). The Economic Planning Unit, functioning under the Prime Minister's Department, is responsible for steering the country's development toward achieving developed nation status by 2020.

Malaysia is a federal state and a constitutional monarchy. The sovereign is elected among the nine Sultans and coopted by his peers every five years. Executive power is in the hands of the prime minister, who is the leader of the party or coalition that has a parliamentary majority.

The dominant political organization, in power since independence, is the Barisan Nasional (National Front) coalition with the United Malays National Organization (UMNO) as its leading partner.

A Multiethnic State

The federation has become home to people of many different ethnic, religious, and cultural origins. There is a Malay majority, but also important Chinese and Indian minorities, a large indigenous population in East Malaysia and smaller ethnic communities of Arabs, Indonesians, Pakistanis, and Filipinos. Since independence one of the country's major challenges has been to maintain harmony among these ethnic communities while fostering economic growth and development.

Malaysia has an historic tradition of segregating economic activity along racial lines. The practice was introduced by the British. In order to simplify administrative control and management, the colonial administration employed Indian immigrants to work on the rubber plantations and Chinese immigrants at the tin mines. Having some experience of trading with the Chinese, the British allowed them to take up certain commercial activities.

Malays were engaged in agriculture and fisheries. They were the only ethnic group allowed into the bureaucracy, albeit on a very limited scale (Ariff 2003). As a result, at the time Malaysia became independent, its society was segregated economically and racially with the majority of Malays at the foot of the social and economic ladder. In order to remedy this inequality, representatives of the three major ethnic groups agreed that upon independence the Malays would be given certain preferential economic and political rights.

The New Economic Policy and Beyond

In 1957–69, economic growth, though quite high, failed to bring a visible improvement in the status of the Malays. In May 1969, violent clashes between Malays and Chinese revealed a wide gap existing between the two communities.

At that time, Malays accounted for 52 percent of the population against 37 percent for the Chinese. The balance of power and prosperity had not changed much since independence. Malays were dominating the political world but their majority population was still engaged in low-income activities, while the Chinese were in control of the more modern sectors of the economy (Menon 2008).

These tragic events were followed by the reassessment of economic and development policies. The New Economic Policy (NEP), which operated from 1971 until 1990, explicitly prioritized the goal of helping the Malays.

The emphasis in all successive five-year plans up until 1990 and beyond, when the NEP was succeeded by the National Development Policy (NDP), was put on increasing Malay ownership, enhancing their access to high-income occupations, and narrowing income inequality. The initial objective was to attain at least 30 percent Malay equity ownership in private companies by 1990. In reality, by the end of the 1980s, it had reached about 20 percent as opposed to 1.9 percent in 1970 (ARC Report Malaysia 2007, 11). The Third Outline Perspective Plan (OPP3) for 2001–10 extended the 30 percent goal until 2010.

Postwar Development

From Import Substitution to Export-Driven Growth

Malaysia inherited a developed infrastructure, efficient administration, and a well-performing, export-oriented primary products sector from the British. In terms of per-capita income, literacy, and healthcare it was more advanced than most of its neighbors. The abundance of land and other natural resources provided favorable initial conditions for growth. The country was already a big exporter of rubber, tin, palm oil, and other natural resources (Athukorala 1997).

From the very start, Malaysia had a relatively open trade and investment policy. However, the authorities pursued import substitution to protect nascent industries, especially the textiles counted upon as an area of competitive advantage.

The second half of the 1960s was marked by a genuine shift to an export-driven economy. In 1968, the Investment Incentives Act was enacted, providing strong incentives to export-oriented, foreign-owned companies.

In the 1970s, Malaysia set up 12 Free Trade Zones (FTZs), not only offering exemption or reduction of corporate tax and customs duties but also waiving regulations regarding the employment of the *Bumiputra* (ethnic Malays and also indigenous people in East Malaysia) and their share in the companies' capital. The FTZs attracted a cohort of leading Japanese, US, and other firms, especially in the electronics sector.

In the mid-1980s, the national economy went through a slowdown, caused by falling world prices on exported commodities. In 1985, the GDP fell by 1.0 percent (ARC Report Malaysia 2007, 83). In the second half of the 1980s, reliance on foreign capital further increased, especially after the 1985 Plaza Accord (the agreement of five leading industrial powers to jointly intervene in the currency markets—first of all to appreciate the yen and depreciate the US dollar to help the US reduce its trade deficit—see page 331) and the subsequent rise of the yen. Dramatically growing inward foreign direct investment (FDI) from Japan, but also from other Asian newly industrialized economies (NIEs) and the West, boosted growth in manufacturing—especially the production of integrated circuits and other electronic products.

In 1988, the share of manufacturing in the GDP surpassed that of agriculture, climbing to 29 percent in 1996 (the same level as in South Korea in 1984). The share of manufactured products in exports exceeded that of the five major primary products in 1987 and in 1996 rose above 80 percent (Watanabe 2003, 138). In the early 1990s, Malaysia became a leading exporter, not only of integrated circuits but also air conditioners, videotape recorders, and color TVs.

The Legacy of Mahathir

From 1981 until 2003, the Malaysian political landscape was dominated by the towering presence of Prime Minister Mahathir bin Mohamad—a fervent advocate of the "Asianization" of Asia's sociopolitical and economic development. Cultivating the position of maverick in the international community, he drove his country along development paths, which, in his view, were rooted in Asian sociocultural heritage and values and, thus, were more attuned to the needs and capabilities of Asian people than were Western models.

Mahathir came up with the vision of a nation transcending existing ethnic identities and loyalties, while providing support to the Malays during a "catch-up" period. It was received positively by the Malays and also, for a while, captured the imagination of the Malaysian-Chinese and Malaysian-Indian middle classes.

Industrial Policy

As part of the NEP, in the first half of the 1980s, Malaysia attempted to promote a range of heavy industries (such as petrochemicals, steel, cement, paper, machinery, transport equipment, and building materials) via the Heavy Industries Corporation of Malaysia (HICOM), a public sector holding company. Among these promotions was the ambitious Proton project, launched in partnership with Mitsubishi Motors (HICOM 70 percent, Mitsubishi 30 percent), aimed at the development of the domestic automobile industry. The production of cars started from 1985. Under the "Look East" policy Malaysia tried to emulate Japan, South Korea, and Taiwan.

These heavy industrialization projects were supported by subsidized credit, government procurement provisions, and heavy tariff protection, without subjecting them to market-based performance norms. Most of them, including Proton, ended up as heavy losers, draining away precious budgetary resources. It was overlooked that the economies that Malaysia had tried to emulate had much more substantial human and financial resources, more sound technological bases and, even in the peak years of industrial policy, allowed much more competition.

New Incentives for Foreign Capital

Luckily, this ill-conceived industrial policy did not affect export-led growth. Mixing pro-*Bumiputra* policy and pragmatism, the government followed a multipronged strategy. On the one hand, it erected barriers to nurture heavy industries. On the other, it was further activating its policies to attract inward FDI.

With the Industrial Master Plan of 1986, regulation of foreign equity participation was relaxed. One hundred percent foreign-equity ownership of export-oriented companies was allowed (Athukorala 1997).

From the early 1990s, Malaysia was one of the most active promoters of the idea of e-government ("paperless government," which means that most documentation is produced, delivered, submitted, and exchanged electronically). In 1993, it began developing the ultramodern new Federal Government Administrative Center in Putrajaya and a few years later started the transfer of government agencies. The prime minister's office moved in 1998. Development of the new administrative capital is to be completed by 2012.

The next big step was the launch of the Multimedia Super Corridor (MSC) in 1995, aiming to attract world class R&D-oriented companies and research institutions. It runs from Kuala Lumpur City Centre (KLCC) in the north to Kuala Lumpur International Airport (KLIA) in the south. Its core, along with Putrajaya, is the information technology (IT) city of Cyberjaya, which began development in 1997. Foreign-owned companies there were given a special legal and fiscal status. They could wholly own their Malaysia-registered subsidiaries and were not subjected to any restriction on the entry and sojourn of foreign skilled workers. In addition to tax holidays for up to ten years and duty-free imports, five cyber laws were enacted—on electronic signatures, intellectual property rights (IPR), telemedicine, Internet infraction, and the promotion of the use of IT.

In another important development, an international offshore financial center was opened on Labuan island, off the coast of East Malaysia.

Encouraging Local Entrepreneurs

The ethnic requirements of the NEP were gradually relaxed and, in 1990, the NEP itself was replaced by the NDP.

A Malay himself, Mahathir initiated various policies favoring his community. Yet, at the same time, he was often very critical of Malay people's behavior and attitudes, reproaching them for passivity and contrasting this with the entrepreneurial spirit of the Chinese and Indian communities. His objective was to boost the development of Malay entrepreneurship.

Only a number of politically sensitive ventures in the automobile, petrochemical, steel, and cement industries were kept under the state's direct control. Privatization, and a stronger emphasis on the role of the private sector, gave Malays a good chance to fill the top positions in the new companies. A number of high-profile *Bumiputra* entrepreneurs appeared, such as Halim Saad of the Renong Group, Tajudin Ramli of TRI (a large telecom company), and Wan Azmi of Land and General (an investment holding company). As a result, Malay attitudes toward entrepreneurship changed. For many of them the group of successful millionaire *Bumiputra* became the new role models, replacing bureaucratic and political figures.

However, the newly born business magnates were not Bill Gates-style technological entrepreneurs (the type of entrepreneurs Mahathir is said to have dreamed of) but typical owners of Asian-style conglomerates, largely relying on strong connections with the state as the major precondition for success.

Structural Reforms

During the Asian crisis, Malaysia's policy was different from the one recommended by the International Monetary Fund (IMF). Having started with an IMF-style package (but without the IMF's involvement) including government spending cuts, a freeze on public-sector investment, and companies' drastic restructuring plans, the government decided to change course. It shifted to an expansionary budget policy, pegged the ringgit to the US dollar (at 3.80 ringgit per US$1), and imposed tight capital controls. It is not widely known, though, that before imposing controls and launching the recovery package, Mahathir and his team held more than 120 consultations with industry groups and experts, including the IMF and the World Bank (Kadir 2007).

The major aim was to stop currency speculation coming from short-selling of the ringgit in offshore markets, particularly Singapore. After the imposition of controls on September 1, 1998, all sales of ringgit assets had to go through authorized domestic intermediaries. All ringgit assets held abroad had to be repatriated (Kaplan 2001). The strategy mostly worked, though Malaysia's image in the eyes of the investment community was put at risk.

Due to rather strict prudential regulations and conservative lending policies, Malaysian banks, though facing difficulties, mostly avoided the troubles faced by their counterparts in Indonesia, South Korea, and Thailand. The nonperforming loans (NPLs) problem and bank restructuring were managed by several state institutions. The Corporate Debt Restructuring Committee (CDRC) worked with corporate loans, Danaharta discounted and bought bad loans from banks, and Danamodal recapitalized banks. Acquisitions of small banks by big ones were encouraged. In reality, it was often used as an excuse for dissolving smaller banks, including those which were properly managed, and expanding politically linked big banks, even when they were in worse shape.

Privatization became a hot topic for Malaysia from the mid-1980s. In 1991, the government announced the Privatization Master Plan. The targets for privatization (complete or partial) included HICOM, Malaysia Airlines (MAS), Proton, the postal and telephone networks, passenger railway services, highways, and hospital support services. They were sold off to well-connected *Bumiputra* tycoons. There was a lot of criticism leveled at patronage, cronyism, and lack of transparency and competitive bidding, as well as an outcry from *Bumiputra* groups that were left out.

In the wake of the Asian crisis, MAS, RapidKL Light Rail Transit company, the national sewage company Indah Water Konsortium, and Proton were renationalized. (At present the government says that it is interested in selling off part of the MAS stock).

Since then, the emphasis has been put on reforming and restructuring government-linked companies (GLCs) rather than on reprivatization or new privatization projects. The government owns around 36 percent of the total stock of the firms listed at the Bursa Malaysia (US Department of State 2007). GLC reform began at the start of the 2000s and is to be completed by 2015. By late autumn 2007, the market value of the 20 GLCs which underwent a major transformation in 2004 had risen by 71 percent (Vinesh 2007).

Present Performance

The Economy is Restoring Its Shape, But...

A *New Straits Times* (Malaysia's major newspaper) report, published on February 6, 2007, stated: "A decade after the Asian financial crisis, the economy is in its best shape." The following impressive figures were presented. Per-capita income rose from 12,079 ringgit in 1998 to 18,039 ringgit in 2005, international reserves rose from US$30.85 billion in 1999 to US$70.48 billion in 2005, and the Kuala Lumpur Composite Index (KLCI) rose from 262.7 points in the dark days of 1998 to 1,225 points on February 5, 2007. In 2006, for the first time ever, foreign trade turnover exceeded the symbolic mark of 1 trillion ringgit (US$306 billion). However, the Singapore-based economist of Standard Chartered, Joseph Tan, was right in his diagnosis: "Benchmarked against itself, Malaysia has made lots of improvement. But compared with other countries ... it needs to act more speedily" (Kadir 2007).

The post-crisis recovery was quite rapid. The pre-crisis GDP level was regained by the mid 2000s (ADB 2007). After a contraction of 7.4 percent in 1998, the economy grew by 6.1 percent in 1999 and 8.9 percent in 2000. Exports, investment, and private consumption started to expand fast (see Table 12.1). Then, the IT recession of 2001 resulted in the decline of exports for two consecutive years.

Table 12.1   Main economic indicators (real annual growth, %)*

Indicator	1999	2000	2001	2002	2003	2004	2005	2006	2007
GDP	6.1	8.9	0.5	5.4	5.8	6.8	5.0	5.9	6.3
Agriculture*	0.5	6.1	–0.2	2.9	6.0	4.7	2.6	5.2	2.2
Industry*	8.8	13.6	2.6	4.2	7.5	7.3	3.4	4.9	3.3
Services*	4.4	6.0	4.1	5.8	4.2	6.4	6.8	7.4	10.0
Gross domestic capital formation	–3.9	29.2	–9.3	7.9	–1.5	6.9	–2.5	11.5	3.9
Private consumption	2.9	13.0	3.0	3.9	8.1	9.8	9.1	6.5	10.8
Consumer prices	2.8	1.5	1.4	1.8	1.2	1.4	3.1	3.6	2.0
Unemployment rate (%)	3.4	3.0	3.5	3.5	3.6	3.5	3.5	3.3	3.2
Exports, fob (billions ringgit)	321.6	373.3	334.3	357.4	397.9	481.3	533.8	589.0	605.1
Imports, cif (billions ringgit)	248.5	311.5	280.2	303.1	316.5	399.6	434.0	480.8	504.8
Average exchange rate (1 ringgit per US$1)	3.80	3.80	3.80	3.80	3.80	3.80	3.79	3.67	3.44

Source: ADB; Key Indicators 2008; Concerns emerged about the country's declining ability to attract FDI.
*Data for agriculture, industry, and services refers to value added.

The growth of private consumption also slowed down. Investment dropped in absolute terms, and the fall was repeated in 2003 and 2005. Concerns emerged about the country's declining ability to attract FDI.

Acceleration

Overall, however, the economy has noticeably accelerated again since 2002. Until 2007, it was growing within the 5–7 percent range.

Exports expanded fast again in 2004–2006. In 2007, however, their growth fell to 2.7 percent, largely due to a slowdown in the US, which negatively affected sales of electronic items. Yet, the growth of private consumption stimulated by the civil servants' wage increase (*The Edge Daily* 2008), significantly accelerated hitting almost 11 percent. The service sector showed new dynamism, led by the booming tourism industry. On the negative side, rising household indebtedness, though still manageable, posed a problem.

In the wake of the growing global demand for primary commodities, Malaysia's position as a net exporter of petroleum and natural gas, as well as a major exporter of palm oil, became an increasingly important factor of its economic strength.

In November, 2006, the government announced the extensive Iskandar Development Plan Malaysia for the southern part of Johor State. The idea was to make the area a new IT and services (digital content and other creative industries, education, financial consulting, healthcare, logistics, and tourism) hub, having close links with Singapore.

In 2007, two more state projects were started: the Northern Corridor Economic Region (NCER), centered on the development of commerce-scale farming and food processing; and the East Coast Economic Region (ECER), aimed at developing a deep-sea fishing port, aquaculture, palm-oil processing, and the petrochemical industry (ADB 2008).

In 2005, the fixed rate of the ringgit to the US dollar was replaced by a managed float against a basket of currencies. The ringgit became more flexible and its exchange rate began to increase.

An Overstrained Budget and Price Controls

To stimulate the economy, in the middle of the 2000s, the government embarked on large-scale, pump-priming measures. In 2006, the non-oil, primary budget deficit was estimated to increase to 9 percent of GDP, from 7.5 percent in 2005. Federal state finances are growing more and more reliant on oil and natural gas revenues (IMF 2007).

In addition, the federal state budget has been overstrained due to continuing price controls and subsidies for many consumer and production goods, such as palm oil, cooking oil, petrol, flour, bread, rice, steel, and cement. Besides purely financial problems, it results in smuggling, hoarding, and even supply shortages. For example, cooking oil is subsidized only for home use, but is hoarded by businesses using it for industrial purposes, which leads to periodical supply shortages (Anis 2008). The government is moving to reduce and eliminate some subsidies, which often turns out to be a socially painful exercise.

Blunders and Problems Unresolved

Attempts to develop heavy industry have brought no tangible success. Proton cars enjoyed a very high domestic market share when the market was protected. Under World Trade Organization (WTO) and ASEAN Free Trade Area (AFTA) obligations the market is now liberalized and it turns out to be just a struggling company with no visible competitive advantage.

The drive to create a developed knowledge society by leveraging the MSC did not provide a strong momentum for innovation (World Bank 2007b). The scheme has not met expectations regarding its role as a vehicle to create a knowledge economy. Though the government-owned Multimedia Development Corporation (MDeC) has set up the MSC Venture Capital Company to provide risk capital to start-ups and promote MSC projects, too few Malaysian companies take advantage of the opportunities it opens (Ariff 2003)—most of them are still unprepared to develop original, brand-name products targeting world markets.

Human Resource Constraints

The country's labor market is tight. Malaysia represents a rare case of an emerging-market country largely relying on immigrant workers. Skilled labor is in short supply, which impedes the climb up the technology ladder. The Malaysian government has spent a lot of money on education, but the results are not that impressive. The level of high schools and vocational training institutions remains relatively low. The chance of a first-class tertiary education is limited, which makes many young Malaysians look for opportunities to study abroad.

Vision 2020, Plans, and Policies

Malaysia's lofty ambition is to graduate from the group of middle-income countries. The "Vision 2020" put forward by Mahathir in 1991, set the target of making it a country developed economically, politically, socially, and culturally by the year 2020. To achieve these objectives Malaysia had to double its GDP every ten years which means a 7 percent annual growth rate (Gomez 1999). Per-capita GDP for 2020 was estimated at US$18,000, provided annual population growth would be 2.5 percent.

Long-term policies to realize this vision are articulated by the National Development Plans (NDPs) covering ten-year periods. The Second NDP, now under implementation, covers the period from 2001 to 2010. The ways to implement long-term policies are specified by Outline Perspective Plans (OPPs) covering the same ten-year periods. Basic policies, or policy priorities for OPPs, are formulated as National Vision Policies (NVPs). The seven basic policies for 2001–10 are: developing the knowledge-intensive society; encouraging domestically driven growth along with attracting FDI into strategically important sectors; invigorating agriculture, manufacturing, and services through knowledge inputs; addressing the poverty problem of national minorities and raising living standards of the 30 percent of households with the lowest incomes; enhancing the *Bumiputra* share in stock ownership to at least 30 percent by 2010; promoting *Bumiputra* engagement in the major sectors of the economy; and human resource development (ARC Report Malaysia 2007).

Finally, there are five-year plans. The plan for 2006–10 was the first for Mahathir's successor, Prime Minister Abdullah Badawi (in March 2009, the premiership is to be transferred to his deputy, Najib Razak), and his cabinet. The target for the average economic growth rate was 6.0 percent. The government articulated five major policies for this period. First, Malaysia had to climb up the value chain through upgrading all industries and generating new sources of wealth in such areas as IT, biotechnology, and high-value-added services. Second, it had to develop a first-class mentality by improving its education and training, including the creation of a world-class university. Third, inequality problems had to be addressed and core poverty alleviated by 2010. Fourth, the country had to work on quality-of-life and sustainability issues. Fifth, public institutions and public service delivery had to be strengthened. It was also declared that the private sector would play a bigger role in economic growth and development.

The Impact of the Global Financial Turmoil

Basically, Malaysia's financial sector has proved to be healthy and has been virtually unaffected by the global financial crisis. The fact that 90 percent of the assets of the domestic banks and insurance companies were ringgit-denominated, reduced the direct influence of the global turmoil even further (JETRO 2008).

Yet, as export industries were hit, economic growth slowed down. In the latter half of 2008, the government changed its growth forecast for 2009 from 5.4 percent to 3.5 percent.

In early November, a 7 billion ringgit (US$1.9 billion) stimulus package for 2009 was unveiled. Out of the total amount, 1.2 billion ringgit were allocated to build 25,000 units of low- and medium-cost houses. Bank Negara was to provide micro credit facilities for SMEs (*Business Times* 2008).

Also, the government decided to temporarily remove import duties on raw materials and intermediate goods (438 items) for manufacturing and to ease licensing requirements for foreign-invested companies (AP 2008). The issue of the liberalization of the service sector, particularly legal and medical services, has also been put on the agenda. The door for additional stimulus measures was left open.

In January 2009, the central bank slashed its overnight policy rate from 3.25 percent to 2.5 percent—the biggest cut since 2004.

Foreign Trade

The Composition of Exports

Malaysia's major export is electronic products. Overall, the machinery sector, with computers and parts and other electronics at its core, accounted for 52.6 percent of total exports in 2006. The share of mineral fuels (petroleum and liquefied natural gas (LNG)) was 13.7 percent, chemicals 5.5 percent, plant and animal oils (mainly palm oil) 4.7 percent, and raw materials 2.9 percent. The main export markets are the US (18.8 percent), Singapore (15.4 percent), Japan (8.9 percent), China (7.2 percent), Thailand (5.3 percent), and Hong Kong (4.9 percent).

The Composition of Imports

Machinery products (including transportation machinery) are also the major import. In 2006, they comprised 55.2 percent of total imports. The share of mineral fuels was 8.9 percent, chemicals 7.8 percent, miscellaneous goods 5.7 percent, and foodstuffs 4.2 percent. The biggest exporters to Malaysia are Japan (13.2 percent), the US (12.5 percent), China (12.1 percent), Singapore (11.7 percent), and Hong Kong and Thailand (5.5 percent each) (JETRO 2007).

The post-Asian crisis decade was marked by a very rapid expansion of trade links with China. Greater China, including Hong Kong, is already the number one exporter to Malaysia's market and the third-largest importer of its products.

FDI and the Business Environment

Malaysia is an attractive place to invest. It is rich in natural resources. Political stability and the rule of law prevail. Financial institutions are reliable. Despite the shortcomings of the educational system, the level of education and training of the workforce is higher than in most neighboring countries. Still, shortages of skilled laborers pose a problem along with heavy regulatory burdens.

Regulations

Regulations, especially those regarding the *Bumiputra* share in foreign-owned companies, are a hindrance. A company seeking to be listed on the Bursa Malaysia has to reserve 30 percent of its initial public offering (IPO) for purchase by *Bumiputra*.

Caps on foreign ownership in the manufacturing industry have been gradually removed. Also, IT and venture capital firms can be 100 percent foreign-owned but each of their investment projects must be approved by the Malaysian Industrial Development Authority (MIDA) or, within the MSC, by MDeC.

In the nonmanufacturing sector, the government restricts foreign equity (usually to 30 percent) and requires foreign firms to establish joint ventures with local businesses. While proposals on FDI in manufacturing have to get approval from MIDA, projects in nonmanufacturing are screened by various related agencies and may need multiple approvals. Guidelines for foreign participation in the nonmanufacturing sector are formulated by the Foreign Investment Committee (FIC) and Securities Commission (the latter regulates mergers and acquisitions). For instance, large retail outlets have to reserve at least 30 percent of their shelf space for products made by *Bumiputra* small- and medium-sized enterprises (SMEs), and these products have to comprise not less than 30 percent of their sales (US Department of State 2007).

Incentives

In 2006–07, the corporate tax rate was reduced by 2 percentage points to 26 percent (ADB 2008). Also, a menu of tax incentives is offered. However, after being widened in 1986, with the enactment of Promotion of Investments Act, they have largely been curtailed since 1991 and are now mainly centered on high-tech sectors and R&D. The system is rather complicated. Tax reductions and exemptions, for up to five years, are available for companies which give a start to new industries and get pioneer status. For companies involved in strategic national projects, or other projects prioritized by the government, taxes can be exempted beyond the five-year limit. Designated companies can get investment tax allowance and reinvestment allowance (in other words, the right to deduct from taxable income part of their investment cost or reinvestment volume), or be eligible for accelerated depreciation. Companies, producing high-tech products, or particular kinds of machinery and equipment, can be eligible for a ten-year tax holiday and a 60 percent investment tax allowance. There is a range of special incentives for the R&D activities, starting with a five-year corporate tax exemption for designated companies (ARC Report Malaysia 2007, 77–80). For companies located in the MSC, tax holidays of up to ten years and a 100 percent investment tax allowance are available. Famous companies get additional incentives.

The Free Zone Act of 1990 gives the Ministry of Finance the right to designate any suitable area as a Free Industrial Zone (FIZ) for manufacturing and assembly or a Free Commercial Zone (FCZ) for warehousing or commercial stock.

In these zones, raw materials, products, and equipment are imported duty-free with minimum customs formalities. To qualify for these zones a company must export 80 percent or more of its output (US Department of State 2007).

Finally, Malaysia is competing with Singapore and Hong Kong to attract multinational corporations (MNCs) to use it as a regional headquarters. Ten-year tax holidays are granted to operational headquarters, international purchasing centers, and regional distribution centers.

Scale and Composition

In the first half of the 2000s, the amount of approved FDI was fluctuating (see Table 12.2), while actual FDI, which is significantly smaller, was rapidly falling—from 8,160 million ringgit in 2001 to a meager 2,400 million ringgit in 2004 (JETRO 2004–07). While the country faced difficulties with attracting foreign investors, China, India, and Vietnam emerged as strong competitors. In 2000–05, total inward FDI stock decreased by over 9 percent. In 1995, the United Nation Conference on Trade and Development (UNCTAD) ranked Malaysia as the sixth-largest FDI destination but in 2005 it was only sixty-second (US Department of State 2007).

Since 2005, by and large, inward FDI has come back on track, though the stock is still below the pre-crisis level. In the manufacturing sector production of electrical and electronic parts is by far their largest recipient. In 2006, its share in total FDI in manufacturing (approval basis) was 42.5 percent. The next biggest recipients were the chemical industry (15.0 percent), the production of basic metal products (11.3 percent), plastics (3.7 percent), nonmetallic mineral resources (4.8 percent), scientific and measuring devices (3.3 percent), and the oil and petrochemical sectors (3.0 percent). The largest investors were Japan (21.8 percent), the Netherlands (16.2 percent), Australia (12.7 percent), the US (12.2 percent), and Singapore (9.3 percent).

Foreign manufacturers are increasing production of high-value-added items and some of them are transferring to Malaysia their R&D and design centers.

In the service industry, where many restrictions on FDI remain, 95 percent of investment was made by domestic companies. According to MITI, approved foreign investment amounted to around 2.5 billion ringgit. Now, FDI in some sectors, especially distribution and finance/insurance, is on the rise.

Malaysia has also become an important outward direct investor—the amount in 2006 was 141.4 billion ringgit. The biggest recipients were Hong Kong, Mauritius, and Singapore (JETRO 2007, 203).

Table 12.2   Amount of inward and outward FDI* (millions of ringgit)

Direction	2001	2002	2003	2004	2005	2006	2007
Inward FDI	18,907.0	11,578.0	15,640.4	13,112.3	17,882.9	20,227.9	33,425.9
Outward FDI	13,107	16,424	10,642	28,302	82,294	143,040	92,462

Sources: JETRO, "Boeki Toshi Hakusho," 2004–07; JETRO Web site: Malaysia Statistics.
*Inward FDI—approval basis, manufacturing sector only; outward FDI—balance of payments basis.

According to UNCTAD, in 2007, for the first time, the country's total outflow of FDI exceeded the inflow. A visible increase in the outward investment was largely driven by cross-border acquisitions, particularly in the financial, telecommunication and other services, and natural resources-excavating industries. Petronas is becoming increasingly active overseas to make up for the depletion of domestic oil resources. Also, Malaysian companies are seeking plantation land, especially in Indonesia (Fong 2008).

Concluding Remarks

The twin Petronas Towers (which tower at more than 1,300 feet tall over Kuala Lumpur), Putrajaya, the Multimedia Super Corridor (MSC), the Kuala Lumpur International Airport (KLIA), and the ultramodern shopping and recreation malls of Kuala Lumpur City Center (KLCC) are symbols of Malaysia's coming of age. Today, it is a relatively affluent, middle-income country with a dynamic economy and a modern mindset.

A group of Malaysian companies, especially in the IT sector, is well positioned to enter the cross-border technological chains of the world's leading MNCs and produce high-value-added items, requiring skill and advanced technology. Perhaps, developing original products and building their own brands could be the next step.

Among other things, as far as the creation of a diversified industrialized economy is concerned, Malaysia turns out to be the most successful performer in the Islamic world. (Not surprisingly, a high-ranking delegation from Saudi Arabia visited the country seeking to learn from its experience.) Yet, to make the dream of becoming a developed nation by 2020 come true, challenging tasks have to be fulfilled.

According to the World Bank, Malaysia has the worst income disparity in Southeast Asia (World Bank 2007a). The time is ripe to look at inequality issues from a new angle. Nowadays, it is not a matter of intra-ethnic relationships—within all the ethnic communities, income gaps are expanding and may become unsustainable in the long term. One of the major reasons for the poor performance of the ruling Barisan Nasional in the March 2008 election was the discontent of Malays at the growing income gap within their own community.

However, affirmative action has blocked many opportunities for representatives of other communities, resulting in their growing migration to developed countries. In turn, this has exacerbated the human resource shortage and worsened prospects for future growth.

Malaysia has to face reality. Becoming a developed nation by 2020 and continuing affirmative action are two ideals which are hardly compatible. The latter has to be dropped—otherwise development will slow down and the country will face the risk of being torn apart by internal conflicts. The future of Malaysia's economy and society strongly depends on whether or not this direction is clearly set and a relevant formula found.

13

Thailand: Rice Bowl, Regional Factory, and Land of Smiles

A Few Basics

Thailand is a middle-income country with a population of 65 million. In 2007, it was the thirty-third largest economy in the world in the International Monetary Fund (IMF) nominal gross domestic product (GDP) ranking. In terms of per-capita GDP (purchasing power parity (PPP)) in 2007, which was US$9,714, it ranked seventy-third between Turkey and Tunisia.

Thailand has a diversified economy with manufacturing industries such as electrical and electronic machinery and auto production (these two sectors are dominated by foreign subsidiaries), petrochemicals, construction materials, the food industry, textiles, and footwear taking the lead. Agriculture, which is largely export-oriented, also remains a very important sector—Thailand is called "the rice bowl of Asia." Other major crops include rubber, corn (maize), cassava, sugarcane, peanuts, soybeans, coconuts, cotton, jute and kenaf, and tobacco. The service sector has been rapidly expanding in recent decades. The tourism, transportation, hotel, and catering industries are strong. Also, Thailand is growing into a financial center for mainland Southeast Asia.

In 2007, agriculture comprised 11.4 percent of GDP, industry 43.9 percent, and services 44.7 percent (ADB 2008). The share of agriculture in the total number of persons employed is very high at 39.5 percent against 15.5 percent for manufacturing and 45. percent for other industries, mainly services (ADB 2008).

The country is rich in natural resources, mainly tin, natural rubber, timber, marine resources, tungsten, tantalum, and lead. It also has resources of natural gas and oil but they are not enough to meet domestic needs and dependence on fuel imports is very high.

Thailand's leading conglomerates include Charoen Pokphand, a giant with 250 companies in 20 countries and 100,000 employees, which is especially strong in agribusiness and is now one of the world's leading producers and suppliers of packaged seafood; Siam Cement Group with an edge not only in cement production but also in petrochemicals, paper and packaging, and ceramics (one of its major stakeholders is the Thai royal family); Minor Group, strong in resort, hotels, and restaurant businesses, the production of dairy products, and the distribution of brand consumer goods; and Teo Hong Group, engaged in the information and communication technology (ICT) and engineering (mechanical and electric systems) businesses, construction, property development, the distribution of medical equipment, and tableware.

The major economy-related agencies are the ministries of Commerce, Industry, and Finance. Also, a very significant role is played by the Board of Investment (BOI).

Thailand is divided into 76 provinces. The most developed ones are located in the very center of the country and include the capital Bangkok and five adjacent provinces Samut Prakan, Samut Sakhon, Pathum Thani, Nonthaburi, and Nakhon Pathom. The BOI designates them as Investment Zone 1. It is encircled by Investment Zone 2, which consists of 12 provinces. The less-developed Investment Zone 3, encompassing the remaining 58 provinces, covers the rest of the country's territory. The northeast and the far south are the least developed regions.

The political history of postwar Thailand has been full of dramatic shifts from military rule to democracy and vice versa. At the time of writing the country has just returned to parliamentary democracy after more than a year of military rule following the September 2006 coup.

It would be safe to say that deep respect and admiration for the King is a key feature of the national culture. Notably, when talking about their monarch, Thai people say "My King."

Thailand is a Buddhist nation. The very south, however, is predominantly Muslim.

Postwar Development

The Historic Perspective

The Kingdom of Thailand has never been a colony. However, until the postwar decades its industrial structure and foreign trade pattern resembled those of the countries under colonial rule. It exported primary products, especially rice, but also tin, natural rubber, teakwood and other tropical timber, and various kinds of plantation fruits and imported industrial products, from textiles to machinery. Rice exports were liberalized in 1851 and rapidly expanded as Thailand became the natural major supplier for the adjacent areas where the British ran large rubber plantations. In the early twentieth century some local industries emerged—namely cement, sugar, and tobacco.

The Phibun Era: Nationalist Policy

In 1948, the administration of Major General Phibun (Luang Pibulsongkhram), an admirer of Benito Mussolini and one of the leaders of the revolution of 1932, which changed the absolute monarchy to constitutional one, assumed power. Challenged with the task of moving on from a colonial-style economy, it embarked on a policy of industrialization, led by state-owned enterprises (SOEs). At the same time, it tightened regulation of the activities of Western trading companies, Chinese capital, and domestic private firms, including businesses where the royal family had a stake. Foreign direct investment (FDI) was effectively blocked.

Although a strong advocate of modernization and Westernization, Phibun will be remembered in Thailand's history as a nationalist leader. His first tenure as prime minister began in 1938, and a year later he presented the "Thailand for the Thai" economic plan. High taxes were imposed on foreign (mainly Chinese) businesses, while Thai-owned enterprises were subsidized.

Between 1948 and 1957, about 80 new SOEs were established—roughly half each in the manufacturing (especially the production of consumer goods) and services (distribution, transport, and finance) sectors (Watanabe 2003, 105). They were run mostly by bureaucrats or former military personnel. Their performance was poor. Corruption "flourished" and competition was restrained. Still, the economy was growing, boosted by the postwar recovery, expanding rice exports, and significant US aid.

The Sarit Regime: A Development Dictatorship

In 1957, Phibun was overthrown in a bloodless coup led by Field Marshal Sarit Thanarat, which marked the start of a radical turnaround in economic policy. The Sarit regime was a typical "development dictatorship." Emphasizing the importance of order, hierarchy, and religion, it proclaimed "Monarchy, Buddhism, and Nation" the major values and the 1960s as the decade of development. The private sector was attached the key role in implementing the development strategy. The country was opened for foreign capital and a number of steps were taken to make it an attractive place to invest. For instance, foreigners were given a limited right to own land. Labor unions were banned. The role of foreign-owned companies in the economy increased very fast—between 1960 and 1971 they accounted for about one-third of paid-in capital of all the companies which got authorization for investment projects from the BOI. Japanese firms were running far ahead of others (Watanabe 2003, 108).

Economic strategies were worked out in close cooperation with the World Bank and technocrats had a big say in articulating them. In 1959, the BOI was established as the key agency responsible for the implementation of the new strategies. It promoted particular investment projects, considered important for national development, through various kinds of tax and other incentives. Textiles and autos were designated as priority industries and were protected by preferentially high import tariffs.

The government promoted not only industry but also agriculture, targeting it as an important export-oriented sector and seeking to raise the living standards of the rural population. However, rural development policies often failed to meet farmers' expectations regarding land reform (many of them remained landless), poverty alleviation, and infrastructure creation. Their bitter disappointment even led to social unrest in some provinces.

Generally, the economic development policies, launched under Sarit, proved to be successful—in the 1960s, average growth rates rose to 8.0 percent as opposed to 4.7 percent in the 1950s (Watanabe 2003, 108). Yet, at the end of the decade, import substitution had exhausted itself—the domestic market was too small to absorb the growing amount of goods that Thai industry was producing.

The 1970s

In the early 1970s, the country shifted toward export-led industrialization. The BOI promoted exporting industries in a conventional way—mainly through tax incentives.

The 1970s, a volatile period in Thailand's history, punctuated by coups, demonstrations, and violence, were also marked by the rise of nationalism—a reaction to the rapidly growing foreign presence in the national economy and increasing trade deficits, especially with respect to Japan. In 1972, the influential National Students Center, along with a number of other organizations, initiated a boycott of Japanese-made goods and 1974 was the year of large anti-Japanese demonstrations. The government tightened regulation of foreign businesses. Liberalization suffered a setback, which in turn exerted a negative influence on FDI. The first oil shock in 1973 pushed annual inflation rates beyond 20 percent.

Overall, however, export-led growth continued throughout the decade at an average annual rate of 6.7 percent. Export gains were boosted by rising prices for primary products and also by the depreciation of the US dollar versus other major currencies—the Thai baht, eventually pegged to the US dollar, was depreciating against those currencies too. Along with primary products and foodstuffs, Thailand increased exports of textiles and footwear, as well as integrated circuits, the latter being produced mostly by the subsidiaries of US companies.

The 1980s

Economic conditions deteriorated during and after the second oil shock (1979). In the first half of the 1980s, world prices for primary products began to plunge, adversely affecting export revenues. A global recession made the situation even worse. In 1983, exports fell by 8.3 percent from a year earlier. The country was struggling with growing deficits of foreign trade, balance of payments, and budget. Foreign debt was increasing. In 1985, it was US$17.5 billion as opposed to US$10.9 billion in 1981 (ADB 1999). In cooperation with the World Bank and the IMF, the government embarked on large-scale deregulation and pursued restrictive financial and monetary policies. IMF loans helped to get the economy back on track by the middle of the decade. Yet, foreign debt remained a pressing issue as the government continued to support SOEs.

Domestic politics entered an era of stability. From 1980 to 1988, Thailand was ruled by several administrations under Prime Minister Prem Tinsulanonda, a retired military officer opposing the military's direct involvement in politics. In 1983, a parliamentary election was held, which left him as the head of a coalition government. Emphasizing the need for dialogue and discussion to address the problems of Thai society in general, and to shape relevant economic policies in particular, he established a council of economic ministers and regularly exchanged views with the business community. Against this backdrop, his administrations steadily proceeded with liberalization and the opening of the economy.

The administration of Prime Minister Chatichai Choonhavan, who succeeded Prem in 1988, put forward the idea of transforming mainland Southeast Asia from a battlefield into a "market-field" with Thailand as the regional economic and financial center.

The Years of Best Performance

Between the mid-1980s and the mid-1990s, growth rates exceeded 8 percent on average. Following the Plaza Accord of 1985, which led to a rapid appreciation of the yen, Japanese FDI increased dramatically. This, in turn, brought about a speedy and significant rise in exports of manufactured products. World prices for exported primary products also started to recover from 1987.

By the middle of the decade textiles had become the major export item, overtaking rice and natural rubber. The years after the Plaza Accord were marked by an expansion in exports of computer and auto parts, as well as home electronic goods. Japanese companies made Thailand their major overseas production base for auto parts.

Generally, the weight of heavy industries in the national economy increased and by the mid-1990s the volume of production of heavy and light industries had virtually equaled (Watanabe 2003, 112). However, heavy industries were critically dependent on imports of machinery, equipment, and intermediate products. As a result, the trade balance remained mostly in the red.

Dynamic economic growth resulted in a rise in household incomes, accelerated the formation of the middle class, and boosted private consumption.

Also, in the early 1990s, the country significantly strengthened its position as a center of world tourism by actively and successfully propagating its "Land of Smiles" image.

The Blows of the Asian Crisis

The smiles faded somewhat in 1997, when Thailand became the catalyst of the Asian crisis. Actually, negative signs had already appeared in 1995, when exports declined and the current account deficit rose to 8 percent of GDP. Foreign debt exceeded US$90 billion, three-quarters of it comprised of the debt of the private sector. In the third quarter of 1998, the key index of the Stock Exchange of Thailand dropped to 253, compared to a 1,200 peak in mid-1996 (Ministry of Foreign Affairs 2000). A number of large enterprises went bankrupt, including the financial company, Finance One, and the property developer, Somprasong Land.

In July 1997, the baht was floated because the Bank of Thailand could no longer support it—foreign exchange reserves had declined to US$800 million. In January 1998, its exchange rate against the US dollar fell to 56 baht versus the pegged rate of 25 baht (Ministry of Foreign Affairs 2000). In 1997, at the start of the crisis, growth fell to just 1 percent and, in 1998, the economy contracted by 10.5 percent (ADB 2008). Unemployment, including the seasonally inactive labor force, increased from 3.6 percent on the eve of the crisis to 6.1 percent in 1998 (ADB 2000). However, in a way, paying attention to the agriculture and rural areas paid off—many Thais, who lost jobs in the cities, returned to their families in the countryside and managed to support themselves through agricultural activities.

After the crisis started, King Bhumibol Adulyadej called on the nation to return to what he called "self-sufficiency," meaning the reduction of dependence on foreign capital and an emphasis on the upgrading of production and better utilization of domestic resources, especially human potential.

Structural Reforms

The Financial Sector

The major part of structural reforms in Thailand was a drastic revamping of the financial sector. In this area, Thai reforms were probably more radical than in any other Asian country except South Korea. The government fully cooperated with the IMF, the World Bank, and the Asian Development Bank (ADB) and got their backing.

One of the main, and most difficult, steps was the closure, by the end of 1997, of 56 insolvent financial companies out of a total number of 89. Financial companies—many of them associated with leading banks—were engaged in a wide range of risky transactions, and were not subject to the prudential regulation and administrative control that the banks were. To restructure and manage the assets of the closed financial companies the government established the Financial Restructuring Authority (FRA), which accepted their bad assets and auctioned them off, and the Asset Management Corporation (AMC) to manage and sell their good assets. Also, six troubled commercial banks were reformed.

Bankruptcy Law Amendments

A milestone of the reforms was the enactment, in 1998, of the amended Bankruptcy Law. The old version of the Law was too favorable to debtors, creating a moral hazard problem. It provided them with leniency and protection, leaving creditors very little room to act against delinquent debtors. Under this state of affairs, the latter often avoided returning their debts, even if they could pay (the practice labeled "strategic nonperforming loans"). The amended version strengthened security for lenders. Among other things, they were allowed to pursue payment from loan guarantors.

State Enterprises

In 1998, the government adopted the Master Plan for State Enterprise Reform. A year later, the State Enterprises Corporatization Act was enacted, setting a schedule for turning SOEs into stock companies. Corporatization is considered an intermediate step toward privatization. Up to now, however, the privatization drive has been slow. As of 2004, there were 61 SOEs, employing 7 percent of the total labor force and accounting for 28 percent of GDP (US Department of State 2006).

In 2001, the oil company, PTT, and Internet Thailand were born as corporations with the state as the major shareholder, but private investors also having a stake. In 2002, Bank Thai, Krung Thai Card (a subsidiary of Krung Thai Bank), Airports of Thailand (AOT), and Telephone Organization of Thailand (TOT) were corporatized, followed by CAT Telecom, in 2003. Private investors also acquired a minority stake in Krung Thai Bank. In 2004, as a result of the initial public offering (IPO), 30 percent of the AOT stock went into the hands of private investors, including foreigners. Also, a second public offering was launched for Thai Airways International. In 2005, the Electricity Generating Authority of Thailand (EGAT) was corporatized but privatization stumbled due to strong resistance from labor unions and other interest groups. In 2006, the government corporatized the Mass Communications Organization of Thailand (MCOT) and listed it on the Stock Exchange with an IPO. At present, the Ministry of Finance remains the major shareholder.

The Financial Sector Master Plan

The new Financial Sector Master Plan, adopted in 2004, was aimed at boosting competition through the elimination of regulatory barriers. Instead of a very complicated system, dividing banks into a number of groups with a strictly regulated range of services for each of them, all the banks were integrated into two groups—commercial and retailing.

In a new development, to stimulate activity in the capital market, from the beginning of the 2000s the government started to create investment funds. For example, the Thai Equity Fund is investing into domestic industrial firms undergoing corporate restructuring. The Thailand Recovery Fund is focused on investment in SMEs. Vayupak Mutual Fund, alongside common stocks and bonds, is also investing in SOEs.

Present Performance

Growth and Industrial Development

After a 10.5 percent drop in GDP, in 1998, the Thai economy rebounded, mainly due to robust exports, reaching more than 4 percent GDP growth in the two following years. The world IT recession and a slowdown in the global economy in 2001 reduced its rate to 1.9 percent but in the next three years growth accelerated again. Thailand became the fastest runner in Southeast Asia, registering a steady expansion of investment, private consumption, and exports (see Table 13.1). By 2001–02 the banking sector had, more or less, gotten over the nonperforming loan (NPL) problem and restored normal lending activities.

Table 13.1 Main economic indicators (real annual growth, %)*

Indicator	1999	2000	2001	2002	2003	2004	2005	2006	2007
GDP	4.4	4.8	2.2	5.3	7.1	6.3	4.5	5.0	4.8
Agriculture**	2.3	7.2	3.2	0.7	12.7	-2.4	-1.9	3.8	3.9
Industry**	9.6	5.3	1.7	7.1	9.6	7.9	5.4	5.7	5.4
Services**	0.4	3.7	2.4	4.6	3.5	6.8	5.0	4.8	4.2
Gross domestic capital formation	8.5	11.3	2.7	6.0	13.5	12.8	12.9	-3.2	0.3
Private consumption	4.3	5.2	4.1	5.4	6.5	6.2	4.5	3.2	1.4
Unemployment rate (%)	4.2	3.6	3.3	2.4	2.2	2.1	1.8	1.5	1.4
Consumer prices	0.2	1.7	1.6	0.6	1.8	2.8	4.5	4.7	2.3
Exports (US$ millions), fob	58,492	68.963	65.113	68,850	80,318	96,214	110,158	130,555	152,459
Imports (US$ millions), cif	50,350	61,924	61,057	64,721	75,824	94,107	118,143	130,605	152,459
Average exchange rate of baht per US$1	38	40	44	43	41	40	40	38	35

Source: World Bank Development Indicators; ADB: Key Indicators 2008, Bank of Thailand.
*Calendar year (fiscal year in Thailand begins October 1)
**Data for agriculture, industry, and services refers to value added.

Industrial growth was led by the electronics and auto industries. The government pledged to make Thailand "the Detroit of Asia," setting ambitious auto production targets. Initially, the interim goal for 2006 was to exceed one million cars and the final goal for 2010 was to hit 1.8 million. Producers ran ahead of schedule, reaching the 1.125 million car mark by 2005. Thus, the final target was elevated to 2 million (JETRO 2006, 197).

In a new development, the BOI has announced that, to support the growth of automotive, electrical appliances, electronics, and other industries, it will promote the high-quality, upstream steel sector.

Thaksinomics

A new era in the country's post-crisis economic development started in 2001 with the administration of Thaksin Shinawatra, after his Thai Rak Thai (Thais Love Thais) won that year's parliamentary election by a landslide. Thaksin's premiership lasted until 2006, when it was overthrown in a bloodless military coup.

During these six years, he came up with a unique set of policies known as "Thaksinomics." They are rather an eclectic set up. The basic idea was—while continuing to attract foreign investment—to focus more on supporting local enterprises and the grassroots economy in order to leverage their unique skills, raise living standards, especially in the countryside, and reduce poverty. Also, Thaksinomics sought to raise the role of the domestic market in economic development and to differentiate from China, conquering market niches where there would be no direct competition with the rising new giant (Looney 2003).

The most popular undertaking was the so-called One Tambon One Product (OTOP) Project (*tambon* means subdistrict in Thai), which covered nearly all of the country's 7,252 districts. The premise was that every *tambon* had a comparative advantage in the production of one or more local products, potentially competitive at the national and international market. The government's role was to help to identify such products and assist in their production.

Achievements and Criticism

Thaksin's policies were widely criticized, at home and abroad, as populist. Such a perception, however, looks one-sided. True, the risk of funds being misused due to inadequate discretionary decisions or vested interests involved was there. The pillars of economic policy, such as support for low-income families, SME promotion, and infrastructure development, were largely made hostage to the political improvisations of the prime minister himself and the people authorized to allocate funds. However, it was in no way a money-wasting undertaking aimed at just getting popular with the masses. The policies were shaped so that they encouraged the beneficiaries' own effort. They got mostly loans, not grants. Thaksinomics was instrumental in addressing such crucial social problems as poverty and the exclusion of many households from the economic development process.

Arguably, Thaksin's ousting from power, caused by purely political and ethical problems, and his economic policy are two entirely different stories. Thaksin was overthrown not because he failed in the economic field but because of the fragility of Thai democracy and his inability to overcome very strong resistance from a wide range of adversaries—opposition parties, influential business groups, a substantial part of the military establishment, and, apparently, also the King and his inner circle.

The Shin Corporation Affair

The prime minister's handling of the Shin Corporation's stock sale issue caused uproar among citizens of big cities, mainly Bangkok, who considered the transaction unfair.

Before January 20, 2005, the Thaksin family owned 38.63 percent of Shin Corporation. On that date, his two children acquired 10.98 percent more from another major shareholder—a family-owned investment company, at a nominal price of 1 baht per share. Three days later the family sold its whole share to two Temasek nominee companies through the Stock Exchange at the market price of 49.25 baht per share. It was by far the biggest transaction on the Stock Exchange, comprising 35 percent of its total annual turnover. No taxes were paid, because in Thailand individuals' transactions on the Stock Exchange are nontaxable. Also, the authorities did not tax the transaction between Thaksin's children and the investment company, though it was carried out outside the Stock Exchange, treating it as the sale and purchase of goods by individuals (IDE-JETRO 2007, 285–286). This was the first dimension to the story—that is, an inappropriate, at least seemingly, mode of action by the Thaksin family.

The second dimension was the presence of a foreign-owned company in a regulated sector. According to the Foreign Business Act, *foreign-owned* means a company where one half or more of the shares, in terms of quantity or value, belong to foreigners. The key daughter company of Shin Corporation is a telecommunication and broadcasting firm, Shin Satellite. The entry of foreign-owned firms into telecommunication and broadcasting sectors is not allowed—Shin Satellite could continue operating only if its parent, Shin Corporation, retained its status as a Thai company. As both of Temasek's nominees were, formally, Thai firms, after they acquired the stake, Shin Corporation, formally, remained 50.01 percent Thai-owned (IDE-JETRO 2007, 285–286).

The Military Coup

Political uncertainty, caused by the Shin affair, began in mid-2005 with mass anti-Thaksin demonstrations in the capital and started to adversely affect the economy. The prime minister dissolved the Parliament for early election in April 2006. The elections were boycotted by the opposition, and the Constitutional Court ruled them unconstitutional (the reason given was the violation of the principle of secret balloting). The election was to be held again in October. However, tensions mounted, and in September 2006, a bloodless military coup ousted Thaksin from power while he was in New York attending the United Nations General Assembly.

The country came under military rule. The new military-appointed cabinet, with General Surayud Chulanont as prime minister, suspended the constitution of 1997 (passing a new one), imposed restrictions on the freedom of speech, information, and gatherings, and promised to hold parliamentary elections in December 2007. (The promise was fulfilled.)

Economic Performance Under the Military Regime

The coup further increased uncertainties about the country's future, exacerbating negative economic trends. Along with political turmoil, the economy had to address tough challenges, caused by natural disasters. A tsunami and devastating earthquake in the six southern provinces, in December 2004, adversely affected the tourist sector and consumer demand. Also, the droughts of 2004–05 were a big blow for agriculture and, in 2006, by contrast, there were floods.

In the middle of the decade, growth rates for both gross capital formation and private consumption started to fall. In 2006, gross capital formation fell in absolute terms (see Table 13.1).

Yet, there was no big slowdown. The negative effect of political destabilization and natural disasters was partly offset by the demand stemming from past wage increases and household income growth, the continuation of investment projects and, especially, rapidly expanding exports. Since the second half of 2007, private consumption has begun to recover too. Investment was also maintained at a comparatively high level and in the manufacturing industry high-value-added subsectors were increasing their share.

As a basic policy concept, the military regime revitalized the above-mentioned notion of a "self-sufficiency economy," introduced by the King in 1997 in reaction to the Asian crisis. However, the government said it didn't mean this in the sense of closing Thailand for foreign investors but providing sustainability of development and inducing market players to respect basic moral principles.

At the end of 2006, the military-appointed government imposed capital controls. It became mandatory for foreigners to keep 30 percent of the amount invested as a reserve in the Bank of Thailand (the regulation was not applied to transactions on the Stock Exchange). The new regulation resulted in the biggest ever one-day sell-off of Thai shares.

Also, the government initiated the Foreign Business Act, tightening regulations on foreign investment, though it was not passed into law. The move was an immediate reaction to problems posed by the Shin Corporation affair.

Naturally, the new government did all it could to distance itself from Thaksinomics in its domestic economic policy too. It reduced budget expenditure by about 20 percent (IDE-JETRO 2007, 289), cutting the above-mentioned reserve fund, widely used by Thaksin to finance spontaneously emerging development projects. Work on the formalization of household property rights for land and other assets, to use them as the loan collateral, was also stopped. Yet, the popular OTOP project was continued under a different name.

To summarize, the military regime had no clear-cut economic policy concept and limited itself to addressing mounting short term issues, which was done in a very spontaneous and often disorderly manner.

A Return to Thaksin-Style Policies

The parliamentary election was held, as promised, in December 2007. The People's Power Party, newly formed by Thaksin loyalists, won in a landslide. Thaksin returned from a self-imposed exile in the UK in late February 2008, and was arrested on his arrival, and then immediately released on bail. He was offered the role of advising the government on financial issues, but rejected it.

The new cabinet, headed by Samak Sundaravej, largely returned to Thaksin-style policies, seeking to restore investors' confidence and boost economic growth to 6 percent. Capital controls imposed by the military were abolished in February 2008, and an increase of capital inflows followed. The "populist policy" of cash handouts to villages for development projects and low-interest loans was restarted. The prime minister also pledged a debt moratorium for the farmers and the poor, vowing to replace "the loan sharks" with the People's Bank and promising to build new homes for low-income families in Bangkok (Reuters 2008).

In early March 2008, the Cabinet announced a large-scale (40 billion baht) economic stimulus package, consisting mainly of various tax cuts. The maximum for nontaxable income was raised from 100,000 to 150,000 baht per year. Deductions for life insurance premiums and investment into retirement and long-term mutual funds were increased. Corporate income tax for listed companies was reduced from 30 percent to 25 percent for three years. Also, for three years, SMEs earning less than 1.2 million baht a year were exempted from paying income tax altogether. To help SMEs, corporate tax was cut for the same period from 30 percent to 20 percent for companies newly listed at the Market for Alternative Investment (an alternative exchange with looser listing rules than the Stock Exchange of Thailand). Company tax deduction for appreciation of machinery and equipment was allowed to be as high as 40 percent of their initial cost (Chatrudee 2008).

Since late May 2008, massive anti-government rallies have begun again. The demonstrators demanded Samak's resignation claiming that he is only a tool in the hands of Thaksin. Samak had to leave office in early September after the court found him guilty of violating the constitution when he accepted pay for hosting a cooking show on TV. He was replaced by Somchai Wongsawat, Thaksin's brother-in-law. Political turmoil continued with anti-Thaksin protesters occupying Government House. The government, having lost control, had to move to the old Bangkok airport, and then to the city of Chiang Mai.

The protests escalated further. In November, the demonstrators occupied the new Bangkok international airport, Suvarnabhumi, paralyzing its activities. They insisted that they would not retreat until the pro-Thaksin People's Power Party regime resigned from power. Eventually, they got what they demanded. In December, the Constitutional Court dissolved PAP and banned Somchai from politics for five years. The premiership went to Abhisit Vejjajiva, the leader of the Democrat Party, associated with the People's Alliance for Democracy, which led the riots.

Inflationary Pressures

From 2006–mid 2008, inflation became an increasingly big headache and, potentially, the strongest growth deterrent, especially with soaring prices for oil and foodstuffs. State subsidies for petroleum products were abolished in 2005, but demands to restore them were growing stronger. On the other hand, the government started to talk directly to producers and distributors to work out comprehensive nonbinding arrangements (in a sense, gentlemen's agreements) to curb consumer price hikes.

For instance, in March 2008, it reached an agreement with pork producers and retailers about the reduction of the retail price for pork from 120 to 98 baht per kilogram for two months, while retaining the farmers' selling price at 58 baht (Phusadee 2008).

The Impact of the Global Financial Turmoil

The impact on the Thai economy was moderate. The national economy was expected to lose around one percentage point of growth in 2009. In October, stock prices plunged about 30 percent. The major blow came from the adverse effect on exporters. In September 2008, year-on-year growth in manufacturing hit a 15-month low of 4.6 percent against 7.6 percent in August (AseanAffairs. com 2008). Also, the services sector's performance worsened because political unrest and uncertainties were driving tourists away from the country.

The GDP growth rate for the whole of 2008 was 3.6 percent, and the Bank of Thailand's forecast for 2009 is only 0–2 percent (Reuters 2009).

Since the start of the global turmoil, domestic political instability prevented the government from taking countermeasures. The Abhisit cabinet announced a 115 billion baht (US$3.28 billion) stimulus package in January 2009. The money is to be allocated to rejuvenating tourism and supporting poor households (*China Post* 2009). Substantial tax cuts for businesses and households were included. Also, plans were announced to borrow US$2 billion to raise funds for state financial institutions.

As inflation ceased to be a threat, the Bank of Thailand considered interest rate cuts. Its one-day bond repurchase rate was reduced from 2.75 percent to 2.00 percent in January 2009.

Foreign Trade

The Composition of Exports

Today, Thailand's exports are led by manufacturing goods, especially electronic products but also autos and parts. The country is an important exporter of natural rubber, tin, rice, timber, tropical fruits, and meat and marine products. In terms of value, the major export items are computers and parts (11.5 percent of total exports in 2006), especially hard disk drives, followed by autos and parts (7.4 percent), integrated circuits (5.4 percent), natural rubber (4.2 percent), plastics (3.5 percent), jewelry (2.8 percent), petroleum products (2.8 percent), iron and steel (2.7 percent), radio and TV sets and their parts (2.7 percent), and chemicals (2.7 percent).

In an important development, Thailand is becoming one of Asia's major exporters of auto vehicles—not only to neighboring countries but also to Australia, the

Middle East, and the European Union (EU) states. Within Southeast Asia it is definitely exporter number one.

As far as the geographical structure of exports is concerned, 60.1 percent of the total went to Asia with Japan as the biggest market (12.7 percent), followed by China (9.0 percent), Singapore (6.4 percent), and Malaysia (5.1 percent). The US remained the biggest single national market for Thai products (15.0 percent). The share of the EU-15 was 13.0 percent (JETRO 2007, 194).

The Composition of Imports

The major import item, in terms of value, is crude oil (15.9 percent), followed by nonelectrical industrial machinery (9.0 percent), electrical products and parts (7.6 percent), chemicals (7.2 percent), integrated circuits (6.8 percent), computers and parts (5.9 percent), iron and steel (5.8 percent), metal waste and scrap (4.8 percent), and auto parts (2.4 percent) (JETRO 2007, 193).

As much as 74.3 percent of imports come from Asia. Japan was the biggest exporter to Thailand (20.1 percent) but the presence of Chinese-made products is visibly growing (10.6 percent). The next most important importers are the US and Malaysia (6.7 percent and 6.6 percent respectively), followed by the UAE (5.6 percent). The combined share of the EU-15 was 8.4 percent.

Inward FDI and the Business Environment

Generally, Thailand's stance toward inward FDI is positive and open, and the environment is mostly favorable. By and large, infrastructure is good and the government doesn't spare any effort to improve it. The commitment of workers is also sufficiently high.

On the negative side, unexpected abrupt policy shifts may occur with changes of regime. In the predominantly Muslim south, the situation is unstable and separatist tendencies are strengthening. Also, reservations about "foreign dominance" in the economy exist, as evidenced by the Shin Corporation affair.

Business Entry Rules

The Foreign Business Act stipulates that, in general, foreigners enjoy the same basic rights as Thai nationals. Businesses where foreign participation is not permitted are comparatively few.

While in the manufacturing sector 100 percent foreign-owned companies are allowed, special acts impose restrictions on foreign ownership in such businesses as commercial banking, insurance, transportation, telecommunication, and commercial fishing. In most service sectors, the share of Thai owners in the business has to be more than 50 percent. Foreign banks can only operate a single branch. However, tax disincentives designed to inhibit the acquisition of stock in domestic banks have been removed.

Also, there is a long list of occupations, which are basically prohibited for foreigners such as legal or litigation services, brokerage or agency work (except in international business), clerical or secretarial work, and civil engineering work.

Investment Promotion

According to the Investment Promotion Act, activities which are important and beneficial for the economic and social development and security of the country are eligible for promotion.

The BOI is the key government agency responsible for promoting investment and setting the rules. It grants approvals for investment projects and chooses projects to be promoted through tax and other incentives. The latter consist of various kinds of government guarantees, special permissions, and services. For example, a promoted company can be allowed to own land to carry on the promoted activities or to bring into Thailand foreign nationals, who are skilled workers, experts, spouses, and dependants, in numbers and for periods deemed appropriate even if they exceed the quotas or periods of time prescribed by the Law on Immigration. The probability of being put on the list of promoted companies is especially high if you bring new technology or invest in less-developed provinces.

The country is divided into three investment zones, depending on the level of income and the availability of infrastructure: Zone 1, Bangkok and five surrounding central provinces; Zone 2, 12 provinces surrounding Zone 1, and Zone 3, the 58 remaining provinces (see the beginning of this chapter). Relocation of projects to Zones 2 and 3 is promoted.

In Zone 1, promoted projects may get a 50 percent reduction of import duty on machinery, which is subject to import duty of 10 percent or more. They also may enjoy a corporate income tax exemption for three years if they are located within an industrial estate or a promoted industrial zone and if the investment is 10 million baht or more (excluding the cost of land and working capital). Finally, there is a one-year exemption of import duty on materials and raw materials used in the manufacturing of export products.

In Zones 2 and 3, all the privileges mentioned are applicable and, furthermore, the corporate income tax exemption period can be extended, respectively, to five and eight years (BOI 2008).

Priority areas, eligible for incentives, are: agriculture and agricultural products; environmental protection and/or restoration; technological and human resource development; basic transportation, infrastructure, and services; and targeted industries, including automotive, information technology (IT) and electronics, semiconductors, fashion, and high-value-added services. In 2007, biotechnology was added to the list. Projects in the priority areas are entitled to exemption from import duty on machinery and the eight-year corporate income tax exemption, regardless of the location.

Recently, the BOI strengthened incentives for companies investing in the auto and electronics industries. In 2001, all auto assemblers, investing 10 million baht (about US$260 million) or more, were eligible for the import duty exemption on machinery. In March 2006, import tariffs were eliminated on parts and materials used in the production of 104 electrical and electronic items. The list included a wide range of products from refrigerators, washing machines, air conditioners, and electric ovens to printing circuits and Braun tubes. Special, generous tax incentives were granted to investors in the electrical and electronics industry, implementing large-scale (more than 15 billion baht, or about US$375 million, land and working capital not included), multiple, high-value projects in Zone 3 (JETRO 2006, 197).

As well as the Investment Zone system, Thailand has 10 export-processing zones (also called free trade zones) for export-oriented production only, where the import of raw materials, materials, and components is duty free and export is entirely tax free, including the exemption of value-added tax (outside these zones it is not exempted).

Hurdles

Foreign businessmen working, or planning to work, in Thailand should be prepared to overcome the following hurdles. Foreigners cannot own land outside the government-approved industrial estates (with the above-mentioned exception for promoted companies). The 1999 amendment made it possible for them to buy up to 1,900 square yards for residential use provided they represent a company investing 40 million baht (around US$1 million) or more. Many foreign companies sign long-term, land-lease agreements.

Before starting a business in Thailand it is recommended to get thorough advice from experts on legal matters. Thai business regulations are governed predominantly by criminal law, rather than civil law, and their violations can result in severe criminal penalties. On the positive side, the country has an independent judiciary, which is rather efficient in enforcing property and contractual rights. However, the legal process is often slow (US Department of State 2006).

Problems may arise with the protection of intellectual property rights (IPR). Patent examination by the Thailand Patent Office may take more than five years. The copyright law is ambiguous about decompilation. Penalties for piracy are often too light to be a deterrent and enforcement procedures leave loopholes (US Department of State 2006).

Thailand has anticorruption laws and an independent National Anti-Corruption Commission. Yet, convictions of public officials on corruption charges are rare. Sometimes, bribes may be considered by your counterparts as an essential part of the business process.

Concerns about the consequences of foreign acquisitions can get rather strong. Domestic companies may defend themselves from acquisitions using cross, or stable, shareholding arrangements. Thai firms are allowed to set their own limits on foreign ownership which may be tighter than those imposed by the government.

Having launched the "Thailand Investment 2008–09 Campaign," the government pledged to amend the laws to make it easier to obtain visas and work permits, to improve services for nonpromoted investors, and to open up a number of service businesses reserved only for Thais. Additional tax incentives are considered for companies locating their regional headquarters in Thailand.

Inward FDI Volume and Composition

Very rapid growth of FDI in Thailand was registered in the first half of the 2000s after the national economy got back on track. In 2003, its volume (flow) increased 2.1 times, followed by a 49.3 percent increase in 2004 (see Table 13.2). In 2005, growth continued, though at a much slower pace. FDI was led by two sectors—autos and electronics—not least because of the strong incentives provided by the BOI. In 2005, they comprised about 70 percent of the total (JETRO 2006, 197). Japanese auto makers have made Thailand their major overseas center of production for both finished products, especially pickup trucks, and parts.

In 2006, inward FDI abruptly fell by 18.2 percent—a direct consequence of political uncertainty, worsened by the coup. Most direct investors abstained from new commitments. Also, to some extent, the reduction can be explained by the investment cycle. Large-scale investments in various sectors were concentrated within the previous three-year period, including massive investment by Japanese heavyweights, Toyota and Nissan, as well as tire makers and the like—and investors took a time-out.

In 2007, inward FDI nearly doubled. Investors' confidence returned, although the military remained in power until December. Presumably, it happened because of the election announcement and also due to the fact that, after all, the regime did not impose new regulations worsening the business environment.

Japan remained the biggest investor with a share of 32.5 percent, followed by the US (20.0 percent) and Singapore (6.8 percent). The share of China (3.1 percent) is noticeably expanding. Other important investors are Canada (3.0 percent), and Malaysia (2.3 percent). The portion of Europe was 12.0 percent, with the Netherlands taking the lead.

Out of the total amount of inward FDI 4.6 percent went into agricultural and fishery products, 24.1 percent into machinery and metal processing, 19.8 percent into the electronic and electrical industry, 19.1 percent into chemicals and paper, 6.4 percent into minerals and ceramics, and 24.1 percent into services (JETRO 2008).

Auto companies, especially Japanese, are reactivating their business in the country. For instance, Suzuki and Siam-Nissan plan to start assembling eco-cars, which will be exported to Asia, Australia, and Africa. Ford-Mazda is also launching a passenger car project.

Table 13.2   Amount of inward FDI (approval projects, billion baht)

Year	2002	2003	2004	2005	2006	2007
Value	101.2	212.5	317.3	325.8	266.6	505.6

Source: BOI; JETRO.

The petrochemical industry is becoming an increasingly important FDI recipient due to a number of big projects including Map Ta Phut Olefin—a joint venture between Dow Chemical and Siam Cement Group; the project of an individual US-based investor, Liu Changfeng, (ethylene and propylene); and the joint venture between Japan's Asahi Glass and the state oil company, PTT (production of acrylonitrile, the raw material for acryl). Map Ta Phut Olefin is planning to develop a large-scale petrochemical production complex in the south (JETRO 2007, 197).

Other sectors absorbing a significant amount of FDI include the textile industry and the processing of agricultural and marine products.

Concluding Remarks

The Thai economy has shown a remarkable ability to resist various kinds of external and domestic shocks. It rapidly rebounded after the Asian crisis, did not slow down in the years of tsunami and droughts, and even performed quite decently amid the political turmoil after the September 2006 coup. Nowadays, it is strong and upgraded enough to expand exports even when the baht significantly appreciates—contrary to the mid-1990s, not to mention earlier years.

Thailand has a diversified and balanced industrial structure. In the electronic, auto, and other machinery industries, Thai-based factories create increasing amounts of value-added (that is, not just assembling products but also producing parts and materials). In the recent years, along with electronics and autos, the chemical and petrochemical sectors have joined the cohort of leading industries, and the food industry and agribusiness have sharpened their competitive edge. The service sector is becoming increasingly competitive, especially in such areas as tourism, recreation, hotels, and catering.

However, there are several difficult issues, of a basic character, that the country has to address. For ASEAN 4 nations, Thailand included, joining the ranks of the newly industrialized economies (NIEs) has been a dream and a major goal for quite a long time. How real is it? Four Asian NIEs have already become developed economies. Which Asian country has the best chance to join this cohort in the foreseeable future? A look at per-capita GDP data prompts the answer—Malaysia. How about Thailand, which follows it in the Asia rankings? Let us face reality—to call it the next solid candidate would be premature. Malaysia has clearly articulated an ambitious target—to become developed by 2020. It is pursuing upgrading very aggressively, trying to focus on R&D, development of original products and technologies, attraction of high-tech companies, and education of people. Thailand is still far from this stage. It stops short of setting ambitious development targets. Its R&D expenditure still comprises only 0.26 percent of GDP as opposed to 2–3 percent in the developed countries. It has about the same number of skilled workers as Malaysia but its population is three times larger (Don 2006). (Also, in contrast to Malaysia, Thailand still has a big informal sector.) It lacks highly qualified engineers, managers, and other specialists, but retains complicated procedures and regulations regarding work permits for foreign talent.

To summarize, the country needs more clear-cut and ambitious goal-setting, with still more focus on innovation, upgrading, and technological progress. It should not forget about the quantitative side too—the record annual growth rate registered in this decade was 7.1 percent, in 2003, the one and only year when it was in the seven percent area. Asian NIEs have much more impressive records.

Unless the country speeds up further and upgrades its economy more efficiently and intensively, it may remain a developing and middle-income nation for an indefinitely long period of time.

One of the major problems Thailand has to tackle is political instability and, in broader terms, an outdated political system and practices. No other Asian country has had so many military coups. Actually, the latter has become a method of exiting from difficult political situations, as well as of overthrowing political rivals. It looked reasonable to expect that in the 2000s, at the level of economic and social development reached and with the democratic experience accumulated, the "practice" would not be used any more. However, the expectations proved to be wrong. As soon as a difficult political situation emerged and the opportunity to overthrow a political foe appeared, the traditional practice was revived.

Obviously, Thailand's political system and practices lag behind its economic development. The country is ruled, eventually, not by law but by elite groups engaged in behind-the-scenes power battles. All this disturbs normal business activities, scares off investors, destabilizes the country's ties with the outer world, and makes it difficult to launch and implement long-term development strategies.

The key question for the coming years is whether Thailand can escape this political deadlock.

14

Indonesia: The Start of the Post-Suharto Era

A Few Basics

Overview

Indonesia is the largest country in Southeast Asia in terms of both territory and population. It is the largest archipelagic state in the world, spanning one-tenth of the equator; the largest Muslim nation; and the world's fourth most populous nation. Its land territory is 741,100 square miles and the population is 240 million people.

The country is spread over more than 17,000 islands, about 6,000 of which are inhabited. However, 60 percent of the population lives on just one—the island of Java. All the other islands, except Java and its close neighbor, Madura, are often referred to as the Outer Islands. Java is densely populated. The Outer Islands are sparsely populated. A big gap in the level of economic development between Java and the Outer Islands is one of the structural problems the country is facing.

Other large islands are Borneo (only the southern part of the island is Indonesian territory and this region is known as Kalimantan), Sumatra, Sulawesi, and the western half of New Guinea which is known as Papua. The east and south of Sumatra and southeastern Kalimantan are the most economically developed parts of the Outer Islands. The island of Bali has become an internationally recognized beach resort. Other territories lag far behind and the fruits of modernization are reaching them at a very slow pace.

By nominal gross domestic product (GDP), in 2007, Indonesia was twentieth in the world. It is a low-middle-income country. In terms of the per-capita GDP (purchasing power parity (PPP)) it was 120th, between the Republic of Congo and Kiribati.

Natural Resources and Industries

The country is rich with natural resources. Its vast areas of fertile land provide favorable conditions for various kinds of agricultural activities. Indonesia is one of the world's major suppliers of tobacco, tea, coffee, palm oil, coconuts, pepper, tropical fruits, and marine products.

Oil and natural gas remain the resources of highest strategic impor- tance. Indonesia is a member of the Organization of Petroleum Exporting Countries (OPEC) and the biggest oil producer in East Asia, with the excep- tion of Russia. However, oil production is falling because of the aging of oil fields and lack of investment in new equipment and exploration. Since 2004, on a monthly basis, the country has ended up being a net oil importer sev- eral times.

Traditionally, tin, bauxite, and silver were the other major mineral resources excavated and exported. Today, Indonesia is noticeably expanding the produc- tion and export of copper, nickel, gold, and coal as well. Another precious natu- ral resource the country has is tropical timber.

The major manufacturing industries are: electronics (mostly assembly), machinery, and transport equipment; fertilizers, chemicals, and rubber products; textiles and footwear; and iron, steel, and other basic metals. The food industry is also very important.

In 2006, agriculture accounted for 12.9 percent of the country's GDP, industry was 47.0 percent, and services were 40.1 percent. The shares in the total number of persons employed were 44.5 percent for agriculture, 12.2 percent for manufac- turing, 1.0 percent for mining, and 42.4 percent for other sectors, mainly services (ADB 2007).

Companies

One of the most famous Indonesian firms is Indofood, the number one processed-food company and the world's largest instant noodles maker (13 billion packs a year) and flour miller (over 3 million tons a year). According to president and director, Anthoni Salim, it is "a food solutions company because Indofood covers all aspects of the food chain from the plantations to processes to logistics—down to the shelf" (*Japan Times* 2005a).

Lippo Group is a leading conglomerate founded by a well-known busi- ness tycoon, Mochtar Riady. He started by establishing Bank Lippo and then expanded into large-scale property development in Indonesia and China. Today, the group provides a wide variety of financial services from insurance to venture capital investment, undertakes big infrastructure projects, and has also entered the education services market.

Astra Group is the country's key player in the auto sector, engaged in the assembly and sales of auto vehicles, as well as the production of components. It has an array of partnerships with the world's major companies, such has Toyota, Isuzu, BMW, and Peugeot.

A number of other Indonesian companies have attracted attention, at home and overseas, by producing competitive products through leveraging the coun- try's natural resources such as timber and rubber.

A Multiethnic State

Three key words are very important to understand postwar developments in Indonesia: nationalism, elite, and unity. Historically, state formation began in the mid-nineteenth century with the colonization of territories, inhabited by a wide variety of ethnic groups, by the Dutch.

In Indonesia, there are 30 distinct ethnic groups speaking more than 300 distinct dialects (*Japan Times* 2007). The largest ethnic groups are the Javanese (40 percent of the total population), the Sundanese (15 percent), and the Madurese (3 percent). While most residents of Java are of Malay origin, in some regions of the eastern part of the country Melanesian ethnic groups comprise the majority.

For a country with such an ethnic diversity, preservation of unity and integrity is a very challenging task. "Unity in diversity" has been Indonesia's major political slogan since independence.

Indigenous ethnic groups across Indonesia, comprising around 95 percent of the population, are called *pribumi* (inlanders). Ever since independence they have enjoyed various kinds of preferential treatment. Overseas Chinese, though playing a key role in the national economy, are not included in this category.

The distinction arises from the Dutch Staat Blaad (State Regulation) No 163, issued in 1917, which divided the population into three categories: European, foreign easterner (Chinese, Arabs, and Indians), and islander (indigenous). Everyone under the colonial jurisdiction was assigned one of these categories at birth. Though officially the rule has been abolished, it still influences Indonesian society. For instance, until recently, only Chinese Indonesians were required to have an Indonesian Citizenship Certificate. Various other kinds of unwritten rules also exist. One of them is that ethnic Chinese are not supposed to work as civil servants.

From the beginning of the twentieth century the Dutch allowed some participation of indigenous people in government. To rule such a vast colony, they needed an extensive administration apparatus, which consisted mostly of the local bureaucratic elite. They educated this elite and delegated to it many important administrative functions. The elite came mostly from Java—the most populous island with the most advanced and well-organized society among the territories that comprise Indonesia. After independence in 1945, the Javanese elite "inherited" the ruling position from the Dutch and became a privileged class.

The Elite and Its Role

The military command and the vast majority of the officers were also a major part of the elite. They proclaimed that the army was the protector of independence and nationalism and that it had the obligation, and the right, to contribute to society—first, by providing national defense and ensuring the safety of its citizens and, second, by participating in politics and social development. This was called the "dual function" doctrine. This doctrine was explicitly declared void only after the emergence of the present administration of President Susilo Bambang Yudhoyono in 2004. On the political scene the elite were represented by the Golkar party, which has had a dominant position in the parliament since 1966 with no strong opposition force to challenge it.

The elite, with President Suharto as its leader, were responsible for the economic development of Indonesia for more than three decades from 1966 until 1998. On the one hand, it launched economic policies beneficial for the country as a whole, which contributed to economic development and the rise of living standards. On the other, it used the state machine it controlled, including numerous state-owned enterprises (SOEs), as a tool for its own enrichment and consolidation of power. To preserve and strengthen its political and economic dominance, it did not hesitate to sacrifice the efficiency and competitiveness of the national economy.

Support for the *Pribumi* and the Dominance of the Suharto Clan

Along with the establishment and expansion of SOEs, the Suharto regime attempted to nurture *pribumi* entrepreneurs. The latter were provided preferential access to government contracts, exclusive licenses for business in lucrative sectors such as distribution and imports, low-interest loans from state-controlled banks, and special rebates on, or exemptions from, customs duties on imported equipment and intermediate products. Such policies would be justified if, at least, they were based on objective criteria for selecting businesses eligible for state support. However, as time went by, it became increasingly obvious that the decisive "criterion" was personal connection. The policy did not succeed that much. Still, promotion of *pribumi* businessmen continues today.

During the 1980s, when Suharto's children grew up, state support began to focus increasingly on businesses run by them. The economy of a huge country was becoming dominated by the Suharto clan. This situation became socially explosive and finally paved the way for Suharto's resignation in May 1998.

However, although it was the end of Suharto clan dominance, the resignation did not mark the end of the system with the elite as its core and nationalism as its ideological framework.

Postwar Development

The Sukarno Years

Indonesia's independence was proclaimed in August 1945, but the Netherlands acknowledged it only in December 1949, after four years of bitter conflict.

The administration of the first president, Sukarno, known for his dislike of colonialism, pursued populist and nationalist policies, which were sometimes confrontational toward the West. Sukarno also showed a rather positive attitude to the ideas of communism.

In the late 1950s, the government eliminated all foreign presence in the private sector. A state-dominated economy emerged. A rapid increase in public, including military, spending and excessive liquidity led to hyperinflation. Economic growth was dynamic in the first half of the 1950s but then slowed down, and in the mid-1960s the condition of the economy became critical. The pro-Maoist Communist Party attempted a coup but it was suppressed by the military, under General Suharto, in one of the worst tragedies in Asia's postwar history. About 500,000 people were killed. Sukarno stepped down and, in 1967, Suharto became president. His rule lasted for 32 years.

The New Order Regime

Suharto's New Order regime started in the "development dictatorship" style. Economic policy was shaped in accordance with the recommendations of the International Monetary Fund (IMF). The World Bank and major developed nations provided massive credits on favorable terms.

Indonesia was prioritized as the recipient of official development assistance (ODA), especially by Japan and the US as its major donors—creating a market economy and consolidating the power of a pro-Western regime in the largest country of Southeast Asia was considered vital for political stability in the region and for neutralizing the communist threat. This gave the regime significant leverage in the West.

The government proclaimed that the private sector would play a pivotal role in economic development and showed its intention to liberalize the economy. However, market-oriented transformation lacked persistence. There were two influential groups in the government with conflicting views about economic policy. The first one, the technocrats, was calling for market-oriented reforms, a smaller government role in the economy, and prudent fiscal and monetary policy. The second group, the economic nationalists, insisted on large-scale government involvement to boost industrialization and growth, advocated trade protectionism, and demanded restrictions on the foreign presence in the economy.

In reality, the economic policy of the regime was aimed at consolidating the elite-centered and elite-dominated economic system with the state playing the major part.

When prices for oil, and the other primary products Indonesia exported, were falling, the government shifted to a more restrictive fiscal policy, curtailing large-scale investment projects in the state sector and deregulating and improving conditions for private business. When prices and export revenues rose, its presence in the economy was increased again.

The 1970s

In the 1970s, the decade of two oil booms, 1973–75 and 1979–80 (oil shocks for importers), the Indonesian economy grew fast. Another key growth factor was preferential loans by the World Bank and developed countries, especially Japan.

Oil revenues were used to promote government-led industrialization. The government launched large-scale projects, seeking to create a full set of industries with SOEs as the major players.

Sometimes, it created partnerships with foreign companies. For example, the government owns 41 percent of the country's only aluminum-smelting company, Indonesia Asahan Aluminum, and a consortium of Japanese companies owns 59 percent (*Japan Times* 2005b).

Government-sponsored projects were usually very costly and the efficiency and profitability of the enterprises were largely ignored. Industries depended on budget financing and were protected by high import barriers. The domestic market was expected to provide sufficient demand.

Import Substitution

Government-sponsored projects were part of an import substitution policy and its contents were rather simple. As soon as imports of a particular product reached a certain level, the government moved to start domestic production. If domestic companies, private and SOEs, could not cope with it by themselves, foreign capital was invited. However, this kind of industrialization policy, launched in the wake of the first oil boom, only really allowed the creation of small-scale assembly factories in the machinery and electronics sectors. Foreign companies were not enthusiastic.

In 1979, the second oil boom started and export revenues surged again. Since 1978, Indonesia had begun to produce and export natural gas and the government worked out a comprehensive schedule for the development of a wide range of other domestic industries, emphasizing the role of SOEs. Really large-scale import substitution industrialization began.

As a result, production in the manufacturing sector (steel, aluminum, cement, textiles, food products, pulp and paper, chemicals and petrochemicals, shipbuilding, the aircraft industry, and the production of durable consumer goods) expanded at a fast pace but structural problems emerged. Expectations regarding the size of the domestic market were too high. As the number of manufacturing companies increased their capacity utilization rates were falling. Domestic products were of higher cost and lower quality than their overseas counterparts.

The Early 1980s: Hard Times

In the first half of the 1980s, as world oil prices fell, Indonesia entered a new stage of its postwar economic history. Declining oil revenues, along with the rising foreign debt service cost, made it impossible to support growth in a wide range of industries by massive government spending. Overall, the economic growth rate for 1982–86 was as low as 3.1 percent (Watanabe 2003, 166). The situation in the manufacturing industries, nurtured by the government's import substitution policy—for example, the production of motorcycles, auto vehicles, and durable consumer goods—became critical.

The Mid-1980s Policy Shift and Acceleration

At this point, it was recognized that such high dependence of industrial growth on oil revenues was no longer relevant. The government began structural adjustment, seeking to promote exports of labor-intensive manufacturing products. First, it engineered a brisk depreciation of the rupiah. In March 1983, its exchange rate fell from 703 Rp to 970 Rp for US$1. Additional incentives were introduced for foreign and domestic private investors. Deregulation progressed.

Indonesia's abundant and cheap labor resource began to work at full strength as a factor attracting foreign direct investment (FDI), especially from Japan and Asia's newly industrialized economies (NIEs). Investment by overseas Chinese conglomerates was also rapidly increasing.

Structural adjustment brought improved results in the second half of the 1980s and the first half of the 1990s—the Indonesian economy was booming. Annual growth rates averaged 6.4 percent in 1987–93 and 7.1 percent in 1994–97 (Watanabe 2003, 166). It was an export-led boom.

The government moved to activate its industrial policy. In 1989, the Agency for Strategic Industries was established with the aim of promoting capital- and technology-intensive industries led by the SOEs. The list of strategic industries included aerospace, marine and land transport, electronics and telecommunications, energy, defense, agriculture, construction, and engineering. Ten SOEs operating in these industries were put under the supervision of the Science and Technology Minister, B. J. Habibie.

Overheating, Overborrowing, and Cronyism

In the early 1990s, the first signs of overheating appeared. As the boom was expected to continue for a long time, land prices soared, largely due to growing speculative demand. In 1991, the government shifted to deflationary policies. However, they were not persistent and did not last long. Nationalists in the government were pressing for policies that would stimulate further growth. As a result, an asset bubble emerged while current account deficits and foreign liabilities were reaching critical levels.

President Suharto took the side of those who called for an expansionary policy. This was largely due to reasons of a very personal character—his children were rapidly expanding their business activities by taking advantage of state support and various kinds of preferential treatment.

It would be safe to say that in the first half of the 1990s cronyism and the abuse of power by the president and his family reached "unprecedented heights." Overheating, overborrowing, tremendous resource allocation biases, and inefficiencies rooted in cronyism and power abuse—structurally, the Indonesian economy was "ripe" for a crisis.

Hardest Hit by the Asian Crisis

Arguably, in 1997–98, Indonesia was hit by the Asian crisis more heavily than any other country in the region. The repatriation of capital by investors brought about the dramatic downfall of the rupiah, which was floated. The bottom for its exchange rate in 1998 was 17,000Rp for US$1 as opposed to the 1997 average of about 2,400Rp. After it bounced bank, more than two-thirds of the value still remained lost. Foreign debt skyrocketed. The activities of most private banks, facing an upsurge of both nonperforming loans (NPLs) and foreign liabilities, were practically paralyzed. Some of the major conglomerates collapsed, including the most powerful one—Salim Group. In 1998, inflation hit 58 percent and GDP fell by 13.1 percent. Unemployment mounted. Worst of all, severe drought led to rice shortages.

All this led to enormous social unrest. Businesses were destroyed by looting and there were widespread anti-Chinese riots. Many shops, banks, and offices, belonging to Chinese Indonesians, were devastated by mobs. The activities of radical Islamic groups were also on the rise. Amid this deep political and social crisis President Suharto stepped down in May 1998.

Structural Reforms

Agreements with the IMF

In its first reaction to the Asian crisis, the government raised interest rates and tightened fiscal and monetary policy. In May 1998, a new Central Bank Act became effective, which gave Bank Indonesia the status and position of an independent state institution, guaranteeing it freedom from interference by the government or any other external party (Bank Indonesia Web site).

The first agreement with the IMF on the rescue package and anti-crisis measures, reached in October 1997, was mostly focused on the tightening of fiscal and monetary policy. Also, it included the termination of the National Car Program, which provided a set of tax and other preferences for domestic "pioneer" auto producers on condition they use Indonesian brands and increase local content, and the dissolution of the clove monopoly agency, the only authorized clove trader established, originally, to protect farmers from fluctuating prices. Both schemes involved Suharto's third son Hutomo Mandala Putra, also known as Tommy Suharto.

After Suharto's resignation, two consecutive agreements with the IMF on an Extended Fund Facility followed.

Banking Reform and the IBRA

Initially, structural reforms were focused on the ailing banking sector. Bank Indonesia prescribed all domestic banks to meet the 8 percent target for capital adequacy ratio and to reduce the share of bad loans in the total amount of outstanding loans to 5 percent by 2001 (Tselichtchev 2004). In 1998, the government issued bonds worth 650 trillion Rp (the figure equals almost 70 percent of GDP for that year), of which around 425 trillion Rp was allocated for the recapitalization of the banks and the rest for repaying customers of the banks which had been closed down (Bhui 2004).

In January the same year, the Indonesian Bank Restructuring Agency (IBRA) was established. It was authorized to take over the ailing banks, restructure them, and collect their NPLs.

The number of banks, which was 239 in pre-crisis 1996, fell to 151 in 2000 and 138 in 2003. The number of domestic private banks decreased from 164 to 81 and 76 in the same respective years (Harada 2005, 33). The government initiated the closure of small banks and injected capital into bigger ones.

The banking system restructuring program, announced in March 1998, divided banks into three categories: A (healthy; exempted from government intervention; 72 banks qualified for this category); B (instructed to submit a business plan; upon its approval the scheme to boost capital adequacy had to be worked out together with the government; the government injected funds; 9 banks were approved, those which failed were put under IBRA control); and C (basically, had to be closed; however, seven banks avoided closure and made a new start) (Harada 2005, 38).

IBRA contributed a lot to the restructuring and revitalization of domestic banks. And not only banks. It also put under government control a number of major conglomerates and pushed through their restructuring, including bankruptcy procedures for companies which were impossible to revitalize or refused to cooperate.

It is important to note that, in order to raise the funds needed, IBRA opened the door to major entries by foreign financial institutions, encouraging them to acquire the stock of the Indonesian banks it had purchased. For example, Temasek Holdings and Deutsche Bank acquired a 51 percent share in PT Bank Danamon Indonesia, a consortium including South Korea's Kookmin Bank acquired PT Bank Internasional Indonesia, and Malaysia's Commerce Asset-Holding Berhad gained control over PT Bank Niaga. However, the privatization bid for Bank Central Asia (BCA) was unexpectedly cancelled on the pretext that the initial bidding price was too low. As a result of the reforms, the management of some leading Indonesian banks has improved.

One of the core elements of the bank reform was the creation, in July 1999, of a new leading state-owned bank, Bank Mandiri, with a newly recapitalized balance sheet through the merger of four other state-owned banks, all of which had become insolvent. After the merger was completed, it became the indisputable number one player in the banking sector—its share of the total amount of both assets and deposits of the national banks was 25 percent (Lasserre 2003, 11). In July 2004, the initial public offering (IPO) for 20 percent of Mandiri's stock was held and 2.6 trillion rupiah was raised (IDE-JETRO 2005, 395–396),

To revitalize the banking sector the government was essentially adhering to the policy of nationalization, restructuring, and selling off. The most challenging task, however, was to make the nationalized banks attractive investment targets and to overcome resistance to foreign acquisitions within the political elite and society in general.

Restructuring SOEs

Another pillar of the reforms is the large-scale restructuring of SOEs. The government is seeking to both reduce their number and raise the efficiency of the companies remaining in the state sector. It is a first attempt to turn SOEs into dynamic market players, capable of competing internationally.

In February 2007, the Ministry of State Enterprise announced a plan to reduce the number of nationalized firms from 139 to 69 within three years through mergers, liquidation, and privatization. Also, the government started to set targets for the annual growth of SOE profits.

As discussed in Chapter 3, the policy of promoting strategic industries has been revived but in a more market-friendly version. Today, it is aimed at raising their international competitiveness, not import substitution.

Present Performance

A Period of Uncertainty

After the fall of the Suharto regime, Indonesia went through a period of political uncertainty and weak governments. The country's third president, B.J. Habibie, led the transitional administration and withdrew his presidential nomination in 1999 after the People's Consultative Assembly rejected his accountability speech—a report on the achievements of the administration. He was succeeded by a Muslim cleric, Abdurrahman Wahid, who had to step down in 2001 in the wake of accusations of involvement in a corruption scandal and misappropriation of funds donated by the Sultan of Brunei. Wahid was replaced by his vice president, Megawati Sukarnoputri, the daughter of Sukarno. In October 2004, for the first time in the nation's history, a direct presidential election was held and Megawati lost to her former Coordinating Minister for Politics and Security, Susilo Bambang Yudhoyono, now often referred to as SBY.

A Picture of Indonesia's Growth

Recovery was slower than in the other crisis-hit countries—the economy continued to struggle with the consequences of the crisis, especially where weaknesses in the financial sector were concerned. Steady acceleration of growth only started from 2002 (see Table 14.1).

In 2006, the pre-crisis level of real per-capita GDP was finally restored. In 2004, the rise in stock prices on the Jakarta Stock Exchange (JSX) was the biggest in Asia at 42 percent. Growth was driven by private consumption along with exports and investment (however, the lion's share of funds was invested into buildings, while investment into machinery and equipment was relatively small). Demand for services has been expanding at the greatest rate, especially telecommunication, transportation, electricity, water, and gas supplies. Sales in the mobile telephony and Internet services sector have been growing 40–50 percent annually (ADB 2008).

Table 14.1 Main economic indicators (real annual growth, %)

Indicator	1999	2000	2001	2002	2003	2004	2005	2006	2007
GDP	0.8	4.9	3.8	4.3	4.8	5.0	5.7	5.5	6.3
Agriculture*	2.2	1.9	4.1	2.6	3.8	2.8	2.7	3.4	3.5
Industry*	2.0	5.9	2.7	4.3	3.8	3.9	4.7	4.5	4.7
Services*	-1.0	5.2	5.0	5.0	6.4	7.1	7.9	7.4	8.9
Private consumption	4.6	1.6	3.5	3.8	3.9	5.0	4.0	3.2	5.0
Unemployment rate (%)	6.4	6.1	8.1	9.1	9.6	9.9	11.2	10.3	9.8
Gross domestic capital formation	-18.2	12.9	8.6	-1.8	10.8	6.9	12.4	1.2	2.0
Consumer prices	20.3	9.3	12.5	10.0	5.1	6.1	10.5	13.1	6.4
Exports (US$ millions), fob	48,665	62,124	56,321	57,159	62,527	69,714	85,660	100,690	114,100
Imports (US$ millions), cif	24,003	33,515	30,962	31,229	33,026	46,180	57,701	61,078	74,473
Average exchange rate (rupiah per US$1)	7,855	8,422	10,261	9,311	8,577	8,939	9,705	9,159	9,143.4

Source: ADB: "Key Indicators," 2008.
*Data for agriculture, industry, and services refers to value added.

In 2005, the exchange rate of the rupiah fell abruptly, as the economy suffered a blow from the rise in the international oil price. In October of the same year, the government cut fuel subsidies, which were to cost US$14 billion, in order to reduce the budget deficit. As a result, prices for consumer fuels more than doubled and inflation became double-digit, peaking at 18.4 percent on an annual basis at the year's end (ADB 2008). In the wake of the price hike the government offered one-time subsidies (direct cash assistance) to low-income families. It was the first significant social security benefits scheme in the country's history.

In 2007, inflation declined. However, in May 2008, administered fuel prices were raised by 28.7 percent in order to cut subsidies (ADB 2008), and year-on-year inflation returned to double-digit levels, causing concerns about its negative influence on consumption, company profits, and employment.

Though the government intended to absorb the rise of global fuel and food prices, it was explained that the budget was overstrained and that funds saved would be used for fighting poverty.

The overall budget deficit was reduced to 0.5 percent in 2005, but rose again to 1.5 percent in 2007 (ADB 2008). The government is noticeably increasing spending on infrastructure and social assistance.

The national economy is not doing well enough in such key areas as reduction of unemployment and poverty. The "open unemployment rate"—which does not take into account latent unemployment (it has to be remembered that in Indonesia the formal sector provides only one-third of total employment)—rose from 9.6 percent in 2003 to 10.3 percent in 2006 (see Table 14.1). The underemployment rate (which refers to people working less than 35 hours a week), as of February 2008, was 27.6 percent (ADB 2008).

Poverty rates increased during the Asian crisis, then gradually fell back below the pre-crisis years' level. But, in 2006, they rose again to become the same as they were in 1996. Since 2006, they have become lower again. According to the Bappenas (National Development Planning Board) report of 2008, 9 percent of the population currently lives below the national poverty line (Indonesian Embassy in the US 2008). Also, 8.5 percent of Indonesians live on less than US$1 a day and about half on less than US$2 dollars (ADB 2008). In other words, though growth is accelerating it is still insufficient to create enough jobs and visibly reduce poverty.

Economic growth in the post-crisis years has also been hindered by recent natural disasters. The biggest one was the devastating tsunami and earthquake of December 2004. The provinces of Aceh and North Sumatra suffered most. This was followed by a great earthquake in central Java in May 2006. Disasters continued in 2006–07, including massive flooding in the capital, Jakarta.

Secessionist or pro-independence movements in several provinces have posed another persistent problem. East Timor became independent in 2002. The separatist movement in the Aceh province intensified its activities at the beginning of the 2000s but, in 2005, the government reached a peace agreement with the Acehnese rebel movement, GAM. There is also a low-profile secessionist movement in Papua.

The Impact of the Global Financial Turmoil

In 2008, the influence of the global turmoil on Indonesia's economic growth was insignificant. In the first half of the year, the annual growth rate was as high as 6.4 percent and, after the turmoil began, the expected figure for the whole year was 6 percent. According to government sources, in 2009, growth was likely to fall to 4.5 percent (*Financial Times* 2008).

Most importantly, growth was supported by robust consumer spending. (Among other things, consumption was increasing fast because the commodity boom of the previous years made people living in the plantation and mining areas wealthier, enabling them to join the ranks of active buyers.) For example, sales of cars and motorcycles were expanding at the fastest pace since the Asian crisis (Suharmoko 2008).

Yet, the economy was negatively affected by the tightening of national banking liquidity and an exports squeeze.

In the financial sector, the big story was the government's November crackdown on Bank Century whose capital adequacy ratio had plunged to −2.3 percent (Xinhua 2008). The bank was nationalized, and its top managers were arrested.

At the end of November, the rupiah weakened to the 12,000 per US$1 level, which is only about two-thirds of the average rate for 2007. The government said that it was comfortable with this rate because it benefited exporters. However, due to the global economic downturn, the positive effect of the currency depreciation on exports was negligible. Indonesian exports were also adversely affected by the fall in the world prices of primary products. Garment exporters lost out because overseas consumers shifted toward more basic and cheaper clothing.

To protect the national currency, the government made it more difficult to buy foreign exchange. It required any purchase worth US$100,000 or more to be supported by underlying transactions in goods and services (Su 2008). In another development, it drastically raised its deposits guarantees limit from 100 million rupiah (US$10,000) to 2 billion rupiah (US$200 million) (Xinhua 2008).

The benchmark interest rate was cut continuously, but cautiously. In January 2009, it reached 8.75 percent. Inflation for the whole year remained double-digit, 11.1 percent, but fell at the year's end.

In 2008, the business community was urging the government to launch a large-scale stimulus package, drastically cut the interest rate, and to provide a full guarantee against all funds deposited in banks, as well as for interbank loans.

The stimulus package, worth 71.3 trillion rupiahs (about US$6.3 billion), or 1.4 percent of the GDP, was announced in late January 2009. It included tax savings, waived taxes and import duties for businesses and certain households, and subsidies and government spending for businesses (Suharmoko 2009).

Indonesia refused to take the loan offered by the IMF to deal with the impact of the turmoil. However, the World Bank moved to create a standby donor facility (Australia, Japan, and the ADB were mentioned as other potential donors) of up to US$6 billion to help the country weather the global crisis by letting it borrow at very low interest rates, avoiding the expensive bond market (*Financial Times* 2008).

The Long-Term State Development Plan

In October 2004, a new Long-term State Development Plan 2005–25 was adopted. While the earlier draft, prepared under Megawati, emphasized fighting corruption, cronyism, and the "policy of force" the Yudhoyono administration attached higher priority to economic development and growth, integrating corruption and cronyism-related problems into the section devoted to the creation of an up-to-date legal system.

The major strategic goals of the plan for Indonesia are defined as: building prosperity and self-reliance; justice and democracy; and safety and unity. Eight tasks are set, mostly in general terms, which have to be addressed to achieve these goals. The first one is high, sustainable, economic growth and the rise of international competitiveness through the promotion of science and technology. The target for 2025 is to raise per-capita income to US$6,000 and to reduce the poverty rate to below 5 percent, from the present 18 percent (Omura 2006). Other tasks include comprehensive infrastructure upgrading, balanced development of the whole national territory and elimination of inter-regional frictions, relevant management of natural resources, preservation of the natural environment, human resource development, an increase in the role of women in society, the formation of a legal state, and clean and efficient government. Decentralization is counted upon as the way to overcome political instability.

The plan also refers to the values and basic principles that government policy will be based upon, especially the paternalistic idea of the country as a big family.

Along with the long-term plan, medium-term, five-year development plans have been adopted, which set more concrete economic targets. The present Five-year Plan covers the period from 2005 to 2009. The government states that the 4–5 percent annual growth of the first half of the decade is not sufficient to create enough good jobs to address the country's poverty problems. The target is to reach 6–7 percent growth on average, which requires substantial acceleration. Key economic policy goals are: macroeconomic stability; promotion of investment, exports and tourism; human resource development; and improvement of infrastructure.

Foreign Trade

Indonesia is both an exporter and importer of oil. The rapid growth of domestic demand, and falling production, has resulted in an equally rapid growth of oil imports. Exports of crude oil slightly exceed imports (US$9,226 million and US$9,057 million, respectively, in 2007). As for petroleum products, the country is a big net importer. In recent years exports of natural gas exceeded those of oil. Yet, as domestic demand has grown, the government has restricted exports, causing doubts about the country's ability to meet its obligations under international contracts.

The Composition of Exports

The total share of the oil and natural gas sector in the country's exports, in 2007, was 19.3 percent (8.1 percent for crude oil, 8.7 percent for natural gas, and 2.5 percent for petroleum products).

In the non-oil sector, animal and plant oils and fats (mostly palm oil) were the major export item (9.0 percent of the total) percent, followed by electrical and electronic machinery and parts at 6.5 percent (their share is lower than in the exports of other East Asian countries), mineral fuels other than oil and natural gas (mainly coal) at 6.2 percent, and natural rubber and rubber products at 5.5 percent. Also, today's Indonesia is a big exporter of copper ore, tropical timber, and wood products. Tropical wood furniture and wood-carving products, especially traditional artifacts, are an area where local producers have a strong competitive edge. However, illegal logging has become a major problem and the authorities' crackdown is limiting exports. Indonesia's other well-known export items include tropical fruit, marine products, canned products, and coffee.

Japan is Indonesia's biggest export market (at 20.7 percent of total exports in 2007). It is followed by the US (10.2 percent), Singapore (9.2 percent), China (8.5 percent), South Korea (6.7 percent), Malaysia (4.5 percent), and India (4.3 percent). The share of the European Union (EU) was 11.7 percent (JETRO Web site 2008).

The Composition of Imports

As part of the total of imports, oil and natural gas comprised 29.4 percent (crude oil was 12.2 percent, petroleum products were 17.1 percent, and natural gas was 0.1 percent). The share of general machinery and parts was 12.5 percent, electrical and electronic products and parts 6.4 percent, iron and steel 5.6 percent, organic chemicals 5.2 percent, and transport machinery and parts 3.2 percent.

At 32 percent, most imports came from the Association of Southeast Asian Nations (ASEAN) countries. The biggest exporter to Indonesia was Singapore (13.2 percent). Recent years have been marked by a rapid increase in imports of auto vehicles and parts from Thailand, whose share reached 5.8 percent. The share of China was 11.5 percent, Japan 8.8 percent, the US 6.4 percent, Saudi Arabia 4.5 percent, and South Korea 4.4 percent. Imports from the EU accounted for 10.3 percent (JETRO Web site 2008).

With the emergence and expansion of the middle class, Indonesia is becoming an increasingly important market for various kinds of products. The law of large absolute numbers works well in this country. For instance, in 2003, Indonesia was the tenth-largest car market in the world for Toyota, outside Japan, and, in 2004, it entered the top five (*Japan Times*, 2005c).

FDI and the Business Environment

Volume and Composition

The amount of FDI in Indonesia (approval basis) increased from US$13,636 million in 2005 to US$15,659 million in 2006, and then surged to US$40,146 million in 2007. The biggest investors in 2007 were the US (33.2 percent of the total) and Singapore (13.9 percent). Malaysia, which was number one in 2006, ran third (5.9 percent), followed by South Korea and China (2.2 percent each). The share of the EU was 33.2 percent.

Manufacturing absorbed 67.8 percent of inward FDI. The largest recipients were chemicals and pharmaceuticals (38.0 percent of the total) and paper and products (17.1 percent). The share of the food industry was 4.3 percent. Metal and the electrical and general machinery sectors combined received 4.0 percent. In nonmanufacturing, the combined share of transportation, telecommunication, and storage services was 12.0 percent of the total, construction 4.3 percent, agriculture 3.0 percent, and mining 2.0 percent (JETRO Web site 2008).

A cheap and abundant labor force, a large domestic market (mainly in the major cities), an expanding, consumption-hungry middle class, and rich natural resources are the major factors attracting investors.

Foreign Companies Operating in Indonesia

There are many examples of foreign companies successfully operating in Indonesia. One of them is the joint venture between Toyota and Astra Group—Toyota Astra Motor (TAM). In 2003, it created two separate companies to cope with growing business (*Japan Times* 2005c). TAM concentrates on local distribution and sales, while Toyota Motor Manufacturing Indonesia (TMMIN) focuses on manufacturing for both domestic and global markets. As part of its global strategy, Toyota has assigned TMMIN to produce the Innova model, the Indonesian-designed multi-purpose vehicle (MPV), sold in Southeast Asia, India, Taiwan, and the UAE.

In 1993, the coal industry was opened up for foreign investors, and PT Kaltim Prima Coal, a joint venture between two UK firms, BP and Rio Tinto, has become the biggest coal producer in the country. In addition, US companies have a predominant position and operate on a large scale in the oil and gas sector.[1]

Rules

The government agency responsible for both domestic and foreign investment is the Investment Coordinating Board. It gives the final approval to investment projects and determines the minimum reasonable paid-up capital, depending on the nature and type of business. A few areas are closed to foreign investment, including natural forest exploitation and lumber contractors, trading services (except large-scale retailers), and the wholesale trade.

Foreign investors can establish both a joint venture with a local company and a 100 percent foreign-owned entity, but the overall number of investors in any foreign-affiliated company has to be two or more. In some areas, the share of foreign capital cannot exceed 95 percent.

Problems

Many attractive opportunities can be found in Indonesia, but the present investment environment in the country is not that favorable by international standards.

One of the major problems is red tape. According to government data as of January 2004, to make an investment in Indonesia one needs to get 12 permits from various agencies and the time needed to go through the formalities required averages out at 151 days. The number of permits doesn't differ that much from most other East Asian countries, but the time span is much longer than anywhere else. Also, Indonesia is the most expensive in terms of the cost one has to bear to get those permits. The government is promising to make formalities more simple and transparent and less costly, as well as to fight widespread corruption. Yet, progress is very slow.

Another problem is a very inflexible labor market. There is a strong belief, rooted in national culture and values, that views a company as a family where all members are bound by mutual obligations to support and take care of one another. Firing an employee is difficult, costly, and time consuming. The employer does not have the right to dismiss a worker without authorization from the Institution on the Settlement of Industrial Relations Disputes (ISIRD). He has to submit a request, presenting the reasons in writing. The permission may be granted only if it is clear that the discussion with the workers' organization, or the non-unionized worker, required by the law, has taken place and failed to produce an agreement (ILO 2007).

Generally, the labor laws attach priority to the rights of workers. Under these conditions, employees sometimes come up with claims which may look excessive. Also, strikes, unauthorized by labor unions, are quite frequent.

The institutions supporting job search and providing vocational training are weak. Hiring of an employee with the skills and qualifications required may be difficult.

Problems also exist with fulfilling the terms of contracts by local transaction counterparts and contract enforcement. The formalities needed to protect your rights, in case a counterpart violates a contract, take a very long time to complete—570 days on average.

As mentioned, the drastic improvement of infrastructure remains a major task, though in and around major cities, especially on Java, it is much better than in small towns and most of the countryside. Only 53 percent of Indonesian households have access to electricity and 78 percent to water supply and sewage systems. Only 4 percent are equipped with a telephone and just 6 percent use mobile phones. The density of roads is also low—just 1 mile per 1,000 persons

(Omura 2006, 185). Foreign companies operating in Indonesia often complain about the network of roads linking industrial zones. It may take one or two hours to transport goods from one zone to another, even though they are less than six miles apart (JETRO 2005, 29).

Another urgent task is to develop and expand the seaports. Indonesia doesn't have ports that are large or developed enough to function as regional transportation hubs, directly linked with the other major ports of the world.

Three Policy Packages and a New Investment Law

In 2006, the government introduced three policy packages to improve the investment climate, infrastructure, and the financial sector.

The investment package seeks improvements in five areas: regulatory regime, taxation, customs and excise, the labor market, and support for small- and medium-sized enterprises (SMEs). Some progress has been achieved in the simplification of investment procedures, including the acquisition of licenses.

Infrastructure reform is aimed at the improvement of the regulatory framework and the promotion of government-private partnerships. Among other things, the government intends to introduce a system of guarantees, to stimulate private investors and reduce their risks.

The financial package is focused on strengthening the financial market infrastructure, and improving the efficiency and liquidity of the capital market. The government wants the private sector to increase its financing of agriculture, forestry, SMEs, and low-cost housing.

In March 2007, a new investment law was enacted. It guarantees equal treatment of domestic and foreign investors and investors' rights to transfer and repatriate capital, profits, and royalties in foreign currency. Investors will be able to obtain various permits more quickly, including those for land rights. The Investment Coordination Board has been authorized to issue a range of incentives for investors, both domestic and foreign, especially exemptions or reductions of income tax, import duties, and value-added, land, and building taxes, as well as accelerated depreciation.

Other measures include the streamlining of business-licencing procedures, and a tax administration law to strengthen taxpayers' rights and limit arbitrary decision-making by officials (ADB 2008). The fight to attract investment is underway.

Concluding Remarks

The Asian crisis syndrome, suffered by Indonesia for a longer time than its neighbors, is over. Under the Yudhoyono administration the country has become more politically stable. Economic fundamentals are improving and growth has been accelerating.

Fiscal discipline has improved. Foreign debt has been reduced. The trade and current account balances have been in the black. High inflation is a headache but efforts to curb it have brought positive results since late 2006. Household consumption is robust, especially in the big cities.

Structural transformation is evident. The banking sector has been restructured and is now managed much better than before the crisis. In the post-crisis years, the government has moved to focus its involvement on such areas as improving infrastructure, fighting poverty, and developing rural areas, while its intervention in business activities in general is declining.

A cohort of dynamic, technologically advanced private companies is emerging, producing for both domestic and overseas markets. They often leverage the country's natural resources.

There is little doubt that, in the medium term, Indonesia will be able to maintain annual growth rates of 4–6 percent. The point, however, is that it is not sufficient and the question is whether or not the economy can grow faster.

The country's huge population turns to be more of a burden than a factor of growth. The annual number of new job seekers is almost two million but the economy is incapable of providing enough jobs, especially good jobs, because of insufficient growth rates, a mismatch between employers' needs and potential employees' capabilities, and the inflexible labor market. The level of education and training of the vast majority of the population remains low. There is also much room to improve in attitudes to work.

Two more factors adversely effect the country's economic growth. First, unlike previous decades, Indonesia cannot capitalize on its position as a big net exporter of oil. Second, in recent years, the country has frequently suffered from devastating natural disasters, and more are expected as it is located in one of the most seismically active areas of the world.

The major preconditions for growth acceleration are the improvement of the business environment, the attraction of more investment (both domestic and foreign), better use of the pool of cheap labor in expanding export-oriented industries, and leveraging a variety of natural resources.

Endnote

1 In Indonesia the state holds all the rights for petroleum and other mineral resources. Foreign companies can participate in their development through production sharing and work contracts. Excavated oil and gas are "shared" by the Indonesian government and the producers. The latter are required to finance all exploration, production, and development costs and are entitled to recover those costs out of the oil and gas they produce.

15

Philippines: Speeding up at Last

A Few Basics

The Philippines is a large low-middle-income country. Its population reached 88.6 million according to the census of August 2007 (Reuters 2008). It was 122nd in the world, in terms of per-capita gross domestic product (GDP) (purchasing power parity (PPP)), in the International Monetary Fund (IMF) ranking for the same year—below Indonesia and Kiribati and above Cape Verde and Mongolia. By nominal GDP it was 47th.

The Philippines is an archipelago of 7,107 islands. The major islands are Luzon in the north, the Visayas group in the center, and Mindanao in the south. Roman Catholics make up 85 percent of the population. The south is predominantly Muslim.

The country is divided into 81 provinces, 136 cities, 1,495 municipalities, and 41,995 barangays (the smallest administrative unit, a village or a district).

The Philippines is rich in natural resources—especially copper, nickel, chromite, and gold, but also silver, cobalt, oil, and coal. Big reserves of natural gas have been discovered at Malampaya field off Palawan island in the southwest and production started in 2001. The mining industry was boosted in 2004 when the operation of 100 percent foreign-owned companies was made possible.

In 2006, agriculture comprised 14.2 percent of GDP, industry 31.6 percent, and services 54.2 percent. The share of agriculture in the total number of persons employed was 33.0 percent, manufacturing 8.5 percent, mining 0.4 percent, and other sectors 50.2 percent (ADB 2007).

Agriculture remains crucially important to the national economy. Major products include rice, coconuts, pineapples, mangoes, bananas, natural rubber, sugarcane, corn, and livestock.

Today, the electronics sector, dominated by Japanese and American subsidiaries, has become the indisputable leader in the manufacturing industry. The Philippines is an important production platform for integrated circuits, hard disk drives, floppy disk drives, and other electronic parts. Manufacturing of auto vehicles and parts is also gaining strength.

Other important industries are food and beverages, textiles and garments, chemicals and petrochemicals, steel, and nonferrous metals. Rapidly expanding new sectors are business-process outsourcing services and call centers.

The national economy is supported by large-scale remittances from more than one million overseas foreign workers (OFWs)—a term for the Filipinos working abroad in the various parts of the world, but most of all in the Middle East.

Domestic economic activities are highly concentrated in the Metro Manila area. The province of Cebu in the Visayas has developed into a new economic center with a wide range of manufacturing and service industries. It aims to become a premier investment, software, and e-services hub in Southeast Asia.

The major economic agencies in the Philippines are the Department of Trade and Industry and the Department of Finance. The National Economic and Development Authority is responsible for economic planning.

One of the most well-known Philippine conglomerates is the Ayala Group, active in the real-estate sector, telecommunications, electronic manufacturing services, vehicle dealership (Ayala Automotive is an agent for Honda and Isuzu), and banking (Bank of the Philippine Islands). JG Summit Holdings is engaged in air transportation, banking, food manufacturing, the hotel business, property development, the production of petrochemicals and textiles, power generation, and publishing. San Miguel is the largest food and beverage group in Southeast Asia. Jollibee is one of the region's most successful fast-food chains offering a wide selection of various items. It has more than 1,000 outlets in the Philippines and 175 overseas—in Asia, the Middle East, and the US.

Postwar Development

The Start of Industrialization

The Philippines became a Spanish colony in the sixteenth century, was ceded to the United States in 1898, and gained independence in 1946. Postwar reconstruction did not take long due to large-scale aid from the US, which considered the Philippines a strategically important ally.

Import-substitution industrialization, already begun in the late 1940s, continued into the 1950s, prompting the Philippines' emergence as the most economically successful country in developing East Asia. Growth was boosted by the entries of American companies, especially into the production of consumer goods.

In the 1960s, import and currency controls were largely lifted but the government protected domestic industries with high tariffs. The average growth rate for the decade was 5.1 percent. However, at its end, the economy began to slow down because the domestic market was too small to sustain growth and there were constraints on imports of machinery, intermediate products, and raw materials due to surging trade deficits. To address the deficit problem, in 1962, the government devalued the peso by about one-half but this only provided a temporary solution.

Mostly, industrialization did not go beyond light industry—food and beverages, textiles, and garments.

The Marcos Era

Ferdinand Marcos became president of the Philippines in 1965. He was expected to exercise the strong leadership needed to speed up industrialization, develop heavy industries, and foster export-led growth. The Investment Incentive Act, enacted in 1967, institutionalized investors' basic rights and guarantees and provided a variety of incentives, including tax exemptions, tax credits, accelerated depreciation, and guarantee protection from the public sector competition. The Export Incentive Act, adopted three years later, marked the first attempt to go beyond import substitution. Export-processing zones were established with the aim of attracting export-oriented firms using special privileges. Nevertheless, the inflow of foreign direct investment (FDI) was sluggish, and new export-oriented industries did not appear.

In 1972, President Marcos declared martial law (which continued until 1981) and prolonged his presidential term (the constitution limits it to six years), effectively establishing dictatorial rule.

In the late 1970s, the government unveiled 11 big projects to be administered by the National Development Bureau. The goal was to construct or expand factories in such areas as the production of copper, fertilizer, steel, heavy machinery, cement, coco-chemicals, diesel engines, aluminum, pulp and paper, and petrochemicals. There was massive investment in infrastructure. State-owned banks, especially the Philippine National Bank (PNB) and the Development Bank of the Philippines (DBP), provided large-scale loans and investments. Such government-sponsored projects opened lucrative business opportunities for Marcos' cronies.

In another major development, the government moved to consolidate control over the sugar and coconut industries—the major foreign exchange earners.

Large-scale government investments and loans boosted domestic demand and stimulated industrial growth. Average growth rates in the 1970s went up to 6.3 percent. However, industrialization did not go beyond import substitution.

Signs of promise for export-led growth were hard to find. From the beginning of the decade, foreign, especially American, companies had begun to assemble and export integrated circuits, but the scale was relatively small. Trade and current account deficits were increasing, along with foreign debt.

The Financial Crisis of the Early 1980s

At the very beginning of the 1980s, a financial crisis erupted—most of the financial institutions were either bankrupt or in distress. Also, practically all the conglomerates run by Marcos cronies were on the verge of bankruptcy. In 1983, foreign debt exceeded US$24 billion (as opposed to only US$1 billion at the start of Marcos' first term as president).

To make things worse, that same year, the Philippines regime became a pariah in the international community after the assassination of Marcos' political rival, former senator and the Liberal Party leader, Benigno Aquino.

The crisis reflected the structural weaknesses of the economy—too much government involvement and inefficient allocation of funds; a volatile financial sector; chronic budget, trade, and balance of payments deficits; and the low competitiveness of companies, especially in the manufacturing sector.

The Philippines economy was dominated by an oligarchy of 15–20 families, which owned land and controlled industry and commerce. The president pledged to put an end to their dominance and build a "new society," but the regime pressured only business empires run by Marcos' foes, while supporting and protecting oligarchs close to him.

Structural Adjustment

From the early 1980s, the administration embarked on a series of structural adjustment programs supported by loans from the IMF, the World Bank, and other institutions. Their implementation continued almost until the end of the 1990s.

The IMF, and other donors, demanded a reduction in the government's involvement in the economy, privatization, and deregulation, the dissolution of the National Sugar Trading Corporation (NASUTRA) and United Coconut Oil Mills (UNICOM) (in reality they were dissolved only after the fall of the Marcos regime), a reduction of budget and trade deficits, and the promotion of exports. Presidential Decree 1177 required the government to pay for its foreign debt before any other expenditure (Villegas 2005).

At the outset of the adjustment, the government drastically cut public spending. Half of the large development projects were suspended. Interest rates were kept high. Along with the world recession, this dragged the economy into a severe contraction. In both 1984 and 1985, GDP fell by 7.3 percent (ADB 2001). A deteriorating economy sped up the regime's collapse.

Corazon Aquino's Term

In 1986, under strong domestic and international pressure, an early presidential election was called. Both Marcos and his opponent, Corazon Aquino, the widow of the assassinated senator, claimed victory and accused each other of counting fraud. The Marcos-dominated National Assembly proclaimed him the winner but a number of key figures in the political and military establishment, as well as the Catholic Church, including Cardinal Jaime Sin, sided with Aquino, who apparently got a majority of votes. Massive anti-Marcos demonstrations sustained opposition to his claim of victory, and, eventually, "the People Power Revolution" installed Aquino as the new president. Marcos fled to Hawaii with the blessing of the Reagan administration, where he passed away in 1989.

Initially, the new administration emphasized helping the poor and creating jobs as the major priorities of its economic policy. However, rather soon the emphasis shifted to liberalization and privatization. Important steps were taken to liberalize trade and foreign investment, especially the enactment of the Omnibus Investment Code of 1987, which introduced a variety of incentives. Land reform, also declared a priority, stumbled before it began.

As part of a new phase of structural adjustment, under the guidance of the IMF, the return of foreign debt was fixed as the major goal. To fulfill its obligations, the government had to borrow from domestic financial institutions. The share of debt servicing in total budget expenditure surged to more than half (Bodegon 1987).

The Economic Recovery Program

The Economic Recovery Program (1987–89) was launched in cooperation with the World Bank and supported by its US$300 million loan. The major aims were rationalization of the tax system (especially broadening of the tax base), improvement of tax collection, and reorganization of the PNB and DBP. Another task was to increase the budget financing of critically important economic and social sectors (infrastructure, education, help to poor families, and livelihood). The results were mixed. Though the tax system was rationalized, problems with tax administration remained, largely due to the lack of adequately trained personnel. The increase in budget revenues was insignificant and the financing of the sectors mentioned did not expand that much.

However, the reorganization of the two state-owned banks turned out to be rather successful. Beforehand, both were technically bankrupt—the ratio of non-performing loans (NPLs) had reached 80 percent. Afterward, their management and condition had significantly improved.

According to the World Bank, the Economic Recovery Program contributed to restoring investors' confidence and a rise in the inflow of foreign capital (World Bank 1993).

The Lost Decade

In 1987, the growth rate reached 4.3 percent and, in 1988, even rose to 6.8 percent (ADB 2001). However, to return the debt and curb budget and trade deficits, the government had to continue and even strengthen fiscal austerity. Thus, in 1990, growth became negative and, in 1991, it was zero. In 1990, economic troubles were exacerbated by a devastating earthquake and drought.

Overall, for the Philippines economy, the 1980s turned out to be the "lost decade," bringing a 7 percent reduction in real per-capita income. The average growth rate for 1980–91 was only 1.2 percent. The country was left out of the East Asian miracle.

The Fidel Ramos Years: Positive Signs

Things changed with the emergence of the Fidel Ramos administration in 1992. The Foreign Investment Act of 1991 decreased the minimum paid-up equity for direct investors, while the Export Development Act (1994) and the Special Economic Zones Act (1995) introduced additional fiscal and other incentives. Continuing the liberalization process, in 1993, the government opened up the telecommunication sector. In 1994, it liberalized new entries by foreign banks and the establishment of new domestic banks, creating a competitive environment in the financial sector. Substantial progress was achieved in building the institutional framework of the securities market. One more breakthrough was the launch of large-scale trade liberalization.

All these measures stimulated FDI, particularly in manufacturing—especially the electronics industry. Japanese companies noticeably increased their investment in the production of computer parts such as floppy disk drives, hard disk drives, and motherboards.

Growth rates during 1994–97 reached 4–5 percent. The national economy was gaining momentum. Unfortunately, it was interrupted by the Asian crisis. In 1998, GDP fell by 0.6 percent.

The Philippines and the Asian Crisis

The mechanism of the crisis was the same as in the other impacted economies—withdrawal of funds by foreign portfolio investors and lenders, falling stock prices, a depreciating peso, rising inflation, squeezed domestic demand and investment, growing unemployment, and declining household incomes. However, the Philippines was hit less hard than its three ASEAN neighbors and South Korea. The blow was mitigated by several factors. First, compared to these four states, the country was less exposed to the inflows of speculative foreign capital simply because its economic problems prompted investors to be cautious. Thus, the asset bubble was much smaller in size and limited mostly to the Metro Manila area. Second, large-scale remittances by the Filipinos working overseas served as a cushion, reducing the scale of both the consumption plunge and the peso depreciation. Third, unlike other Asian countries, the Philippines had started structural adjustment long before the Asian crisis erupted—since the early 1980s it had been fighting with crises of its own.

Structural Reforms

Banking and Fiscal Reforms

In 2000, the parliament adopted the General Banking Law and, in 2002, the Special Purpose Vehicle (SPV) Act. The former institutionalized banking reforms with regard to such activities as risk management, corporate governance, competition, and microfinance. The latter created the legal framework for SPVs and introduced incentives for the disposal of banks' nonperforming assets. The framework does not involve public funds, fully relying on the private sector.

Since 2006, banks in the Philippines have begun the transition to international accounting standards. A phased program of capital increases was implemented. A new capital adequacy framework was introduced, based on the risk assessment of various types of assets. As of March 2006, the capital adequacy ratio of commercial banks was 19 percent, which is much higher than the central bank's target of 10 percent and the 8 percent Bank for International Settlements (BIS) norm (Tetangco 2007).

As a result of fiscal reform, carried out during 2005–06, the rate of value-added tax, the major source of the budget revenue, was raised from 10 percent to

12 percent and its base was broadened. Measures were also taken to improve tax administration.

Agricultural Reform

Agricultural reform remains one of the difficult issues. It was started in the 1970s under Marcos and then put very high on the priority list by the Aquino administration. The Comprehensive Agrarian Reform Program (CARP) was launched in 1988. A special Department of Agrarian Reform (DAR) was established. The basic idea of the reform is to transfer land from landlords to poor farmers, who actually manage and till it as either tenants or farm workers (largely *sacadas*, or seasonal workers). The reform is implemented through both mandatory purchases of land by the state from landlords and voluntary sales by the latter.

However, due to strong resistance from landowners, representing the richest and most influential families and clans, the pace of this reform is slow and the scale is limited.

Energy Sector Reform

In 1987, power generation was opened up to the private sector. The number of independent power producers has noticeably increased.

In the early 1990s, severe power shortages occurred on the island of Luzon. In 1997–98, in the wake of the Asian crisis, electricity demand plunged, and the debt burden of the National Power Corporation (NPC, though generally known as Napocor) surged to unsustainable levels. The government decided to restructure and privatize the power industry. In 2001, the Electric Power Industry Reform Act (EPIRA) was enacted. It unbundled the power sector into generation, transmission, distribution, and supply and provided the legal framework for privatizing Napocor. The Power Sector Assets and Liabilities Management Corporation (PSALM) was formed to oversee and manage the privatization of Napocor's generating assets (41 plants), award the concession for National Transmission Corporation (TransCo) transmission operations, and take over Napocor's debt liabilities (ADB 2004). PSALM had to sell 70 percent of Napocor's generating assets within three years. However, up to August 2006, only six small hydroelectric power plants were sold (US Department of State 2007).

It would be premature to say that market and competition forces are already at work. For instance, independent power producers are closely protected by the government and critics indicate that large vested interests are involved. Not surprisingly, high electricity costs remain a heavy burden for the economy.

Present Performance

Quick Recovery and New Troubles

The post-Asian crisis recovery was quick due to the strong performance of the agricultural sector, a rapid increase in government spending and rising exports.

However, new troubles soon appeared. In 2000, two important financial institutions, Urban Bank and Urbancorp Development Bank (UDB), collapsed. Also, in 2001, President Joseph Estrada had to step down as a result of his impeachment on large-scale corruption and graft charges and he was replaced by his vice president, Gloria Macapagal-Arroyo. (In 2007, she pardoned Estrada soon after he was sentenced to life imprisonment.) This political instability negatively influenced the economy. Along with the global information technology (IT) recession it caused a big drop in GDP growth rate (see Table 15.1).

The banks' ratio of NPLs peaked, not during or immediately after the Asian crisis, but in 2001, reaching 19 percent. After that it began to fall and comprised less than 7 percent in 2006 (Tetangco 2007). Yet, the growth of bank lending remained moderate.

The Start of Rapid Growth

From 2002, the economy was back on track. The Philippines finally did what it could not do in the years of the Asian miracle—it joined the ranks of Asia's fastest runners. Especially remarkable was the 7.2 percent growth in 2007, the fastest in 31 years and a rate that exceeded the government's targets. Growth had been stimulated by an unprecedented boom in the service sector—most of all business outsourcing and call centers, although production in industry and agriculture was also rising at a fast pace. In 2000, there were only four call centers in the Philippines but, in 2005, the number surged to more than 1,000, with 112,000 persons employed (IDE-JETRO 2007, 214).

Private consumption has been expanding steadily all through the post-crisis years too. However, the growth of investment is uneven and, on average, sluggish.

Improving Fundamentals

The Arroyo administration deserves credit for drastically reducing the level of the fiscal deficit. It declined from 5.3 percent of GDP in 2002 to 1.2 percent in 2006 (Tetangco 2007). However, the reduction was largely achieved by government asset sales, and further improvement in tax collection is needed. Improvements in the fiscal position made it possible to drastically increase spending on infrastructure, which remains the Philippines' weak point.

Consumer price growth was brought down from 6.8 percent in 2001, when the central bank, the Bangko Sentral ng Pilipinas (BSP) started inflation targeting, to 3.0 percent in 2002 (see Table 15.1). Since 2004, however, it has accelerated again due to rising oil and food prices.

Part of the foreign debt has been paid back ahead of schedule. Debt service payments are falling. Still, the long-term debt of more than US$50 billion remains a headache. International reserves increased from a meager US$15 billion at the end of 1999 to US$34 billion at the end of 2007 (ADB 2008).

The improvement of the macroeconomic performance also resulted in the reduction of the country's risk premium, thus cutting foreign borrowing costs.

Somewhat unexpectedly, the Philippines has entered the group of Asian countries with the soundest economic fundamentals. In early 2007, CalPERS, the

Table 15.1 Main economic indicators (real annual growth, %)

Indicator	1999	2000	2001	2002	2003	2004	2005	2006	2007
GDP	3.4	4.4	1.8	4.4	4.9	6.4	5.0	5.4	7.2
Agriculture*	6.5	3.4	3.7	4.0	3.8	5.2	2.0	3.7	4.9
Industry*	0.9	4.9	-2.5	3.9	4.0	5.2	3.8	4.8	7.1
Services*	4.0	4.4	4.3	5.1	6.1	7.7	7.0	6.5	8.1
Gross domestic capital formation	-2.0	5.5	-7.3	-4.3	3.0	7.2	-8.8	5.0	11.2
Private consumption	2.6	3.5	3.6	4.1	5.3	5.9	4.8	5.5	5.8
Consumer prices	5.9	4.0	6.8	3.0	3.5	6.0	7.6	6.2	2.8
Unemployment rate (%)	9.8	11.2	11.1	11.4	11.4	12.1	7.8	7.9	6.3
Exports, fob (US$ millions)	35,037	38,078	32,150	35,208	36,231	39,681	41,255	47,410	50,466
Imports, cif (US$ millions)	32,568	33,807	34,939	41,092	42,576	46,102	49,487	54,078	57,996
Average exchange rate (peso per US$)	39.1	44.2	51.0	51.6	54.2	56.0	55.1	51.3	46.2

Source: ADB: Key Indicators 2008; Philippines Government Web Portal; Bangko Sentral ng Pilipinas (BSP).
*Data for agriculture, industry, and services refers to value added.

biggest US pension fund for retired civil servants and one of the global leaders in the investment business, raised the country's rating as an investment destination, placing it above other ASEAN 4 states, China, and India (*The Manila Times* February 15, 2007).

The rise in the inflow of both direct and portfolio investment, as well as remittances by OFWs, has led to a rapid appreciation of the peso, starting in late 2005. Its appreciation pace became the highest among Asian currencies, posing problems for exporters.

Although the Philippines' foreign trade balance remains in the red, its current account balance has shown a surplus since 2003—OFWs' remittances exceed the trade deficit and inflows from call services are rising.

The number of OFWs increased from 842,000 in 2000 to 1,092,000 in 2006 (IDE-JETRO 2007, 315). More and more Filipinos—information and communication technology (ICT) professionals, teachers, and caregivers—are getting higher paid jobs.

Growth Benefits are Not Felt by the Poor

As yet, accelerated growth has not brought visible benefits for poor families. According to official data, the share of households living below the poverty line, about 25 percent, has not significantly changed in this decade. The vast majority of Filipinos consider themselves poor or very poor (Xinhua 2008). Income gaps remain among the widest in East Asia. The unemployment rate, double-digit until 2004, is also one of the highest.

Food and Energy Problems

The Philippines' population growth rates remain among the highest in the world, posing various problems. Today, the most acute one is food supplies. It was further exacerbated by worldwide food-price inflation. In the second half of the 2000s, rice shortages occurred, especially in the areas hit by droughts and floods. In April 2008, the Philippines called for an emergency ministerial-level meeting of Asian countries to discuss means to increase food production and provide interim food aid (AFP 2008).

Like its neighbors, the country has struggled with soaring oil prices too. The government intends to increase production of alternative energy sources, including ethanol from corn.

Economic Policy Priorities

The Medium-Term Philippines Development Plan for 2004–11 names fighting poverty as the main national goal. It emphasizes the need to support micro-, small-, and medium-sized enterprises (SMEs) and agribusiness as the major job creators. One of the key strategies is to develop 4,942,000 acres of new land for agribusiness, which is expected to provide 2 million new jobs and contribute to a rise in farmers' incomes and productivity. Another target is to create 3 million micro-enterprises and provide them with credit, technology, and marketing support.

The government will seek to improve the accessibility of poor households to essential services, such as clean water and healthcare, and to reduce their medicine costs by half. Another strategic goal is the facilitation of investment in the mining industry, as well as natural gas and oil exploration.

A new feature of today's economic policy is the emphasis on regional development. In July 2006, President Arroyo articulated the concept of five super regions. North Luzon and Mindanao are to be centered on agribusiness, Metro Luzon (including Metro Manila) and the Central Philippines are to focus on industry and services, and, finally, the Cyber Corridor will concentrate on ICT technologies and education. This corridor will encompass all the major cities of the other super regions, stretching from Baguio City in North Luzon to Davao in Mindanao.

The Impact of the Global Financial Turmoil

The Philippines' economic growth had already begun to lose momentum in early 2008, most of all because of mounting inflation, caused by surging oil and food prices. (At its peak, in August, the year-on-year inflation rate hit 12.5 percent.) Private consumption lost much of its dynamism. Investment also weakened. The major adverse effect of the financial turmoil was the slump in exports, especially in the electronics industry.

Direct damage from exposure to the US subprime mortgage loans market was negligible. The Philippines' banks were well-capitalized and their management was mostly sound. To shield the domestic financial market from possible external shocks, the Philippines' banks have agreed to take measures to boost liquidity. Particularly, to avoid the credit crunch, the Bankers' Association of the Philippines (BAP) encourages more active lending between its members through the interbank repurchase (see endnote on page 167) facility, requiring them to release more US dollars into the banking system (*People's Daily* 2008).

The business-process outsourcing (BPO) industry has received a fresh boost, as the global financial crisis makes companies around the world actively seek cost-effective outsourcing opportunities. Not only American, but also the UK, Australian, and other financial institutions and firms are intensifying the transfer of their back office jobs to the Philippines. Remittances from OFWs were helpful to maintain consumption levels.

A healthy budget and increased foreign currency reserves have also helped to cushion the global turmoil's negative effects. The government has increased spending on infrastructure, social services, and agriculture. Contrary to other Asian countries, the central bank initially refrained from interest rate cuts as inflationary pressures remained high, amplified, among other things, by the weakening of the peso and rising electric power rates. Yet, as the inflation outlook improved, in January 2009, its overnight borrowing rate and lending rate were slashed by 0.5 percentage points to 5.0 percent and 7.0 percent respectively.

In January 2009, the government announced that in 2008 the economy had grown by 4.6 percent. The target for 2009 was set at 3.7–4.7 percent. Despite having lost almost three percentage points of growth, the Philippines' economy has proved to be structurally strong enough to mitigate the adverse effects of the global financial crisis. It is in a good position to accelerate again after the turmoil is over.

Foreign Trade

A significant part of the country's exports and imports is accounted for by the intrafirm trade of multinational corporations (MNCs), especially cross-border deliveries of electronic parts.

The Composition of Exports

In 2007, electronic products comprised 61.6 percent of total exports. The next most important item was garments with a 4.6 percent share. The share of cathodes, sections of cathodes, and refined copper was 2.6 percent, petroleum products 2.2 percent, woodcrafts and furniture 2.0 percent, and mineral products, mainly copper concentrate, iron, chromium, and nickel ores, was 4.5 percent. The country is also an important exporter of iron, chromium, and nickel ores, coconut oil, and tropical fruits.

The US was the biggest market for the Philippine goods, comprising 17.0 percent of total exports. Japan followed with 14.5 percent, Hong Kong 11.5 percent, China 11.4 percent, Singapore 6.2 percent, the Netherlands 8.2 percent, and Taiwan 3.9 percent (National Statistics Office 2008).

The Composition of Imports

As for imports, electronic products accounted for 44.3 percent of the total, mineral fuels, lubricants, and related materials 17.3 percent, transport equipment 4.4 percent, industrial machinery and equipment 3.8 percent, iron and steel 2.2 percent, cereals and cereal preparations 2.1 percent, and chemicals and textiles 2.8 percent each. Today, the Philippines is the biggest importer of rice in the world.

In 2007, the US provided 14.1 percent of the country's total imports. It was followed by Japan (11.7 percent). Other major import partners were Singapore (11.2 percent), Taiwan (7.3 percent), China (7.2 percent), South Korea (5.9 percent), Malaysia (4.5 percent), and Hong Kong (4.0 percent) (National Statistics Office 2008).

Inward FDI and the Business Environment

FDI Volume and Composition

The Philippines attracts foreign investors by its low labor costs and the pool of educated and quick-to-learn laborers with a good command of English. The amount of FDI was falling at the beginning of the 2000s but noticeably increased in 2004 and then again in 2006–2007 (see Table 15.2).

Table 15.2   Approved inward FDI (peso millions)

Year	2000	2001	2002	2003	2004	2005	2006	2007
Amount	80,374.2	64,436.1	46,048.7	34,010.3	173,895.2	95,806.2	165,880.0	215,230.8

Source: Department of Trade and Industry.

Japanese and American companies are constantly present among the leading investors. Both are active in the electronics sector. For Intel, and other leading US semiconductor producers, the Philippines has become one of the major sites for assembly and testing. Japanese firms, such as Fujitsu, Toshiba, and Hitachi, are active in the production of hard disk drives and other data processing devices. Practically all electronic parts are exported. Also, Japanese companies have a strong presence in the auto industry. US firms are taking the lead in business outsourcing.

Recently, the presence of South Korean, Singaporean, Taiwanese, and Chinese firms has noticeably increased, and they have risen to the leading position in terms of investment volume. In 2006, South Korea was the largest investor, mostly due to entries of its companies into heavy industries. In 2007, the largest amount of FDI—20.6 percent of the total—came from Singapore. Japan followed with 17.9 percent, the US 16.8 percent, Taiwan 9.5 percent, the Netherlands 6.7 percent, South Korea 5.6 percent, and the UK 4.7 percent.

In terms of industry sectors, 37.6 percent of the total went to manufacturing with the electronics industry leading. The share of the electric power sector was 34.7 percent, individual and business services 12.9 percent, and mining 4.5 percent (JETRO 2008).

Investment Laws and Regulations

FDI regulations in the Philippines are rather complicated but, as time goes by, conditions for investors are gradually improving. Several agencies are authorized to approve foreign investment projects: the Board of Investments (BOI) and the Philippines Economic Zones Agency (PEZA) in the economic zones; the Subic Bay Metropolitan Authority (SBMA) in the Subic Bay Freeport Zone; and the Clark Development Corporation (CDC) in the Clark Freeport Zone. Foreign investors are required to register with the Securities and Exchange Commission (SEC).

The Foreign Investment Act of 1991 introduced the concept of the negative list, opening up the country for 100 percent foreign-owned companies in the sectors the list does not cover. As for the sectors on the negative list, some of them are reserved for Philippine nationals only (for example, small-scale retailing or utilization of marine resources), in others limits on foreign ownership are imposed. Foreigners are not allowed to own land. They can lease it for fifty years and then renew the arrangement for another twenty-five.

For a company which is more than 40 percent foreign-owned and caters to the domestic market, the minimum capital requirement is the peso equivalent of US$200,000. It can be reduced by half in cases where advanced technologies are used or at least 50 people are directly employed. For export companies (exporting 60 percent or more of their produce) the rule is not applicable.

Incentives

A number of incentives are provided by the Omnibus Investments Code of 1987. An enterprise, engaged in an activity included in the Investment Priorities Plan and registered with the BOI, can get an income tax holiday of up to six years, with a possible extension for one year if local raw materials are used and conditions regarding foreign-exchange earnings and the ratio of capital equipment to the number of workers are met. The code also provides additional tax deduction for labor expenses and infrastructure work; tax credit for taxes paid on raw materials, supplies, and intermediate products used in the manufacture of export products; and access to the bonded warehouse system.

Extra incentives are offered by the Special Economic Zones Act of 1995. The government's policy is to promote the creation of world-class, environment-friendly economic zones (in the Philippines they are called "ecozones") all over the country.

The Export Development Act of 1994 provides tax credits for imported materials, which are primarily used for export production, and tax credit for the increase in the current year's export revenue.

In the Subic Bay Freeport Zone, enterprises are exempt from all national and local taxes provided they pay a final tax of 5 percent of the gross income earned within the zone. Taxes and duties on imported raw materials are also exempted.

Problems and Impediments

Infrastructure remains a difficulty. Unpaved village roads comprise around 60 percent of all roads. As for the national road network, 30 percent of it remains unpaved (Library of Congress 2006). Port and interisland shipping facilities also require attention. Electricity shortages are forecasted in the near future unless new power plants and transmission lines are constructed.

Electricity costs are the second highest in the region after Japan. Transportation costs are also higher than in neighboring countries.

The efficiency of bureaucracy is low. Regulations are often inconsistent and opaque. Regulatory authority is weak and ambiguous. Starting a business takes 15 procedures and 58 days as opposed 9 and 47, respectively, for the Asia-Pacific region on an average, but related costs are relatively low (Business Anti-Corruption Portal).

Sometimes interpretations of business rules appear to be more than flexible. For instance, though 100 percent foreign ownership in the mining industry was allowed in 2004, some court decisions challenged the extent of foreign participation. Investment disputes are not frequent, but when they occur, it may take years to reach a settlement (Balana 2007). Protection of intellectual property rights (IPR) is weak, but improving. The government is cooperating with the Asian Development Bank (ADB), the World Bank, USAID, and the Japan International Cooperation Agency (JICA) on anti-corruption reforms. According to estimates, more than 20 percent of the funding for government projects is lost to corruption (Business Anti-Corruption Portal).

Safety issues also require attention. For example, in March 2008, the new commander of the Philippines Army 10th Infantry Division called on mining companies running banana plantations in southern Mindanao to organize their own militias to protect themselves from the pro-communist New People's Army rebels (Tolentino 2008).

Concluding Remarks

In the post-crisis decade, the Philippines economy was put back on track and became one of the fastest runners in the region. In fact, it completed the shift, started in the early 1990s, to export-oriented growth fostered by inward FDI—especially where the electronics industry is concerned. Yet, as its neighbors had already reached this benchmark level in the 1970s or the 1980s, the country still has to catch up.

For its own part, the Philippines has generated a number of important advantages, which differentiate it from other regional economies and contribute to economic growth. It is capitalizing on its pool of literate and trained laborers with a good command of English. A strong edge has been developed in the business-process outsourcing and call center sectors. Reduction of budget deficits and the foreign debt burden make it easier to address key development problems. However, the major "attack" on poverty is still to be launched. Much will depend on the government's ability to stimulate micro-entrepreneurship, provide better education, and build up infrastructure. Another urgent task is to improve governance and strengthen notoriously inefficient government institutions. Corruption also remains an enormous impediment.

All through the decade, the Philippines remained one of the least politically stable countries of the region. Military coup attempts followed one another. Though none of them succeeded, they revealed the fragility of the Philippines democracy and underscored the legacy of the military's involvement in politics.

As long as democracy remains fragile, political parties weak, and legal institutions inefficient, "people power" retains a role, both in fighting corruption and preventing a shift back to dictatorship. Yet, it is not a panacea and, of course, not an alternative to building efficient and reliable institutions.

The business community also has a lot of urgent tasks to address. A big gap exists between the sectors directly involved in the supply chains of leading MNCs and the rest of the economy. Related and supporting industries producing materials, components, and equipment remain underdeveloped. The dissemination of key technologies, such as metal processing or die forming, has advanced less than in the neighboring states.

In our view, a realistic target for the Philippines, in the foreseeable future, would be to become a middle-income country with competitive advantages in a wider range of sectors—services, agriculture, mining, and manufacturing—much less poverty, lower unemployment, and more efficient state institutions.

16

Vietnam: A New Magnet for Investors?

A Few Basics

Vietnam, with its 85 million people, is the fifteenth most populated country in the world, just ahead of Germany. By nominal gross domestic product (GDP), in 2007, it was fifty-ninth, by per-capita GDP (purchasing power parity (PPP)), 129th—below Pakistan and above East Timor and Uzbekistan. For now, the national goal is to become a middle-income country with a per-capita GDP of around US$10,000 by 2020.

Vietnam is rich in natural resources such as offshore coal and natural gas, coal, manganese, chromium, bauxite, salt, timber, and marine resources.

Agriculture is still playing a vitally important role in the economy. Major crops include rice, sugarcane, coffee, cassava, corn (maize), peanuts, and soybeans. The country is also a producer of natural rubber and tropical fruits.

The major industrial products are foodstuffs and beverages (including canned fruits, marine products, and a variety of tropical juices), textiles, wood and wood products, bicycles and bicycle tires, cement, steel, chemicals, fertilizer, sugar, and sugar syrups. The machinery industry, including electronics, has been growing fast in recent years.

In 2006, agriculture contributed 20 percent to GDP, industry 41.6 percent, and services 38.1 percent. Their shares in total employment were 52.2 percent for agriculture, just 12.5 percent for manufacturing, and 35.3 percent for other sectors (ADB 2007).

Vietnam is divided into 58 provinces and 5 municipalities. The major cities are the capital Hanoi, Ho Chi Minh City, Haiphong, and Da Nang. The country's only political party is the ruling Communist Party of Vietnam. Other parties are not allowed.

Postwar Development

Division and Reunification

In the middle of the nineteenth century, Vietnam was colonized by France. During World War II it was occupied by the Japanese, but they let the French stay and retain some influence.

In 1945, Ho Chi Minh, the leader of the Communist organization, Viet Minh, proclaimed independence. However, the French regained control and, in 1946, the First Indochina War between Viet Minh forces and France broke out. It continued until 1954. The Vietnamese won and French control ended in May 1954. The country was divided into North Vietnam and South Vietnam. The former, run by Ho Chi Minh's Communist administration from Hanoi, opted for Soviet-style socialism, the latter, under the government of Ngo Dinh Diem, backed by the US, chose capitalism.

The Viet Cong, the Communist forces in the south, supported by North Vietnam, and the South Vietnamese regime, supported by the US and its allies, were at war (this was the Second Indochina War, though it is more widely referred to as the Vietnam War) from 1954 till 1975.

The 1973 Paris Agreement officially put an end to the Vietnam War and called for free elections in South Vietnam and peaceful reunification. US forces were withdrawn. However, two years later the North Vietnamese captured Saigon and reunited the country under its own rule. The South Vietnamese army surrendered. Saigon was renamed Ho Chi Minh City. (Ho Chi Minh himself died in 1969.) This did not bring complete political stability, as relations with neighbors, Cambodia and China, were strained.

The transition to a planned socialist economy, as required by the Communist Vietnamese government, met strong latent resistance in the south, which had a certain tradition of private entrepreneurship. Around one million southerners fled the country, fearing persecution and the seizure of their businesses (Library of Congress 2005). About the same number of people were relocated to previously uncultivated land for "re-education," including a significant number of intellectuals, professionals, and skilled workers.

The Failure of the Planned Economy

In the first half of the 1980s, the situation in the economy became disastrous. Even basic foodstuffs and consumer goods were in deficit. Enterprises, small-scale and poorly managed, had to struggle with chronic shortages of raw materials, materials, and other capital goods.

The Second Five-Year Plan (1976–81), seeking to economically integrate the south, set very ambitious growth targets for both agriculture and industry, but was unfulfilled. Goals for the next five years were much more modest.

The Doi Moi Reforms

In 1986, a political and economic renewal campaign was launched, known as the Doi Moi reforms. The goal was to mix planning with elements of a market economy. As in China, "market socialism" was the conceptual frame.

A landmark law, passed in 1987, paved the way for a *de facto* decollectivization of agriculture. Peasants were given long-term land-use rights. Individual farmers became the major players in the rural economy. Productivity and earnings increased. The following year the legitimacy of the nonagricultural private sector was recognized. In 1990, the encouragement of the private sector was raised to the level of official government policy.

In early 1989, a comprehensive reform package was launched to address enormous macroeconomic imbalances (Ronnas 1997). Interest rates were dramatically raised and government expenditure curtailed. The government put an end to the practice of printing money to cover budget deficits. The Vietnamese dong was devalued from 425 to 4500 dong per US$1. This wiped out the black currency market. Foreign trade restrictions were significantly reduced.

As a result, hyperinflation was brought to a halt. Empty shelves in the shops were suddenly filled with a variety of goods and open-air markets mushroomed (Ronnas 1997). The quick success of the reforms created momentum, radically changing the country's image in the eyes of the international business community.

A Shaky Aftermath

Initially, the objective of the Vietnamese reforms was not the creation of a new economic system. Central planning was to remain its core, while the market segment was deemed necessary to speed up technological change and industrialization. However, these two notions do not go together well and the reforms lacked dynamism and persistence.

After a few years of euphoria, enthusiasm faded. In the first half of the 1990s, Vietnam was again looked upon as a country in which it was difficult to do business. Investors were upset by corruption, red tape, and the authorities' bias toward a regional development policy favoring the north.

The leadership was still wary of genuine pro-market reforms, fearing that they could erode its power base. Also, the legacy of the recent past was still in evidence. Vietnamese military forces stayed in Cambodia until 1989 and the relationship with China remained uneasy, with small border incidents continuing until the early 1990s. And Cold War repercussions were still being felt—the fall of the Berlin Wall and the implosion of the Soviet Union were a shock, while the US economic embargo was maintained until 1994.

Structural Reforms (The 1990s and the 2000s)

Toward a Multisectoral Economy

In December 1997, the Communist Party of Vietnam Central Committee articulated the policy of building "a multisectoral economy operating in a market managed by the state in the direction of socialism." It pledged to encourage both "the state capitalist economy" and "the private capitalist economy." The intention to build a market-oriented socialist economy was confirmed at the 9th Party Congress in 2001, which endorsed the Ten-Year Socioeconomic Development Strategy for 2001–10. The latter set the goals of doubling GDP within this period and becoming an industrialized country by 2020.

Financial and Monetary Reform

In 1999, following the example of China, after decades of direct credit control the State Bank of Vietnam began to use open-market operations as a tool of monetary policy. A road map for banking sector reform was drawn. Supervision improved and public confidence in the banking system was restored.

The Law on Financial Institutions came into effect in 1998. It clearly defined credit institutions, dividing them into state credit, joint-stock credit, cooperative, joint-venture, non-bank wholly owned by foreigners, and foreign bank branches.

The Enterprise System

In 1990, Vietnam adopted its Company Law and the Law on Private Enterprise. Enterprises were divided into three groups: state-owned enterprises (SOEs), non-state, and foreign-invested. Amid calls from within the government for equal treatment of private, collective, state-owned, and foreign-owned firms, the two laws were replaced by the Law on Enterprises, or the Unified Enterprise Law. Since 2006, all types of companies have been treated on an equal footing. SOEs have to be transformed into limited liability or shareholding companies within four years. The Common Investment Law also came into effect in 2006. All investors, domestic and foreign, are now treated and promoted in the same way.

The private sector now accounts for more than 60 percent of GDP. However, its competitiveness is still low. Key sectors, such as auto assembly and the production of motorcycles, banking, and retailing, are heavily protected.

Entrepreneurship

The idea of creating a company was discouraged in Vietnam until the early 1990s when the Law on Private Enterprise was enacted. Since then, many private enterprises have been established by former employees of state companies and civil servants. Simultaneously, a class of young entrepreneurs, full of enthusiasm and energy, has been emerging. However, many Vietnamese entrepreneurs still lack business experience. Also, unclear and frequently changing government regulations often result in cheating and corruption.

Growth in non-state manufacturing has been achieved primarily through an increase in the number of enterprises. Very few private companies have reached a size large enough to become significant market players. The scope of industries with a significant presence of private firms is still limited to a few traditional sectors, such as manufacturing of food and beverage products, ceramics and glass, garments, and wood and leather products (Xuan 2005).

SOE Reform

The restructuring of SOEs is already under way. Thousands of companies have gone through corporatization, from such sectors as electricity, post and telecommunication, and banking and insurance. The *leitmotiv* is to improve their transparency and accountability and to create an effective corporate governance system (Meyer 2006). For the time being, SOEs remain key players in almost all the sectors of the economy.

In early 2006, Vietnam had 4,086 operating SOEs—one-third of this number still in their pre-reform structure. They accounted for only 3.6 percent of the total number of active companies and 53 percent of total company capital. The share of the private sector in company capital increased to 25 percent, from 12 percent in 2001. The average number of employees at SOEs was 499 workers against 28 at domestic private companies and 330 at foreign-owned companies. The total number of SOE employees declined from over 4 million in 2002 to 2 million and the SOE share of the total number of employees from 54 percent to 33 percent.

The number of SOEs managed by provincial and municipal governments is larger than that controlled by the central government—55 percent and 45 percent respectively. This type of SOE is generally smaller and its technological level and efficiency are lower. The money-losing SOEs are mostly located in the countryside and engaged in the agriculture, paper, textiles, sericulture, sugar and sugarcane, and seafood sectors (VietnamNet Bridge, October 15, 2007).

The Vietnamese government emphasizes its strong commitment to foster private sector participation in all the sectors of the economy. Yet, Vietnam is very keen to nurture a group of competitive state companies in the Singapore fashion.

A New Openness

In 1991, the Paris agreement on Cambodia opened the way for Vietnam to establish, or re-establish, economic and diplomatic relations with West European, Asian, and other countries. In 1993, it normalized its relationship with the International Monetary Fund (IMF), the World Bank, and the Asian Development Bank (ADB). In 1994, the US lifted its economic embargo in a major step toward the normalization of bilateral relations the following year. Also in 1995, Vietnam became a member of the Association of Southeast Nations (ASEAN) and, in 1998, the Asia-Pacific Economic Cooperation (APEC). In 2007, it joined the World Trade Organization (WTO).

Present Performance

A Picture of Vietnam's Growth

Until the beginning of the 2000s, Vietnam pursued an import-substitution policy, relying on SOEs in the heavy industries, such as chemicals and petrochemicals, and encouraging exports of labor-intensive goods, such as textiles, by emerging private enterprises. Later in the decade, the strategy changed to active promotion of foreign investment in export-oriented industries and the opening of domestic markets for competition.

Vietnam has enjoyed an impressive 7–8 percent GDP growth rate since 2002 (see Table 16.1)—higher than any other major Asian economy except China. Growth has been driven by rising consumer spending and fixed-capital investment. Exports have been growing fast too but the country's trade balance is in deficit. Inflation has been brought under control, falling from three-digit levels in the late 1980s to single digits in the 1990s and the 2000s.

Table 16.1　Main economic indicators (real annual growth, %)

Indicator	1999	2000	2001	2002	2003	2004	2005	2006	2007
GDP	4.8	6.8	6.9	7.1	7.3	7.8	8.4	8.2	8.5
Agriculture*	5.2	4.6	3.0	4.2	3.6	4.4	4.0	3.7	3.4
Industry*	7.7	10.1	10.4	9.5	10.5	10.2	10.7	10.4	10.6
Services*	2.3	5.3		6.5	6.5	7.3	8.5	8.3	8.7
Gross domestic capital formation	1.2	10.1	10.8	12.7	11.9	10.5	11.2	11.8	24.2
Private consumption	2.6	3.1	4.5	7.6	8.0	7.1	7.3	8.3	9.6
Consumer prices	4.2	−1.6	−0.4	4.0	3.2	7.8	8.4	7.4	8.3
Unemployment rate (%)	4.4	2.3	2.5	2.2	2.2	2.1	2.5	2.3	2.0
Exports, fob (US$ billions)	11.5	14.5	15.0	16.7	20.1	26.5	32.4	39.8	48.6
Imports, cif (US$ billions)	11.6	15.6	16.2	19.7	25.3	32.0	36.8	44.9	62.7
Average exchange rate (dong per US$1)	13,943	14,168	14,725	15,280	15,510	15,777**	15,859	15,994	16,179

Source: ADB; Key Indicators 2008, General Statistics Office of Vietnam.
*Data for agriculture, industry, and services refers to value-added.
**As of the end of the year.

During 2000–01, the economy was in deflation. However, inflationary pressures have significantly increased from 2004. The situation deteriorated further, in 2007, due to surging commodity and food prices.

Vietnam is increasingly benefiting from its rich offshore oil and natural gas reserves.

In financial terms, the country's external position is essentially sound. Though the trade balance remains in deficit, the current account is close to equilibrium. Capital inflows contribute to a comfortable surplus in the overall balance of payments. The economy is also supported by large-scale remittances from Vietnamese working overseas.

Foreign exchange reserves significantly increased since the middle of this decade reaching US$23.9 billion by the end of 2007 (ADB 2008). From the beginning of the decade until 2007 Vietnam's stock exchange, though still quite small, was one of the most buoyant in Asia. However, since early 2008, stock values have begun to plunge.

So far, growth has benefited both urban and rural areas. Access to electricity, tap water, and telephone services in the countryside has improved significantly, although it still falls short of the levels attained in the cities.

In 1993, two-thirds of the rural population was considered poor. In 2007, the share declined to one-sixth (UNDP 2007). However, 20–30 million people still live "just above" the poverty line.

Toward a Mass Consumption Society

The Doi Moi reform has changed the traditional set of values nurtured under a centrally planned and subsidized economy. Among other things, it became the first step to the formation of a mass consumption society.

Today, more than 15 million Vietnamese use the Internet and 12 million are subscribed to mobile phone services (VietnamNet Bridge, January 15, 2008). Consumers have access to a wide variety of products and services of different quality, design, and price. Franchise fast-food chains are expanding. Modern supermarkets and shopping centers supplant traditional distribution channels. About 20–30 percent of the population of the two major cities, Hanoi and Ho Chi Minh City, can afford regular shopping in the modern distribution outlets (VietnamNet Bridge, January 15, 2008). A. T. Kearney's *2007 Global Retail Development Index* ranks Vietnam as the fourth most attractive country for mass retailers after India, Russia, and China (A.T. Kearney 2007).

In Hanoi and Ho Chi Minh City the luxury goods market is developing. Consumption standards in the provincial cities, and especially the countryside, are lagging far behind. The income gap between urban and rural areas has widened dramatically (Hy 2003).

Changes in the Industrial Structure

Until recently, in the economic field, Vietnam has been known mainly for its exports of catfish, pepper, coffee, rice, and other agribusiness products. It is also positioned as a low-cost manufacturer of products such as Nike sneakers,

Liz Claiborne blouses, and wooden furniture. Today, it is about to make one more important step forward. Growing investment by high-tech companies has opened an opportunity to become Southeast Asia's new center for electronics manufacturing.

Also, in the 1990s, Vietnam's machinery sector met only 10 percent of domestic demand. Now it covers 40 percent, and its output is growing by 40 percent a year. For instance, 40 percent of automobile parts and light trucks, sold in the domestic market, are now produced locally.

Another sector demonstrating potential for expansion is the information technology (IT) industry. In 2005, production of software surged 50 percent. It has already created 15,000 jobs. Today, the idea of developing a "Vietnamese Bangalore" is in the air.

Hurdles

The reform strategy attaches an important role in generating employment, income, and growth to the infant non-state industrial sector. So far, the results have been mixed. Though the number of private manufacturers has increased dramatically, the sector has not met the high expectations.

The government argues that the current trade deficit is nothing to be concerned about since a significant part of imports is accounted for by the equipment and machinery used by local manufacturers. However, it uncovers the structural weakness of the economy—industrial production is mostly limited to assembly and processing.

Large-Scale Infrastructure Development

One of the major stories of today's Vietnamese economy is large-scale infrastructure creation—the construction and development of roads, railways, waterways, and airports. Airport capacity is expected to grow 2.5 times by 2015 and four times by 2020. As many as 24 airports are projected to be built by 2015, including ten international ones. In addition, projects have been launched to increase the capacity of the public transportation system—buses and urban mass rapid transit.

The government is encouraging private investment in a wide range of infrastructure-related sectors, including investment under the build-operate-transfer (BOT) and build-transfer (BT) models.[1]

The Asset Bubble and Inflation

In the summer of 2007, clear signs of an asset bubble appeared but the government stopped short of shifting to an anti-inflationary policy, prioritizing growth stimulating measures.

The first half of 2008 was marked by a dramatic plunge of stock values—in the middle of the year they fell to just one-third of the October 2007 peak level. As of mid-May 2008, the rate of the dong at the money changers had dropped by 10 percent from the peak. Inflationary pressures increased. In February 2008, the government chose to raise centrally controlled prices for petroleum products, thus exacerbating the trend. In the middle of the year the inflation rate hit 25 percent on an annual basis, the highest level since the start of the reforms in 1986. Prices for rice, wheat, and pork doubled (*Nikkei Shimbun* 2008). In a number of foreign-owned companies, workers went on strike demanding pay raises. After such mounting pressure, the government finally switched to an anti-inflationary policy in mid-2008.

The Impact of the Global Financial Turmoil

In the second half of 2008, Vietnam's direct losses that could be linked to US sub-prime mortgage loans were close to none, but the national economy suffered a blow due to the squeeze on export markets. Along with crude oil, the biggest foreign currency earner, world prices for other major export commodities, such as rubber, coffee, pepper, seafood, and rice were falling. The growth of textile and apparel exports stopped short of meeting the government's targets and exports of furniture plunged. Rising unemployment and labor unrest began to threaten social stability. Though there was no mass exodus of foreigners from the financial markets, they became net sellers of Vietnamese stocks and bonds. Thus, the plunge of stock values continued. It has been announced that growth in 2008 was 6.23 percent (VietnamNetBridge 2009a), the lowest since 1999, but very high for the year of the global crisis. In spite of the worsening global conditions, exports rose to a record of US$60 billion, trade deficits decreased, and the inward FDI commitments also reached the record of US$60 billion (VietnamNetBridge 2009c).

In October, the government again shifted to an expansionary policy. In October–November, the State Bank of Vietnam cut its benchmark rate twice, bringing it down to 12 percent. Still, the scale and the scope of the stimulus measures were limited by high inflation. In 2008, it reached 23 percent, up from 8 percent in 2007, though since September, its rate was declining (AFP 2009). One of the government's major policy goals was to keep it below 15 percent in 2009 (Intellasia 2008).

The stimulus package to be implemented from 2009 will be worth US$1–2 billion and will target large, labor-intensive projects (VietnamNetBridge 2009b).

Foreign Trade

Liberalization

In 2007, Vietnam joined the WTO. Trade liberalization is clearly progressing. Import duties for most items have been reduced to 20–30 percent. Under the ASEAN Free Trade Agreement (AFTA), the country has abolished quantitative import restrictions. In 2004, tariffs on manufactured goods from ASEAN states were cut by 50 percent on average. In 2006, Vietnam was granted the Permanent Normal Trade Relations Status by the United States.

As a member of the WTO, Vietnam will be treated as a most-favored nation without any conditions. At the same time, domestic industries, especially the light ones such as garments and footwear, will face fierce competition because of tariff reductions and subsidy cuts.

The Composition of Exports

Vietnam's major export item is oil. In 2006, it accounted for 20.8 percent of total exports. At present the country does not have oil-refining facilities, it only exports crude oil and imports petroleum products. Other major exports are textiles and clothing (14.6 percent), footwear (9.0 percent), marine products (8.4 percent), wood and wood products (4.9 percent), computers and electronic parts (4.3 percent), rubber (3.2 percent), rice (3.2 percent), coffee (3.1 percent), and coal (2.3 percent).

Primary goods remain the key items. Exports of agricultural, forestry, and fishery products increased from US$4.2 billion in 2000 to more than US$12 billion in 2007 (IMF 2008). Vietnam has become the world's largest exporter of pepper, the second-largest exporter of rice, and Brazil's competitor in the coffee markets. Yet, the potential of agricultural exports is still not realized fully. Small Vietnamese farms have high production costs, lack a clear-cut marketing strategy, and use outdated technologies.

The share of electronic goods (and other manufacturing items) in Vietnam's exports is still low, but in recent years it has been growing rapidly.

The most important export markets are the US (19.7 percent of the total in 2006), Japan (13.6 percent), Australia (9.2 percent), China (7.6 percent), Singapore (4.1 percent), Germany (3.6 percent), and Malaysia and the UK (3.0 percent each).

The Composition of Imports

The major imports are machinery, equipment, and parts (14.8 percent), petroleum products (13.3 percent), steel (6.5 percent), computers and electronic parts (4.6 percent), textile products and leather (4.3 percent), and plastics (4.2 percent).

The biggest exporter to Vietnam is China (16.5 percent). It is followed by Singapore (14.0 percent), Taiwan (10.7 percent), Japan (10.5 percent), South Korea (8.6 percent), and Thailand (6.8 percent) (JETRO 2007).

FDI and the Business Environment

In its 2007 report, PricewaterhouseCoopers (PwC) put Vietnam at the top of 20 emerging-market countries, in terms of attractiveness for manufacturing investment (PwC 2007).

The Low-Labor-Cost Advantage

Vietnam's major advantage as an FDI destination is its low labor costs (see Table 16.2). For the time being, this favorable factor remains, although high growth is starting to produce the same kind of skilled, and recently also unskilled,

Table 16.2   Cost comparison in selected Asian cities (US$)

	Hanoi	Bangkok	Kuala Lumpur	Shanghai
Worker's monthly wages (general industry)	79–119	184	202	109–218
Mid-level engineer's monthly salary	171–353	327	684	269–601
Mid-level manager's salary (section chief or department chief)	504–580	790	1,892	567–1,574

Source: JETRO (2004).

labor shortages as in India and China and, consequently, to exert upward pressure on cost. Illegal strikes are also growing into a big problem.

The high turnover of managers, engineers, and regular skilled workers is another serious issue (*Mizuho Global News* 2008). Only 20 percent of all Vietnamese workers have received training. The government hopes to double the number of qualified IT workers to 330,000 by 2015. However, in view of the constraints inherent in the educational system, this goal will not be easy to achieve.

Improving Conditions for Investors

In 1999, a charm offensive was launched to stop the exodus of disenchanted multinationals (the list of those who said good-bye included ExxonMobil, Cable and Wireless, and other big names) and to lure new foreign investors. It included a cut in telecommunication costs and an end to discrimination against foreign-invested companies with respect to electricity and water charges. Preparation for WTO entry entailed a range of commitments to protect the latter's trading and investment rights.

The Foreign Investment Code was amended to ease some procedures. The new law allows foreigners a 70-year-plus land lease, which is longer than in most other Asian countries (VietnamNet Bridge, November 19, 2007). Leasing arrangements can be extended without additional payment. Overseas developers have been provided with the same treatment as their Vietnamese counterparts.

Since 2007, fully foreign-owned banks are allowed to compete on an equal footing with domestic banks. In January 2009, the retailing sector was to be completely opened for overseas companies (IMF 2008).

Vietnam has also been working on intellectual property rights (IPR) regulations and laws, though protection is still weak.

Impediments

Vietnam remains among the countries with the lowest degree of protection against directors' misuse of corporate assets. Also, it is still very difficult to close down a business. In addition, foreign entities are not permitted to acquire more than 30 percent of the capital of a local company, which seriously constrains merger and acquisition deals.

As far as noninstitutional impediments are concerned, infrastructure shortcomings are among the most serious. In particular, electricity supply cuts can pose a big problem.

Inward FDI Amount and Composition

FDI in Vietnam has been noticeably growing, especially since 2004 (see Table 16.3). In 2006, it was more than twice the amount of the previous year. In 2007, FDI more than doubled once again, reaching US $ 18.7 billion (IMF 2008). As the FDI recipient, Vietnam has grown into a serious competitor for the ASEAN 4 states.

Most of the investment goes into heavy industry (51.4 percent of the total in 2006), followed by light industry (10.4 percent), the hotels and tourism sector (9.1 percent), transportation and telecom (7.0 percent), and services (3.1 percent).

In 2006, the biggest investor in Vietnam was South Korea (31.8 percent of the total), followed by Hong Kong (13.4 percent), the UK (12.9 percent; including British-ruled territories), Japan (12.0 percent), the US (8.7 percent), Singapore (5.0 percent), and China (3.9 percent).

Examples of South Korean investment include leading steel producer, Pohang Iron and Steel Company (POSCO), getting approval for investment in a large-scale steel mill construction (US$1,128 billion by 2010) and a consortium, led by Daewoo Construction, putting money into a Hanoi city development project (US$314 million) (JETRO 2007, 219). Major investment from Hong Kong came from the local affiliate of Intel, investing US$650 million in a semiconductor factory, and the Japanese-owned firm Meiko, allocating US$300 million for the production of electronic parts.

The list and sequence of major investing countries may differ a lot from year to year, depending on the number and magnitude of projects they put money into. In 2007, the leading position went to India through investment in a large-scale steel mill construction project by Essar Steel, and number two was Singapore, as Banyan Tree invested in the construction of an integrated tourist complex.

Overall, the foreign-invested sector's share of GDP increased from 7.5 percent in 1996 to 17 percent in 2006 (IMF 2008).

Investing Companies

Many large companies, such as Canon, Sony, Alcatel-Lucent, Fujitsu, Panasonic, Siemens, and Yamaha, are setting up or expanding their operations. Chinese companies are also active, including leaders like TCL and Konka (one of the

Table 16.3   Amount of inward FDI (approval basis, US$ million)

Year	2001	2002	2003	2004	2005	2006
Amount	2,529.1	1,557.7	1,914.3	3,222.1	4,268.4	8,827.2

Source: JETRO, "Boeki Toshi Hakusho;" JETRO Web site: Vietnam Statistics.

leading TV manufacturers). Since 2004, Japan's Renesas Technology has been manufacturing integrated circuits here for applications in consumer electronics, mobile products, and automobiles.

Since 2000, FDI has been increasingly focused on export-oriented sectors, including garments, footwear, furniture, and electronic assembly. Vietnam is betting on investment by large contract manufacturers. Taiwan's Hon Hai, with clients such as Hewlett-Packard, Dell, and Apple, has applied for an investment of up to US$5 billion.

In fact, many further investment projects have been waiting in line to be realized as Vietnam is not able to accommodate all of them at once. Also, a growing number of foreign companies, especially Japanese, target the country as part of their "China plus One" strategy.

Concluding Remarks

Essentially, the "market socialism" exercise has been a success. Today's Vietnam is one of the fastest-growing economies in the region, and the world. It is also among the leaders in terms of the growth of inward FDI. Yet, there is still a lot to be done to bridge the gap with ASEAN 4 countries in two respects: the development of the private sector (along with the cleaning-up of the state sector) and the intensity and scale of export-oriented industrialization. Fulfilling these two tasks holds the key to future growth and development.

As times goes by, more emphasis is put on privatization and the promotion of entrepreneurs. Yet, progress is not speedy. Companies lack external financing, though most of them get official assistance during the start-up period. The reason is that state-owned commercial banks remain fragile and have very little experience in working with the private sector. Private financial institutions of any importance are still extremely rare.

The opening of the economy, institutional reforms, and efforts to create a relevant legal framework have significantly improved the environment for businesses and brought about an inward FDI boom. However, it is not given that the boom will continue. The legal system needs further improvement in accordance with international norms and infrastructure remains underdeveloped. Human resource constraints are growing. Serious regulatory hurdles remain and complaints about corruption are still too frequent. Low labor and other costs are the major, and in many cases the only, trump card to attract investors, but the advantage may gradually erode.

Endnote

1 Build-operate-transfer is a form of project financing, meaning that a private company receives a concession, usually from the public sectors, for financing, designing, and constructing a facility and then operating it for a specified period of time. After it ends, the facility is transferred back to the entity which granted the concession. In the build-transfer model the facility is transferred back right after the end of construction.

17

North Korea: Utter Orthodoxy or Attempts to Reform?

A Few Basics

North Korea, or the Democratic People's Republic of Korea (DPRK) as it is officially known, with its population of 23.5 million, remains generally a poor country, suffering from shortages of food and basic consumer goods. The estimates of its gross domestic product (GDP) (purchasing power parity (PPP)) in 2007 range from US$40 billion (CIA 2008) to US$71 billion (the econometric consultancy firm Global Insight), and per-capita GDP, from US$1,900 to US$3,094, respectively. If we stick to the Central Intelligence Agency (CIA) figure, the DPRK's GDP would be close to that of, for example, Cambodia, Kenya, or Tajikistan.

The central bank of South Korea estimated the DPRK's nominal GDP for the same year at US$20.1 billion (Lee 2008), which would be a little smaller than in Iceland and a little larger than in Panama.

The share of agriculture in the GDP was estimated at 30 percent, industry 39 percent, and services 31 percent (Nanto 2008).

After the division of the Korean Peninsula following World War II the North became a militarized Stalinist state with the Korean Workers' Party (KWP) as the dominant force. Kim Il-sung, the founder of the state and its leader for almost five decades, wielded absolute power through the development of his personality cult as "Great Leader." After his death in 1994, his son, Kim Jong-il, inherited the position of leader.

The North Korean planned economy used to be tightly controlled by the party and the state. However, since the late 1990s elements of a market economy have begun to appear.

The country is rich in natural resources such as coal, lead, zinc, molybdenum, tungsten, copper, gold, rare metals, gravel, salt, and marine resources and in the agricultural sector the major crops are rice, corn, potatoes, and soybean.

From the birth of the North Korean state in 1948, until the 1990s, heavy industries were attached an absolute priority. The major ones included mining, general and electrical machinery, chemicals, and metallurgy. As the leadership had always propagated the notion of self-reliance, foodstuffs and consumer goods were also mostly produced inside the country. Today, in a new development, labor-intensive contract manufacturing is taking its initial steps in the sectors of electronics and textiles.

On its official Web site, the government of the DPRK presents a list of major products available for export, which includes ships and ship parts, general machinery products, cosmetics, garments, trucks, cars, motorbikes, engines, spirulina, cold-cast iron, tiles, mineral water, and stainless steel tubes (The Democratic People's Republic of Korea Official Web site 2008a).

Defense industries are the core. North Korea has emerged as an exporter of weaponry and weapons-production technology (including nuclear technology). It poses a threat to stability in various parts of the world, as Pyongyang's counterparts are usually the regimes with poor reputations in the international community.

North Korea's nuclear program has become a major destabilizing factor in Asia. To address the issue, and bring North Korea's nuclear program to a halt, the six-party talks mechanism was launched in 2003 with the participation of the two Koreas, the US, China, Japan, and Russia. In 2005, Pyongyang withdrew and, in 2006, it test-fired ballistic missiles and conducted a nuclear test. After the talks resumed, it closed the nuclear facilities in Yongbyon and promised to disable them and provide correct and complete information on its nuclear programs. In June 2008, the declaration on the nuclear programs and activities was handed to China, the host of the six-party talks, via the US, and in October the same year the United States removed North Korea from its list of states sponsoring terrorism. Pyongyang was also exempted from the Trading with the Enemy Act, which basically opened the way for international aid, joining international financial institutions and getting loans from them, and wider external economic ties.

Postwar Development

After World War II, North Korea started building a conventional, socialist, planned economy with a nationalist flavor. The idea of *juche*: self-effort, self-reliance, or, in broader terms, "doing it ourselves" became the guiding principle (in part, to check Soviet and Chinese influence). The reality was, however, that the economy depended on its ties with, and aid from, the former USSR, East European socialist states, and China.

After the end of the Korean War in 1953, directive planning was started in the form of three-, six-, and seven-year plans. Heavy industries led the economy in terms of production volume but their efficiency was low. Light industries and agriculture were lagging behind. Consumption was mostly limited to basic goods and services. However, in the tradition of socialist planned economies, healthcare and education were made free and housing was almost free.

In 1993, it was officially announced that the Third Seven-Year Plan, adopted in 1987, was unfulfilled. The three following years were proclaimed as a period of adjustment. The government pledged to balance the economy by promoting agriculture, light industry, and foreign trade.

The 1990s: A North Korean Tragedy

From 1990 to 1998, for nine consecutive years, growth in the North Korean economy was negative. While, in the second half of the 1990s, East Asia in general "only" went through a deep financial and structural crisis, the North Korean people suffered a tragedy.

Generally, economic conditions sharply deteriorated with the break up of the USSR and the pro-market shift of the former socialist economies. In the first half of the 1990s their interest in economic links with North Korea declined to the minimum level.

Almost every plant or factory ceased operating for some time between 1995 and 1997. By early 1997, the average production of a major plant was only 46 percent of its capacity (Lankov 2006). To make things worse, the DPRK suffered from devastating floods in 1995 and 1997 and drought in 1996.

A deep crisis erupted with even basic foodstuffs and consumer goods in short supply. Famine began and continued until the end of the decade. Estimates say that 600,000–1 million people perished. According to the Bank of Korea, gross domestic product (GDP) fell by 4.6 percent in 1995, 3.7 percent in 1996, and 6.8 percent in 1997 (ARC Report DPRK 2007, 27).

Structural Reforms

Amid the crisis of the second half of the 1990s the North Korean leadership embarked on reforms.

More Emphasis on the Economy

To begin with, in today's North Korea, economic development is ranked higher (and ideological issues lower) on the scale of the government's policy priorities than before the crisis. As far as the economy is concerned, the solution of the food problem and an improvement of consumer goods supply are attached primary importance, along with the traditional "Four Priority Sectors"—electricity, coal, metal, and railway transport.

The government also began to emphasize the importance of science and technology, including information technology (IT), nanotechnology, and biotechnology. Substantial progress was made in introducing computers—both at production sites and in the service sector.

More Autonomy for Enterprises

As a principle of economic management, along with "self-reliance," the KWP started to emphasize "practical gain." The importance of economic incentives was recognized. Enterprises were guided to be financially viable and even profitable.

From 1999 to 2001, the restructuring of state-owned enterprises (SOEs) was carried out. The powers of managers were expanded. A system was introduced which allowed, and even encouraged, enterprises to be engaged in the direct sale and purchase of capital goods at market prices.

Production planning authority and decision-making rights regarding export-import transactions were largely transferred from the state and the ruling-party level to enterprise managers. In agriculture, collective farms have been given the right to determine what crops to cultivate and what technology to use. Mandatory deliveries of agricultural goods to the state have been replaced by payments for the use of land.

July 1, 2002 Adjustment

A large-scale adjustment of wages and prices was implemented on July 1, 2002. State purchasing prices for rice were raised almost 50 times from 0.82 won to 40 won per kilo, while sales prices went up 550 times from 0.08 won to 44 won. The average prices for industrial goods surged 25 times. Price hikes for rice and other agricultural products were greater to stimulate farmers. The average wages of blue and white collar workers were raised 18 times and of miners and other workers engaged in physically hard labor 20-30 times (ARC Report DPRK 2007, 31).

In other words, an attempt was made to "let prices work," reflecting supply and demand, and to get over the economy of super-low, often merely symbolic, prices and rationing of goods. That's why, naturally, price hikes were bigger than the rise in wages—a typical set-up for a planned economy making a market transition. However, the adjustment did not mean a shift to market prices as such. It was only a price correction with centralized control remaining in place.

In parallel, currency reform was carried out. Previously, domestic currency won could not be used for purchasing imported goods or goods on the list of exported items. To buy them, foreign currency certificates had to be used and these were given in exchange for foreign currency—that is, if anyone had it. As very few North Koreans could earn or get foreign currency, such items remained unavailable for the vast majority of households. From July 2002, foreign currency certificates were abolished and it became possible to pay for all goods and services in won. The exchange rate of the won itself was reduced from 2.2 to 150 won for US$1, which is much closer to market realities (ARC Report DPRK 2007, 32). It was announced that the rate would be adjusted depending on market trends.

Markets and Petty Entrepreneurship

Markets and Rationing.   But perhaps the most important step was the reform of "farmers' markets," legalized throughout the country in 2003. Markets in North Korea practically disappeared in the 1960s. From the 1970s nearly all food and consumer items were handed out through the Public Distribution System (PDS). Prices were just symbolic.

In the 1980s street markets began to appear again but essentially they were considered inappropriate, especially for "the socialist paradise" of Pyongyang. There they were only located on the outskirts of the capital.

Due to the impact of the economic disaster of the late 1990s markets began to spread at a remarkable pace. In fact, there was no other way to survive as the rationing system did not work any more—one could have a coupon but there was not enough food available in exchange for it.

A Mini-Boom of Markets.   In June 2003, the name "farmers' markets" was changed to "general markets," and more recently the term has become "local markets." Sales of all kinds of consumer goods were legalized. For some goods, price caps are imposed, but for the majority of items prices are set freely depending on supply and demand (Mimura 2007, 12–13).

In Pyongyang, more than 60 markets have been established—one in virtually every neighborhood. Each market hosts around 50 traders. Service is getting better. In the clothing stores, mannequins and attractive price tags have appeared. A variety of seafood is sold, which is delivered by private entrepreneurs running refrigerator trucks from the coast to the capital (Institute for Far East Asian Studies 2008a).

A big new market has been opened just five blocks away from the Tower of Juche Idea, in the very center of the capital (*North Korea Economy Watch* 2008).

The Rise of Private Commerce.   The 2000s have been marked by a rapid rise in private commerce, including petty foreign trade. More and more people have begun to leave their home areas in search of better access to food and better opportunities to earn a living. Many women—housewives or those engaged in less-demanding and time-consuming jobs than their husbands—have turned into petty capitalists, running canteens, food-stalls, small shops, and inns.

In the past, to go abroad a North Korean citizen had to get a travel permit, which was a long and burdensome procedure. From the mid-1990s controls were eased. It became possible to buy the permit from a police officer for a bribe of US$5–10 (Lankov 2006). As a result, new opportunities appeared for petty trade with the neighboring provinces of China. Today, cross-border trade is booming.

Commercial activities are also getting a boost from growing investment in trading ventures by Japan-based Koreans and the rise of businessmen of Chinese origin, leveraging their family ties in China.

The Ruling Elite: Seeking to Benefit.   Generally, the ruling elite is no longer impeding commercial activities of this kind. Its significant part seems to be somewhat tired of imposing ideological dogma on society. It is more interested in benefiting from the *de facto* market transition, using its power and access to financial and material resources to get a big piece of the pie.

Present Performance

A Shift to Positive, But Slow, Growth

In 1998, the DPRK economy hit rock bottom, but the following year the recovery started. Budget expenditure began to grow and so did foreign trade, especially with China and South Korea.

Policies, articulated in 1998, were focused on boosting production in agriculture, coal, steel, electricity, and basic consumer goods. In 1999, the economy grew by 6.2 percent, but the following year the growth rate fell due to the poor performance of agriculture and the steel industry and declining imports of oil. In the first half of the 2000s, production has been growing at a slow pace within a 1–4 percent range (see Table 17.1).

In 2005, a significant increase was registered for domestic investment in the power sector, mining, construction of irrigation facilities, heavy industries, and food production. However, in 2006, the economy contracted again due to the negative effect on its external ties of missile test-firing in July and, especially, the nuclear test in October. Agriculture suffered from summer floods.

In 2007, the situation deteriorated further due to flooding, rising commodity prices, chronic energy shortages, and worsening relations with its major donor, South Korea. Production in the agriculture, forestry, and fisheries sector contracted by 9.4 percent, while the increases in mining, manufacturing, and services were 0.4, 0.8, and 1.7 percent respectively (Lee 2008). A big food shortage loomed again.

Overall, economic performance depended most crucially on foreign aid, which in turn was closely related to Pyongyang's stance regarding the nuclear issue and missile testing and, since 2003, the situation at the six-party talks. For its part, the North Korean side sought to leverage its nuclear and military potential in order to obtain more financial and economic assistance.

Initially, at the beginning of the 2000s, growth in the agricultural sector got a big boost when South Korea started supplying fertilizer after the first North–South summit in 2000. Then, from 2004, Seoul further activated its Sunshine Policy, not only increasing supplies of food and fertilizer, but also cooperating in building infrastructure and developing local industries.

The acceleration of growth since 2003 has largely been the result of expanding trade from China in the wake of the start of the six-party talks. However, economic relations with Japan are paralyzed because of the unresolved issue of

Table 17.1   The economic growth of North Korea*

Year	1999	2000	2001	2002	2003	2004	2005	2006	2007
% growth	6.2	1.3	3.7	1.2	1.8	2.2	3.8	−1.1	−2.3

Source: ERINA Report 78, 2007 November, p. 13; CRS Report for Congress, August 2008.
*Estimates by the Bank of Korea. North Korea does not provide its own information on economic growth.

the Japanese citizens, abducted by North Korean agents in Japan and Europe in the 1970s and 1980s, and forced to live and work in the DPRK (mostly to teach Japanese language and culture at spy schools).

Foreign Trade

After 1999, the amount of foreign trade grew in parallel with the growth of production. In 2007, it reportedly reached US$5,101 million, which is 17.3 percent more than in the previous year (trade with South Korea included) but was still below the US$5,240 billion peak level of 1988. Exports were US $ 1,854 million and imports US$3,242 (Nanto 2008). North Korea's foreign trade has never been in surplus.

The major exports (excluding South Korea)[1] are mineral resources (24.4 percent of the total in 2005), especially coal and metallic ores, nonferrous metals (18.7 percent), textile products (12.3 percent), machinery and electrical and electronic devices (13.3 percent), and chemicals and plastics (7.2 percent) (ARC Report DPRK 2007, 38). Since 2004, exports of mineral products (especially iron, zinc, magnesium, and other ores) have been growing rapidly—largely due to growing Chinese investment in the mining industry. Exports of chemicals and plastics are also on the rise, the latter due to the increase in production on commission. Contract manufacturing and the export of textiles (one of the most competitive sectors of the economy) are growing too. Marine products were leading in terms of volume in 2000–04, but then their exports dropped due to falling prices in China, sanctions imposed by Japan, and falls in the catch due to fuel shortages.

The major imports (also excluding South Korea) are petroleum and other mineral products (25.1 percent in 2005), machinery (15.0 percent), nonferrous metals (8.0 percent), textiles (7.6 percent), chemicals (5.7 percent), and plastics (5.4 percent). Imports of capital goods have been rising since 2000. Textiles are imported largely for contract manufacturing. The share of agricultural products was 13.9 percent (ARC Report DPRK 2007, 39). Imports of foodstuffs and consumer goods remain small due to foreign exchange constraints.

In 2007, 41.2 percent of total exports went to South Korea and 31.5 percent to China. The share of Russia and Thailand was 1.8 percent each. Also, recently, Brazil has emerged as a new and important counterpart.

Dependence on trade with South Korea is growing. In 2005–06 exports to all other countries combined were falling.

Among the exporters to North Korea, China is leading (43.0 percent of total imports in 2007) and South Korea is number two with 31.8 percent. The share of Thailand was 5.7 percent and Russia 3.9 percent (Nanto 2008). Since 2004, Russia and Thailand have exported more than Japan, whose share is declining significantly.

FDI and the Business Environment

Propagated Merits and Scale

To lure investors, North Korea emphasizes the fact that the country has the lowest labor costs in Asia and the lowest tax schemes, especially for high-tech industries. Another advantage is defined as qualified and motivated personnel (Democratic People's Republic of Korea Official Web site 2008b).

Undoubtedly, cost merits are very significant. The DPRK has the potential to become East Asia's next (maybe last) frontier for the very low cost production of labor-intensive products.

The amount of foreign direct investment (FDI) inflow is small but it has started to grow in the wake of the July 1, 2002 adjustment. According to the US Congress Research Service Report, it was US$158.2 million in 2003, US$196.9 million in 2004, US$50.4 million in 2005, and US$135.2 million in 2006 (Nanto 2008).

Legal Framework

The legal framework for FDI was initiated in 1984, when the law on joint ventures was enacted. The Free Trade Zone Act of 1993 was adopted to foster the development of the Rajin-Songbong Special Economic Zone (SEZ) around the Sea of Japan port of Rajin in the northeastern part of the country (in 1999, its name was changed to Rason).

The basic law on foreign investment was adopted in 1992 and amended in 1999. It allows joint ventures between foreign and North Korean companies anywhere in the country and 100 percent foreign-owned companies in the Rason SEZ.

Rason SEZ

In the Rason SEZ, foreign-owned companies producing goods can import materials and export products duty free and get a three-year income tax holiday plus a 50 percent reduction for the following two years. The basic corporate tax rate in the zone is 14 percent, which is lower than in other areas.

The zone has been counted upon as a center of transportation and logistics, export processing, tourism, and financial services—mostly in the context of multilateral cooperation between China, Japan, the Russian Far East, the two Koreas, and Mongolia.

From 1996, the government started to call in foreign investors and made certain steps to improve infrastructure. For the time being the results are modest. However, the building of infrastructure is now progressing at a fast pace with the active involvement of Russia and China. Russia is repairing the railroad tracks. China is constructing a new highway and investing in the redevelopment of the port. Both link their respective borders with Rajin.

Expanding Links with China and Russia

In other developments, since 2005, China has increased its investment in the development of North Korean natural resources. Also, another important trend is emerging. As wages in China are increasing and labor legislation amendments make it more difficult to fire employees, Chinese companies, largely small- and medium-sized enterprises (SMEs), are turning their attention to North Korea as a production site for labor-intensive, low-cost items. Lastly, Russia is providing jobs for tens of thousands of North Korean immigrant workers.

Economic Relations with South Korea

Growing Scale

Relations with South Korea play a crucial role in national economic development. After the first North–South Summit in 2000, a shift was made from economic ties based mostly on private sector initiatives to ones based on intergovernment agreements. In 2006, commercial deals accounted for 69 percent of North–South trade and noncommercial ones, mainly assistance from South Korea (especially supplies of food and fertilizer), 31 percent (Mimura 2007, 14).

In 2005, for the first time, bilateral trade exceeded US$1 billion. General trade with the North engaged 379 South Korean firms and 136 were engaged in trade transactions related to contract manufacturing at North Korean factories (ARC Report DPRK 2007, 43).

The North is enhancing its exports of marine and mineral products and also steel. Likewise, the South is increasing its exports of general machinery, electrical and electronic items, and textiles.

Personal exchanges are also visibly expanding. In 2006, their scale (the total number of South Koreans who visited the North and vice versa) exceeded 100,000 people.

However, after the emergence of the Lee Myung-bak administration in the South, political relations have become much more strained, which adversely affects economic ties. In late January 2009, Pyongyang announced it was scrapping a nonaggression pact and all other peace accords with Seoul.

Kaesong Industrial District

The basic agreement on the Kaesong Industrial District was reached at the North–South Summit in 2000. Kaesong, the location for the first capital of a unified state on the Korean Peninsula, is situated just 40 miles from Seoul and 80 miles from Pyongyang. It has been developed by Hyundai Group companies, which have invested almost 10 trillion won in the project (Salmon 2006). The complex is run by a South Korean management committee under a 50-year lease arrangement, effective from 2004. Construction has to be completed by 2012. Kaesong is expected to become an export-oriented zone producing textiles, footwear, watches, and other labor-intensive products. It is planned to build trading, tourist, and international business facilities as well as a residential area for 50,000 people.

In June 2006, the first group of 15 South Korean companies entered the area and started production activities. From March 2005, South Korea's electric power company, Korea Electric Power Corporation (KEPCO), began to supply electricity. As of the end of July 2007, the number of companies operating in the zone was 45.

The Kaesong project has a chance of developing into a genuine export-processing zone and, thus, setting a precedent for the establishment of more zones of this kind, speeding up economic development and market transformation. However, in early 2008, North Korea expelled South Korean officials in protest against the tougher policy in North–South relations of the Lee Myung-bak administration.

Other Schemes and Plans

In 2004, South Korea's SME South–North Investment Council and North Korea's Association of National Economic Cooperation agreed to create the Pyongyang industrial estate, where South Korean SMEs are producing glass, construction materials, and furniture.

In recent years the two sides have also expanded cooperation in the development of North Korea's mineral resources: such as iron ore, sand, gravel, magnesium, and zinc.

There are plans to open high-tech zones and bonded factories in Nampo on the west coast and Unsan on the east coast. At the North–South Summit, in October 2007, some new ideas were put on the table, including the creation of a joint shipbuilding cooperation zone for repair services and parts manufacturing.

Concluding Remarks

North Korea has two faces. On the one hand, economically, it is the sick man of East Asia, and politically, a reclusive dictatorial state with a criminal record. On the other, in the late 1990s and early 2000s, it has made a structural breakthrough, shifting from a centrally planned and tightly controlled economy with the Public Distribution System at its core to a new economy containing a significant market element. Today, entrepreneurial activities support the majority of North Korean families by both giving work to earn a living and providing basic consumer goods and services. The transition has gotten an implicit, and to some extent also explicit, blessing from the authorities.

As a result of the reforms, SOEs and collective farms are also now operating in an environment that is not so different from a market economy as it used to be.

Conditions are ripe for fostering reforms in the Chinese or Vietnamese fashion. Notably, the leadership does not object. During an unofficial visit to China in January 2006, Kim Jong-il once again showed interest in Chinese-style economic reforms and recognized the need to apply their experience in his country. In October 2007, receiving the Vietnamese Communist Party chief, Nong Duc-Manh, he praised the economic achievements of Vietnam.

However, the main problem lies in the inability of the present leadership to launch the necessary reform initiative and set its direction. It is too weak, old-fashioned, corrupt, and preoccupied with preserving its power in the short term. Today's pro-market drive is made by "people from the street" and, maybe, by rank-and-file government officials. By no means does this create a solid foundation for economic progress.

Since late 2008, one more factor of uncertainty has appeared—Kim Jong-il's health. The leader has ceased to appear in public.

In our view, the international community, especially the big powers, can do much more to facilitate North Korea's market reforms through their support in articulating policies, training people, improving the legal system, and developing entrepreneurship. To address these tasks, Pyongyang could work with international organizations, such as the World Bank, the International Monetary Fund (IMF), and the Asian Development Bank (ADB).

Endnote

1 The data on foreign trade by product, compiled by the (South) Korean Trade-Investment Promotion Agency (KOTRA), does not include exports to, and imports from, South Korea because they are considered internal trade.

18

The Russian Far East: Yes, It Is Also East Asia!

A Few Basics

Asian Russia

About 75 percent of the Russian Federation's territory is in Asia. In contrast, about 75 percent of its population lives in the European part. Asian Russia consists of three vast regions: West Siberian, East Siberian, and Far Eastern. The latter is also known as the Russian Far East (RFE). In this chapter, we will focus on the RFE. The region is located in close proximity to the major regional economic powers, has deepening relations with them, and is becoming a noticeable economic player in Asia, especially in northeast Asia.

With its remarkably rich natural resources—oil and natural gas, metallic ores, timber, and marine products—the RFE has the potential to become one of the leading suppliers of fuel and raw materials for Japan and other East Asian countries.

Territory and Administrative Divisions

The territory of the RFE is 2.4 million square miles—36.4 percent of the total territory of the Russian Federation (for comparison, it is about 16 times larger than the territory of Japan). However, its population is small—only 6.5 million people as of January 1, 2008 (FSSS 2008). Furthermore, its decline since the early 1990s poses a major problem for economic development.

The RFE, consists of nine major administrative entities—Russia's equivalents of states or provinces: Amur Oblast, Chukotka Autonomous District, the Jewish Autonomous Oblast, Kamchatka Krai (both oblast and krai mean province), Khabarovsk Krai, Magadan Oblast, Primorsky Krai, Sakha (Yakutia) Republic, and Sakhalin Oblast. In the context of the economic policy of the Russian government and regional business activities two administrative units east of Lake Baikal, which geographically are part of East Siberia, (Buryat Republic and Zabaykalskiy Krai), are often considered a part of the region's economy. In this case the term "Far East and Zabaikal" is used ("Zabaikal" means "Transbaikal").

297

Natural Resources and Industry

Major metallic ores excavated include gold, silver, platinum, copper, tungsten, lead, and zinc. In recent years, the excavation of iron ore and titanium has begun too. The Sakha Republic is one of the most important centers of the world's diamond industry. Deposits of many metal ores and other mineral resources still remain untouched.

The role of the oil and natural gas sector was small until the beginning of the 1990s saw the development of the shelf deposits in the Sea of Okhotsk, off Sakhalin Island (Sakhalin 1 and Sakhalin 2 projects). The implementation of these projects opens the way for the region to become one of the major energy resource suppliers to northeast Asia and beyond. Coal and hydro-energy resources are also important.

The RFE has rich and diverse timber resources and its marine economic zone is home to a wide variety of fish and other seafood, from cod and herring to the famous Kamchatka crab.

Major industries in the Russian Far East are fishery and timber, and excavation of metallic ores and diamonds; coal, oil, and natural gas. The transportation sector is also very important, especially the 11 major ice-free ports, which handle most of the export, import, and transit cargo. The manufacturing sector is weak, with the exception of a group of defense enterprises. The role of agriculture is insignificant. Service industries, underdeveloped for decades, have made significant progress in the 2000s.

The RFE in the Soviet Economy

The status of the economy of the RFE depended on its ranking on the scale of priorities of the Communist Party leadership in Moscow and the amount of investment it received from the state budget. However, its location far away from the country's major economic centers, small population, severe climatic conditions, and underdeveloped infrastructure made any attempt to stimulate its economic development a very difficult and costly exercise with unpredictable results. The leadership needed compelling reasons to make such policies worthwhile.

During World War II, the region was considered strategically important because of the danger of military confrontation with Japan. After the war, especially with the emergence of the Communist regime in China, the situation changed. The RFE was a supplier of natural resources for other regions of the USSR and one of the centers of defense production, but its role in the national economic and defense policy declined.

With the emergence, in 1964, of a new Soviet leadership with Leonid Brezhnev at its head, the government began to pay more attention to developing the RFE's natural resources. Also, the deterioration of relations with China provided a strong "negative incentive" to strengthen the Far Eastern economy.

In 1967 and 1972, the Central Committee of the Communist Party and the Council of Ministers (the government) adopted two important ordinances concerning the economic development of the RFE. Their major contents were

a significant rise in state investment in the region, construction of new factories (especially machine-building and timber-processing), development of new
deposits of mineral resources, and the promotion of fishery and energy sectors. As a result, the region's economic growth accelerated.

Also, from the middle of the 1960s, bilateral Soviet–Japanese resource development, in the form of "compensation projects," was started. The Japanese
side provided loans and equipment, while the Soviet side paid back by
resource deliveries.

In the second half of the 1970s the Soviet economy began to worsen. A
growing portion of oil export revenues was used for defense purposes and the
import of foodstuffs, to make up for the poor performance of the domestic
agricultural sector. Allocation of significant funds for the development of the
RFE became problematic. Production growth rates in the region started to fall.

The new era for the RFE, as well as for the USSR as a whole, began in the
perestroika (restructuring) years. In an historic speech in Vladivostok in 1986,
new leader, Mikhail Gorbachev, articulated a strategic shift of the Soviet foreign and economic policy toward a rapidly growing Asia-Pacific region. The
expansion of economic ties with regional states was proclaimed a priority goal
and development of the RFE, the country's gateway to the Asia-Pacific region,
obtained a new significance. In September 1987, a long-term program for the
region's development until 2000 was adopted.

However, relatively high 4.4 percent industrial growth rates were maintained
only during 1986–87. At the end of the decade the RFE economy was entering a
crisis, together with the other regions of the USSR. In 1991, the implementation
of the program was effectively stopped.

The Market Transition of the 1990s

Market reforms in the newly independent Russia were started in 1992 by the
administration of President Boris Yeltsin. They are compared to "shock therapy,"
as price liberalization for most goods and services was implemented in one step.
As a result, consumer prices rose 26 times in 1992 and 9 times in 1993. Also in
1992, massive privatization of state-owned enterprises (SOEs) began. Between
1992 and 1994, more than 100,000 SOEs were privatized (including buy-outs by
workers and other untraditional methods), with about 20,000 large companies
among them (Tselichtchev 1995). Foreign trade activities were also liberalized.

To reduce fiscal deficit, combat inflation, and stimulate the companies'
self-financing, the government abruptly reduced subsidies and low-interest loans
to enterprises as well as budget expenditure in general, including infrastructure,
welfare, and education. Tight fiscal and monetary policy both strengthened companies' financial constraints and squeezed domestic demand. Shortage of liquidity resulted in the growth of barter transactions and wage deferrals. Negative
growth of GDP and industrial production continued from the very start of the
market reforms in 1992 until 1996. However, inflation was gradually brought
under control, and companies were accumulating necessary experience in

operating within a new framework by learning to raise funds and establish ties with suppliers and buyers without guidance from the state.

In 1997, for the first time, Russia's new market economy registered positive growth, albeit minimal, but, in 1998, the country was hit by the financial crisis, in much the same way that South Korea and the ASEAN 4 had been. GDP fell by 5.1 percent and consumer prices soared by 84 percent (FSSS 2002).

However, like the crisis-hit East Asian states, the Russian economy recovered fast and entered a period of rapid growth from 1999. In the first half of this decade, it was growing 6.2 percent on average (FSSS 2006). In 2007, the growth rate rose to 8.1 percent.

In the 1990s, the RFE's economy suffered a blow from a breakdown of traditional ties with other regions of Russia and shrinking support from the central government. In particular, transportation and energy costs ceased to be subsidized from the central budget. The blow was mitigated by a rapid expansion of links with adjacent Asian countries.

Natural resources-related industries proved to be the most competitive and their share in the regional economy significantly increased (as did the share of the transportation and electricity sectors—largely because of the rising tariffs).

In 1996, private enterprises comprised about half of the total number of companies registered in the RFE, not to mention many third sector firms which were on the way to complete privatization. The share of "purely" state and municipal enterprises in the gross regional product (GRP) was 23.4 percent (Minakir 1999, 89).

Also in 1996, the Russian government adopted a new RFE and Zabaikal Region Development Program. However, implementation was sluggish, and the federal government's commitments to funding remained unfulfilled.

Present Performance

The Russian Economy East Asian-Style—Growing Fast

The Russian economy has continued to grow rapidly all through the 2000s without interruptions (see Table 18.1).

Initially, growth was driven by the depreciation of the ruble and rising oil exports. However, in the first half of the 2000s, Russia not only already exploited its advantage as a major oil exporter but also capitalized on an unprecedented expansion of domestic demand.

Table 18.1   GDP of the Russian Federation and GRP of the RFE–Zabaikal Region (% growth)

	1999	2000	2001	2002	2003	2004	2005	2006
Russian Federation	6.4	10.0	5.1	4.7	7.3	7.2	6.4	7.7
RFE-Zabaikal	5.6	4.6	6.0	3.8	6.1	6.1	4.5	5.1

Source: FSSS; Ishaev 2007.

Most macroeconomic indicators have been sound and the fiscal balance is in the black. The major macroeconomic problem is inflation, remaining above the 10 percent level.

In the wake of the global financial turmoil, Russia's growth slowed down, but not that much. In October 2008, the year-on year growth rate was 5.9 percent, and in the January-October period 7.5 percent versus 8.1 percent for the whole of 2007 (*The Moscow Times* 2008). The economy was negatively affected by falling oil and other commodity prices, dwindling exports, and the outflow of foreign capital. The latter was driven not only by the global risk aversion trend, but also by investor concern due to a week-long war with Georgia and the authorities' tough stance in particular cases regarding the disputes between domestic and overseas owners of joint ventures and the application of the anti-monopoly law.

The Two Faces of the RFE Economy

Today's RFE economy has two faces. On the positive side, since 1999, it has been growing quite fast, along with other provinces of Russia, taking advantage of intensifying links with Asian countries—especially China, Japan, and South Korea. Sakhalin Oblast has made a big step forward toward becoming a key supplier of oil and natural gas for Japan and other regional economies. The development of the shelf resources in the Sea of Okhotsk, with the participation of leading Russian and overseas firms, has grown into a very large-scale project by any standards.

On the negative side, the RFE remains a "problematic region" with a relatively weak economy. The development gap with other regions, especially the European part of Russia is increasing. The RFE's growth rates are below the national average. It has never exceeded the 5–6 percent level, while the Russian economy as a whole was growing at around 7 percent a year in 2003–2006 (see Table 18.1).

Real household incomes in the RFE-Zabaikal region, in 2006, were 27.8 percent higher than in 2003, while in Russia as a whole they grew by 38.2 percent. In 2005, the RFE-Zabaikal region's per-capita GRP comprised only 89.5 percent of the national average as opposed to 117.5 percent in 1998, though its prices were higher (Ishaev 2007). Living infrastructure in the region—housing, utilities, roads, healthcare, and social welfare facilities—also remains underdeveloped.

The incomes of 21.2 percent of the RFE-Zabaikal population are still below the living minimum—the Russian term for the poverty line. The share for Russia as a whole is 17.6 percent (Government of Russia 2006).[1] In some RFE provinces— for example, Chukotka Autonomous District, Kamchatka Krai, and Sakhalin Oblast—nominal per-capita GRP exceeds the national average by 50 percent or more, but the seeming advantage is completely offset by higher prices for consumer goods and services, a much smaller selection of the same, and underdeveloped infrastructure.

Thus, in relative terms, the region is becoming a less and less attractive place to live in, which results in population outflow from all its provinces. A significant number of those choosing to leave are highly qualified specialists and skilled workers. Especially worrisome is the outflow of young people, who do not see attractive job opportunities in the RFE.

In other words, the story of today's RFE economy features great new opportunities but also exacerbating problems and growing risks.

A Picture of the RFE's Economic Growth

GRP growth in the 2000s has been led by the service sector. Growth rates in industry, both mining and manufacturing, are lagging behind. Textiles, food (other than processed marine products), and other consumer goods-producing industries, which used to produce for the domestic market in the Soviet era, have practically disappeared. The defense industry has also significantly declined in scale.

However, the GRP share of transportation and logistics, finance, domestic and foreign trade, catering, and tourism is rising. Quite often former factory buildings are used as storage or distribution facilities. Sakhalin Oblast is the only exception—growth there is driven by the Sea of Okhotsk shelf oil and natural gas development project, attracting large-scale foreign direct investment (FDI). Sakhalin's oil industry appears to be about the only rapidly growing industrial sector, and the extraction of natural gas is emerging as one more.

Other mining industries, especially excavation of metallic ores, face constraints due to the exhaustion of resources in easily accessible fields, rising costs, and insufficient prospecting.

High energy and transportation costs—a product of the region's severe climatic conditions and its long distance from Russia's major economic centers, remains another major growth constraint. For example, electricity costs in the RFE are 1.8–1.9 times higher than the national average (*Financial Izvestia* 2007).

The development of manufacturing industries, especially those processing local raw materials, to increase the value created within the RFE, is recognized as an important task both at the regional and federal levels.

Deepening Engagement with East Asia

In the Soviet era about 75 percent of the RFE's produce was supplied to other regions of the country, while the share of exports was only 6 percent. The remaining 19 percent were consumed within the region. Market reforms brought about a radical change. Most goods are exported or consumed within the RFE, and trade with China, Japan, and South Korea has become much bigger than domestic trade with other regions of Russia. In terms of value, the latter receive only 4 percent of the products made in the RFE (*Financial Izvestia* 2007).

Today, the region is supplying more and more raw materials to neighboring Chinese provinces, especially for petrochemical and wood-processing industries, and a proportion of the final goods produced there return to the RFE as Chinese exports.

The vast majority of businessmen in the RFE, whose activities relate to foreign trade or investment, work with counterparts from East Asia. The foreign ties of provinces and municipalities, as well as human contacts, are also Asia-focused.

A New Development Program

Amid a significant improvement in the country's macroeconomic and financial performance, in November 2007, the administration of President Vladimir Putin announced a new Far East and Zabaikal Development Program for 2008–13.

The major goal is to build necessary infrastructure and create a favorable investment environment in areas where the region has a competitive advantage. Within this period, the GRP is expected to double and capital formation to triple. The total amount of funds to be allocated for the region's development within its framework is 567 billion rubles, or about US$21.8 billion. From this sum, 75 percent will come from the federal budget. The remaining part is to be provided by local budgets (around 10 percent) and private investors. The allocation for building transportation infrastructure will be 218.9 billion rubles, 138.1 billion rubles are earmarked for the development of the energy sector (construction of power plants, gas pipelines, and electricity transmission lines), and 148.5 billion rubles will be assigned to the development of Vladivostok, which is to host the 2012 APEC Summit (Minakir 2008).

Foreign Trade

The Composition of Exports

In 2006, the total exports of the RFE reached US$7,152 million (including items produced in other regions of Russia and delivered overseas through the RFE). The major export items were fuels, minerals, and metals (especially coal, oil, steel, and nonferrous metals), which comprised 60.4 percent of the total, marine products (16.9 percent), and timber (16.6 percent).

The major export market for the RFE is China with 35.9 percent of the total, followed by Japan (22.6 percent) and South Korea (16.6 percent). The US comes in fourth with 3.0 percent. Japan has become the major exporter to the region with 24.6 percent of total imports, though it is closely followed by China (24.4 percent) and South Korea (23.0 percent). The share of the US was 6.2 percent (Roshia-NIS Boekikai 2007b, 69).

The Composition of Imports

In 2006, the value of imports was US$6,972 million. The major imports were machinery and equipment (including transportation machinery) with a share of 59.3 percent and consumer goods at 23.6 percent (including 10.3 percent for foodstuffs). The share of fuels, minerals, and metals was 9.4 percent and chemicals 5.8 percent (Roshia-NIS Boekikai 2007b, 69).

Initially, after the market reforms in the 1990s, booming exports from China played a crucial role in the supply of key consumer goods. It is difficult to imagine today's Vladivostok, Khabarovsk, or Blagoveshchensk (the capital of Amur Oblast) without long rows of Chinese trading lots. However, as time went by, incomes rose, the middle class expanded, and the stratum of the super-rich was becoming more and more visible. As a result, South Korean and, especially, Japanese products, including high-end items, became increasingly popular.

The growth of imports from Japan and South Korea has also been boosted by purchases of equipment, machinery, and other capital goods, especially for the Sakhalin projects.

Inward FDI and the Business Environment

FDI Volume and Composition

The amount of inward FDI into the RFE is steadily growing (see Table 18.2). Especially dramatic growth was registered in 2003–04, when it exceeded US$2 billion and almost reached US$4 billion, respectively. The lion's share of the total goes to the oil and natural gas development projects in Sakhalin Oblast. Consequently, the share of the mining industry in total FDI, in 2006, was as high as 92.4 percent, as opposed to 3.0 percent for finance, trading, and real estate, 1.8 percent for transport and telecommunication, and 1.2 percent for manufacturing. As far as the breakdown by country is concerned, 54.1 percent of the total came from the Netherlands—Shell is the major player in the Sakhalin 2 project. The share of the Bahamas, a Caribbean tax haven, was 9.3 percent, India 8.3 percent (the Indian state company, Oil and Natural Gas Corporation (ONGC), has joined Sakhalin 1), and Japan 8.1 percent (Roshia-NIS Boekikai, 2007a; 10, 17).

In Sakhalin Oblast, FDI comprises 75 percent of total investment (Government of Russia 2006). In the Sakha Republic the FDI share is 16.5 percent—the diamond industry being the major target. In other provinces the share and role of FDI are still relatively small.

The Sakhalin Projects

The Sakhalin 1 and Sakhalin 2 projects are among the most large-scale resource development schemes in the world. They are important not only because of the scale of investment and expected production volumes but also the state-of-the-art technology applied.

Sakhalin 1. The Sakhalin 1 project (at a total estimated cost of US$12 billion) is run by ExxonMobil, Japan's Sakhalin Oil and Gas Development Company, India's state company, ONGC Videsh, and two affiliates of Russia's state oil giant Rosneft, Sakhalin Morneftegas and RM Astra. In February 2007, Phase One of the project reached its targeted oil production level of 250,000 barrels

Table 18.2   Inward FDI in the RFE (US$ millions)

	1999	2000	2001	2002	2003	2004	2005	2006
RFE	1,096.7	304.7	458.4	724.2	2,092.9	3,972.1	3,942.3	4,027.1
Sakhalin Oblast	1,022.4	246.1	374.6	679.8	2,007.7	3,396.5	3,800.8	3,834.5

Source: Roshia-NIS Boekikai: Roshia-NIS Chosa Geppo, 2007, No. 9–10.

a day (Sakhalin-1 Project Website 2008a). Oil exports started in 2006. A pipeline has been built, linking Sakhalin Island to the De-Kastri Marine Terminal on the mainland of Russia, where oil is loaded into tankers for deliveries to East Asian markets. Production of natural gas started in 2005, initially for the domestic market.

Direct revenues received by the Russian state during the lifetime of the project are expected to reach US$50 billion. The Russian economy, including the RFE, will also benefit from infrastructure development, technology transfer, and job creation. The Russian content of the project (the value of goods to be supplied by domestic producers) reached US$5 billion as of October 2008 (Sahkalin-1 Project Website 2008b).

In 2007, Sakhalin 1 set a world record—the extended-reach-drilling well at Chayvo field reached a depth of 37,014 feet. A year later it broke its own record, reaching 38,320 feet. As of early 2008, Chayvo field accounted for 17 out of the 30 longest extended-reach-drilling wells in the world (Watkins 2008a).

Sakhalin 2. The Sakhalin 2 project's (the total estimated cost is US$20 billion) operator is Sakhalin Energy. In December 2006 (a turbulent year when the project came under criticism over its environmental impact), the Russian state gas giant, Gazprom, bought 50 percent, plus one share, from Shell and the other parties and became the main stakeholder. The move reflected the determined intention of the Russian government to be a major player in the strategically important resource development schemes and to preserve Gazprom's dominance in the natural gas sector. Gazprom has the exclusive right to export natural gas. The other major stakeholders are Shell with 27.5 percent minus one share, Mitsui Trading (12.5 percent), and Mitsubishi Corporation (10 percent).

Along with the development of two fields—Piltun-Astokhskoye and Lunskoye—the project includes the construction of a pipeline to Prigorodnoye in the south of Sakhalin Island and a liquefied natural gas (LNG) plant and terminal. The state-of-the-art LNG plant (construction was completed in late 2008) is the first in Russia and the largest in the world.

The production and export of oil started in 1999, albeit only in summer. The production volume, in 2006, was 1.65 million tons. Export deliveries of natural gas are to start in early 2009. Sakhalin Energy has signed long-term supply contracts with Japanese, South Korean, and US buyers for nearly all of the LNG from the 10.6 million tons a year capacity plant. About 60 percent will be exported to major electric power and gas companies in Japan (Watkins 2008b).

Negotiations and preparatory work for consecutive projects up to Sakhalin 9 are under way.

Business Climate

The investment environment in Russia is improving. Today, as the country has become strong economically and financially, its bargaining power is significantly increasing and, unlike in the 1990s, both the government and business can speak to foreign investment partners from a position of strength.

The Foreign Investment Code provides national treatment for foreign-owned firms. The grandfather's clause protects them from unfavorable changes in tax and other legislation until the project reaches a breakeven point, but for no more than seven years. Prior approval is needed for ventures using the assets of existing Russian enterprises, for investment in the exploration of natural resources and in the defense industry (the latter may be prohibited in certain cases), as well as for all investment over 50 million rubles and enterprises with a foreign share of more than 50 percent. Investments in some sectors, such as mining, banking, or telecommunications, require licensing, and procedures may take a long time.

Business registration procedures have been streamlined. These are completed through the Ministry of Economic Development and Trade in a one-stop service mode. One hundred percent foreign ownership is allowed, but joint ventures are preferred. In some sectors, such as aerospace and electric power, caps on foreign ownership are imposed. Foreign companies are barred from acquiring a majority stake in the development of natural resource deposits which are considered strategically important. Otherwise, the new Law on Natural Resources provides better conditions for investors. It guarantees that licenses will carry over from the exploration to the development stage, stipulates that they will be based on civil rather than administrative law, and limits the number of possible reasons for license revocation.

The tax burden (the major federal taxes are value-added tax, profit tax, and social tax) on companies remains comparatively heavy, though significant progress in tax reduction has been made. (As for individual income tax, Russia has a very liberal system—a flat 13 percent rate.) The basic corporate tax rate today is rather low—24 percent, with 6.5 percent going to the central budget and 17.5 percent going to the regions. The latter can reduce this to no less than 13.5 percent. At the federal level, tax incentives for foreign investors are very few as the government sticks to the level playing field principle. However, many regions are actively providing them to attract investors.

A number of significant impediments also exist. Problems with infrastructure remain significant. For instance, the Trans-Siberian Railroad and Baikal-Amur Mainline (BAM) are the only major railroads running through the RFE. In the vast area to the north of BAM, comprising more than half of the RFE's territory, there are no railroads at all. The capacity of existing railroads is not enough to handle efficiently the growing amount of cargo going through the RFE's seaports (*Financial Izvestia* 2007). The density of roads is also low.

Business rules are often difficult to understand, and much depends on the interpretation of law or ordinance provisions by the particular person in charge. Procedures are often opaque and regulations inconsistent. Compliance with contract terms may also be a problem. Courts are mostly inefficient. Corruption remains a very big issue.

Today's Russia, the RFE included, offers a lot of very lucrative, often unique, business opportunities. It is important, however, to create a solid network of local contacts and establish relations of mutual trust with the key figures upon whom the success of your project depends.

Concluding Remarks

Ever since Russia's market reforms were initiated, the RFE has begun to develop, through trial and error, a new and much deeper economic relationship with East Asia, especially with the three major northeastern economies of China, Japan, and South Korea.

In the short term, Russia's major regional role will be that of the main supplier of energy resources, especially oil and natural gas. However, horizons are widening. A US$1 billion nuclear power plant construction contract with China, signed in May 2008—the first big international business scheme to be blessed by the new president, Dmitry Medvedev—is a good example. Russia has excellent opportunities to supply both raw materials and manufactured products to China and other East Asian countries. Such commodities include not just crude oil but also petroleum and petrochemical products and not just raw timber but also wood products and pulp and paper. Much will depend on its ability to strengthen its processing capacity.

The RFE's position in the national economic strategy is changing. Today, it is no longer just a "problematic region," located far away from the major economic centers and requiring huge subsidies to keep going. It looks like it is turning into Russia's economic gateway to East Asia. As the country has become economically and financially strong, the federal government is ready and willing to provide the support the region needs to play this role.

The process of recognizing Russia as an East Asian nation will be long and slow. The reason is not only geography but also the still low degree of its involvement in regional affairs, in areas other than diplomacy and security. However, the start of large-scale supplies of oil and gas and the forthcoming APEC 2012 Summit in Vladivostok have set the stage for a big breakthrough. New developments will follow. It is possible that in the foreseeable future Russia will move to establish free economic zones in the RFE and conclude some sort of free trade agreements (FTAs) with its neighbors.

Endnote

1 The figures are for 2004.

19

India: The Next-Door Neighbor Knocking at the Door

A Few Basics

Overview

In terms of gross domestic product (GDP) (purchasing power parity (PPP)) India lies fourth after the US, China, and Japan. By nominal GDP, in 2007, it was twelfth between Russia and South Korea, and by per-capita GDP (PPP) it was 126th—above Nicaragua and below Moldova.

The share of agriculture in the GDP is 17.5 percent, for industry it is 27.9 percent, and for services it is 54.6 percent (Dutz 2007). Shares in the total number of persons employed are 55 percent, 18 percent, and 27 percent, respectively (ADB 2007).

However, as formal laborers account for only about 15 percent of the total, employment composition figures may be misleading. With a lot of people going back and forth from the countryside to the cities, the absence of monitoring of the grassroots situation by the authorities, and enormous numbers of micro-enterprises appearing and disappearing, the real situation with labor is difficult to grasp (Datt 2007).

Since independence, India has upheld an electoral system, with regular and fair elections, that has provided the foundation for give-and-take parliamentary policy. Defeated parties have always been ready to vacate office in an orderly manner. Contrary to its politically unstable neighbors, the country did not suffer military coups or civil wars.

More than 80 percent of India's population is Hindu. However, people of all religions can, and do, hold high office or wield significant political power—a commendable political set-up.

India has a highly sophisticated intelligentsia, rich cultural traditions, a world-famous film industry, and an active community abroad whose contribution to the country's development is rapidly increasing. The media is free. The country has the largest number of TV channels in the world and, against the grain of world trends, its print media is also expanding.

India also has a vibrant civil society with nongovernmental organizations (NGOs) actively defending human rights, promoting environmentalism, educating poor children, and fighting injustice.

Industries and Companies

The major agricultural crops include rice, wheat, oilseed, cotton, jute, tea, sugarcane, and potatoes. Among the industries the most important are automotive, cement, chemicals, consumer electronics, food processing, machinery, mining, petroleum, pharmaceuticals, steel, transportation equipment, and textiles.

The textile industry is the largest in terms of scale. It contributes about 4 percent of GDP, 14 percent of total industrial output, and provides employment for 35 million people. Its contribution to gross export earnings is about 25 percent while it adds only 2–3 percent to the gross import bill. It is the only Indian industry that is completely self-reliant, from raw materials to final products, including high-value-added items. (Datt 2007).

Until a few years ago, India was known as one of the most protected automobile markets in the world. Today, the situation is changing dramatically. Practically all large auto makers are keen to enter into what promises to become one of the most exciting markets in the years to come.

India is the seventh-largest steel producer in the world, with a production volume of more than 55 million tons per year (ADB 2008). ArcelorMittal, based in Luxembourg with famous Indian entrepreneur Lakshmi N. Mittal as chairman and CEO, is already the number one steel maker in the world.

Pharmaceuticals is the leading knowledge-intensive industry with wide-ranging capabilities in manufacturing and R&D. Leading companies, such as Argenta Pharma or Ranbaxy, are shifting away from pure generic business and embarking on ambitious international strategies.

Software and business process outsourcing (BPO) services also play an important role in the national economy. Today, they are India's most globally competitive sectors.

India's corporate world is a mix of old companies, established during the colonial period, and of newcomers that have emerged since independence.

Administrative Divisions and Regional Development

India consists of 28 states (and seven territories) and, in parallel with democracy at the national level, state governments are elected directly. Within the states the administrative units are districts. Their total number is over 600. The states are very different from one another in terms of population, territory, language, and economic development.

Overall, the southern and western states are doing better economically and socially. Large-scale industries are highly concentrated in the states of Maharashtra, West Bengal, Gujarat, and Tamil Nadu. Within these states the industries are further concentrated in a few large cities, such as Mumbai, Kolkata, and Chennai. Information technology (IT) companies are mainly found in the cities of Bangalore, in Karnataka state, and Hyderabad, in Andhra Pradesh state. Bangalore is also the center of the defense industry and the location of the most prestigious public research institutions. Hyderabad is a major center for pharmaceuticals. Initiatives such as Genome Valley, Fab City, and the Nano-Technology Park are aimed at boosting the biotechnology and nanotechnology sectors.

The richest states are Maharashtra (which includes the city of Mumbai), Punjab, Gujarat, Tamil Nadu, and Haryana with per-capita GDP between 17,000 and 14,000 rupees. Mumbai is the commercial and entertainment center of India, generating 5 percent of GDP and accounting for 25 percent of industrial output, 40 percent of maritime trade, 33 percent of tax revenues, and 70 percent of capital transactions. It is home to such important financial institutions as the Reserve Bank of India (RBI), the Bombay Stock Exchange (BSE), the National Stock Exchange of India (NSE), and the corporate headquarters of many domestic and foreign-owned companies. The city is also famous for its film and television industry.

The income gap between the richest states and the poorest ones, such as Assam, Jharkhand, Mizoram, or Manipur, is around 10 to 1. Almost all states enjoyed economic growth during the 1990s but the gap widened because the rich states grew much more rapidly than the poor ones (Ahluwahlia, Montek S., 2000).

Postwar Development

The Command Economy

India fell under British colonial rule in the eighteenth century and after almost 200 years became independent in 1947. The new nation's economic structure was outdated and its manufacturing sector was weak (Ahluwahlia, Isher, 1995). Large merchant houses were more interested in making money on trading and lending than investing in heavy industry with its long payback periods. The banking sector was more concerned with commerce than industry. There was no securities market. The development of modern companies and entrepreneurship was stifled.

During the early post-independence years, India's economic record was lackluster, in terms of growth, and weak, in terms of income distribution and poverty alleviation. Growth rates were well below the level of other less-developed economies during this period.

The pre-reform era before the mid-1980s is associated with a centrally planned economy. To proceed toward orderly economic and social development, India's first prime minister, Jawaharlal Nehru, advocated the adoption of a Soviet-style five-year planning system. Technology was considered the key to improving the Indian economy.

India did not become like the Soviet Union, though. A number of large private companies played an important role, although the government strictly regulated their investments and entries into new business areas. Based on the import-substitution principle, the whole economic system had a strong focus on self-sufficiency coupled with skepticism about inward foreign direct investment (FDI) (Khandwalla 2002). Indians were encouraged to buy made-in-India goods, while the consumption of imported products was discouraged by regulations and high duty rates.

Progress in Technology and Production

From the 1960s, efforts were made to mobilize foreign aid and technology for basic industries, agriculture, and technical education. The Soviet bloc countries helped India to build up its heavy industry sharing expertise in steel production, aircraft, tanks, and other military production technology. They also provided assistance to the oil, machinery, and power generation equipment sectors. With US support, India adopted high-yielding breeds, new pesticides, and agricultural implements. Consequently, by the late 1970s, the growth rate in agriculture rose to 3 percent a year, outpacing population growth for the first time since independence and facilitating a dramatic fall in rural poverty from 60 percent in the late 1960s to 40 percent in the late 1980s (Datt 2007).

Institutions of higher education in management, technology (engineering), and medicine also developed. A network of forty national R&D laboratories was created (Indiresan 2007). In 1967, the Electronics Corporation of India Limited (ECIL) was formed. Its strategy was to tie up with international companies for the local manufacture of computers and to increase the local value-added to the point of self-reliance. The same policy was followed in other sectors. It allowed India to enjoy respectable growth and to become 90 percent self-sufficient in capital goods by the late 1970s, mastering a range of sophisticated technologies (Das 2001).

The Low Efficiency of the Economic System

Yet, productivity in domestic industry remained low while costs were high. Indian-made computers, for example, had limited applications and were more expensive than foreign models. The emphasis on industrial goods and import substitution led to a substantial shortage of consumer goods.

Underdeveloped capital markets constrained the ability of companies to access risk capital from potential investors. Tough labor regulations made it difficult to lay-off employees when necessary and to recruit when needed, especially qualified personnel. The legal system needed for a market economy was almost nonexistent. Enforcement of contracts was also a problem (Virmani 2004).

Overall, the efficiency of the economic system was low. One of the major impediments was the policy of reserving production of certain items for small-scale enterprises. From the late 1970s, this covered about 800 items. Investment into plant and machinery at any individual production unit could not exceed US$250,000. Many of the reserved items, such as garments, shoes, and toys, had high export potential and the failure to permit production units with a larger scale of production and more modern equipment restricted India's export competitiveness (Ahluwahlia, Montek S., 2002).

The Start of Reforms

The mid-1980s marked the start of economic reforms aimed at deregulation, the reduction of state ownership and control, and the liberalizing of trade and foreign capital inflows.

Economic growth gradually accelerated to 5 percent a year in the second half of the 1980s, which was much faster than in the earlier decades. In the 1990s, it rose further, reaching 6 percent on average (Ministry of Finance 2001–02).

However, in 1990–91 India faced big problems with foreign-debt servicing and had to be rescued by the International Monetary Fund (IMF) and the World Bank. Also in 1990–91, the combined fiscal deficit of the central and state governments climbed to 9.4 percent of GDP and its reduction became a top priority (Ahluwahlia, Montek S., 2002).

Structural Reforms

Regulatory and Public Sector Reform

From the mid-1990s, the government embarked on more large-scale regulatory and public sector reforms, pressed by the IMF and the World Bank. The latter initiated a number of measures aimed at stabilization and structural adjustments: cuts in fiscal spending; deregulating production, investment, and prices; liberalizing cross-border flows of goods, services, technology, and capital; and gradual reduction of import duties. Licensing requirements for setting up or expanding businesses were eased. Unviable public sector firms were closed. Telecommunications and domestic airline services were opened to private companies, which now control about 75 percent of the market in both sectors.

To facilitate private R&D, the government introduced several programs to support utilization of imported technology; develop, demonstrate, and commercialize indigenous technology; and encourage technological entrepreneurs.

Loss-Making State Companies

In the "formal" sector of the economy, publicly-owned companies accounted for 38 percent of value added in 2006. Many of them are losing money, particularly at the state level. Their productivity and profitability are lower than in the private sector (McKinsey 2007).

The scale of privatization remains modest due to political constraints. Mostly, it is limited to sales of minority shares. The state retains a big stake in banks, insurance, coal, and electricity companies.

Tough regulations remain. For instance, though today most banks have private shareholders and private banking is progressing, the central bank, the Reserve Bank of India (RBI), retains control over lending activities—banks can only freely extend 41 percent of their loans (OECD 2007).

The Need for Financial Reform

With its extremely wide range of cultures and diverse economic structures India represents a set of different regional markets. This is reinforced by the strong influence of state governments on taxation and investment rules, as well as the "internal tariffs" they impose on goods and services. Reforms of public finance and tax are necessary to create a "real" single national market. Despite a degree of national sharing of tax revenues, gaps in public revenues and expenses among the states are widening.

The Pro-Reform Drive of the Business Community

Dynamic Indian companies, both old and new, are keen to curb the regulatory powers of the bureaucracy and bring about significant tax reduction, especially on imported intermediate and capital goods. They also want higher institutional security in terms of contract enforcement, better property registration, and stronger fiscal discipline. For their part, would-be start-up entrepreneurs want to be able to create a company faster, at a lower cost, and with less red tape. They are also pushing for the easing of restrictions on foreign collaborations and a faster and wider liberalization of capital markets.

For a long time, old business groups, such as Tata or Birla, were taking advantage of the informal linkages with the political establishment. This provided easy access to sources of finance, irrespective of the underdeveloped capital market. Today, the new generation of business leaders insists on strict implementation of clear rules and regulations.

In the 1980s, professional managers of new-wave companies (not family-owned) had already started to discuss corporate governance reforms with the government and took a number of initiatives in this regard. In 1996, the initiative propelled the Securities and Exchange Board of India (SEBI), the capital market regulatory authority, to introduce a statutory code to elevate the level of corporate governance to international standards.

Return on Equity

Since the mid-1990s Indian companies have been providing one of the highest returns on equity (ROE) in Asia. In 2006, ROE in India was about 21 percent, compared with 9 percent in China (McKinsey 2007). Private investors and venture capital, both domestic and foreign, showed growing interest in such sectors as technology consulting, healthcare, food, real estate, travel, jewelry, and animation. Usually, they acquire a 10–30 percent stake. The younger generation of India's family businessmen is showing a positive attitude to such investments as they bring not only cash but also valuable expertise and help to establish strategic global partnerships.

Present Performance

New Economic Strength

In the 2000s, growth rates increased remarkably (see Table 19.1). Private consumption has been robust and capital investment has been expanding very fast, with its ratio to GDP on the rise. Exports have expanded but imports have followed suit and the trade balance remains in the red.

Table 19.1 Main economic indicators (real annual growth, %)*

Indicator	1999	2000	2001	2002	2003	2004	2005	2006	2007
GDP	6.4	4.4	5.8	3.8	8.5	7.5	9.4	9.6	8.7
Agriculture**	2.7	-0.2	6.3	-7.2	10.0	0.0	5.9	3.8	2.6
Industry**	4.6	6.4	2.7	7.1	7.4	10.3	10.1	11.0	8.9
Services**	9.5	5.7	7.2	7.5	8.5	9.1	10.3	11.1	10.7
Gross domestic capital formation	20.6	-3.5	-2.9	17.0	19.9	19.5	19.4	10.9	16.0
Private consumption	6.1	3.2	6.1	2.7	5.8	5.2	8.7	7.1	6.8
Consumer prices	4.7	4.0	3.8	4.3	3.8	3.8	4.2	6.2	6.3
Exports (billions of rupees), fob	1,595.6	2,035.7	2,090.2	2,551.4	2,933.7	3,753.4	4,454.6	5,717.8	6,254.7
Imports (billions of rupees), cif	2,152.4	2,308.7	2,452.0	2,972.1	3,591.1	5,010.7	6,604.1	8,405.1	9,491.3
Exchange rate (millions of rupees per US$1)	43.1	44.9	47.2	48.6	46.6	45.3	44.1	45.3	41.3

Source: ADB: Key Indicators 2008; National Council for Applied Economic Research (NCAER); United Nations Public Administration Network (UNPAN).
*Fiscal year, beginning April 1.
**Data for agriculture, industry, and services refers to value added.

Real per-capita income (in 2007 US dollars and adjusted for PPP) increased from US$917 in 1980 to US$2,534 in 2007 (Cox 2008). Today, India has the largest number of listed companies in the world. In December 2007, the total value of stock, listed on the BSE, reached US$1.79 trillion (BSE Web site 2008).

Also, the country has emerged as the world's fastest wealth creator. In 2006, it boasted the largest number of billionaires in Asia—36, collectively valued at US$191 billion—and also had more than one million millionaires. The emerging middle class not only actively participates in consumer market development but has also given birth to a new cohort of entrepreneurs. According to the National Council of Applied Economic Research (NCAER), in 2005, the number of people belonging to the middle class (households with an annual income of US$5,000–30,000) was about 100 million.

Economic growth has also translated into improvements in social indicators—such as reduced poverty and mortality rates and higher literacy levels.

On the negative side, the budget deficit remains high by international standards, though it dropped from 10 percent of GDP in 2001 to 7.5 percent in 2006. The government's target for the next 20 years is 5–6 percent (Ministry of Finance 2006–07). More significant reductions are unlikely because a wide range of state companies continue to be subsidized and important vested interests are involved.

Unemployment is increasing. On the basis of current daily status (the unemployed average in a particular reference week), during the reference period (from 1993–94 to 2004–05), unemployment rates for males increased from 5.6 percent to 8 percent in rural areas and from 6.7 percent to 7.5 percent in urban areas. Similarly, unemployment rates for female workers increased from 5.6 percent to 8 percent in rural areas and from 10.5 percent to 11.6 percent in urban areas (Ministry of Finance 2007).

Poverty Remains High

In spite of all the progress made, a very large segment of India's population is still excluded from a decent human life. It cannot be denied, however, that the number of people living below the poverty line is rapidly declining. Households across the income spectrum are improving their living standards. In 2004, the poverty rate was about 22 percent (UNDP 2006).

There is still a long way to go. Successive governments have under-emphasized the development of basic living infrastructure—schools, hospitals, and rural medical centers, water supply systems, and other facilities.

Some failures are huge, such as continuing undernourishment, particularly of children. Forty-seven percent of Indian children under the age of five are either malnourished or stunted (UNDP 2007). Also, child labor continues to plague the country. India accounts for one-quarter of the world's child labor population.

On the public health front, there are more people in India with HIV than anywhere else in the world (UNDP 2006). It also has the largest slum population. In Mumbai, half of the population lives in slums, largely due to massive migration from rural areas and skyrocketing real-estate prices (Dutz 2007).

Competitiveness: Achievements and Problems

India's leading companies are rapidly becoming full-fledged global players, but overall many of the basic factors needed for international competitiveness are still not present.

For instance, the country has one of the lowest percentages of computer users in the world. Only 0.7 percent of the population has computer access as opposed to 2.8 percent in China (World Bank 2005).

India's engineering schools are among the best in the world but it still has a lot to do to upgrade the technological and managerial capabilities of company people. BPO and software successes have been built on deregulation in the telecommunication sector, falling technology costs, and human resources availability. It is not enough anymore. Competition in the low-cost IT segment from Brazil, Malaysia, Vietnam, and East European countries is growing. The Indian IT industry may be in trouble if it does not create a sustainable competitive advantage based on higher value-added products and services, rather than just adding more people to address the tasks.

A Growth Opportunity and Human Resource Constraints

By 2030, India is expected to overtake China as the most populous country in the world. Annual population growth has slowed from the 1.93 percent per year during the 1990s, to an average of 1.63 percent in 2002–07. It is projected to fall further to an average of 1.41 percent in 2007–12 and to 1.2 percent in 2012–17 (Census of India 2001). Nevertheless, it remains high by international standards. For instance, China's expected average population growth rate for the period between 2000 and 2020 is 0.8 percent (Dutz 2007).

In the next 20 years or so, India's dependency ratio, that is, the ratio of the economically dependent part of the population to its productive part (the economically dependent part includes, generally, individuals under 15 and over 65) will drop. This ratio is important because its increase strains the productive part, which has to spend more money and time on the upbringing of children and support for the elderly. In India, the child dependency ratio will fall from 65 percent in 1985 to 36 percent in 2025 (Datt 2007). All this opens up an excellent growth opportunity.

Yet, rapid population growth is a double-edged sword—it also amplifies pressure on strained infrastructure and healthcare and education systems. A growth opportunity can materialize only if India is able to properly educate its growing population and if its labor markets prove to be flexible enough to absorb new entrants. At present, the existence of elite engineering schools cannot hide the fact that the university system is underperforming. Indian universities have no money and many of them are unable to provide a decent level of tertiary education to young people from middle-class families (Indiresan 2007).

To provide a sustained supply of knowledge workers, a more relevant education system has to be developed, starting from primary school. About 40 million children, aged from 6 to 15, do not go to school. Furthermore, in 2006, the school enrollment ratio declined (UNDP 2006). Despite some improvement, public expenditure on education is inadequate—in 2002–04 total expenditure comprised 3.3 percent of GDP as opposed to the 6 percent target (UNDP 2006). The level of education at public schools has deteriorated over the past decades. In 2005, expenditure on tertiary education amounted to 0.85 percent of GDP, about half the level of most emerging-market countries.

Access to education and career opportunities for women has improved but big interregional gaps remain. In many parts of the country, discrimination is still firmly in place. About half of all Indian women remain illiterate (Census of India 2001).

India's constitution bluntly states that the government should practice social engineering to uplift the "backward" castes. However, Indian politics has become so obsessed with present or even past discrimination issues that "reverse discrimination" has emerged, creating obstacles for economic development (Indiresan 2007). The priority access to energy and water given to poor farmers constrains their supply to industry, hindering job creation. Likewise, many jobs in industry, the civil service, and academia are reserved for people from low castes, irrespective of whether or not they have relevant skills (Indiresan 2007).

Employment Problems

Huge migration from rural to urban areas poses acute employment problems. To accommodate the migrants, India cannot rely only on services. Historically, no Asian nation has achieved economic success without promoting export-oriented, labor-intensive manufacturing. The latter allows poor but labor-abundant countries to specialize in labor-intensive products, effectively using limited capital. India cannot skip this stage either. However, insufficient effort to upgrade secondary education limits the number of workers having the basic skills needed to work in industry.

About ten million Indians enter the labor market every year. However, the number of employees in the organized manufacturing sector is only seven million. Tight labor regulations (especially regarding lay-offs) discourage employment.

Services-Driven Growth

As mentioned, unlike most East Asian countries, where economic growth was indivisible from industrialization, India's growth is services-driven. The services sector leads in terms of market liberalization, technological change, and access to well-educated human resources (World Bank 2006).

In industry, the picture is more complicated. Some manufacturing sectors, such as pharmaceuticals and the auto industry, are growing quite fast. Overall, during 1992–2003, growth in manufacturing averaged 6.8 percent per annum, and in 2003–06 it accelerated to 8.5 percent (Ministry of Finance 2007). However, China's industrial growth is 1.5 times higher.

In the 1980s, under Prime Minister Rajiv Gandhi, economic reforms were launched, centered on the electronics industry, including consumer electronics and software. Technology trade was liberalized, paving the way for imports of key components and technology as well as software exports.

The new government policy underlined the importance of comprehensive development of the software sector for both domestic and export markets. Computerization of all government departments and enterprises generated large-scale demand. The government also involved the private sector to expand and upgrade the telecommunication industry. Bangalore was turned into a major base for partnerships between domestic firms and foreign multinationals. The emphasis on software, which is not a capital-intensive sector, made it possible to grow without a rapid rise in capital formation.

In the service industries, where deregulation progressed—telecommunications, portfolio management, and IT—domestic sales and exports have increased fast. While in the 1990s and early 2000s growth was driven mostly by IT-related services and offshoring, in the second half of the 2000s several new sectors showing double-digit growth rates have emerged—aviation, entertainment, real-estate development, financial services, medical tourism, and hospitality.

As the services sector pays the highest wages, its expansion boosted household incomes and stimulated consumption. India is less dependent on exports than other emerging Asian countries as it has such a large home market.

Agriculture and the Rural Economy

As mentioned, growth in agriculture has been picking up since the late 1960s. Growth rates, between 1980 and 1992, averaged 3.2 percent (Ministry of Finance 2006). It was boosted by the green revolution, which significantly raised yields. However, big productivity gaps remained between regions and farms of different sizes. Overall, modernization was sluggish. The living standards gap between cities and the countryside remains considerable.

In 1992–2003, agricultural growth decelerated to an average of 2.4 percent and in 2003–06 to 1.2–1.3 percent (Ministry of Finance 2007). The trend is common for all crops and probably reflects a deceleration in productivity growth. The agricultural economy is still backward and yields in most states are low. Rice production per hectare is lower than in Myanmar. The land is very fragmented. Farmers are heavily indebted.

To solve the agricultural crisis, the government launched large-scale infrastructure development projects. Efforts have been made to provide low-cost inputs, introduce innovative logistics, and support grassroots innovation. Encouraged by the government's effort to bring about the second green revolution, companies have started to conclude direct agreements with farmers to grow specific high-quality crops and provide technical know-how and related services.

One more important direction for the modernization of the rural economy, and also a way to create jobs, is the development of nonagricultural sectors. Today, services and industry combined comprise 54 percent of the rural value-added. Thirty-seven percent of factories are located in rural areas, employing 41 percent of organized industrial workers (McKinsey 2007).

The Impact of the Global Financial Turmoil

The direct effect of the global financial crisis on India's banking sector was negligible, largely because it is still dominated by state-owned banks (consequently, there was no crisis of bankers' confidence). In addition, the RBI maintains strict regulations and adheres to conservative policies. Indian banks are well-capitalized, their nonperforming loans (NPLs) ratio is low and the capital adequacy ratio is high—in the 10–20 percent range (Kundu 2008).

The main problem is falling foreign investor confidence—especially as India belongs to the group of Asian countries that are most strongly dependent on external financing. From January to November 2008, foreign investors withdrew US$13.5 billion from India's stock market and the benchmark Sensex index plunged by 57 percent (AP 2008). Foreign banks squeezed their loans.

The growing outflow of capital brought about a steep depreciation of the rupee. In October 2008, it breached the 50 rupees for US$1 mark, while on April 1, the rate was 39.9 rupees for US$1 (Kundu 2008). To support the currency, the authorities embarked on massive sales of US dollars and other foreign exchange (in October net sales of foreign exchange in the spot market hit US$7.6 billion (Kundu 2008), which largely offset the effect of the measures taken by the central bank to inject more liquidity into the economy.

Capital outflows and the overseas lending squeezes prompted Indian corporations to rely more on the loans extended by domestic banks. Yet, in the second half of 2008, although the latter were rising around 30 percent year-on-year, businesses still complained of the credit crunch (Kundu 2008).

In the July-September quarter, the annualized economic growth rate was 7.6 percent—the slowest pace since the last quarter of 2004 (Bloomberg 2008). Export-oriented sectors, the production of consumer goods, and infrastructure-related industries slowed down most. On the other hand, the services sector retained growth dynamics, and some of its sectors, such as IT, education, and organized retail, were growing at 10–20 percent (Indiapcwire.com 2008). Overall, domestic demand helped to sustain growth. For the 2008–09 financial year (April 1, 2008–March 31, 2009) estimates predict growth of around 7 percent. Government sources were upbeat about the prospects for the 2009–10 financial year, anticipating, as of January 2009, a 7.5 percent growth. Most private forecasters expected a further slowdown (*International Business Times* 2008), and so did the IMF.

As the economy was cooling off, the annual inflation rate (measured as growth of wholesale prices) came down to below 6 percent in January 2009, from its peak of 12.9 percent in August 2008, (Financial Express 2009).

To stimulate credit, in October, for the first time in four years, the RBI cut the repo rate, at which it lends to commercial banks, from 9 percent to 7.5 percent and in December, again to 6.5 percent. Reserve requirements for commercial banks were drastically reduced to 5.5 percent. The RBI also raised limits imposed on foreign borrowing by private companies (external commercial borrowing (ECB)).

A large budget deficit limited the room for fiscal stimulus measures. However, in December, the government announced an extra US$4 billion of spending for the 2008–09 financial year and pledged to increase expenditure in 2009–10.

The US$4 billion package included value-added tax cuts, additional allocations for export promotion (including labor-intensive exports, such as textiles and handicrafts), and infrastructure projects. There was also support for small businesses and relief for people who have to pay back housing loans.

Foreign Trade

India's share in the world trade of goods and services remains insignificant—around 1 percent in 2006 (Dutz 2007).

The main imports, in the 2007–08 financial year, were oil and oil products (33.4 percent of the total), electronic products (8.5 percent), general machinery (8.2 percent), gold and silver (7.5 percent), steel (3.4 percent), and transport machinery (3.4 percent). The largest exporters to the Indian market were China (11.4 percent), Saudi Arabia (8.1 percent), United Arab Emirates (5.6 percent), the United States (5.5 percent), Iran (4.6 percent), Switzerland (4.1 percent), Germany (4.0 percent), and Singapore (3.4 percent).

Between 2003 and 2007, the volume of merchandised exports almost doubled (see Table 19.1) although they still equal only 28 percent of GDP as opposed to 41 percent in China. The most important export items were oil and oil products (15.6 percent), textiles and clothing (12.0 percent), general machinery (5.5 percent), transport machinery (4.4 percent), and metal products (4.4 percent) (JETRO 2008a). The export of services roughly equals the exports of goods (Chauvin and Lemoine 2004). Among them, exports of IT-related services are growing especially fast.

Unlike China, foreign-affiliated companies do not currently play the leading role as exporters. However, there are plans to create Chinese-style special economic zones (Special Economic Zone Act of 2005) that would welcome export-oriented FDI (Ministry of Finance 2006).

The country is becoming increasingly integrated into East Asian production chains, most of all in such key knowledge-based segments as R&D and product design.

India used to be a high-tariff country until the beginning of the 1990s. For some products the tariff rates were in the range of 150–170 percent with an average close to 70 percent (Planning Commission 2000). To stop or slow down imports, the government also widely used anti-dumping procedures. Agriculture-related tariffs remain in the range of 30–40 percent but industrial and services sectors are now almost as open as in China.

Over the next two decades, India's attractiveness as an export market will increase rapidly. According to McKinsey, the annual real-income growth per household is expected to accelerate from 2.8 percent over the last two decades (1985–2005) to 3.6 percent over the next two decades (2005–25). Today, India is the twelfth–largest consumer market in the world. By 2025, it is expected to be in the top five and equal that of Germany. However, per-capita spending will still be very modest by international standards—about the same as in today's Egypt (McKinsey 2007).

At the top, the rise of India's rich is noticeable. The world's luxury brand makers, such as Gucci, Cartier, and Louis Vuitton, are targeting India as one of their major stops. In 2006, the upscale, premium, and luxury market hit US$15.6 billion (Technopak 2006).

Rural markets may open new opportunities too. More and more companies are targeting the "Bottom of the Pyramid (BOP)" markets. The most well-known examples are Procter & Gamble and Hindustan Unilever Limited who both sell packaged consumer goods. Nestle and Britannia are selling small chocolate and biscuit packages for about two cents each.

FDI and the Business Environment

Rules

In most sectors, 100 percent foreign ownership is allowed automatically. However, in some areas, such as banking, insurance, print media, broadcasting, and tele-communication, there are caps varying from 24 percent to 74 percent. In these industries, FDI proposals are examined under the regulatory framework of the Foreign Exchange Management Act (FEMA) enacted in 1999. The institution in charge is the Foreign Investment Promotion Board (FIPB), part of the Department of Economic Affairs at the Ministry of Finance. Another organization, the Foreign Investment Implementation Board (FIIB), is responsible for implementation at state level (Ministry of Commerce and Industry 2008).

One of the sectors difficult for investors is retailing, the country's second-largest employer after agriculture. Its growth potential has already attracted international retailers, such as Wal-Mart, Starbucks, Marks & Spencer, Tesco, Metro AG, and Liberty International, as well as South Africa's biggest food retailer Shoprite Holdings and Singapore-based CapitaLand. Yet, as there are about six million small retail shops all over the country, political opposition to complete liberalization of FDI remains strong. State governments retain the right to allow or disallow the setting up of a retail establishment.

Single-brand retailers such as The Body Shop are not permitted to invest more than 49 percent and have to establish joint ventures with local companies. No FDI is allowed in multibrand retailing.

The Scale and Composition of Inward FDI

Overall, the growth of inward FDI has dramatically accelerated since the second half of the 2000s (see Table 19.2). Prospects for the following years are good.

According to the Ministry of Commerce and Industry, in the calendar year of 2007, 18.0 percent of the total amount of inward FDI went into the service sector (primarily financial services), 12.6 percent into computer hardware and software-related sectors, 7.9 percent into housing and real estate, 6.6 percent into construction, 5.6 percent into the telecommunications sector, and 3.1 percent into electrical machinery. As far as composition by country is concerned,

Table 19.2   Inflow of FDI* (US$ millions)

Financial year	2000	2001	2002	2003	2004	2005	2006**	2007**
Inward FDI	4,029	6,130	5,035	4,322	6,051	8,961	22,079	32,475

Source: Reserve Bank of India, 2008.
*Balance of Payments Basis—Includes equity capital as well as reinvested earnings (retained profits of FDI companies) and "other capital" (debt transactions between related entities). Financial Year: April 1–March 31.
**Preliminary.

40.3 percent of the total came from Mauritius. The share of Singapore was 7.6 percent, the US 4.6 percent, the Netherlands 3.6 percent, Japan 3.5 percent, and the UK 2.5 percent (JETRO 2008b). The high percentage of FDI from Mauritius, made by investors of various national origins, is explained by the agreement with that country, which has a very liberal tax system, to avoid double taxation (Ministry of Commerce and Industry 2008).

FDI is heavily concentrated in a few megacities, especially Mumbai, Delhi, Bangalore, Chennai, and Hyderabad. At the state level, the main recipients for FDI are Andhra Pradesh, Gujarat, Karnataka, Maharashtra, and Tamil Nadu, where the investment climate is better (Stern 2001). Investors perceived a cost difference between states up to 30 percent depending on the availability of infrastructure and the quality of governance (Ahluwahlia, Montek S. 2002).

Over 100 multinational companies, including GE, General Motors, Intel, Texas Instruments, Microsoft, and IBM, have set up R&D operations in India.

Impediments

One of the major impediments to investment is infrastructure. Many regions suffer from electricity and water supply interruptions due to inadequate distribution facilities. Demand for electricity constantly exceeds its supply.

India has one of the highest electricity costs among major emerging economies— US$0.80 per kwh for industry against US$0.10 in China. The reason is, not least, the highest level of transmission and distribution losses in the world—about 25 percent of gross electricity output (Datt 2007).

Transportations costs are also a burden. They account for 25 percent of total import costs as opposed to only 10 percent in comparable countries.

The labor market remains tightly regulated despite the reforms. Permanent employment contract requirements are strict. Public authorization is still required to lay off even one worker in manufacturing companies with more than 100 employees (Panagariya 2002). In the public sector, nationwide industry-level bargaining is common in core industries, such as coal, steel, banking, insurance, and ports. In the private sector, industry-level bargaining on a regional scale is usual for industries such as textiles, plantations, and engineering. Professional managers, representing the Confederation of Indian Industry (CII), negotiate regional and industry-based agreements for its member companies (Kuruvilla 1996). Ever since the 1980s, private companies have been trying various new approaches to cope with the restrictive labor legislation.

324 Asia's Turning Point

Table 19.3 Monthly salary per occupation (US$)

Occupation	US$
General manager	8,000
Division manager	3,000
Factory manager	3,000
Section manager	1,800
Factory engineer	1,000
Secretary	1,000
Service engineer	620
Employee	600
Line worker	300

Source: *Mizuho Global View*, 2008.

The rising turnover of workers and growing labor costs may also pose a problem. The demand for skilled laborers exceeds supply and job-hopping is on the rise. Many companies have to deal with turnover rates as high as 70 percent.

Since 2000, Indian workers have enjoyed very high annual salary increases—12–14 percent in nominal terms and 7–9 percent in real terms (Hewitt Associates 2006). In the IT sector, during the last decade (1995–2005) wages were growing 20–30 percent a year. In 2000–05, IT engineers' wages quadrupled (Oxford Analytica, November 14, 2005). Intel now recruits engineers in Vietnam, saying that there is no reason to employ Indian engineers anymore as their salaries are as high as those in the United States. Well-paid jobs are no longer limited to the IT industry. Other sectors—financial services, retail, and hospitality—are also bidding them up as they have to employ higher-skilled laborers to respond to the growing affluence and requirements of consumers. Examples of current average monthly salaries are given in Table 19.3.

Outward FDI

India's outward FDI began to grow fast from 2006 (see Table 19.4). In April–December 2007, it exceeded US$18 billion. Big deals, such as the acquisition of Arcelor by Mittal Steel and Corus Group by Tata Steel, have increased the profile of cross-border mergers and acquisitions (M&A) activities by Indian companies. A number of Indian firms have embarked on cross-border acquisitions to tap new overseas markets, buy brands, and access niche technologies.

Indian companies (including small ones) often acquire high-tech start-ups in such areas as clinical research, bio-equivalence, and data management. Also, they are becoming increasingly active in the exploration and development of overseas natural resources. As a result, in a wide range of sectors from oil exploration to

Table 19.4   The amount of outward FDI (US$ millions, approval basis)

Financial year	2003	2004	2005	2006	2007 (April–December)
Amount of outward FDI	1,466.3	2,804.3	2,854.8	15,060.0	18,437.3

Source: India Onestop.com, 2008. (http://www.indiaonestop.com/FDI/outwardfdiflow.htm).

mining, India and China compete with each other in such places as Zambia, West Africa, and Latin America.

Along with M&A, Indian companies are fostering cross-border strategic alliances. For example, Ranbaxy formed an alliance with the US multinational Eli Lilly in the pharmaceutical business (Kedia 2006). Outward FDI in R&D is also on the increase. Tata Consultancy Services (TCS), the largest Indian exporter of computer services, has opened 19 R&D centers all over the world.

In the April–December 2007 period, 43.3 percent went into manufacturing, 9.5 percent into nonfinancial services, and 3.5 percent into trading (India Onestop.com 2008).The biggest recipients were Singapore (37 percent), the Netherlands (26 percent), and the British Virgin Islands (8 percent) (Rediff News 2008).

Concluding Remarks

India is a democracy run by coalition governments, representing constituencies with diverging agenda. Not surprisingly, the reform process in the country is slow. Nevertheless, the cumulative change it has brought about is remarkable. Parties which opposed the reforms when they were in opposition, vote for many of them when they come to power. In West Bengal or Kerala, local Communist parties are showing readiness to open their doors to FDI. A number of trade unions are ready to accept compromises and more labor market flexibility.

State governments are becoming more pragmatic. The states actively attracting domestic and foreign investment and supporting entrepreneurs are in much better economic shape than others. They have more liberal legislation and a much better record of enforcing the rule of law. The message is quite clear for everyone.

Competition has spread to a widening range of sectors and industries. If and where this is not the case, be it the utilities or education, more often than not the private sector's presence is becoming more visible too.

The reforms have entered the stage where vested interests are threatened more directly than ever before. The stakes are getting higher every day. Thus, the political will to continue the reforms and the consolidation of pro-reform forces will become increasingly important.

The key competitive advantage of India is the youth of its population. Whether this advantage is made to work or not, will largely depend on the country's success in improving education, infrastructure, and governance at corporate, state, and national levels.

20

Japan: Forgotten Giant

A Few Basics

Japan's population of 128 million is the third largest in East Asia after China and Indonesia. In terms of nominal gross domestic product (GDP) the national economy remains the second largest in the world after the US. By GDP (purchasing power parity (PPP)) Japan ranks third—between China and India. In 2007, according to the International Monetary Fund (IMF), in terms of per-capita GDP (PPP), it ranked twenty-fourth, below Germany and above France.

The main islands of Japan are Hokkaido, Honshu (the biggest island where Tokyo and most other major cities are located), Shikoku, Kyushu, and Okinawa. Administratively, the country is divided into 47 prefectures. The geographical (not administrative) regions are Hokkaido, Tohoku, Koshinetsu, Kanto (including Tokyo), Hokuriku, Tokai (including Nagoya), Kinki (also called Kansai, and including Osaka plus the two ancient capitals of Kyoto and Nara), Chugoku, Shikoku, Kyushu, and Okinawa. The population and economic activities are very highly concentrated in the Kanto region (Tokyo, Kanagawa, Chiba, and Saitama prefectures account for more than one-third of the total population). In relative terms, the north and the very south are lagging behind in their economic development, and the Sea of Japan coastal region is less developed than the Pacific coast.

Japan does not have significant mineral resources. On the industrial front, the country maintains an almost full set of manufacturing and service sectors, though the role and share of textiles and other light industries have been declining over time, while those of electrical, transportation, general and precision machinery, production of new materials (like optical and carbon fibers), and biotechnology are growing. The services sector is also becoming increasingly important. Today, the country's economic strategy emphasizes the role of manufacturing and services as equally important "twin engines" of growth (METI 2006). Agricultural production retains its importance in terms of both food supply and the preservation of rural communities and culture. However, the majority of farms are small scale (with the exception of the northern island of Hokkaido the average area of cultivated land is less than 2.5 acres). The food self-sufficiency ratio is low.

As of 2006, the share of agriculture in the GDP was 1.5 percent, manufacturing 21.0 percent, construction 6.3 percent, wholesale and retail trade 13.8 percent, finance and insurance 7.0 percent, real estate 12.0 percent, and services 21.5 percent (MIC 2008b, 151). The share of primary industry in the total number of persons employed was 4.3 percent, secondary 27.0 percent, and tertiary 67.7 percent (MIC 2008a).

Major Japanese corporations—Toyota, Nissan, or Honda in the auto industry; Sony, Fujitsu, Matsushita (whose name has recently been changed to Panasonic), Hitachi, or NEC in electrical goods; Canon in precision machinery; Mitsukoshi and Isetan (recently merged by forming a joint holding) in retailing; NTT Docomo in mobile telephony; and many others—are well known all over the world, as are the biggest banks, especially Mitsubishi Tokyo UFJ, Sumitomo Mitsui, and Mizuho. Yet, the strength of the Japanese economy is also rooted in the exceptional capabilities of a pool of technologically advanced small- and medium-sized manufacturers, who often lead world markets in particular products.

For just one example out of many, let us take Chuetsu region at the center of Niigata Prefecture in northern Honshu. Within this tiny territory, around the cities of Sanjo and Tsubame Sanjo, we find a cohort of technologically advanced and innovative SMEs. For instance, Tsubamex, engaged in the production of mold models (prototypes which produce objects) and auto parts, was the first company in the industry to introduce a three-dimensional CAD-CAM system to speed up product development and raise its quality. It also developed a new technology for the processing of magnesium.

Nagata Seiki, one of the world's leading producers of knitting machinery, also offers state-of-the-art surface modification/thin film technologies. Snow Peak is a producer of outdoor goods (especially for dedicated hikers, anglers, and mountain climbers) popular not only in Japan, but also in Asia, the US, and Europe. It developed the world's smallest gas stove (you can put it into your pocket)—a great gadget for hikers.

Japan is a constitutional monarchy and a mature parliamentary democracy. However, the Liberal Democratic Party has rarely relinquished its position of ruling party since 1955, when it was formed (with the exception of a very short period in the early 1990s). At present, it governs in coalition with the New Komeito Party, the political arm of the influential Buddhist organization, Soka Gakkai.

The major economic agency in Japan is the Ministry of Economy, Trade and Industry (METI). It is responsible for articulating economic strategies and for all issues related to external economic relations, including foreign investment. Other major economy-related agencies include: the Ministry of Finance; the Ministry of Health, Labor and Welfare; the Ministry of Internal Affairs and Communications; the Ministry of Land, Infrastructure, Transport and Tourism; the Ministry of Education, Culture, Sports, Science and Technology; and the Ministry of the Environment. The Council on Economic and Fiscal Policy, chaired by the prime minister, with both key ministers and private sector experts as members, is consultative body, articulating policies regarding structural reforms and fiscal management.

Postwar Development

Postwar Reconstruction and the Three Reforms

In 1945, after defeat in World War II, Japan embarked on postwar reconstruction under the administrative control of the Allied forces' General Headquarters (GHQ), the US playing the leading role. Reforms carried out at that time were also mostly initiated by Americans. The following three reforms were particularly important.

First, large financial–industrial groups, called *zaibatsu* (such as Mitsui, Mitsubishi, Sumitomo, and Yasuda), with family-controlled holdings at the top, were dissolved. Second, a set of labor laws provided basic rights for employees, raised employment standards, and strengthened the bargaining power of labor unions. Third, agricultural reforms facilitated the transfer of land from landowners to farmers (the government bought land from landowners and resold it to farmers at a low price). This virtually put an end to tenancy in the countryside and made farmer households key players in the agricultural sector.

During 1945–49, the national economy began to recover, stimulated by government investments and loans. Massive government spending resulted in big budget deficits and strong inflationary pressure. GHQ demanded a shift to a deflationary policy and restoration of fiscal discipline.

The government complied, and tightening of fiscal and monetary policies was about to drag the economy into a contraction, when the Korean War (1950–53) began, bringing Japanese producers an unforeseen windfall—a big market for parts, materials, trucks, and repair services, as well as consumer goods and foodstuffs for the US-led United Nations forces. The economy entered a period of boom.

Rapid Growth and Heavy Industrialization

The post-Korean War pause was very short. From 1955, Japan entered an 18-year-long period of rapid growth, labeled "Japan's economic miracle," when the real GDP growth rate averaged almost 10 percent.

In the first half of the 1950s, textiles and other light industries still prevailed. The second half was marked by rapid heavy industrialization. Steel, shipbuilding, heavy machinery, and the chemical and petrochemical industries became the frontrunners, and in the early 1960s they were joined by the automotive, electronics, and precision machinery sectors.

From the mid-1960s, exports began exceeding imports and, in 1968, Japan became the second-largest economic power in the capitalist world.

Nonmanufacturing sectors were also expanding fast and undergoing rapid modernization. For example, the opening, in 1956, of the first supermarket, Kinokuniya, in Tokyo gave impetus to a revolution in the distribution industry, led by the big supermarket chains.

Rapid growth also generated a rise in household incomes and consumers did not think twice about taking their chances. A consumption rush was stimulated by massive purchases of key durable goods—refrigerators, washing and sewing machines, TVs, and later air conditioners and audio systems.

However, the downside of rapid industrialization was that it exacerbated environmental problems. Air pollution and water contamination reached critical levels.

The Role of the Government

The government, especially the Ministry of Trade and Industry (MITI) (now METI), played a key role in orchestrating growth through a set of industrial and macroeconomic policies. Modernization of particular industries was supported by various tax incentives (especially accelerated depreciation). From the early 1950s, the Financial Loans and Investment Program (FILP) was institutionalized as part of the national budget. It provided massive funding for a wide range of industries, sectors, and regions. Its scale reached about half the size of the budget's general account. The major sources of financing for the program were postal savings (Japan's postal savings network developed into the biggest financial institution in the world in terms of the volume of deposits), along with National Pension and Postal Insurance funds. The funds were transferred to the Trust Fund Bureau, an account run by the Ministry of Finance, and then either invested in the operations of public sector companies, mostly in the infrastructure and natural resources-related sectors, or lent to state-owned financial institutions (such as Development Bank of Japan (DBJ), Export-Import Bank, Japan Finance Corporation for Small and Medium Enterprise (JASME), Agriculture, Forestry and Fisheries Finance Corporation, and Housing Finance Corporation). The latter, in turn, extended preferential loans (at a lower interest and for a longer term than commercial loans) to the particular sectors and industries they were responsible for.

MITI closely guided private companies on matters such as volumes of investment and production, disposal of outdated equipment, and export-related activities. It also initiated a number of mergers and acquisitions (M&A) to boost Japan's international competitiveness.

The First Oil Shock and Beyond

Rapid growth was abruptly interrupted by the first oil shock in 1973. As the fourth Arab-Israeli war broke out, world oil prices quadrupled, hitting the Japanese economy hard due to its high dependency on oil imports, mostly from the Middle East. Severe stagflation resulted. In 1974, GDP fell by 0.4 percent for the first time in the postwar era. In 1975, consumer prices went up by 25 percent and wholesale prices by 33 percent.

However, Japan was very quick to get over the shock and, although, in the second half of the 1970s, growth rates halved to about 5 percent a year, the nation took large strides toward becoming a world leader in terms of production efficiency, quality of products, and the level of customer services. The decade was marked by a notable rise in the influence and role of the service sector.

Japan also became an indisputable world leader in such frontier areas as robotics, numerically controlled machine tools, and optical and carbon fibers. The rising competitiveness of leading manufacturing firms facilitated exports and large trade surpluses became a constant irritant in relations with the US and major West European countries.

To boost economic growth and stimulate domestic demand, in the second half of the decade, the government increased public works spending to unprecedented levels and the budget deficit surged.

The Slowdown of the Early 1980s

The second oil shock came in 1979–80, in the wake of the Iranian revolution and the onset of the Iran–Iraq War. Oil prices doubled. Its negative effect on the national economy was much smaller than that of the first shock—technological progress and the remaking of the industrial structure had made it much more oil shock-resistant. Still, growth rates at the beginning of the 1980s—around 3 percent—were low by Japanese standards of that time.

One major development was administrative–financial reform in the Reagan–Thatcher fashion, launched by Prime Minister Yasuhiro Nakasone. It was aimed at reducing the size of government and its role in the economy, as well as at balancing the budget. A privatization program was unveiled with the National Railways (Kokutetsu) and Nippon Telegraph and Telephone Public Corporation (Nippon Denshin Denwa Kosha) as the major targets. Both were privatized in the middle of the decade.

The Golden Years of the Japanese Economy

The acceleration of growth began again in 1984 and in the second half of the 1980s growth rates approached 5 percent once more. It was the time when Ezra Vogel's motto "Japan as number one" enjoyed popularity worldwide. While the US was fighting with stagnating productivity, falling competitiveness, low labor motivation of workers, and skyrocketing budget and current account deficits, and the status of West European economies was described as "Euro-sclerosis," steadily growing Japan was reaching new heights in productivity, product quality, and technological innovation. Besides, it had low inflation and unemployment rates, still tolerable budget deficits, and large trade and current account surpluses. "Learn from Japan" became a slogan in the US and Europe, not to mention Asia.

For Japan, a landmark event of the decade, reflecting and recognizing its unprecedented economic strength, was the signing of the Plaza Accord in September 1985 (the venue was the Plaza Hotel in New York). The finance ministers and heads of the central banks of the five leading developed nations (the US, Japan, West Germany, the UK, and France) agreed to jointly intervene in the currency markets to appreciate the yen and to depreciate the US dollar. In fact, it was an emergency step, aimed at rescuing the US economy, which was incapable of curbing soaring trade deficits. (In 1985, the trade deficit with Japan reached US$46 billion.) The average annual exchange rate of the yen against the US dollar went up from 200.6 yen for US\$1 in 1985 to 160.1 yen in 1986 and to 122.0 yen in 1987 (MIC 2008a).

Two post-Plaza Accord developments were especially significant for the Japanese economy. First, as a result of a very brisk appreciation of the yen exports stumbled, but only in the short term. From 1987, they surged again, reflecting a remarkable rise of Japan's non-price competitiveness: the goods it produced remained in demand due to their high quality and often uniqueness. The second major development was Japan's emergence as the world's leading financial power. Appreciation of the yen stimulated the country's outward investment, as the yen-denominated cost of everything Japanese investors were acquiring overseas dramatically decreased—be it real estate, labor force or other production inputs, and stocks or bonds.

In some sensational developments during those years, reflecting Japan's emergence as a major financial power house, Sony acquired Columbia Pictures, and the Rockefeller Group, the owner of Rockefeller Center and other office buildings in Manhattan, sold control of the company to Mitsubishi Estate.

Psychological tensions in the US, caused by Japan's rise, increased. For instance, there were incidents where gangs of vandals were destroying Japanese-made cars in some US cities. However, both the federal US government and individual US states were keen to promote Japanese foreign direct investment (FDI), which contributed much to America's growth and job creation.

The US, supported by Western Europe, was pressing Japan to stimulate domestic demand and raise imports. In response, the government launched an import promotion campaign (even the inscription on the luggage carts at Narita International Airport said "Import Now"). Though the economy was expanding fast, monetary policy was kept loose and public investment high.

The Bubble

The late 1980s will be remembered in Japan's economic history as the years of the bubble economy—a product of skyrocketing land and stock prices. Land prices soared as a consequence of the rush to construct factories, houses, and offices, especially in the Tokyo and Osaka areas. Among other things, demand for office space in Tokyo was burgeoning due to the growing role of Japan's capital as an international finance and business center. The rise in land prices looked endless and enormous speculative demand emerged.

Nearly all stock prices were increasing too, in anticipation of continuing economic growth. Stocks of practically any Japanese corporation were looked upon as a precious asset, investors not caring that much about checking the soundness of company management.

Those companies and individuals owning land or stock felt very confident about their financial status (whenever you need liquidity you can get it by selling land or stock at a high price) and this confidence (the "assets effect") bolstered the expansion of both investment and private consumption. In the business world, the word *zaitech* (financial technologies) became a popular term, meaning making money on aptly arranged transactions with land and other assets. Reliance on *zaitech* undermined incentives to raise the efficiency and profitability of the main business. Having plenty of cash at hand, companies saw no limits to expanding their investments and often diversified widely, sometimes including business sectors where they did not have strong capabilities.

For consumers it was an unprecedented boom time, marked by a quest for luxury. However, the widening gap between households which owned land and stock and those which did not questioned the sustainability of the middle class.

Though asset inflation was accelerating, the government did not divert from its loose monetary policy until the very end of the decade. Provided with easy access to liquidity, banks were extending large-scale loans, including ones for speculative real-estate transactions. Often, they did not bother to properly screen their borrowers as land and other real estate served as the loan collateral.

What were the reasons behind the government's tardy response to the asset bubble threat? Bureaucratic inefficiency and lack of political will? Maybe. The promise made to the US to boost domestic demand in order to expand imports? Definitely. However, there is one more reason—very important but rarely mentioned because vested interests were involved. The rising value of assets, prompted by the bubble, enriched people influential in the world of business and politics—including businessmen who were closely linked with politicians (in Japan the most deeply rooted image of such a businessman is the owner-manager of a construction firm).

Stock prices reached their peak in 1989 and land prices in 1990. Then, in early 1990, the bubble burst, and the economy was dragged into an unprecedented, long recession, which, with short breaks in 1995–96 and 2000, continued until 2002. Average growth rates in the 1990s, labeled "the lost decade," were only about 1 percent. The country became the slowest runner among the major developed economies.

"The Lost Decade"

In the late 1980s, the rise in land and stock prices stimulated both investment and consumption. In contrast, in the 1990s, falling prices brought about their squeeze. It was the "asset effect" with a minus sign.

Banks accumulated enormous nonperforming loans (NPLs), while deflated land, or other real estate, ceased to serve as relevant collateral. The disposal of NPLs required cost and time (mostly it was done through depreciation). Lending policy was fundamentally reconsidered and became ultra-conservative. It brought about a credit crunch, adversely affecting a wide range of industries, especially small- and medium-sized enterprises (SMEs). In 1998–99, the government injected public funds into large banks.

For their part, companies had to struggle with "excessive debts" (they had borrowed too much during the bubble years), "excessive production assets" (resulting from overinvestment), and "excessive employment" (the product of overexpansion). Large firms moved to sell off nonprofitable business units and focus on areas of core competence. Though avoiding American-style, large-scale lay-offs, Japanese companies drastically cut personnel in order to reduce labor costs. Encouraging early voluntary retirements, they squeezed the employment of new full-time workers, increasingly relying on part-timers and introducing fixed-term labor contracts.

From the very start of the recession, the government tried to boost growth through an unprecedented expansion of public works spending. As tax revenues were falling, it resulted in a skyrocketing budget deficit—the biggest among major developed nations. As, in 1995–96, comparatively high growth rates (2.5 percent and 2.9 percent, respectively) were reached, it was reckoned that the time was ripe to focus on balancing the budget as a priority goal. In 1997, the cabinet of Prime Minister Ryutaro Hashimoto raised consumption tax from 3 percent to 5 percent, increased social insurance premiums, and ramped up the co-payment ratio for medical services (the part of the medical charge covered by the patient directly and not by the insurance). This "triple whammy" brought new pressure on household consumption.

Also, caps on fiscal expenditure were imposed. However, they had to be hastily removed as, from 1998, the economy contracted again, putting in its worst performance in the postwar era. A new headache was deflation.

The era had its positive side though. Prices in Japan were (and are) among the highest in the world and overpriced goods and services (not necessarily of high quality either) were eventually brought down, providing breathing space for households.

Deflation was largely brought about by growing competition from cheap imports and by the efforts of companies in the technologically advanced sectors, such as electronics or precision machinery, to produce high-end items at a lower cost. However, the deflationary trend drove the political and business establishment into a state of panic, as it was associated with falling demand and its consequent negative effect on economic activity.

Overcoming deflation was proclaimed the major economic policy goal. The central bank shifted to a zero real-interest-rate policy (the targeted rate for overnight interbank loans) and took steps to provide abundant liquidity. The discount rate was reduced to just 0.1 percent.

Outward FDI fell far below the pre-recession level. Japan not only lost its position as the world's top direct investor but also dropped out of the top five. Nevertheless, continuing relocation of production by manufacturing firms, to China and other Asian countries with lower production costs, became a matter of grave concern as it was accompanied by the closure of factories inside Japan. When the Asian crisis came, Japan was already fighting with a structural crisis of its own.

Structural Reforms

Major structural reforms were launched by the cabinet of Prime Minister Junichiro Koizumi, who took office in 2001. The key figure in articulating the content of the reforms and fostering their implementation was a prominent economist, Heizo Takenaka.

Banking Reform

The key issue was the revitalization of the banking sector, struggling with huge NPLs and undercapitalization. In July 1998, the Financial Supervisory Agency was formed as an independent institution of fiscal authority (from 2000, it was called the Financial Services Agency). The Financial Reconstruction Act and Prompt Recapitalization Act were passed in October the same year. The major contents were an injection of public funds into banks to prevent financial crises, nationalization of failing banks, and protection of depositors. The government nationalized the insolvent Long-Term Credit Bank, later reselling it to a group of private investors.

In 2002, the Financial Revitalization Program (also known as the "Takenaka Plan") was announced, seeking to accelerate and deepen bank reform and strengthen supervision. The government strongly urged the banks to accelerate disposal of NPLs and to improve the transparency of financial information, disclosing the amount of NPLs on a stricter basis. The policy allowing banks to engage in regulatory arbitrage for meeting minimum capital requirements was stopped. They were requested specifically, not to overstate deferred tax assets (tax credits from past losses that banks expect to claim in the future) as their capital. Also, a scheme was arranged to inject public funds into weak but solvent banks (Sakuragawa 2008).

In addition, the Bank of Japan announced a package of monetary policies, including an ample supply of liquidity and an increase in the amount of equity holdings it was ready to purchase from commercial banks.

By the second half of the decade the NPL problem was mostly resolved.

New Fiscal Policy

The key point of the Koizumi–Takenaka reforms was a shift to "small government." Fiscal policy was fundamentally reconsidered—massive budget spending on public works ceased to be used as a tool to overcome the recession. On the contrary, eliminating the deficit of the primary fiscal balance (fiscal balance without revenues from issuance of government bonds and expenditure on the servicing of the public debt), by 2011, was proclaimed a priority goal. Between 2001 and 2006 budget spending on public works was reduced by 24 percent and the primary balance deficit reduced by half (Kanamori 2007, 20).

Privatization

The core of the structural reforms was the privatization of public entities—the largest in scale since the mid-1980s. It began with the privatization, in October 2005, of the National Highway Public Corporation, which engaged in highway construction and management. It was split into three regional companies. Three other expressway companies went private simultaneously.

The next step was the corporatization, in April 2003, and then privatization, on October 1, 2007, of the postal network. The Japan Post Group was born consisting of four companies—Japan Post Bank, Japan Post Insurance, Japan Post Service (mail deliveries), and Japan Post Network (managing post offices and their real estate), with Japan Post Holdings at the top. Post privatization became a major political issue and met strong resistance, even within the ruling Liberal Democratic Party. In 2005, after the bill was defeated in the upper house of the Diet (parliament), Koizumi dissolved the lower house (the upper house cannot be dissolved) and scheduled a general election in September, calling it a national referendum on postal privatization. The Liberal Democrats won by a large majority, which paved the way for the continuation of the privatization process.

Initially, the government will own all the shares of Japan Post Holdings, which in turn will own all the shares of the four newly born firms. In 2010, the Japan Post Bank and Japan Post Insurance are to go public and, by 2017, all their shares will be traded on the market. The government stake in Japan Post Holdings will be reduced to 33 percent (Takahara 2007). Japan Post Service and Japan Post Network companies will not be listed.

Also, a program for the reorganization of state-owned financial institutions was launched, including their transformation into independent public entities (such entities have to be self-sustainable), mergers, and privatization. Eventually, only one state-owned lending institution—the Japan Finance Corporation (JEF), inaugurated in October 2008, will remain.

Corporate Sector Reforms

One more important set of reforms concerns the corporate sector, especially in the fields of accounting standards and corporate governance. Consolidated accounting was made mandatory. In other words, corporations were obliged to disclose financial data for the whole business group, including daughter and related firms. The aim was to increase transparency and prevent large corporations from hiding losses using accounting chemistry to pass them onto their group companies. It also became mandatory to record all marketable financial assets held for trading purposes at their market value.

The revised Company Law, adopted in 2003, gave Japanese corporations the option to introduce an American-style governance system with compensation, nomination, and audit committees, that consisted of independent board members only (in this case the Auditing Board is unnecessary) (Oba 2008).

Post-Koizumi Policy Change

After Prime Minister Koizumi left office in 2006, the major vectors of economic policy were largely reconsidered. The priorities of his successor, Shinzo Abe, were rather vague. He resigned after only a year in office, mostly as a result of failures in the selection of relevant people for government posts and the organization of the cabinet's work.

Yasuo Fukuda, who assumed the premiership in September 2007, turned out to be, in many ways, Koizumi's exact opposite. Wary of abrupt change, he preferred consensus-building and compromises between various interest groups.

A year later another new prime minister, Taro Aso, shifted the emphasis to the short-term goal of stimulating the weakening economy.

Present Performance

Getting Back on Track

Having overcome the recession in 2002, the Japanese economy started to get back to normal, entering what turned out to be the longest period of uninterrupted, steady growth in its postwar history. In 2004–07, it was expanding at a pace of around 2 percent a year—a bit slower than the US, but faster than a number of leading European economies. Unlike in the past, the recession was overcome without pump-priming measures on the part of the government—the private sector had managed to do it all by itself.

Initially, the return to steady growth was brought about by surging exports, especially to the rapidly growing economies of China and other East Asian countries. It was not least the result of the intensifying transfer of production sites by Japanese manufacturers themselves. Their newly emerging, foreign-based subsidiaries imported a lot of parts, materials, and equipment made by factories inside Japan.

More Domestic Factories Built

The post-recession years were marked by a rise in the number of newly built factories inside Japan. Having hit a low figure of 844 in 2002 (factories with an area of 10,500 square feet and more), the number started to grow again, and, in 2005, reached 1,544—the early 1990s level. The major reason stated by companies for choosing to produce domestically was the growing number of sophisticated products that were difficult to make overseas (Mitsuhashi 2007, 419).

Manufacturing firms are getting back to basics, capitalizing on the traditional Japanese culture of worshipping high-quality manufacturing. In so doing they are positioning domestic factories as production sites for high-end final and intermediate products, as well as centers of product development and design.

Robust Exports and Sluggish Consumption

Exports remained robust in the wake of the upturn in the world economy and the depreciation of the yen in 2001–002 and again, in 2005–07.

Until 2003, domestic investment mostly continued to fall and private consumption was sluggish (see Table 20.1). From 2004, both recovered, and the contribution of domestic demand to growth became more significant. Investment rose as companies restored confidence through increasing sales and profitability. This led to improvements in the labor market. Especially important was the return of companies to hiring regular employees—with an implicit long-term engagement guarantee. Along with the rise in the nominal wages of regular workers in 2005–06, it contributed to the growth of private consumption.

However, since the middle of 2006, and especially in 2007, consumer energy had begun to fade again, largely because the rise in workers' earnings did not last long. Overall, the average earnings of all workers' households (not only those of regular employees) have been mostly falling all through this decade. Besides, consumer sentiment worsened due to the rise in the prices for foodstuffs and some other products.

As in 2007, domestic investment stagnated too, and economic growth became decisively dependent on exports once again.

Table 20.1 Main economic indicators (real annual growth, %)*

Indicator	1999	2000	2001	2002	2003	2004	2005	2006	2007
Real GDP	-0.1	2.9	0.2	0.3	1.4	2.7	1.9	2.4	2.1
Agriculture**	1.0	2.1	-2.4	6.0	-5.9	-7.1	3.6	-2.6	n/a
Industry**	-0.6	2.7	-4.2	-1.8	2.4	4.8	3.8	3.1	n/a
Services**	0.6	1.9	2.1	1.7	1.2	1.1	1.9	0.6	n/a
Private consumption	0.9	0.9	1.6	1.0	0.3	1.5	1.3	2.0	1.5
Gross domestic capital formation	-0.8	1.2	-0.9	-4.9	-0.5	1.4	3.1	1.3	-0.6
Consumer prices	-0.3	-1.8	-0.7	-0.9	-0.3	0.0	-0.3	0.3	0.0
Average monthly cash earnings per regular worker	-4.7	0.5	-0.2	-2.5	0.5	-3.3	0.9	1.1	-1.7
Unemployment rate (%)	4.7	4.7	5.0	5.4	5.3	4.7	4.4	4.1	3.9
Exports (billion yen), fob	47,548	51,654	48,979	52,109	54,548	61,170	65,657	75,246	83,931
Imports (billion yen), cif	35,268	40,938	42,416	42,228	44,362	49,217	56,949	67,344	73,136
Average exchange rate (yen per US$1)	113.9	107.8	121.5	125.3	115.9	108.2	110.2	116.3	117.8

Source: Ministry of Internal Affairs and Communications Statistics Bureau (2008): ADB: "Key Indicators 2008."

*Calender year (fiscal year in Japan begins April 1)

**Data for agriculture, industry, and services refers to value added.

The Impact of the Global Financial Turmoil

By mid-2008 the symptoms of the economic downturn appeared. The major reasons were faltering exports and declining consumer demand. The global financial crisis sapped the confidence of investors, producers, and consumers even further.

In the second quarter of the fiscal year (July–September), the economy technically entered recession, as the GDP had been declining year-on-year for two quarters in a row (by 3.7 percent in the first quarter and 1.8 percent in the second quarter).

The yen sharply appreciated, hitting a thirteen-year high and entering the range of around 90 yen for US$1. The major reason was active buying by international investors looking at Japan as an island of stability while the US and Europe were going through the turmoil. However, the strong yen adversely affected exporters, adding to the blow they had suffered from the fall in global demand. Weak domestic demand was also pushing the GDP growth down as both investment and private consumption were declining. As a result, corporate profits plunged, and the employment situation worsened. In November, the "Toyota shock" occurred as the flagman of Japanese industry slashed its profit forecasts by 56 percent due to a steep fall in sales in the US and other major markets. In late October, the benchmark Nikkei stock index plunged to its lowest level in 26 years. Deepening of the recession is inevitable. In January 2009, the Bank of Japan cut its GDP growth forecast to –1.8 percent for the 2008 fiscal year (April 2008–March 2009) and to –2 percent for the 2009, fiscal year. Concerns about deflation re-emerged.

Still, Japan was hit by the financial turmoil much less than the US and Western Europe. Its financial sector was exposed to the subprime loans market to a much lower degree and, in relative terms, as their Western counterparts were facing big troubles, the Japanese financial institutions got a chance to strengthen their position as global players and did not miss it. In particular, Nomura Securities acquired the operations of Lehman Brothers, both in Asia-Pacific and Europe, taking a dramatic step toward becoming one of the leading global financial companies. Mizuho Corporate Bank invested US$1.2 billion in Merrill Lynch, and Sumitomo Mitsui Financial Group put 500 million pounds into Barclays plc of the UK.

In August, the Fukuda administration announced economic stimulus measures worth 11.7 trillion yen to offset the negative effects of the surges in prices of energy and raw materials.

In late October, the Aso cabinet unveiled a much larger 26.9 trillion yen stimulus package. It included an increase in the scale of tax breaks for those paying housing loans, an extension of the tax breaks on capital gains, and a cut in expressway tolls. To facilitate lending, the state's credit-guarantee scheme for small businesses was expanded by 21.8 trillion yen and reached 30 trillion yen. Also, 600 billion yen were allocated to prefectural administrations to build up infrastructure. To stimulate private consumption expenditure, the government pledged to deliver a total of 2 trillion yen in cash or purchase coupons to all households by the end of the financial year (end of March 2009). The prime minister also announced that tax cuts and other economy-boosting measures would be implemented for three years, and then, once the economy recovers, the tax system would be reformed to secure revenues, including the consumption tax hike (Kyodo News 2008; *Nikkei Shimbun* 2008).

To boost confidence in the country's financial system, as a preventive measure, the scheme for the injection of public funds into the banking sector, was expanded from 2 trillion yen to 10 trillion yen and the range of possible recipients was widened. However, as of the early 2009, only one Japanese bank is going to apply.

In November, the Bank of Japan cut its discount rate from 0.5 percent to 0.3 percent.

The Decline and Aging of the Population

In 2005, Japan's population began declining. According to the estimates of the National Institute of Population and Social Security Research (basic scenario), the fertility rate will drop from 1.3 in the early 2000s to 1.26 in 2055, and the country's population will fall to 90 million. The share of elderly people, aged 65 and over, will rise from 20.8 percent in 2006 (MIC 2008a) to 27.8 percent in 2025 and 37.5 percent in 2050 (International Longevity Center-Japan 2006). However, the "young population," aged 20–34, will decrease by 31 percent by 2020 (METI 2006). The large-scale retirement of the postwar, baby-boomer, demographic bulge started in 2007–08.

In 2025, there will be only two working people per one pensioner, as opposed to four at the beginning of the 2000s. The increasing financial burden on working families, especially people in their thirties and forties, who have to spend a great deal on such commitments as bringing up and educating children and buying an apartment or a house, is becoming a substantial growth deterrent.

Pension Reform

In 2004, the pension reform was launched. Japan's system consists of the national pension, giving universal coverage, and the employees' pension. In the employees' pension, subsystem insurance premiums are to be gradually increased from 13.58 percent of the monthly income to 18.3 percent in 2017 and fixed at this latter level. The national pension's monthly premiums are to be increased from 13,300 yen prior to the reform to 16,900 yen in 2017 and also fixed. The pensions benefit level of a standard pensioner household, adjusted on the basis of wages and consumer prices at the time of payment, is to be reduced from around 59 percent to roughly 50 percent of income during working tenure (Mitsuhashi 2007, 202).

For the employees' pension, the retirement age will be gradually raised from 60 to 65 between 2013 and 2025 (with a five-year lag for women). For the national pension, this raise will take place between 2001 and 2013. Also, working people aged between 65 and 70 will be required to pay the pension premium.

One of the most difficult issues is the financing of the basic pension plan. Under the current system it is funded by both social insurance premiums and the state budget. The latter covers one-third of the total. However, a significant number of pension-plan holders refuse to pay premiums. In fiscal 2006, for example, 43.7 percent of self-employed, part-time workers and other holders of the national pension program failed to pay (Yumoto 2008). In 2009, the state burden is to be lifted to 50 percent. The viable option discussed is to provide all the funding from the state budget.

To make things worse, 2007 brought a new big shock. It turned out that the pension records of more than 50 million households had simply disappeared from the database of the Ministry of Health, Labor and Welfare when the computer system was changed.

Healthcare Reform

Another headache is the status of the medical insurance system. Generally, Japan's healthcare and health insurance system is considered one of the best in the world. According to the World Health Organization (WHO), Japan's healthy life expectancy of 74.5 years is the highest. The WHO Report of 2000 also ranked Japan first in terms of health system attainment and performance (WHO 2000).

Costs in relation to GDP are lower than in other developed countries. However, they are now skyrocketing with the aging of the population and the consequent growing expenses of medical treatment for the elderly. In June 2006, the Health Insurance Act and a number of related laws were significantly amended to curb the uncontrolled rise in costs and improve healthcare system finance. The co-payment rate (the portion of the medical charge borne by the patient) for people under 70 was raised from 20 percent to 30 percent and for those aged 70–74 from 10 percent to 20 percent. Elderly people aged 75 and over were obliged to bear 10 percent of the cost within a newly established Advanced Elderly Health Care System (previously the total cost was covered from the state budget and contributions from the national and employees' insurance).

Trying to Revitalize the Regions

A crucial issue that Japan has tried but failed to resolve since the 1960s is balanced regional development. The economic gap between the Tokyo–Yokohama, Osaka, and Nagoya areas on the one hand and, as they are called in Japan, the *chiho*—"regions" (the term applied to all the other areas of the country)—on the other, is widening (for instance, per-capita income in Tokyo is twice that of Okinawa). The population of the regions is declining more quickly and getting older faster than the national average. The outflow of people to the bigger cities continues.

In most regions, the production volumes of local industries are declining, and the number of SMEs is falling too. The government is trying to strengthen local autonomy and encourage initiatives on the part of provinces themselves. It has called for competition among the regions in revitalizing local economies and providing better livelihoods.

The Koizumi administration (2001–06) launched a decentralization policy with a set of three reforms as its core. First, subsidies for local administrations from the central budget, including those for public works, were drastically cut. Second, national tax revenue transfers were reduced. Third, the central government "conceded" to prefectures the sources of tax revenues.

Also, to improve the efficiency of administration and provide synergies, mergers of cities, towns, and villages are encouraged—between March 1995 and August 2006 their number decreased by as much as 40 percent, from 3,232 to 1,819 (Kanamori 2007, 333).

The government is showing a willingness to increase the funding of various projects in the regions. However, unlike in the past, proposals are expected to come from the localities themselves. Primary importance is attached to projects aimed at technological and business innovation, especially if they are carried out jointly by local companies, administrations, and academia.

Innovation-Led Growth

Once the recession was over, the issue of the country's ability to provide innovation-led growth came back into focus. In the 1990s, during the recession, the pace of innovation at Japanese companies slowed down. R&D spending in the corporate sector was reduced. In the 2000s, corporate R&D activities visibly intensified.

The country's latest innovation achievements cover quite a wide range of sectors such as mobile telephony (especially i-mode), online shopping, hybrid cars, advanced robotics, and plasma TVs. Japanese manufacturers are leading in the production of advanced auto, electronic, and machinery parts.

The New Industry Promotion Strategy prioritizes such areas as fuel cells, robots, and digital consumer electronics as well as R&D in cutting-edge industries, such as lithium-ion batteries for next-generation cars, advanced medical equipment, and next-generation environmental aircraft (METI 2006).

However, until now, Japan has failed to get over a number of structural and institutional barriers hampering innovation activities. About 90 percent of the R&D expenditure of all companies is accounted for by big firms with capital of 1 billion yen or more. On the whole, the role of SMEs, is negligible. Venture business remains weak.

Nevertheless, it has to be remembered that Japan has a pool of technologically advanced SMEs, often with a long history, who command important technological and production niches not only domestically, but on a global scale.

Japanese companies have not developed a culture of encouraging and stimulating talented people capable of leading innovation activities and achieving outstanding results. Furthermore, conflicts emerge between innovators and the companies they work for over property rights on the technologies they develop and the reward they get for it—quite often corporations are ready to pay only a symbolic remuneration but wish to get all the benefits.

Though the total number of researchers remains high by international standards, the share of researchers with a doctorate is low. The share of Japanese in the total of the world's patent holders remains the second-largest after the Americans

(25.7 percent and 36.4 percent respectively, as of 2003), but is noticeably falling (Cabinet Office 2007).

Innovation Strategy

Within its New Economic Growth Strategy, METI has launched the Innovation Super Highway initiative. Emphasis is put on the interaction and exchange of ideas between the parties involved, linkages between various R&D fields and the provision of an "exit"—real value creation based on R&D results. The strategic goal is to capitalize on the achievements of science and technology to create new industries, upgrade information and telecommunication infrastructure, find solutions for energy and environmental problems, provide better healthcare and welfare services, and improve public safety (METI 2006). METI has also launched the industrial clusters promotion plan.

The first success stories are emerging. For instance, in the Tohoku Manufacturing Corridor a former electronic parts assembler, Inspec, which was linked with venture capital, successfully developed a processor for product-testing devices. In 2006, the firm was listed. Now it produces high-speed, high-precision inspection equipment for semiconductor manufacturing.

For its part, the Ministry of Education, Culture, Sport, Science and Technology (MEXT) is promoting knowledge clusters aimed at developing competitive innovative technologies in the regions through collaboration between universities, research institutions, and knowledge-intensive companies. Around 500 million yen has been allocated for every cluster for the five-year period (MEXT 2008).

Foreign Trade

The Composition of Exports

In 2007, exports to East Asia comprised 46.0 percent of the total. China provided the biggest Asian market with a share of 15.3 percent. It was followed by South Korea (7.6 percent), Taiwan (6.3 percent), Hong Kong (5.5 percent), and Singapore (3.3 percent). The US remained the biggest single export market (20.1 percent of the total). The share of the 27 European Union (EU) countries was 14.8 percent, including 3.2 percent for Germany (JETRO 2008a).

In terms of sectors, Japan's exports are dominated by machinery products (transportation equipment, electric machinery (including electronic products) and general machinery)—combined they account for about two-thirds of the total. As the intra-industry division of labor in the machinery sector, especially with East Asian countries, is deepening, the role of electronic and auto parts as major export items increases. In 2006, the share of transportation equipment was 24.2 percent of the total (including 16.3 percent for motor vehicles and 4.0 percent for parts), electric machinery 21.4 percent (including 6.5 percent for semiconductors and other parts), and general machinery 19.7 percent. The share of scientific and optical equipment was 3.5 percent.

Other export items with significant shares are chemicals (9.0 percent) and iron and steel products (4.6 percent) (MIC 2008a).

It can be argued that the composition of Japan's exports is too biased toward machinery products and that the export activities of most other industries are too small-scale for an economy of that size.

A number of items do not command a high share of the export total but serve as representative made-in-Japan products in various parts of the world. These include high-end kitchenware from Noritake and sportswear from Mizuno.

The Composition of Imports

East Asian goods also dominate the country's imports (40.9 percent of the total imports in 2007). Today, China is by far the biggest exporter to Japan (20.6 percent). The next most important Asian exporters are South Korea (4.4 percent), Indonesia (4.3 percent), and Taiwan (3.2 percent). The share of the US was 11.4 percent, Saudi Arabia 5.7 percent, United Arab Emirates 5.2 percent, Australia 5.0 percent, and Germany 3.1 percent (JETRO 2008a).

As far as sectors are concerned, in 2006, mineral fuels accounted for 27.7 percent of the import total (including 17.1 percent for crude and partly refined petroleum), foodstuffs 8.5 percent, and raw materials 7.0 percent. Naturally, Japan remains one of the biggest importers of those primary products and their share of total imports (43.2 percent) is higher than in most other developed countries.

The share of general machinery was 9.3 percent and for electric machinery 12.8 percent (including 4.2 percent for semiconductors and other parts). Japan is also one of the biggest importers of clothing and clothing accessories (4.1 percent). The share of transportation equipment is comparatively low at 3.4 percent, including only 1.4 percent for motor vehicles (MIC 2008a).

A Reluctant Importer

Until the late 1980s, Japan was importing more primary products than manufactured goods and was criticized for exporting too many manufactured products and importing them too little.

Since 1989, the share of imported manufactured goods has been exceeding that of primary products. When the Japanese economy lost its tempo in the early 1990s, while the US, and to some extent European, economies accelerated and China emerged as a major exporter, Japan's trade surpluses ceased to be an irritant to other nations. However, it does not mean that they are getting smaller.

As for imports, though in absolute terms the country provides one of the biggest import markets in the world, import intensity (especially regarding manufactured goods) measured, for example, by import value per capita or import ratio to GDP, remains significantly lower than virtually in all other developed states. In spite of very low tariffs for most products, it is still often difficult to export to Japan because of the complex domestic distribution channels that foreign companies cannot access. Even today (though less than in the past), Japanese manufacturing and trading firms often prefer long-term transactions with one another, keeping the door shut to foreign newcomers. Those invisible import barriers exert a negative influence on consumption and living standards (Tselichtchev 2004).

FDI and the Business Environment

Policies and Targets

The merits of investing in Japan include the world's second-largest domestic market, the availability of technologically advanced suppliers of production inputs, well-trained laborers, and access to high technology. Infrastructure is also generally good, though problems remain. For multinational corporations (MNCs) Japan often serves as a venue for developing and testing new products and technologies. And increasingly, foreign companies use their Japanese subsidiaries as a base for business activities in East Asia as a whole.

Until recently, the promotion of inward FDI was not high on the economic policy priority list. On the contrary, entries by large foreign companies were looked upon mostly as a threat to domestic producers.

However, during the Koizumi era (2001–06), this changed and the promotion of inward FDI was proclaimed an important goal and a tool to invigorate the economy. In 2003, in a policy speech at the Diet, the prime minister announced the government's intention to double inward FDI stock between 2001 and 2006. In reality, the result turned out to be a little bit below the target. In March 2003, the Japan Investment Council was established, and chaired by the prime minister himself. It articulated the promotion program, consisting of five pillars: providing information at home and overseas; creating a favorable business environment; reconsidering administrative procedures; improving the working and living environment; and improving the regulatory system at the national and local levels.

In May 2006, the government set a new target—to double the ratio of inward FDI balance to GDP by 2010, lifting it to 5 percent.

Entry Rules and Changes in the Legal Environment

Back in 1991, the system of prior notification about FDI (meaning case-by-case approval) was replaced by ex-post facto notification for non-restricted industries.

Positive changes in the legal environment came with the 2005 revision of the Corporate Law. Minimum capital requirements for establishing a new company were abolished. Triangular mergers (a foreign subsidiary as a surviving company acquires the stock of a Japanese firm, providing to its shareholders the shares of its parent foreign company) and cash-out mergers (shareholders of the acquired company are compensated by cash) were allowed, which is expected to facilitate acquisitions of Japanese companies by foreign firms. From May 2007, the latter were permitted to use the triangular scheme.

Deregulation measures, which opened to private business a number of utility and welfare-related sectors, will widen the scope of business opportunities for foreign companies too.

The introduction of international accounting standards started in the 1990s. Especially significant improvement has been achieved since the start of the "Big Bang" reform in 1998. Japan has also enacted several laws to strengthen intellectual property rights (IPR) protection and, in 2005, established the Intellectual Property High Court.

Incentives

The system of incentives for foreign investors is complicated. At the national level there are none, as foreign companies are supposed to operate under the same conditions as domestic ones. However, there are factory zones where land for factory use is set aside, business zones providing office space for industry and research institutions, and industrial parks.

Special incentives are offered by local governments at their own discretion through various ordinances and programs. Several prefectures provide incentives for foreign business activities in particular industries, such as autos and auto parts, retailing, information and communication technology (ICT), biotechnology, healthcare, and environment. For instance, Aichi Prefecture, one of the centers of the auto industry, supports FDI into advanced automobile-related industries (including fuel cells, information technology (IT), and, of course, parts) by local establishment promotion subsidies, reductions in the real-estate acquisition tax, and land-leasing schemes.

Japan External Trade Organization (JETRO), functioning under METI, provides a "one-stop service" for foreign investors, including information and advice, organization of events, and assistance in establishing business networks.

Impediments

Yet, though the business environment is improving, the scale of inward FDI remains small, if not inadequate, for an industrially developed country of this size. Significant impediments are still present. They include high costs (real-estate prices, distribution, and labor), complexities in administrative procedures, and the tendency of Japanese businesses to maintain long-term, sometimes exclusive, ties among themselves. Complicated decision-making mechanisms at Japanese firms, sometimes making it difficult to understand who is in charge of what, coupled with the disinclination of managers to take personal responsibility, the ambiguous manner of negotiating, and the conservative mindset of managers in large organizations ("why should I run a risk and take responsibility doing something new—for example, establishing a new partnership with a foreign firm, when things are fine the way they are?") also add to the problems faced by a foreign businessman in the Land of the Rising Sun.

Establishing business contacts requires time and patience. Your partners may well believe that, since you've come to Japan you must adhere to Japanese standards of doing things rather than your local counterparts should adhere to *de facto* global standards. Finally, English language skills generally remain low, which inhibits communication.

Attitudes to acquisitions of Japanese companies by foreigners (especially invest-ment funds) are largely negative. A growing number of companies are introduc-ing defense schemes against such takeovers.

If disputes occur, it may be very difficult and costly to resolve them through the courts. Procedures are very slow, good lawyers are difficult to come by, and the fees they charge are very high by international standards.

As far as everyday life is concerned, housing standards in Japan remain com-paratively low, though, conversely, the costs of renting or buying a house are high. The living environment, in such respects as availability and size of green zones, space for informal sports activities, sports and recreation facilities, kindergartens, and other facilities for children is often unsatisfactory.

Success Stories and Withdrawals

Despite the impediments, the list of foreign companies successfully operating in Japan is quite long. It includes Texas Instruments, Saint-Gobain of France (Europe's largest apparel corporation), Inditex Group from Spain (with its famous Zara brand), Microsoft, Cisco Systems, Citibank, and GAP to name just a few.

However, large-scale withdrawal stories are also not that rare. In 2006, Vodafone sold its cellular phone business to Softbank, run by the star of Japan's business world, Masayoshi Son. It became the biggest acquisition in the country's history. Carrefour started a number of hypermarkets, but was unsuccessful and sold them off to the domestic supermarket chain Ion. Wal-Mart made Seiyu its Japan unit and started a discount store business, but is reporting big losses.

Inward FDI

Overall, fluctuations in the amount of inward FDI are very big (see Table 20.2). In 2006, it was even negative—mostly because of the disinvestment by Vodafone. However, in 2007, it reached a record high.

In 2007, 59.8 percent of FDI came from the US and 21.6 percent from Western Europe, with Switzerland as the leader (5.3 percent). The share of Asian coun-tries is still relatively low, though growing (7.2 percent). Almost all of Asia's investment comes from the newly industrialized economies (NIEs)—Hong Kong, Singapore, South Korea, and Taiwan.

Finance and insurance got 79.6 percent of total FDI, wholesale and retail trade 7.5 percent, the oil sector 4.2 percent, and the glass and ceramics industry 3.0 percent (JETRO 2008b).

Table 20.2   Japan's outward and inward FDI (balance of payments basis, US$ millions)

Direction	1999	2000	2001	2002	2003	2004	2005	2006	2007
Inward FDI	12,308	8,226	6,191	9,089	6,238	7,808	3,223	−6,789	22,181
Outward FDI	22,366	31,534	38,495	32,039	28,767	30,962	45,461	50,165	72,483

Source: JETRO Web site 2008.

FDI in Japan is very highly concentrated in the Tokyo area, the next most important destination being Osaka. The presence of foreign capital in the prefectures remains negligible. The reasons cited are difficulties in finding appropriate personnel and business partners, communication problems, insufficient infrastructure (especially transportation), and an unsuitable living environment.

Outward FDI

Japan's outward FDI was the largest in the world in 1990 but, during the recession of the rest of that decade, its volume fell significantly and the leading position was lost. Its growth remained sluggish in the first half of the 2000s but has accelerated since 2005 (see Table 20.2). The largest portion of Japan's FDI goes to the US, the EU countries, and East Asia. Their order, in terms of the amount received, changes from year to year. Basically, in recent years, manufacturing companies are more focused on East Asia and nonmanufacturing enterprises on Europe and the US.

In 2007, Western Europe was the major destination for Japan's outward FDI (28.2 percent), closely followed by Asia (26.7 percent). The share of the US was 21.6 percent. The next biggest recipient, on a country basis, was the Netherlands (17.2 percent), followed by China (8.6 percent), the UK (4.2 percent), Thailand (3.6 percent), and Singapore (3.1 percent). The share of India is also noticeably increasing (2.1 percent).

As for the breakdown by industry, in the manufacturing sector automotive and electric machinery (especially electronic) industries usually take the lead (in 2006, their shares of total outward FDI were 17.1 percent and 14.0 percent, respectively). However, in 2007, the leader was the food industry with 17.4 percent, while transportation machinery followed with 11.8 percent, and electrical machinery with 6.4 percent. The share of general machinery was 3.6 percent. In the nonmanufacturing sector, finance and insurance was the indisputable leader with 26.5 percent. It was followed by wholesale and retail trade at 6.5 percent. Mining accounted for 5.5 percent (JETRO 2008b).

Concluding Remarks

Japan's economic success was a sensation from the 1960s to the 1980s. In the late 1980s, excitement about the nation's emergence as the world's economic leader reached its peak. Those days are gone. In the 1990s, the country's position in the global economy began to decline and, in parallel, interest in it began to fade. Expectations about Japan's leadership proved to be too high and apprehensions about its victories in international competition and its drive to economic dominance exaggerated. Excitement was largely replaced by skepticism. Then the focus of attention drifted toward the new economy in the US and the emergence of new giants like China and India and, in a way, the world started to forget about Japan as an economic giant.

Two important things have been happening to the Japanese economy since the 1990s. First, it is losing its position as the number two economy in the world in terms of size. The country's shares in world GDP, trade, and investment are all declining. It is no longer the number one provider of official development assistance (ODA). Its per-capita GDP (PPP) is already lower than those of Singapore and Hong Kong.

Second, Japan has lost its dynamism. This applies not only to growth rates but also to the dynamism of positive change as a whole—in living standards, international competitiveness, innovation, business models, infrastructure, and education.

Economic strategies are being adapted to the conditions of a mature economy whose dynamism has been lost. From now on, even in the good times, growth rates will hardly exceed the 2 percent level. Naturally, the government's strategy emphasizes the upgrading of production and quality of life, not quantitative growth, as the major goals (METI 2006). The first major task is to make Japan a global and regional center for innovation, R&D, and the production of high-value-added products. The second is to enhance per-capita GDP and make people's lives more affluent, stable, and safe, capitalizing on the country's technological strength.

As far as breakthrough innovation is concerned, in most areas Japan is still far from the top. Also, it is much stronger in process (technological) innovation than in product innovation. Becoming a center of innovation requires the active promotion of those talented individuals capable of leading it but in Japan this is not happening. Without new approaches to education, including the nurturing of an "intellectual elite," advanced courses, and fast tracks for the most talented students, creating this new talent cadre looks unlikely.

On the quality of life front, Japan has reached the status of a slowly growing "mature" economy, still bearing the burden of "quality of life problems" it should have resolved when it was growing fast. Living infrastructure remains largely outdated. Houses are small and inconvenient, but also expensive. The retailing sector is incapable of providing a spectrum of goods meeting the standards expected in a developed country. Many Japanese continue to work long hours with surprisingly short vacations. Conversely though, especially in the case of white-collar workers, efficiency remains low.

Yet, in spite of all the problems mentioned, we should not forget that, though dynamism has been lost, stocks also matter. In terms of accumulated stocks of capital and technology, Japan remains the undisputed leader in Asia and will remain so for the foreseeable future.

Today, the giant is running slower but in many respects he is still far ahead of the followers. Don't forget about the giant.

Epilogue

The dawn of the new century marks Asia's turning point. East Asian economies have started to grow fast again but today's growth is largely different from the one in the years of the economic miracle.

In the 1980s, Japan led the world in terms of efficiency and competitiveness. The Japanese model seemed more capable of handling not only an economic catch-up but also a highly developed economy. In the West, "learn from Japan" became a catchphrase. American and European businessmen and management experts, invited to visit Japanese firms, admired the way the latter worked with suppliers, trained personnel, and controlled the quality of products. US congressmen were calling for imitation of Japan's cooperative government–business relations and scholars discussed scenarios for the formation of American financial–industrial groups in the fashion of Japanese *keiretsu*.

Most other Asian countries were willing to follow Japan's example. It was believed that East Asia, though definitely having opted for the market, not the socialist planned economy, would be capable of building an economic system more workable and relevant for its societies than anything Western capitalism could offer.

An emphasis on stability and long-term growth rather than on maximization of investors' returns; on cooperation and teamwork rather than on individualism; on trust and personal relationships rather than on blind and "heartless" contracts and rules seemed to pave the way for achieving social harmony, enhancing workers' commitment, and raising international competitiveness. This was thought to be instrumental in addressing the problems Anglo-Saxon capitalism was failing to resolve: inequality; low labor motivation; high unemployment and other forms of social exclusion; human relations ruled by the "law of the jungle" and, consequently, a growing number of people losing direction in their lives; and increasing crime and suicide rates, mounting social unrest, and so on.

By and large, until the 1990s, Asian capitalism did meet such high expectations. However, in the 1990s its weaknesses, from cronyism and resource misallocation to "irresponsible" diversification, overborrowing, and poor corporate governance, became obvious for all who wanted to see. The Asian crisis underscored the need for far-reaching change.

351

At the turning point, modernization is bringing Asian capitalism—sometimes gradually, sometimes rapidly—much closer to, not further from, the capitalist system established in the West. The process is stimulated by globalization and the growing presence in Asian economies of Western multinational corporations, banks, and investment funds.

The basic things comprising the economic model—the role of government and its relations with the private sector, corporate ownership, the way companies are governed and the goals they pursue, corporate finance, and employment practices—increasingly resemble Western patterns. Business-related laws and rules are also becoming closer to those established in America and Europe.

In the 2000s, Asia is actively pursuing competition, self-responsibility, and self-reliance, letting the market decide who wins and who loses.

The profitability of Asian companies has dramatically improved and the dividends they pay turn out to be not lower, but higher than in the West. Their dependence on debt financing has significantly decreased, while banks have become much more selective and demanding toward borrowers. The governments may support high-tech sectors or the modernization of rural areas but they won't bail out ailing conglomerates or look after particular industries and groups of companies the way they did before.

Increasingly, Asia and the West are speaking the same business language, which makes working with each other easier than ever.

Westernization of the economic model does not mean that Asia is becoming like the West. The transformation is systemic, not cultural.

As far as consumption patterns, fashion, music, or movies are concerned, Asian and Western cultures are increasingly penetrating into one another's territory and exerting a growing mutual influence. Currently, the degree of penetration of Western culture in Asia is higher than the degree of penetration of Asian culture in the West. Nevertheless, at a basic level—customs, values, mentality, and the modes of action they produce—Asia retains its specificity. Quite often Asian businesses pursue the same goals as their Western counterparts, but use somewhat different means.

However, after the turning point it has become increasingly difficult to follow "the Asian way," as used to be the case. Emphasizing profitability and introducing more flexible and merit-based employment and compensation systems, most Japanese managers still oppose the emergence of strong outside directors. They also do their utmost to prevent acquisitions of their companies by overseas investment funds when "danger" is in the air. They even initiate the exchange of stock with their long-term business counterparts, which is a new spin on the old habit of cross shareholding. However, these days they cannot forget about the shareholders and let this kind of action harm the company value. For instance, not to disturb the shareholders, they adjust their policy regarding cross shareholding partners, limiting them to highly performing companies, in terms of value and profitability.

In most of the conglomerates that survived the blows of the Asian crisis (and the majority did survive) the founders and their families retain a dominant position. However, they have to accept the growing role of outside shareholders, work with professional managers, and focus on areas where they can do better rather than expand their empires by entering one business field after another.

The Westernization described does not mean the "triumph of Western capitalism." It brings not only positive change but also "Western-style" problems that Asian economies and societies must tackle, such as growing income gaps, inequality, worsening employment conditions for many workers, and the alienation and despair of those who lose out in competition, or, in broader terms, in the bitter fight to survive. Also, the school of thought and mode of action, biased toward reliance on market mechanisms, putting profitability first, and making a shareholder—especially a large shareholder—"a king" is, naturally, causing a lot of resistance in Asian societies—interestingly, largely in the same way that it has done in the West. An economy dominated by investment funds does not seem to be a very popular idea anywhere. The "human dimension" of an economy—the social responsibilities of all the parties involved, the mission of a business organization and the way it should be managed and governed, and support for the poor and the weak—presents very complicated issues that mankind is obliged to work on in the search for relevant solutions. Undoubtedly, from now on, Asian societies will continue searching for such solutions, compatible with their culture, values, and ideals.

There is another reason why the dawn of the twenty-first century became Asia's turning point. Gone are the days when the region's growth was boosted mainly by a rise in the volumes of industrial production. Today, most of the Asian economies are industrialized. Not much, if any, room is left for further industrialization, perceived as the rise of the share of manufacturing in GDP.

At the dawn of the new century growth is most dependent on the ability of Asian countries to upgrade their economies. Notably, in spite of the fierce competition to attract foreign capital, their interest in investment in low-value-added sectors is decreasing. Channeling funds into higher-end production, research, and development has become the primary policy goal.

As far as the production of higher value-added goods is concerned, progress in the post-Asian crisis years has been remarkable. Not only developed but also developing Asian countries have become capable of expanding their exports, even when national currencies appreciate—a definite sign of the newly acquired ability to compete on quality and product differentiation.

However, the upgrading challenge is not limited to producing higher value-added goods. Growth will lose much of its significance if Asian nations do not take big steps forward in enhancing the quality of life in the broader meaning of the phrase. They have to provide better housing and living infrastructure, education, healthcare, and leisure, as well as more urban green zones and cleaner air, rivers, and lakes. They have to narrow enormous gaps between exclusive clubs of their largest cities on the one hand and the rest of their territories on the other.

They have to improve the basic training of their laborers so that there are no money changers failing in basic calculations, no airport check-in staff unable to understand what is written in a passenger's passport, no hotel room-service staff unable to open a bottle of wine, and no tourist guides ignorant of a country called Russia ("I will ask my cousin, maybe he knows").

Upgrading means the creation of economies which are environment-friendly and resource-saving. Unfortunately, with very few exceptions, Asia has not yet made a visible shift in this direction. With China and India at its core, today's Asia resembles a chronically hungry genie, just released from the bottle. He demands more and more "food": petroleum, natural gas, coal, metals, or whatever. He devours it all, emitting loads of hazardous waste in the process. The need to change this pattern of growth has been recognized but the road map has still not been drawn.

Today, it is clear that the 2000s have posed a great new structural challenge, which is both regional and global—overstrained fuel, mineral resource, and food markets, creating permanent latent (and sometimes explicit) shortages and very strong inflationary pressures. It would not be an exaggeration to say that a commodity (fuel-food-mineral resources) crisis is knocking at the door—not least because of the natural resource-intensive pattern of growth of the large Asian economies and the unprecedented rise in demand that they generate.

Tight commodity markets bring down living standards and exacerbate poverty problems, largely devaluing growth benefits. At the company level, they push up production costs and squeeze profits. At the macroeconomic level, they make governments resort to anti-inflationary policies, which turn into growth constraints. On the financial front, all this weakens the confidence of investors, leading, since late 2007, to a massive stock price plunge.

Negative economic developments spur riots, strikes, anti-government demonstrations, and other forms of social unrest.

The situation in the Asian economies deteriorated further under the blows of the global financial turmoil, started in autumn 2008 with the Lehman Brothers' collapse. Yet, at the same time the latest developments underscore the importance of the turning point Asian economies are going through: they are becoming structurally stronger. Asian countries managed to curtail the negative influence of the external shock and China, India and developing ASEAN countries are preserving decent economic growth. (Though, inevitably, its speed is slowing down and 2009 may well become for Asian economies the worst year of the decade.) Thus, they contribute to the growth of the world economy, "making up" for the devastating effect of the downturn in the West. Furthermore, today, we even can hear calls for Asian governments and financial institutions to use their financial might to help the West restore stability.

The global financial turmoil has not put an end to the wave of growth of Asian economies since the 1997–98 crisis. It has brought only a short interruption, and by the beginning of the next decade at least, they will be back on a higher growth track. In relative terms, the shift of economic power from the West to the East, not least to East Asia, is accelerating.

References

Chapter 1

Asanuma, Banri. 1992. Interfirm Relationships in Japanese Manufacturing Industry. *Keizaigaku Ronshu* (Ryukoku University) 32 (3).

Asian Development Bank (ADB). 2008. Key Economic Indicators.

Cabinet Office of the Government of Japan. 2006. *Keizai Hakusho 2006.* Tokyo: Government of Japan.

Cheong Kee Cheok and Wong Choong Kah. 2006. *Asia Resurgent.* Kuala Lumpur: University of Malaya Press.

Claessens, Stijn, Simeon Diankov, and Larry Lang. 2000. East Asian Corporations Heroes or Villains? World Bank Discussion Paper No, 409. Washington, DC: World Bank.

Council of Economic Planning and Development, Republic of China, 2002. Taiwan Statistical Data Book 2008. Taipei

Economic Report of the President. 1999. Washington, DC: US Government Printing Office.

Gerson, Philip. 1998. Poverty and Economic Policy in the Philippines. *Finance and Development.* 35 (3).

Murakami, Yasusuke. 1992. *Han-koten-no Seiji Keizaigaku.* Tokyo: Chuo Koronsha.

Nationalmaster.com. 2008. Economy Statistics. GDP by Country (1970, 1990). (http://www.nationmaster.com/graph/eco-gdp-economy-gdp&date=1970; http://nationmaster.com/graph/eco-gdp-economy-gdp&date=1990).

Omura, Keiji. 2006. *Indonesia Keizai: Yakushintekina Saiken Keikaky.* Tokyo: Tosho Shuppankai.

Takushoku University, Azia Joho Center. 2000. *Higashi Azia Choki Tokei.* Tokyo: Takushoku University. 9 (12) 502–503, 512–513.

Tselichtchev, Ivan. 1992. Japanese-Style Interfirm Ties and Competition. *Keizaigaku Ronshu* (Ryukoku University) 32 (3).

Tselichtchev, Ivan. 1994. Rethinking Interfirm Ties in Japan as a Factor of Competitiveness. In H. Schütte ed. *The Global Competitiveness of the Asian Firm.* New York: St Martin's Press.

World Bank, The. 1993. *The East Asian Miracle: Economic Growth and Public Policy.* New York: Oxford University Press.

World Economic Outlook Data Base. International Monetary Fund. (accessed April 2008).

Chapter 2

Cheong Kee Cheok and Wong Choong Kah. 2006. *Asia Resurgent.* Kuala Lumpur: University of Malaya Press.

Collins, Susan and Barry Bosworth. 1996. Economic Growth in East Asia: Accumulation Versus Assimilation. *Brookings Papers on Economic Activity.* (2).

International Monetary Fund (IMF). 2006. World Economic Outlook: Financial Systems and Economic Cycles. (http://www.imf.org/external/pubs/ft/weo/2006/02/index.htm).

Krugman, Paul. 1994. The Myth of Asia's Miracle. *Foreign Affairs.* 73 (6).

Ministry of Economy, Trade, and Industry (METI). 2006. Tsusho Hakusho 2006 (White Paper on the International Economy and Trade). Tokyo.

Mitsuhashi, Tadahiro, Shigeo Uchida, and Yoshiki Ikeda. 2007. *Nihon Keizai Numon.* Tokyo: Nihon Keizai Shimbunsha.

Tejada, Carlos. 2008. Sliding Asian Currencies Spur Central Banks Actions. *The Wall Street Journal (Asia)*, November 23.
Thaichareon, Kitipong and Seo Eon-Kyung, 2008. Asia's Tiger Economies Falter. *Business Inquirer*, November 28 (http://business.inquirer.net/money/brekingnews/view.2008/).

Chapter 3

AFP. 2007. Malaysian Government Launches Chip With Radio Technology. *The China Post*. February 26.
AFP-Jiji. 2008. FT: Morgan Stanley in Talks with China SWF to Sell Up to 49% Stake. *The Daily Yomiuri*. September 20.
ANTARA News. 2007. Bio-Fuel To Power Indonesia's Anti-Poverty Drive. *Jakarta Post*. February 19.
Board of Investment (BOI). 2001. A New Era. *BOI Investment Review*. 10 (3).
China.org.cn. 2003. Market-Oriented Reforms of China's Enterprises in Retrospect. (http://www.China.org.cn/english/2003chinamarket/79520.htm).
ERINA. 2005. *Gendai Kankoku Keizai*. Tokyo: Nihon Hyoronsha.
Farrell, Diana, Ulrich Gersch, and Elizabeth Stephenson. 2006. The Value of China's Emerging Middle Class. *The McKinsey Quarterly*. June. (http://www.mckinseyquarterly.com/The_value_of_Chinas_emerging_middle_class_1798).
Hakim, Zakki P. 2005. Indonesia Finally Has Industrial Policy. *Jakarta Post*. July 4. (http://www.thejakartapost.com/news/2005/07/04/indonesia-finally-has-industrial-policy.html).
Hudiono, Urip. 2007. Government Reviving Peatland Program. *Jakarta Post*. February 15.
Jakarta Post. 2007. We Must Eradicate Poverty: Badawi. February 21.
Khazanah Nasional. 2008. Portfolio Companies. (http://www.khazanah.com.my/portfolio.htm).
Koh, Tommy, Timothy Auger, and Jimmy Yap eds. 2007. *Singapore: The Encyclopedia*. Singapore: Editions Didier Millet, National Heritage Board.
Ministry of Internal Affairs and Communications (MIC). 2008. *Japan Statistical Yearbook 2008*. Statistical Bureau. Tokyo: Government of Japan.
Sekai Nenkan 2006. 2006, Tokyo: Kyodo News.
Shameen, Assif. 2007. Building an Oil Giant. *Asia Incorporated*. February, No 19, 41.
Straits Times, The. 2007. China's Small Steel Mills Spurn Shutdown Order. February 22.
Tselichtchev, Ivan. 2004. East Asian Economies: Westernization, Liberalization and New Regionalism. In *Trust and Antitrust in Asian Business Alliances*. ed. John Kidd and Frank-Jurgen Richter. 32–60. Basingstoke and New York: Palgrave Macmillan.

Chapter 4

Agami, Abdel. 2002. The Role That Foreign Acquisitions of Asian Companies Played in the Recovery of the Asian Financial Crisis. *Multinational Business Review*. Spring 2002. (http://findarticles.com/p/articles/mi_ga3674/is_200204/ai_n9042916).
Anderson, Jonathan. 2005. The Great Chinese Bank Sale. *Far Eastern Economic Review*. September.
AsiaPulse News. 2006. Chinese Mainland Poised to See Surge in M&A Activities: PwC. January 25.
Burton, David. 2007. Asia and the International Monetary Fund: Ten Years After the Asian Crisis. In *Ten Years After: Revisiting the Asian Financial Crisis*. Bhumika Muchhala, ed. Washington, DC: Woodrow Wilson International Center for Scholars Asia Program.
Chan-Fishel, Michelle. 2007. Time to Go Green: Environmental Responsibility in the Chinese Banking Sector. Friends of the Earth-US. (www.foe.org/pdf/Chinese_Bank_Report5–9–07pdf).
Crowell, Todd. 2005. Ever Heard of Lenovo, Haier, CNOOC? You Will. *Christian Science Monitor*, June 30.
Desai, Ashok V. 2005. His Name Was Sukses. *The Telegraph* (Calcutta, India). September 20.
Economist, The. 2002. Monsters Still, But Prettier: Globalization is Forcing Conglomerates in Poor Countries to Change. January 3.
ERINA. 2005. *Gendai Kankoku Keizai*. Tokyo: Nihon Hyoronsha.
Garnout, Ross, Ligang Song, Stoyan Tenev, and Yang Yao. 2005. *China's Ownership Transformation*. Washington, DC: International Finance Corporation.

Guo, Sujian. 2003. The Ownership Reform in China: What Direction and How Far? *Journal of Contemporary China*. 12 (36), August.

Imai, Ken'ichi. 2002. Kigyo Kaikaku-no Shoten to WTO Kameigo-no Tembo. *Zaimusho Chugoku Kenkyukai.* January 11.

Kaye, Chris and Jeffrey Yuwono. 2003. Conglomerate Discount or Premium? Marakon Associates. (http://www.marakon.com/ideas-pdf/id_030830_kaye.pdf).

Khanthavit, Anya, Piruna Polsiri, and Yupana Wiwattanakantang. 2003. Did Families Lose or Gain Control?: Thai Firms After the East Asian Financial Crisis. Social Science Research Network. (http:/papers.ssrn.com/sol3/papers.cfm/abstract_id370120).

Knowledge@Wharton. 2006. The Long and Winding Road to Privatization in China. May 10. (http://knowledge.wharton.upenn.edu/article.cfm?articleid=1472).

Korea Exchange. 2008. Statistics: Stocks—Shareholdings. (http://eng.krx.co.kr/index.html).

McKinsey & Company, Thai Institute of Investors. 2002. Strengthening Corporate Governance Practices in Thailand. April.

Ministry of Economy, Trade, and Industry (METI). 2003. White Paper on International Trade and Economy, 2003. Tokyo.

Nikkei Shimbun. 2006. Kabunushi to wa. Yuka Shoken Kanri-no Shitakugin ga Jyoi. October 25.

Purfield, Catriona, Hiroko Oura, Charles Kramer, and Andreas Jobst. 2006. Asian Equity Markets: Growth, Opportunities, and Challenges. IMF Working Paper (http://www.imf.org/external/pubs/ft/wp2006/wp06266.pdf).

Ramirez, Carlos D. and Ling Hui Tan. 2003. Singapore, Inc. Versus the Private Sector: Are Government-linked Companies Different? IMF Working Paper (http://www.imf.org/external/pubs/ft/wp/2003/wp03156.pdf).

Tselichtchev, Ivan. 2004. East Asian Economies: Westernization, Liberalization and New Regionalism. In *Trust and Antitrust in Asian Business Alliances* ed. John Kidd and Frank-Yurgen Richter, 32–60. Basingstoke and New York: Palgrave Macmillan.

Williamson, Peter. 2004. *Winning in Asia: Strategies for Competing in the New Millennium.* Cambridge, MA: Harvard University Press.

World Bank, The. 2004. Report on Observance of Standards and Codes (ROSC). Corporate Governance. Country Assessment. Indonesia. August. (http://www.worldbank.org/ifa/rosc_cg_idn.pdf).

World Bank, The. 2005. Report on Observance of Standards and Codes (ROSC). Corporate Governance. Country Assessment. Malaysia. June. (http://www.worldbank.org/ifa/rosc_cg_malaysia.pdf).

Chapter 5

Aoki, Masahiko, and Masahiro Okuno. 1996. *Keizai Shisutemu-no Hikaku Seido Bunseki (A Comparative Analysis of Economic Systems).* Tokyo: University of Tokyo Press.

Bae, J and C. Rowley. 2004. HRM in South Korean. In *Managing Human Resources in Asia-Pacific.* ed. Pawan S. Budhwar. London: Routledge.

Benson, John, and Chris Rowley. 2004. Conclusions: Changes in Asian HRM—Implications for Theory and Practice. In *Managing Human Resources in Asia-Pacific.* ed. Pawan S. Budhwar. London: Routledge.

Bloom, David, and David Canning. 2004. Global Demographic Change: Dimensions and Economic Significance. Working Paper Series 1. Cambridge, MA: Harvard Initiative for Global Health.

Cabinet Office of the Government of Japan. 2006. *Keizai Hakusho* 2006. Tokyo: Government of Japan.

Caspersz, Donella. 2006. The 'Talk' versus the 'Walk': High Performance Work Systems, Labor Market Flexibility and Lessons from Asian Workers. *Asia Pacific Business Review.* 12, (2): 149–161.

Debroux, Philippe. 2003. *Human Resource Management in Japan.* Aldershot: Ashgate Publishers.

Debroux, Philippe. 2004. Internal Corporate Governance Discipline and the HRM System in Large Japanese Companies. *Asia Pacific Business Review.* 10, (3–4): 346–359.

Debroux, Philippe. 2006. *The Shift Towards a Performance-based Management System: From Noryokushugi to Seikashugi.* London: Palgrave.

Fang Lee Cooke. 2004. HRM in China. In *Managing Human Resources in Asia-Pacific.* ed. Pawan S. Budhwar. London: Routledge.

Frost, Stephen. 2006. IFC and ILO Team up to Improve Supply Chains. *CSR Asia Weekly.* 2 (3).

Guest, David. 1995. Human Resource Management, Trade Unions and Industrial Relations. In *Human Resource Management: A Critical Text.* ed. John Storey. London: Routledge.

Hofstede. Geert. 2001. *Culture's Consequences: Software of the Mind.* London: McGraw-Hill.

Khan, Ahmed. 2005. *Matsushita's Turnaround.* ICFAI Knowledge Center.

Jie Shen and Vincent Edwards. 2006. *International Human Resource Management in Chinese Multinationals.* London: Routledge.

Jie Yu and Hendrick Meyer-Ohle. 2006. Working for Japanese Companies in China: A Qualitative Study. Proceedings of the 23th Annual Conference of the Euro-Asia Management Studies Association, Seoul, November 22–25.

Legge, Karen. 1995. *Human Resource Management, Rhetorics and Realities.* London: Palgrave.

Lynton, Nandani. 2006. Chindia's Workforce Worries. *Business Week Online.* June 31.

Rousseau, Denise. 1995. *Psychological Contracts in Organizations: Understanding Written and Unwritten Agreements.* London: Thousand Oaks.

Storey, John. 1995. *Human Resource Management: A Critical Text.* London: Routledge.

Tomer, John. 2001. Understanding High-Performance Work Systems: The Joint Contribution of Economics and Human Resource Management. *The Journal of Socio-Economics.* 30(1): 63–73.

Torrington, Derek, and Tan Chwee Huat. 1998. *Human Resource Management for South-East Asia and Hong Kong.* Singapore: Pearson.

Towers Perrin. 2003. *Worldwide Total Remuneration 2002–2003.*

Truong Quang and Le Chien Thang. 2004. HRM in Vietnam. In *Managing Human Resources in Asia-Pacific.* ed. Pawan S. Budhwar. London: Routledge.

Umashanker, Shastry. 2005. *Jong Yong Yun, Samsung Electronics' CEO: Competing through Catastrophe Culture.* IBS Case Development Centre.

Yukongdi, Vimolwan, and John Benson. 2005. Women in Asian Management: Cracking the Glass Ceiling. *Asia Pacific Business Review.* 11 (2): 139–148.

World Bank, The. 2004. *East Asia Update: Strong Fundamentals to the Fore.* Washington, DC: World Bank.

World Bank, The. 2006. *World Development Report 2007: Development and the Next Generation.* Washington, DC: World Bank.

Chapter 6

Asia Regional Integration Center. 2008. FTA by Country/All. Asian Development Bank (ADB). (http://aric.adb.org/FTAbyCountryAll.php).

Association of Southeast Asians Nations (ASEAN). 2008a. Protocol to Amend the Agreement on the Common Effective Preferential Tariff (CEPT) Scheme for the ASEAN Free Trade Area (AFTA) for the Elimination of Import Duties. AFTA and FTAs. (http://www.aseansec.org/14183.htm).

Association of Southeast Asians Nations (ASEAN). 2008b. Database on the Cooperation Progressing in the ASEAN plus Three and the ASEAN plus One Cooperation Frameworks. (http://www.aseansec.org/ASEAN+3Database.pdf).

Association of Southeast Asians Nations (ASEAN). 2008c. The Joint Ministerial Statement of the ASEAN + 3 Finance Ministers Meeting. (http://www.aseansec.org/6312.htm).

China Economic Review. 2007. Sino-ASEAN Trade to Go Nearly Zero Tariff by 2010. August 1. (http://www.chinaeconomicreview.com/finance/2007/08/01/sino-asean-trade-to-go-nearly-zero-tariff-by 2010).

China Post, The. 2007. ADB Urges Asian Trade Bloc, More Financial Cooperation. January 16.

Hatakeyama, Noboru. 2008. How Should We Deal With 3 FTA Proposals in Asia? The Chairman's Article (excerpts from JEF's Magazine *Japan Spotlight*) Japan Economic Foundation. (http://www.jef.or.jp/en_act/act_article_topics.asp?cd=114&num=1).

Hirakawa, Hitoshi, Koichi Ishikawa, Atsuji Ohara, and Naoaki Kobayashi eds. 2007. *Higashi Azia-no Gurobaruka to Chiiki Togo*. Tokyo: Mineruba Shobo.

JETRO. 2007. *Sekai Boeki Toshi Hakusho 2007*. Tokyo: JETRO.

Kyodo News. 2008a. ASEAN–Japanese FTA to Take Effect December 1. *The Japan Times*, October 22. (http://search.japantimes.co.jp/rss/nb20081022a6.html).

Kyodo News. 2008b. East Asian Leaders Eye Upgraded Currency Swap Scheme. *The Daily Yomiuri*. October 25.

Tselichtchev, Ivan. 2004. *Nihon-o Yuataka-ni Suru Mitsu-no Hoho*. Tokyo: Shogakukan.

Zhang Yunling. 2006. How to Realize EAFTA: Views from Joint Experts Group. (http://www.isis.org.my/files/eaec/Sess_2.4_Zhang_Yunling.ppt).

Chapter 7

Asian Development Bank (ADB). 2008. Key Economic Indicators.

Associated Press. 2007. China Says Energy Efficiency Slowly Improving. *International Herald Tribune*. July 30. (http://www.iht.com/articles/ap/2007/07/31/business/AS-FIN-China-Saving-Energy.php).

BBC News. 2007. China "Buried Smog Death Finding." July 3. (http://news.bbc.co.uk/2/hi/asia-pacific/6265098.htm).

Chambers, Sam. 2005. Critical Time Ahead for Hong Kong's Role. *Lloyds List*. February 21. (http://www.fusionc.com/pdf/articles/lloyds_list_critical_time_ahead_for_hong_kong_050221.pdf).

Chung, Olivia. 2007. Carlyle Saga Puts Spotlight on China Takeovers. *Asia Times Online*. (http://www.atimes.com/atimes/China_Business/IC24Cb02.html).

Daily Yomiuri, The. 2008. "China Problem" Merits Global Attention. January 6. (http://www.yomiuri.co.jp/editorial/neworder/dy20080106.htm).

Fujitsu Research Institute. 2008. Gendai-no Chugoku Keizai (2). *Nihon Keizai Shimbun*. January 8.

IDE-JETRO. 2007. *Azia Doko 2007*. Tokyo: Institute of Developing Economies.

Institute of Chinese Affairs (Chugoku Kenkyusho). 2006. *Chugoku Nenkan 2006*. Tokyo: Soshisha.

Institute of Chinese Affairs (Chugoku Kenkyusho). 2008. *Chugoku Nenkan 2008*. Tokyo: Soshisha.

JETRO. 2007. *Boeki Toshi Hakusho 2007*. Tokyo: JETRO.

Kahn, Joseph, and Jim Yardley. 2007. As China Roars, Pollution Reaches Deadly Extremes. *The New York Times*. August 26. (http://www.nytimes.com/2007/08/26/world/asia/26china.html).

Ministry of Commerce. 2003. National Economic and Technological Development Zones. China.org. (http://www.china.org.cn/english/SPORT-c/76751.htm).

Ministry of Economy, Trade, and Industry (METI). 2006. Tsusho Hakusho 2006. Tokyo.

National Bureau of Statistics of China. 2007. *China Statistical Yearbook 2007*.

Roberts, Dexter. 2007. China's Emerging Global Brands. *BusinessWeek*. (http://images.businessweek.com/ss/07/10/1008_chinabrands/index_01.htm).

People's Daily. 2004. China Becomes World Third-Biggest Hi-Tech Producer. February 4. (http://english.peopledaily.com.cn/200402/04/eng20040204_133870.shtml).

Sino Daily. 2008. China Uncovers Thousands of Illegal Land Grabs: Report. April 14. (http://www.sinodaily.com/reports/China_uncovers_thousands_of_illegal_land_grabs_report_999.html).

Williamson, Peter. 2004. Buying the Brand: China's Shortcut to World Markets. *Asia Today Online*. February 16. (http://www.asiatoday.com.au/feature_reports.php?id=158).

Xinhua. 2008. China Plans 10 Major Steps to Spark Growth. Gov.cn. November 10. (http://www.gov.cn/english/2008-11/10/content-1144563.htm).

Chapter 8

Baark, Erik, and Naubahar Sharif. 2006. Hong Kong's Innovation System in Transition. In Bengt-Ake Lundvall, Patarapong Intarakumnerd, and Jan Vang J eds. *Asian Innovation Systems in Transition*. Cheltenham: Edward Elgar.

Census and Statistics Department. 2006. Trade Statistics. The Government of Hong Kong SAR.

Census and Statistics Department. 2008a. Hong Kong in Figures. The Government of Hong Kong SAR.

Census and Statistics Department. 2008b. Trade Statistics. The Government of Hong Kong SAR.

Chambers, Sam. 2005. Critical Time Ahead for Hong Kong's Role. *Lloyd's List.* February 21. (http://www.fusionc.com/pdf/articles/lloyds_list_critical_time_ahead_for_Hong_Kong_050221.pdf)

Common, Richard. 2001a. Civil Service Reform in Hong Kong: Conforming to the Global Trend? *Public Administration and Policy: A Hong Kong and Asia-Pacific Journal.* 8 (2): 37–56.

Common, Richard. 2001b. Globalization and Urban Government: New Perspectives on the Local Politics of Global City Formulation, (Globalization and the Governance of Hong Kong). Paper for the 51th Political Studies Association Conference, April 10–12, Manchester, United Kingdom.

Economist, The. 2007. One-horse Race, A Special Report of Hong Kong. June.

Fong, Cherise. 2008. Hong Kong Cyberport Refocuses on Digital Community. *CNN.com.* March 29. (http://www.cnn.com/2008/BUSINESS/03/25/digitalbiz.cyberport/index.html).

Fuller, Douglas. 2007. Reinvigorating Hong Kong's Innovation System: A Project Proposal. Savantas Policy Institute. August 16.

Hong Kong Monetary Authority. 2006. Hong Kong's Economic Integration and Business Cycle Synchronisation with Mainland China and the US. (http://www.info.gov.hk/hkma/eng/research/RM11-2006.pdf).

Hong Kong Tourism Board. 2007. Hong Kong Tourism Sees Steady Growth in 2006. January 22. (http://www.travel2hk.com/2007/jan/pdf/Stat_E.pdf).

People's Daily. 2008. Shanghai Port Second in TEU Throughput in 2007, Surpasses Hong Kong. January 19. (http://english.people.com.cn/90001/90776/6341186.html)

Tao, Z, and R.Y.C. Wong. 2002. Hong Kong: From an Industrialized City to a Center of Manufacturing-related Services. In HKIEBS Working Papers. Hong Kong University.

United Nations Development Program (UNDP). 2008. *Human Development Report 2008.* New York: UNDP.

Chapter 9

Asian Development Bank (ADB). 2008. Key Economic Indicators.

AFP. 2008. Taiwan Banks Insulated from Global Turmoil; Facing Challenges. October 30.

Associated Press. 2008. Taiwan, China Ink Landmark Flight Deal. *The Daily Yomiuri.* June 14.

Chen Yi-Chi. 1998. Asian Crisis Project: Country Report on Taiwan. University of Washington. (http://faculty.washington.edu/karyiu/Asia/booklet/tn-report.pdf).

Council for Economic Planning and Development (CEPD). 2007. Development Vision for 2015: First-Stage Three-Year Sprint Program (2007~2009). June 1. (http://www.cepd.gov.tw/encontent/m1.aspx?sNo=0007382&key=&ex=%20&ic=&cd=).

Einhorn, Bruce. 2005. Why Taiwan Matters. *BusinessWeek.* May 16.

Government Information Office. 2008. Enterprises to be allowed to invest raised funds in China. *Taiwan Headlines.* June 20. (http://www.taiwanheadlines.gov.tw/ct.asp?xItem=122030&CtNode=39).

Heritage Foundation, The. 2008. Index of Economic Freedom 2008. Taiwan. (http://www.heritage.org/research/features/index/country.cfm?id=Taiwan).

Huang, Joyce. 2004. Planner Says Firms Need Deregulation. *Taipei Times.* June 7. (http://www.taipeitimes.com/News/biz/archives/2004/06/07/2003174146).

JETRO. 2007. *Boeki Toshi Hakusho 2007.* Tokyo: JETRO.

Kyodo News.2008. Taiwan's Ruling Party Chief Meets Hu. *The Daily Yomiuri,* May 29.

Reuters 2009. Chronology–Taiwan Moves to Stimulate the Economy. February 2. (http://www.sharewatch.com/story/php?storynumber=190164).

Ridley, Scott. 2004. Taiwan Tackles High Credit Card Default Rate. *Asia Times Online.* August 18. (http://atimes.com/atimes/China/FH18Ad04.html).

Sino Daily. 2008. Taiwan May Ease China-Bound Investment Restrictions: Reports. January 21. (http://www.sinodaily.com/reports/Taiwan_may_ease_China-bound_investment_restrictions_reports_999.html).

US Department of State. 2007. 2007 Investment Climate Statement—Taiwan. (http://www.state. gov./e/eeb/idf/2007/88188.htm).
Watanabe, Toshio, ed. 1995. *Azia Keizai Yomihon.* Tokyo: Toyo Keizai Shimposha.
World Economy Information Service. 2008, ARC Report Taiwan 2007. Tokyo.
Yin, Norman. 2007. Rebar Case Exposes Shortcomings. *Taipei Times.* January 14. (http://www.taipeitimes. com/News/editorials/archives/2007/01/14/2003344784).

Chapter 10

AFP 2009. SKorea Economy in Worst Shapre for a Decade: Central Bank, January 21. (http:// www.timesoftheinternet.com/39595.html).
Asian Development Bank (ADB). 2007. Key Economic Indicators.
Asian Development Bank (ADB). 2008. Key Economic Indicators.
Cho, Kyung Bok. 2007. Koreans Say Crisis Worse Than 1997 as Stocks Tumble. *Bloomberg.com.* November 3. (http://www.bloomberg.com/apps/news?pid=20601080&sid=al.vjyuQ6F_Q&refer=asia).
Chosun Ilbo, The. 2006. Korean Shipbuilders Sweep Global Top Five Rankings. December 18. (http://english.chosun.com/w21data/html/news/200612/200612180024.html).
The China Post. 2009. South Korea Hit by Record Export Fall in Downturn. February 2. (http:// www.chinapost.com.tu/business/asia/korea/2009/02/02).
Evertiq. 2007. Top 10 Semiconductor Producers in 3Q07. October 29. (http://www.evertiq.com/ news/read.do?news=9186&cat=2).
Haggard, Stephan, Wonhyuk Lim, and Euysung Kim. 2003. *Economic Crisis and Corporate Restructuring in Korea: Reforming the Chaebols.* Cambridge: Cambridge University Press.
Heritage Foundation, The. 2008. Index of Economic Freedom 2008: Korea, South. (http://www. Heritage.org/research/features/index/country.cfm?id=KoreaSouth).
Hirano, Shinichi. 2007. South Korea Split Over Approach to North. *The Daily Yomiuri.* November 22.
Invest Korea. 2008a. Government Policy and Incentives. (http://www.investkorea.org/ InvestKoreaWar/work/ik/eng/bo/content_print.jsp?code=102010201).
Invest Korea. 2008b. FDI Incentives. (http://www.investkorea.org/InvestKoreaWar/ik/eng/).
JETRO. 2007. *Sekai Boeki Toshi Hakusho.* Tokyo: JETRO.
Kim Joongi. 2005. Anatomy of an Asian Conglomerate: The Rise and Fall of Daewoo and the Formation of Modern Corporate Governance. Asian Corporate Governance Study Series (Korea). Seoul: Hills Governance Center at Yonsei. (http://hills.yonsei.ac.kr/conference/ s_03_01_05/HGCY_session3_Daewoo.pdf).
Korea National Statistical Office. 2007. *Korea Statistical Yearbook, 2007.*
Korea.net. 2008. Tax Incentive System on Foreign Investment in Korea. (http://search.Korea. net:8080/central/686_en.pdf).
Lee Jong-wha. 1997. Economic Growth and Human Development in the Republic of Korea, 1945–1992. UNDP. Occasional Paper No. 24. (http://hdr.undp.org/docs/publications/ocational_ papers/oc24aa.htm).
Lovgren, Stephan. 2006. A Robot in Every House by 2020, South Korea Says. *National Geographic News.* September 6. (http://news.nationalgeographic.com/news/2006/09/160906-robots.html).
Mehta, Stephanie. 2007. Samsung's Climb to No. 2. *Fortune.* August 29. (http://money.cnn. com/2007/08/28/technology/samsung_rises.fortune/index.htm?postversion=2007082907).
Ministry of Finance and Economy. 2006. Republic of Korea Economic Bulletin: The Green Book. November. 28 (11). (http://english.mofe.go.kr/media/etc/etc_file_library_18636443334557 ahd807598.pdf).
Purfield, Catriona, Hiroko Oura, Charles Kramer, and Andreas Jobst. 2006. Asian Equity Markets: Growth, Opportunities, and Challenges. IMF Working Paper. (http://www.imf.org/external/ pubs/ft/wp2006/wp06266.pdf).
Watanabe, Toshio ed. 1995. *Azia Keizai Yomihon.* Tokyo: Toyo Keizai Shimposha.
World Economic Information Services. 2008. ARC Report Republic of Korea 2007. Tokyo.

Chapter 11

Asian Development Bank (ADB). 2008. Key Economic Indicators.

Biomed Singapore. 2008. Venture Support. (http://www.biomed-singapore.com/bms/sg/en_uk/index/financial_support/venture_capital.html).

Chew Xiang. 2008. Average Monthly Household Income Grows at Fastest Pace in 10 Years. *The Business Times*. February 14. (http://www.asiaone.com/Business/News/My%2BMoney/Story/A1Story20080215-49841.html).

Chia Siow Yue. 2000. Singapore: From the Asian Crisis to the New Economy. IUJ Research Institute Working Paper, Asia Pacific Series No. 18. December. (http://www.iuj.ac.jp/research/archive/wpaper/wpap018.html).

Koh, Tommy, Timothy Auger, and Jimmy Yap. eds. 2007. *Singapore: The Encyclopedia*. Singapore: Editions Didier Millet, National Heritage Board.

Ministry of Trade and Industry. 2003. Main Report. Economic Review Committee. (http://app.mti.gov.sg/data/pages/507/doc/ERC_Comm_MainReport_Part1_v2.pdf); (http://app.mti.gov.sg/data/pages/507/doc/ERC_Comm_MainReport_Part2_v2.pdf).

Singapore Budget 2009. Budget Speech 2009. (http://www.singaporebudget.gov.sg/speech-toc/index.html).

Singapore Department of Statistics. 2006. Singapore's Invest Abroad 2006. (http://www.singstat.gov.sg/pubn/business/sia2006.pdf).

Singapore Department of Statistics. 2008a. Singapore in Figures 2008. (http://www.singstat.gov.sg/pubn/reference/sif2008.pdf).

Singapore Department of Statistics. 2008b. Statistics: GDP at 2000 Market Prices. (http://www.singstat.gov.sg/stats/themes/economy/hist/gdp1.html).

Singapore Department of Statistics. 2008c. Singapore Yearbook of Statistics 2008.

SPRING Singapore. 2000. National Plan to Boost SMEs. January 4. (http://www.spring.gov.sg/newsarchive/news/releases/00_01_04.html).

Watanabe, Toshio, ed. 2003. *Azia Keizai Yomihon*. Tokyo: Toyo Keizai Shimposha.

Wijaya, Megawati. 2008. A Dent in Singapore's Financial Hub Dream. *Asia Times Online*. November 6. (http://www.atimes.com/Southeast_Asia/JK06Ae01.html).

Chapter 12

Anis, Mazwin Nik, Sylvia Looi, Sira Habibu, Carolyn Ooi, and Steven Daniel. 2008. 5 Kg Buying Limit on Cooking Oil. *The Star*. June 5. (http://thestar.com.my/news/story.asp?file=/2008/1/5/nation/19925382&sec=nation).

Ariff, Mohamed, and Syarisa Yanti Abubakar. 2003. Strengthening Entrepreneurship in Malaysia. Mansfield Foundation Project on Entrepreneurship in Asia. (http://www.mansfieldfdn.org/programs/program_pdfs/ent_malaysia.pdf).

Asian Development Bank (ADB). 2007. Key Economic Indicators.

Asian Development Bank (ADB). 2008. *Asian Development Outlook 2008*. Manila: Asian Development Bank.

Associated Press (AP). 2008. Malaysia Exempts Manufacturers From Import Duties. November 14. (http://www.sfgate.com/cgi-bin/article.cgi?f=/n/a/2008/11/14/financial/f022536S80.DTL&feed=rss.business).

Athukorala, Prema-chandra, and Jayant Menon. 1997. Export-led Industrialisation, Employment and Equity: The Malaysian Experience. *Agenda*. 4 (1): 63–76.

Business Times. 2008. Malaysia Unveils RM7b Stimulus Package. November 4. (http://www.btimes.com.my/Current_News/BTIMES/articles/Malaysia_unveils_RM7b_stimulus_package20081104170726/Article/index_html).

Edge Daily, The. 2008. Malaysia Resilient Against Global Economic Slump. (http://www.theedgedaily.com/cms/content.jsp?id=com.tms.cms.article.Article_7a3ef830-cb73c03a-c1186f00–95cc4clf1).

Fong, Kathy. 2008. Malaysia's FDI Outflow Surpasses Inflow. *The Edge Daily.* September 25. (http://www.theedgedaily.com/cms/content/jsp?/id=com.tms.cms.article.Article-9761d85e-cb73c03a-if195fco-3d8c8c30#).

Gomez, Terence, and Jomo K.S. 1999. *Malaysia's Political Economy: Politics, Patronage, and Profits.* Cambridge: Cambridge University Press.

International Monetary Fund (IMF). 2007. IMF Executive Board Concludes 2006 Article IV Consultation with Malaysia. Public Information Notice No. 07/34. March 16. (http://www.imf.org/external/np/sec/pn/2007/pn0734.htm).

JETRO. 2004–07. *Boeki Toshi Hakusho.* Tokyo: JETRO.

JETRO. 2008. Kabu Kaiage Nado- no Sogo Keizai Seisaku-o Happyo-e. Tokyo: JETRO.

Kadir, Jasin. 2007. Malaysia in Its Best Shape? *Malaysia Business.* February 16.

Kaplan, Ethan, and Dani Rodrik. 2001. Did the Malaysian Capital Control Work? Cambridge, MA: Harvard University, J. F. Kennedy School of Government. (http://ksghome.harvard.edu/~drodrik/Malaysia%20controls.pdf).

Menon, Jayant. 2008. Macroeconomic Management amid Ethnic Diversity: Fifty Years of Malaysian Experience. ADB Institute Discussion Paper No. 102. April. (http://www.adbi.org/files/dp102.macroeconomic.management.malaysia.pdf).

US Department of State. 2007. 2006 Investment Climate Statement—Malaysia. (http://www.state.gov/e/eeb/ifd/2006/62012.htm).

Vinesh, Derrick. 2007. GLCs Attain 71% Increase in Share Market Value. *The Star.* November 24. (http://thestar.com.my/news/story.asp?file=/2007/11/24/nation/20071124163934&sec=nation).

Watanabe, Toshio, ed. 2003. *Azia Keizai-no Yomihon.* Tokyo: Toyo Keizai Shimposha.

World Bank, The. 2007a. *World Bank Development Indicators.* Washington, DC: The World Bank.

World Bank, The. 2007b. Malaysia and the Knowledge Economy: Building a World-class Higher Education System. Report No. 40397. (http://web.worldbank.org/external/wbcat/main?pagePK=219264&piPK=219251&theSitePK=222993&menuPK=249316&entityID=000020439_20071003115258).

World Economy Information Service. 2008. ARC Report Malaysia 2007. Tokyo.

Chapter 13

AseanAffairs.com. 2008. Thai Economy Looking Weak Despite Trade Surplus. November 1. (http://www.aseanaffairs.com/thai-economy-looking-weak-despite-trade-surplus).

Asian Development Bank (ADB). 1999. Key Economic Indicators.

Asian Development Bank (ADB). 2000. Thailand. In *Asian Development Outlook 2000.* Manila: Asian Development Bank. (http://www.adb.org/Documents/Books/ADO/2000/thailand.pdf).

Asian Development Bank (ADB). 2008. Key Economic Indicators.

Board of Investment (BOI). 2008. About BOI; How to Do Business. (http://www.boi.go.th:english).

Chatrudee Theparat, and Wichit Chantanusornsiri. 2008. Government Pledges Package to Lift Grassroots Economy. *Bangkok Post.* March 5.

The China Post. 2009. Thai Cabinet Agrees on US$3.28 bil Stimulus. January 14. (http://www.chinapost.com/tw/business/asia/thailand/2009/01/14/191961/thai-cabinet.htm).

Don, Sambandaraksa. 2006. Thailand Ranks 41st in the EIU's IT Competitiveness Survey. *The Nation.* March 5.

IDE-JETRO. 2007. *Azia Doko 2007.* Tokyo: Institute of Developing Economies.

JETRO. 2006. *Boeki Toshi Hakusho 2006.* Tokyo: JETRO.

JETRO. 2007. *Boeki Toshi Hakusho 2007.* Tokyo: JETRO.

JETRO. 2008. Chokusetsu Toshi Tokei. Thai. Tokyo: JETRO.

Looney, Robert. 2003. Thailand Thaksinomics: a New Asian Paradigm? *Strategic Insights* Center for Contemporary Conflicts. 2 (12), December. (http://www.ccc.nps.navy.mil/si/dec03/east-Asia.asp).

Ministry of Foreign Affairs. 2000. Thailand Road to Recovery. Business Handbook for Royal Thai Embassies and Consulates-General. (http://www.mfa.go.th/internet/document/h_sec1-fin.pdf).

Phusadee, Arunmas. 2008. Price of Pork Cut by 18 Percent. *Bangkok Post.* March 6.

Reuters. 2008. Thailand Revives Popular Economic Policies. *Business Times.* February 19.

Reuters. 2009. Thailand Plans to Borrow $2bln to Boost Economy. January 31. (http://malaysia.news.yahoo.com/rtrs/20090131/the-thailand-economy-debt-56757el.html).

US Department of State. 2006. 2006 Investment Climate Statement—Thailand. (http://www.state.gov/e/eeb/ifd/2006/62040.htm).

Watanabe, Toshio, ed. 2003. *Azia Keizai-no Yomihon.* Tokyo: Toyo Keizai Shimposha.

Chapter 14

Asian Development Bank (ADB). 2007. Key Economic Indicators.

Asian Development Bank (ADB). 2008. *Asian Development Outlook 2008.* Manila: Asian Development Bank.

Bank Indonesia. 2008. Status and Position of Bank Indonesia. (http://www.bi.go.id/web/en/Tentang+BI/Fungsi+Bank+Indonesia/Status+dan+Kedudukan/).

Bhui, Aloysius. 2004. IBRA's Closure Leaves Indonesia Major Challenges of Avoiding New Crisis. *AFX- Asia.* February 26. (http://www.infid.be/ibra_afx.htm).

Financial Times. 2008. Facility Will Let Jakarta Avoid Bond Market. November 27. (http://www.ft.com/cms/s/o/d9cdab2c-bc26-11dd-80e9-0000779fd18c.html).

Harada, Kimie, and Takatoshi Ito. 2005. Rebuilding the Indonesian Banking Sector: Economic Analysis of Bank Consolidation and Efficiency. *JBCI Review.* August, No. 12: 32–59. (http://www.jica.go.jp/jica-ri/publication/archives/jbic/report/review/pdf/report12_2.pdf).

IDE-JETRO. 2005. *Azia Doko Nempo 2005.* Tokyo: Institute of Developing Economies.

Indonesian Embassy in the US. 2008. Government Continuing Effort to Achieve Poverty Reduction Target. August 14. (http://www.embassyofindonesia.org/news/2008/08/news060.htm).

International Labor Organization (ILO). 2007. Social Dialogue, Labor Law and Labor Administration. (http://www.ilo.org/public/english/dialogue/ifpdial/info/termination/countries/indonesia.htm).

Japan Times. 2005a. Attention to Detail Is the Perfect Ingredient for Success. October 22.

Japan Times. 2005b. Indonesia Asahan Aluminum Shows the Way to Joint Ventures. October 22.

Japan Times. 2005c. Toyota Maintains Pole Position for Expansion. October 22.

Japan Times. 2007. Indonesia Offers the Ultimate in Diversity. August 17.

JETRO. 2005. *Boeki Toshi Hakusho 2005.* Tokyo: JETRO.

JETRO Web site. 2008. Indonesia. Tokei. (http://www.jetro.go.jp/world/asia/idn/stat-{02–07}).

Lasserre, Philippe, and Sam Garg. 2003. *Bank Mandiri: Case in Corporate Transformation.* Singapore: INSEAD.

Omura, Kenji. 2006. *Indonesia Keizai: Yashintekina Saiken Keikaku.* Tokyo: Tosho Shuppankai.

Su, Harry. 2008. Bahana: 1998 vs 2008: A Tale of Two Crises, Their Impacts on Indonesia., *The Jakarta Post.* November 26. (http://www.thejakartapost.com/news/2008/11/26/bahana-1998-vs-2008-a-tale-two-crises-their-impacts-indonesia.html).

Suharmoko, Aditaya. 2008. RI Economy to Remain Robust in Third Quarter. *The Jakarta Post.* October 3. (http://www.thejakartapost.com/news/2008/10/03/ri-economy-remain-robust-third-quarter.html).

Suharmoko, Aditya. 2009. Govt Unveils Final Stimulus Plan to Boost Economy. *The Jakarta Post.* January 28. (http://www.thejakartapost.com/news/2009/01/28/govt-unveils-final-stimulus-plan-boost-economy.html).

Tselichtchev, Ivan. 2004. East Asian Economies: Westernization, Liberalization and New Regionalism. In *Trust and Antitrust in Asian Business Alliances.* ed. John Kidd and Frank-Jurgen Richter. 32–60. Basingstoke and New York: Palgrave Macmillan.

Watanabe, *Toshio* ed. 2003. Azia Keizai Yomihon. Tokyo: Toyo Keizai Shimposha.
Xinhua. 2008. Indonesian VP Calls on Bank Owners to Share Burden With Central Bank. November 29. (http://english.eviewweek.com/Indonesian-VP-calls-on-bank-owners-to-share-burden-with-central-bank.shtml).

Chapter 15

AFP. 2008. Philippines Calls For Asia Food Meet. (http://www.asiaone.com/News/Latest%2BNews/Asia/Story/A1Story20080411-59387.html).
Asian Development Bank (ADB). 2001. Key Economic Indicators.
Asian Development Bank (ADB). 2004. "Proposed Technical Assistance to the Republic of the Philippines for Institutional Strengthening of Energy Regulatory Commission and Privatization of National Power Corporation. December. Manila: Asian Development Bank. (http://www.adb.org/Documents/TARs/PHI/tar-phi-37752-01.pdf).
Asian Development Bank (ADB). 2007, Key Economic Indicators.
Asian Development Bank (ADB). 2008. Key Economic Indicators.
Balana, Cynthia. 2007. US State Dep't Report: RP Losing Edge in English. Global Nation, September 8. (http://globalnation.inquirer.net/news/breakingnews/view_article.php?article_id=81472).
Bodegon, Sophia. 1987 "Aquinomics" or Marcos Revisited? IPS-International Press Service/Global Information Network. February 25. (http://www.sjsu.edu/depts/sociology/living/aquino-870225.html).
Business Anti-Corruption Portal. Philippines Country Profile. (http://www.business-anti-corruption.com/normal.asp?pageid=337).
IDE-JETRO. 2007. *Azia Doko Nempo 2007.* Tokyo: Institute of Developing Economies.
JETRO. 2008. Firipin. Tokei. Tokyo: JETRO.
Library of Congress. 2006. Country Profile: Philippines. Federal Research Division. March. Washington, DC: Library of Congress. (http://lcweb2.loc.gov/frd/cs/profiles/Philippines.pdf).
Manila Times, The. 2007. CalPERS Lifts RP Rating. February 15. (http://www.manilatimes.net/national/2007/feb/15/yehey/top_stories/20070215top1.html).
National Statistics Office. 2008. Philippines in Figures 2008. (http://www.census.gv.ph/data/publications/PIF2008-final.pdf).
People's Daily. 2008. Philippines Banks Agree on Liquidity Boost Amid Financial Turmoil. October 31. (http://english.peopledaily.com.cn/90001/90778/90858/90863/6525388.html).
Reuters. 2008. R.P. Population Climbs Above 88 Million. *The Daily Yomiuri.* April 18.
Tetangco Jr, Amando M. 2007. The Philippines Economy Ten Years After the Asian Currency Crisis. Speech by Mr Amando M. Tetangco, Jr, Governor of the Bangko Sentral ng Pilipinas (BSP), at the International Symposium "Ten Years After the Asian Currency Crisis: Future Challenges for the Asian Economies and Financial Markets." hosted by the Center for Monetary Cooperation in Asia (CeMCoA), Bank of Japan, Tokyo. January 22, Basel: Bank for International Settlements (BIS). (www.bis.org/review/r070511f.pdf).
Tolentino, Gani. 2008. Philippines Can't Protect Foreign Investors? *The Filipino Express.* March 17–23. 22 (12). (http://www.filipinoexpress.com/22/12_op-ed.html).
US Department of State. 2007. 2007 Investment Climate Statement—The Philippines. (http://www.State.Gov/e/eeb/ifd/2007/80731.htm).
Villegas, Edberto. 2005. The Philippine Fiscal Crisis and the Neo-Colonial State. *Yonip.* (http://www.yonip.com/main/articles/fiscalcrisis/html).
World Bank, The. 1993. Support for Economic Recovery in the Philippines Washington, DC: World Bank. (http://lnweb90.worldbank.org/oed/oeddoclib.nsf/DocUNIDViewForJavaSearch/8B3BF0F24B61E91D852567F5005D84EC).
Xinhua. 2008. Most Filipinos Feel Life Worse Despite Record Economic Growth. *Philippines News Archives.* March 31. (http://www.Topix.com/world/philippines/2008/03).

Chapter 16

Asian Development Bank (ADB). 2007. *Asian Development Outlook 2007: Growth Amid Change.* Manila: Asian Development Bank.

Asian Development Bank (ADB). 2008. Key Economic Indicators.

A.T. Kearney. 2007. *2007 Global Retail Development Index.* Chicago: A.T. Kearney.

Hy Van Luong. 2003. Wealth, Power, and Inequality: Global Market, the State, and Local Sociocultural Dynamics. In *Postwar Vietnam: Dynamics of a Transforming Society.* Hy Van Luong ed., Lanham, MD: Rowman and Littlefield Publishers.

Intellasia. 2008. Vietnam Walks Tightrope Between Inflation and Downturn. November 18. (http://www.intellasia.net/news/articles/economy/111252275.shtml).

International Monetary Fund (IMF). 2008. Vietnam: New Challenges Amid Signs of Overheating. *IMF Survey Magazine: Countries and Regions.* March. (http://www.imf.org/external/pubs/ft/survey/so/2008/CARO3708A.htm).

JETRO. 2007. *Boeki Toshi Hakusho 2007.* Tokyo: JETRO.

Library of Congress. 2005. Country Profile: Vietnam. Federal Research Division. December. Washington, DC: Library of Congress. (http://www.lcweb2.loc.gov/frd/cs/profiles/Vietnam.pdf).

Meyer, Klaus E., Yen T.T. Tran, and Hung Vo Nguyen. 2006. Doing Business in Vietnam *Thunderbird International Business Review.* 28 (2): 263–290.

Mizuho Global News. 2008. Vietnam Investment Environment, Light and Shadow. (translated from Japanese), March 12.

Nikkei Shimbun. 2008. Tenken.Shinkokoku Keizai. Betonamu. Infure Kasoku, Shijyo Konran. June 25.

PricewaterhouseCoopers (PwC). 2007. Balancing Risk and Award: The PricewaterhouseCoopers EM20 Index. July.

Ronnas, Per, and Bhargavi Ramamurthy. 1997. *Entrepreneurship in Vietnam: Transformation and Dynamics.* Copenhagen and Singapore: Nordic Institute of Asian Studies (NIAS) and Institute of Southeast Asian Studies (ISEAS).

United Nations Conference on Trade and Development (UNCTAD). 2007. World Investment Report 2007: Transnational Corporations, Extractive Industries and Development. Geneva: UNCTAD. (http://www.unctad.org/en/docs/iteiit20074a5_en.pdf).

United Nations Development Program (UNDP). 2007. *Human Development Report 2007.* New York: UNDP.

VietnamNet Bridge. 2007. The Decline of the SOEs. October 15.

VietnamNet Bridge. 2007. Vietnam Opens Property Market Further. November 19. (http://english.vietnamnet.vn/biz/2007/11/755592/).

VietnamNet Bridge. 2008. The Consequences of a Competitive Society. January 15. (http://english.vietnamnet.vn/reports/2008/01/764236/).

VietnamNet Bridge, 2009a. Vietnam Economy to Pick Up in 2009. January 24. (http://english.vietnamnet.vn/biz/2009/01/825656/).

VietnamNet Bridge, 2009b. Vietnam Economy Not Immune to Global Crisis. January 26. (http://english.vietnamnet.vn/biz/2009/01/825806/).

VietnamNet Bridge, 2009c. Outlook for Vietnam's Economy in 2009. January 29. (http://english.vietnamnet.vn/biz/2009/01/826100/).

Xuan Dung Cao and Thi Anh-Dao Tran. 2005. Transition et Ouverture Economique au Vietnam: une Différentiation Sectorielle. *Economie Internationale.* Volume 104: 27–43.

Chapter 17

Central Intelligence Agency (CIA). 2008. CIA World Factbook. (https://www.cia.gov/library/publications/the-world-factbook/geos/kn.html).

Democratic People's Republic of Korea Official Web site. 2008a. Business in DPR Korea: Exports. (http://www.korea-dpr.com/exports.htm).

Democratic People's Republic of Korea Official Web site. 2008b. International Trade Office of Korea. (http://www.korea-dpr.com/users/switzerland/international_trade_office_korea/itok_index_en.php).

Institute for Far Eastern Studies (IFES). 2008a. Market Activity Flourishes in the DPRK. *North Korean Economy Watch.* Brief No. 08-4-21-1. April 21. (http://www.nkeconwatch.com/2008/04/24/market-activity-flourishes-in-the-dprk/).

Lankov, Andrei. 2006. The Natural Death of North Korean Stalinism. *Asia Policy.* No. 1, January: 95–121. (http://www.nbr.org/publications/asia_policy/pdf/ap1-lankov.pdf).

Lee Jong-Heon. 2008. North Korea Economy Shrinks Due to Floods. *UPI Asia.com.* June 18. (http://www.upiasia.com/Economics/2008/06/18/north_korean_economy_shrinks_due_to_floods/8923/).

Mimura, Mitsuhiro. 2007. Chyosen Minshushugi Jimmin Kyowakoku Keizai-no Genjo. *ERINA Report.* 78, November: 2–14.

Nanto, Dick K. and Emma Chanlett-Avery. 2008. The North Korean Economy: Leverage and Poilicy Analysis. Congressional Research Service (CRS) Report to Congress. (updated August 26). (http://www.fas.org/sgp/crs/row/RL32493.pdf).

North Korea Economy Watch. 2008. Pyongyang's Newest Market. April 25. (http://www.nkeconwatch.com/2008/04/25/pyongynags-newest-market/).

Salmon, Andrew. 2006. Kaesong Zone a Troubled Korean Jewel. *Asia Times.* April 6. (http://www.atimes.com/atimes/Korea/HD06Dg01.html).

World Economic Information Service. 2008. ARC Report DPRK 2007. Tokyo.

Chapter 18

Federal State Statistics Service (FSSS). 2002. *Rossiyskiy Statisticheskiy Ezhegodnik 2002.* Moscow: Goskomstat.

Federal State Statistics Service (FSSS). 2006. *Rossiyskiy Statisticheskiy Ezhegodnik 2006.* Moscow: Goskomstat.

Federal State Statistics Service (FSSS). 2008. Otsenka Chislennosti Postoyannogo Naseleniya Rossiyskoy Federatsii. (http://www.gks.ru/free-doc/2008/demo/popul08.htm).

Financial Izvestia. 2007. Gubernator Khabarovskogo kraya Viktor Ishaev o Razvitii Regiona: Nuzhna Ekonomicheskaya Perestroika. August 8.

Government of Russia. 2006. Programma Razvitiya Dalnego Vostoka I Zabaikaliya.

Ishaev, Viktor. 2007. Strategicheskie Voprosi Dolgosrochnogo Razvitiya Dalnego Vostoka i Zabaikalya. Report at the Second Far East International Economic Forum. (http://www.adm.khv.ru/invest2.nsf/AllNewsRus/839CE7C2F8B7E3C9CA25736E000EB604).

Minakir, Pavel, and Natalia Mikheeva eds. 1999. *Dalniy Vostok Rossii: Ekonomicheskiy Potentsial.* Vladivostok: Dalnauka.

Minakir, Pavel. 2008. Roshia Kyokuto Keizai to Shin-Kyokuto Hatten Puroguramu. *Chosa Geppo.* Roshia NIS Boekikai. No. 5.

Moscow Times, The. 2008. Government Cuts Economic Growth Forecast. November 25. (http://www.themoscowtimes.com/article/1009/42/372628.htm).

Roshia-NIS Boekikai. 2007a. *Chosa Geppo.* No. 7.

Roshia-NIS Boekikai. 2007b. *Chosa Geppo.* No. 9–10.

Sakhalin-1 Project Web site. 2008a. It's a Big World—But There's Only One Sakhalin! (http://www.sakhalin-1.ru/en/home.asp).

Sakhalin-1 Project Web site. 2008b. Sakhalin-1 Project Continues to Achieve Milestones. (http://www.sakhalin1.com/en/news/press/20081002.asp).

Tselichtchev, Ivan. 1995. *Roshia Keizai-ni Nani ga Okotteiru ka.* Tokyo: Nikkei Shimbunsha.

Watkins, Eric. 2008a. ExxonMobil Drills Record Extended-Reach Well at Sakhalin 1. *Oil & Gas Journal.* February 11.

Watkins, Eric. 2008b. Sakhalin-2 Deliveries Are to Start in Early 2009. *Oil & Gas Journal.* October 21.

Chapter 19

Asian Development Bank (ADB). 2007. Key Economic Indicators.

Asian Development Bank (ADB). 2008. Key Economic Indicators.

Ahluwahlia, Isher. 1995. *Industrial Growth in India: Stagnation Since the Mid-Sixties.* New Delhi: Oxford University Press.

Ahluwahlia, Montek S. 2000. Economic Performance of States in Post-Reforms Period. *Economic and Political Weekly.* 35 (May 6): 1637–1648.

Ahluwahlia, Montek S. 2002. Economic Reforms in India Since 1991: Has Gradualism Worked? *Journal of Economic Perspective.* 16 (3): 67–88.

AP. 2008. Indian Economy Seen Weathering Attacks. *The Daily Yomiuri.* November 29.

Bloomberg. 2008. Economy Slows Most Since '04. *The Daily Yomiuri.* November 29.

Bombay Stock Exchange (BSE). Introduction. (http://www.bseindia.com/about/introbse.asp).

Census of India. 2001. Government of India.

Chauvin, Sophie, and Francoise Lemoine. 2005. L'économie Indienne: Changements Structurels et Perspectives à Long-Terme, Centre d'Etudes Prospectives at d'Informations Internationales (CEPII), Document de travail No. 2005-04. (http://www.cepii.fr/francgraph/doctravail/pdf/2005/dt05-04.pdf).

Cox, W. Michael, and Richard Alm. 2008. China and India: Two Paths to Economic Power. *Economic Letter—Insights from the Federal Reserve Bank of Dallas.* Federal Reserve Bank of Dallas. 3 (8). (http://dallasfed.org/research/eclett/2008/el0808.html).

Das, Suranjan. 2001. The Nehru Years in Indian Politics. *Edinburgh Papers in South Asian Studies.* Working Paper No. 16. Centre for South Asian Studies. (http://www.csas.ed.ac.uk/fichiers/DAS_Nehru.pdf).

Datt, Ruddar, and K.P.M. Sundharam. 2007. Indian Economy. TPK.

Dutz, Mark A. 2007. Unleashing India's Innovation: Toward Sustainable and Inclusive Growth. Washington, DC: The World Bank.

Financial Express. 2009. No Fear of Recession: Government. January 27. (http://www.financialexpress.com/news/no-fear-of-recession-government/415752/).

Hewitt Associates. 2006. *Managing Compensation in Asia 2006.* Hewitt Associates: Hong Kong.

IndiaOneStop.com. 2008. India's Outward Foreign Direct Investment. (http://www.indiaonestop.com/FDI/outwardfdiflow.htm).

Indiaprwire.com. 2008. Services Sector Will Prop Growth Rate: Industry Report. December 2008. (http://www.indiaprwire.com/businessnews/20081228/36291.htm).

Indiresan, P.V. 2007. Prospects for World Class Research Universities in India. In *Transforming Research Universities in Asia and Latin America: World Class Worldwide.* Philip G. Altbach and Jorge Balan, eds. Baltimore: John Hopkins University Press.

International Business Times. 2008. India Sees Growth Accelerating to 9% Next Year. November 18. (http://in.ibtimes.com/articles/20081118/india-economy-global-financial-crisis-chidambaram-india-economic-summit.htm).

JETRO. 2008a. Indo Boeki Tokei.

JETRO. 2008b. Indo Tokei. Tainai Chokusetsu Toshi.

Kedia, Ben, Debmalya Mukherjee, and Somnath Lahiri. 2006. Indian Business Groups: Evolution and Transformations. *Asia Pacific Journal of Management.,* 23: 559–577.

Khandwalla, Pradip. 2002. Effective Organizational Response by Corporates to India's Liberalization and Globalization. *Asia Pacific Journal of Management.* 19: 423–449.

Kundu, Sridhar. 2008. Can the Indian Economy Emerge Unscathed From the Global Financial Crisis? (http://www.orfonline.org/cms/export/orfonline/modules/issuebrief/attachments/meltdown_1227252052108.pdf).

Kuruvilla, Sarosh. 1996. Linkages Between Industrial Strategies and Industrial Relations/Human Resource Policies: Singapore, Malaysia, the Philippines, and India. *Industrial and Labor Relations Review.* 49 (4) (July): 635–657. (http://digitalcommons.ilr.cornell.edu/cgi/viewcontent.cgi?article=1005&context=cbpubs).

McKinsey & Co. 2007. *The 'Bird of Gold': the Rise of India's Consumer Market.*

Ministry of Commerce and Industry. 2008. Foreign Direct Investment—Policy and Procedures.

Ministry of Finance. 2002. Economic Survey 2001–02. (http://indiabudget.nic.in/es2001-02/welcome.html).

Ministry of Finance. 2006. Economic Survey 2005–06. (http://indiabudget.nic.in/es2005-06/esmain.htm).

Ministry of Finance. 2007. Economic Survey 2006–07. (http://indiabudget.nic.in/es2006-07/esmain.htm).

Ministry of Finance. 2008. Economic Survey 2007–08. (http://indiabudget.nic.in/es2007-08/esmain.htm).

Organization for Economic Cooperation and Development (OECD). 2007. *Economic Survey of India 2007*. Paris: OECD.

Oxford Analytica. 2005. November 14, quoted in Inclusive Growth and Service Delivery: Building on India's Success, India Development Policy Review, May 29, 2006, The World Bank.

Panagariya, Arvind. 2002. India's Economic Reforms: What has Been Accomplished? What Remains to be Done? ERD Policy Brief Series No. 2. Asian Development Bank (ADB). (http://www.adb.org/Documents/EDRC/Policy_Briefs/PB002.pdf).

Planning Commission. 2000. Report of the Task Force on Employment. Government of India.

Rediff News. 2008. Singapore Makes Most of India's Outward FDI. April 15. (http://www.rediff.com/money/2008/apr/15fdi.htm).

Stern, Nicholas. 2001. Building a Climate for Investment. Growth and Poverty Reduction in India In *A Strategy for Development*. Washington, DC: The World Bank. (http://siteresources.worldbank.org/INTPOVERTY/Resources/335642-1130251872237/BuildingAClimateForInvestment.pdf).

Technopak. 2006. *India's Luxury Trends 2006: A Report on India's Luxury Market.*

United Nations Development Program (UNDP). 2006. Asia-Pacific Human Development Report 2006. New York: UNDP. (http://www.pcij.org/blog/wp-docs/HDR2006/Prelim.pdf).

United Nations Development Program (UNDP). 2007. *Human Development Report 2007*. New York: UNDP.

Virmani, Arvind. 2004. India's Economic Growth: From Socialist Rate of Growth to Bharatiya Rate of Growth. Working Paper No. 122. Indian Council for Research on International Economic Relations (ICRIER). (http://www.icrier.org/pdf/wp122.pdf).

World Bank, The. 2005. *Reforming Services in India, Drawing from Lessons of Success*. Washington, DC: The World Bank.

World Bank, The. 2006. *Inclusive Growth and Service Delivery: Building on India's Success*. Washington, DC: The World Bank.

Chapter 20

Cabinet Office of the Government of Japan. 2007. *Keizai Zaisei Hakusho 2007.*

International Longevity Center-Japan. 2006. Reform of the Health Care System in Japan. (http://longevity.ilcjapan.org./pdf/Reform%20of%20the%20health%20care%20system%20in%20Japan.pdf).

JETRO. 2008a. Doru-Date Boeki Jyokyo. Tokyo: JETRO.

JETRO. 2008b. Chokusetsu Toshi Tokei. Tokyo: JETRO.

Kanamori, Hisao, Yutaka Kosai and Haromi Kato. 2007. *Nihon Keizai Yomihon*. 17th ed. Tokyo: Toyo Keizai Shimposha.

Kyodo News. 2008. Aso Unveils ¥26.9 Trillion Stimulus Plan. *The Daily Yomiuri*. October 31.

Ministry of Economy, Trade, and Industry (METI). 2006. New Economic Growth Strategy (Outline). Tokyo: Government of Japan. (http://www.meti.go.jp/english/report/download-files/NewEconomicGrowthStrategy(outline).pdf).

Ministry of Internal Affairs and Communications (MIC). 2008a. *Japan Statistical Yearbook 2008*. Statistical Bureau. Tokyo: Government of Japan.

Ministry of Internal Affairs and Communications (MIC). 2008b. Tokei-de Miru Nihon-no Sugata 2008. Statistical Bureau. Tokyo: Government of Japan.

Ministry of Education, Culture, Sport, Science and Technology (MEXT). 2008. Chiiki Kurasta Sosei Jigyo. (http://www.mext.go.jp/a_menu/kagaku/chiiki/cluster/index.htm).

Mitsuhashi, Tadahiro, Shigeo Uchida, and Yoshiki Ikeda. 2007. *Nihon Keizai Numon*. Tokyo: Nihon Keizai Shimbunsha.

Nikkei Shimbun. 2008. Jigyo Kibo Saidai-no 27 Cho Yen. October 31.

Oba, Tokiko, and Julian Satterthwaite. 2008. Who's in Charge of Big Companies? *The Daily Yomiuri*. April 19.

Sakuragawa, Masaya, and Yoshitsugu Watanabe. 2008. Did the Japanese Stock Market Appropriately Price the Takenaka Financial Reform? National Bureau of Economic Research. (http://www.nber.org/books_in_progress/ease18/sakuragawa-watanabe4-2-08.pdf).

Takahara, Kanako. 2007. All Eyes on Japan Post as Privatization Begins. *The Japan Times*. September 29. (http://search.japantimes.co.jp/cgi-bin/nn20070929f1.html).

Tselichtchev, Ivan. 2004. *Nihon-o Yutaka-ni Suru Mitsu-no Hoho*. Tokyo: Shogakukan.

World Health Organization (WHO). 2000. *The World Health Report 2000—Health Systems: Improving Performance*. Geneva: World Health Organization. (http://www.who.int/whr/2000/en/whr00_en.pdf).

Yumoto, Hiroshi, and Hiroshi Ishizaki. 2008. Talks on Basic Pension Plan Intensify. *The Daily Yomiuri*. March 6.

Index

K

Kaesong Industrial District, 293–294
Kerry Group, 202
Khazanah Nasional, 63, 77
Kim Il-sung, 285
Kim Jong-il, 285, 294–295
Kim Young-sam, 172
Koizumi, Junichiro, 49, 50, 59, 106,
    334–336, 342, 345
Kookmin Bank, 74, 243
Korean Asset Management Corporation
    (Kamco), 173
Krakatau Steel, 15
Krugman, Paul, 33–34
Kuok Group, 202
Kuomintang (KMT), 146, 155

L

labor market, 88, 91–94, 166, 175, 182,
    194, 197, 209, 251–252, 317–318, 323
labor relations, 1–2, 13–16, 19, 87–96
Laos, 2–3, 7, 27, 105–106, 110
Latin America, 9, 26, 34
Lee Hsien Loong, 188
Lee Kuan Yew, 187, 190, 194
Lee Myung-bak, 107, 177, 179, 293–294
Lee Teng-hui, 158
Lenovo, 73, 89, 117, 132
leverage (ratio of total debt to equity),
    19, 65
LG, 92, 95, 169
Liberal Democratic Party, 58, 328, 335–336
liberalization, 11, 19, 48, 59, 105–106,
    158, 181, 196, 211, 218, 259, 279–280,
    299, 314, 318
light industry, 13, 155–156, 171, 219, 257,
    282, 287, 327, 329
Li Ka Shing, 83, 144
Lippo Group, 236

M

Ma Ying-jeou, 163–164
Macau, 2–3, 71
Mahathir, bin Mohammad, 18, 108–109,
    204–206, 210
Malaysia, 2–3, 7–9, 15–17, 25–26, 28–29, 31,
    41, 43, 51, 56, 58–60, 63, 65, 74, 76,
    78–81, 90–91, 94, 102, 105, 108, 152,
    187–188, 196, 201–214, 232, 243, 317

manufacturing, 9, 13–14, 42, 47, 52,
    59–60, 117, 124, 135–136, 138–139,
    144, 146, 149, 161–163, 165, 169,
    171, 183, 186, 189, 191, 194,
    198–199, 201–2-2, 204, 210–213,
    215, 217, 225, 227–229, 236,
    240–241, 250, 255–256, 258, 260,
    269, 271, 274, 278, 280, 286,
    290–291, 293–294, 298, 302, 304,
    310–311, 318, 323, 327, 331, 334,
    337, 343–344, 348, 353
Mao Zedong, 11, 118–120
Marcos, Ferdinand, 257–258, 261, 265
Medvedev, Dmitry, 307
Megawati, Sukarnoputri, 244, 248
middle class, 36, 45, 58, 85, 93, 139,
    172, 204, 219, 249–250, 302–303, 316,
    333
mining industry, 255, 265, 268, 291, 302,
    304
Ministry of Economy, Trade and Industry
    (METI), 328, 330, 343, 346
minority shareholders, 12, 80, 81
Mongolia, 2–3, 8, 11, 255, 292
Multimedia Super Corridor (MSC), 205,
    209, 212, 214
Myanmar, 2–3, 7, 27, 105–106, 156, 179,
    319

N

National Development and Reforms
    Commission, 55, 72, 118, 124
natural resources, mineral resources,
    127–128, 155, 201, 211, 235–236, 255,
    271, 285, 291, 298, 327
Nehru, Jawaharlal, 311
New Economic Policy (NEP), 203–205
new mentality and mode of action, of
    dominant stakeholders, 81–85
New Zealand, 75, 107, 110, 112
newly industrialized economies (NIEs),
    3, 7–9, 16, 24–26, 28, 30, 34, 36–38,
    44, 65, 98, 100, 102, 204, 232–233,
    241, 347
North American Free Trade Agreement
    (NAFTA), 97–99
North Korea, People's Democratic
    Republic of Korea (DPRK), 3, 11,
    179, 285–295